Ornithologies of Desire

Ornithologies of Desire
Ecocritical Essays, Avian Poetics, and Don McKay

Travis V. Mason

WILFRID LAURIER
UNIVERSITY PRESS

This book has been published with the help of a grant from the Canadian Federation for the Humanities and Social Sciences, Humanities and Social Sciences, through the Awards to Scholarly Publications Program, using funds provided by the Social Sciences and Humanities Research Council of Canada. Wilfrid Laurier University Press acknowledges the support of the Canada Council for the Arts for our publishing program. We acknowledge the financial support of the Government of Canada through the Canada Book Fund for our publishing activities. This work was supported by the Research Support Fund.

Library and Archives Canada Cataloguing in Publication

Mason, Travis V., 1977–
     Ornithologies of desire : ecocritical essays, avian poetics, and Don McKay / Travis V. Mason.

(Environmental humanities series)
Includes bibliographical references.
Issued also in electronic formats.
ISBN 978-1-55458-630-1 (hardcover). —ISBN 978-1-77112-348-8 (softcover)

     1. McKay, Don, 1942– —Criticism and interpretation. 2. Birds in literature. 3. Ecology in literature. 4. Ecocriticism. I. Title. II. Series: Environmental humanities series

PS8575.K28Z87 2013   C811'.54   C2012-907174-9

Electronic monographs.
Issued also in print format.
ISBN 978-1-55458-647-9 (PDF)—ISBN 987-1-55458-371-3 (EPUB)

     1. McKay, Don, 1942– —Criticism and interpretation. 2. Birds in literature. 3. Ecology in literature. 4. Ecocriticism. I. Title. II. Series: Environmental humanities series (Online)

PS8575.K28Z87 2013   C811'.54   C2012-907175-7

First paperback printing 2018

© 2013 Wilfrid Laurier University Press
Waterloo, Ontario, Canada
www.wlupress.wlu.ca

Cover design by Blakeley Words+Pictures. Cover image: *The Goldfinch*, a painting in oil on panel by Carel Fabritius (1622–1654), courtesy of the Royal Picture Gallery Mauritshuis, The Hague, Netherlands. Text design by Angela Booth Malleau.

Excerpts from the poetry of Don McKay reprinted with permission of McClelland & Stewart and the author. Excerpts from *Mean* (1999), by Ken Babstock, reprinted by permission of House of Anansi Press. Excerpt from "Bird Landing," by W. H. New, from *Riverbook and Ocean* (2002), reprinted by permission of Oolichan Press. Excerpt from *Pigeon* (2009), by Karen Solie, reprinted by permission of House of Anansi Press. Excerpts from "Understory" and "The Tide," both from *Habitat* (2005), by Sue Wheeler, reprinted by permission of Brick Books.

Every reasonable effort has been made to acquire permission for copyright material used in this text, and to acknowledge all such indebtedness accurately. Any errors and omissions called to the publisher's attention will be corrected in future printings.

No part of this publication may be reproduced, stored in a retrieval system, or transmitted, in any form or by any means, without the prior written consent of the publisher or a licence from the Canadian Copyright Licensing Agency (Access Copyright). For an Access Copyright licence, visit http://www.accesscopyright.ca or call toll free to 1-800-893-5777.

Contents

vi	*List of Abbreviations*
vii	*Acknowledgements*
ix	*A Note on the Cover*
xi	*Beginnings : An Introduction*

PART ONE

3	Chapter One • Nesting
15	Chapter Two • Naming
31	Ecotone One • Field Marks

PART TWO

45	Chapter Three • Homologies
63	Chapter Four • Flight
81	Chapter Five • Gravity
99	Ecotone Two • Field Guides

PART THREE

115	Chapter Six • Notes
129	Chapter Seven • Birdsong
147	Chapter Eight • Listening
161	Ecotone Three • Field Notes

PART FOUR

177	Chapter Nine • Birder-Poet
195	Chapter Ten • Science
215	Ecotone Four • Field Trips
223	Ending • Ravens

227	*Appendix • Bird Concordance*
237	*Notes*
259	*Works Cited*
277	*Index*

List of Abbreviations

A	*Apparatus* (1997)
AG	*Another Gravity* (2000)
AOS	*Air Occupies Space* (1973)
B	*Birding, or desire* (1983)
DW	*Deactivated West 100* (2005)
F	*Foglio a foglia/Leaf to Leaf* (2010)
L	*Lependu* (1978)
LS	*Long Sault* (1975)
M	*The Muskwa Assemblage* (2008)
MC	*Moccasins on Concrete* (1972)
NF	*Night Field* (1991)
P	*Paradoxides* (2012)
S	*Songs for the Songs of Birds* (2008)
SD	*Sanding Down This Rocking Chair on a Windy Night* (1987)
ST	*The Shell of the Tortoise* (2011)
S/S	*Strike/Slip* (2006)
V	*Vis à Vis: Field Notes on Poetry & Wilderness* (2001)

Acknowledgements

This book would not have been possible if not for the helpful guidance and patient listening of many people. Laurie Ricou has compelled me to take risks I would likely have avoided (and surely would have regretted not taking) without his challenging provocations and selfless attitude. He has taught me the value of paying attention to habitat—and all it entails—and the importance of writing as a way of thinking. Laura Moss knows what questions to ask and what accomplishments to celebrate. Mike Healey (the "alien" scientist in the ranks) offered astute, slightly suspicious commentary that has made this work stronger. Bill New has been a model of openness, humility, wisdom, and constant encouragement without which I would not be writing.

I am grateful to friends and colleagues whose conversations along the way have made my work enjoyable, including Sarah Banting, Nicholas Bradley, Jennifer Delisle, Matt Huculak, Eddy Kent, Alyssa MacLean, Shurli Makmillen, Taiwo Adetunji Osinubi, Shane Plante, Tyson Stolte, Katja Thieme, Terri Tomsky, Angela Waldie, and Onjana Yawnghwe. Maia Joseph and Lisa Szabo-Jones generously shared their time, knowledge, and editing prowess; Duffy Roberts offered unflagging support and willingness to read anything and respond with candour. Kitty Lewis at Brick Books has been generous and open with her time; Kieran Kealy shared many bird books; and Simon Bonner provided birding companionship and expertise.

I benefited a great deal from my time spent at Rhodes University, Grahamstown, South Africa, where I revised much of this manuscript while red-winged starlings and cape weavers sang just outside my office. The Andrew Mellon Foundation made my time there possible. Dan Wylie and Ann Smailes shared some of their favourite birding spots and game drives. The Department of English at Dalhousie University provided a welcome and accommodating space in which to complete this manuscript. I am grateful to the Killam Trusts for financial support; to Carrie Dawson for offering sage advice; to Dean Irvine for listening; to Erin Wunker for uplifting and for reminding that sparrow is also a verb.

Parts of this book have been published elsewhere and appear here in revised form. Parts of Chapter Two were published as "Naming and Knowing in Don McKay's Poetry," *The Dalhousie Review* 90.1 (2010); parts of Chapters Nine and Ten appeared in "Toward an (Avian) Aesthetic of (Avian) Absence," *Alternation: Interdisciplinary Journal for the Study of the Arts and Humanities in Southern Africa* 16.2 (2009); part of Chapter Eight appeared in "Listening at the Edge: Homage and

Ohmage in Don McKay and Ken Babstock," *Studies in Canadian Literature/Études en littérature canadienne* 33.1 (2008); parts of Chapter Two and Seven appeared in "Lick Me, Bite Me, Hear Me, Write Me: Tracking Animals between Postcolonialism and Ecocriticism," *Other Selves: Animals in the Canadian Literary Imagination*, University of Ottawa Press, 2007; and shorter versions of Ecotones One through Three were published as "West-Coast Birding as Postcolonial Strategy: Literary Criticism in the Field," *Kunapipi: Journal of Postcolonial Writing & Culture* 29.2 (2007).

Lisa Quinn, acquisitions editor at Wilfrid Laurier University Press, has worked tirelessly to ensure publication of this book. I am thrilled to be included in WLUP's Environmental Humanities Series, which is led by intrepid series editor Cheryl Lousley. Leslie Macredie and copy editor Rob Kohlmeier have helped shape this book in ways I could not have envisioned or articulated. The suggestions from the two anonymous readers have been invaluable in turning a manuscript into a book. Any remaining errors are mine alone.

My family deserves credit for nurturing my work by virtue of accepting it for what it is. That my mother, who died in 2011, can no longer express her happiness at my accomplishments makes this work bittersweet, to say the least. My father, Kerry Mason, has always supported me, and for that I'm grateful.

Finally, this book would not be possible without the patience, intelligence, and humour of my partner and my wife, Maryann. I dedicate this book to her, as if that were enough.

A Note on the Cover

The bird depicted in Carel Fabritius's *The Goldfinch* (1654), the painting reproduced on the cover of this book, is a European goldfinch. It is not a bird likely to be encountered in Canada. Because this book interrogates a particular kind of attention to specific bird species in the context of Canadian poetry, some explanation for the choice of this image is in order. As soon as I saw the painting, I knew I wanted it for the cover. Its Europeanness is in keeping both with my discussion of British Romantic poets (and McKay's own response to that tradition; McKay doesn't limit his avian subjects to Canadian species, though most of the birds he writes about are encountered in Canada) and with my concept of multiple ornithologies of desire (scientific and literary), which emerge from and connect to a kind of Enlightenment rationality not limited to Canada. Fabritius's painting demonstrates both the historical and the very immediate trajectory of a human desire to know the avian other by capturing and looking ... and painting and writing, I suppose. One of my goals with this book is to position McKay within a Canadian as well as an international (mostly European and American) tradition of eco- and avian poetry/poetics. In that sense, the Fabritius cover anticipates that broader scope.

Beginnings

An Introduction

> what dew yu write abt   abt
> treez n birds n nature I sd
>   yu ar an idealist she sd
> iuv bin thru that
> – bill bissett [untitled poem]

> "Geoffrey Chaucer made conventional use of bird imagery," intones the teacher who knows something about Chaucer and somewhat less about birds.
> – Michael Jenied, *Chaucer's Checklist*

What follows is a book in which I make a case for the value of critical attention across disciplinary lines, for the value of reading ecocritically. Though the work of Don McKay forms a central part of these essays, and poetry and poetics more generally receive a great deal of attention, the book as a whole argues for the capacity of ecocriticism to read across genres and disciplines, to listen to many different stories, and to speak/write polyphonically.[1] It assumes, that is, that more than one discipline provides evidence, more than one story offers knowledge, and more than one writing style—more than one voice—expresses ideas. My strategy relies on two interconnecting focuses: one is an ecocriticism that refers to the language and the epistemological contributions of science (especially the life sciences);[2] the other is the biological and ecological specificity evident in McKay's writing, particularly as it relates to a tradition of English-language nature poetry and to a phenomenological response to the world. But my strategy also announces a scepticism that is meant to question the value of unchecked anthropocentric behaviour and reading practices. If Northrop Frye's focus on Canadian poets' "terror in regard to nature" (Conclusion

342) and Margaret Atwood's claim that "Canadian writers as a whole do not trust Nature" (49) indicate anthropocentric as opposed to ecocentric models of Canadian identity formation, then McKay's poetry and poetics operate in contradistinction to these progenitors of Canadian literary criticism. By looking back to the British and American poetry that informed much early Canadian poetry and continues to inform the work of someone like McKay, I hope to reveal the dynamics at work in those poems that clearly voice a simultaneous indebtedness to and suspicion of what has come before. I draw attention to the science and philosophy of ecology in the same spirit of connectedness. Poetry does not get written in a temporal, political, or epistemological vacuum.

If science gets taken up as a subject in literary criticism, it tends to occupy a contrary position. "It is never what a poem *says* which matters," writes I. A. Richards in *Poetries and Sciences* (1970), "but what it *is*. The poet is not writing as a scientist" (33). Frye helped devise a modern literary criticism by comparing nascent work in arts and humanities to earlier developments in science. "Science learns more and more about the world as it goes on: it evolves and improves," he claims in *The Educated Imagination* (1963). "But literature begins with the possible model of experience, and what it produces is the literary model called the classic. Literature doesn't evolve or improve or progress" (7). Nevertheless, both Richards and Frye think that writing about such perceived differences is a worthwhile practice, that, indeed, the places where science and literature meet reveal commonalities as well as differences. I offer these responses to science by literary critics to remind that "science" as a term has necessarily been vague while being rhetorically dominant. Neither Richards nor Frye defines science—Richards considers such a task to be "foolish" (8); Frye prefers listing examples of scientific fields, of which even literary criticism qualifies (*Anatomy* 8). While I understand the difficulty of accurately defining science and rather like the idea of identifying "a scientific element in criticism" (*Anatomy* 8), I want to clarify how I use the term in this book. When I refer to science, I refer to an inclusive epistemological and political entity: scientific ideas, language, and methodologies; the history and philosophy of science (more particularly of ecology and ornithology); the inventories of natural history; and the current taxonomies that enable access (through field guides and popular writing) to the material world. Such a broad, still somewhat vague definition is necessary, since one goal of this book is to develop a strategy for getting closer to the source material for ecopoetry, including field guides, scientific writing, and, in the case of Don McKay, birds themselves.

Because the bulk of this book will engage with avian poetics directly, through readings of McKay's birder-poet and bird poems,³ and indirectly, through the development of an ecocritical attention related to McKay's poetic attention, I want to introduce McKay's avian poetics by looking at some poems that respond to McKay and his work. A number of poems that have been dedicated to McKay address birds and/or the physical world as a way of addressing McKay. Sue Wheeler's "Understory," for example, embraces field guide and listening tropes in McKay's oeuvre by articulating the imperative "To walk out of the field guide / and listen" (11). David Seymour's "In the Absence of Birds," seemingly following Wheeler's suggestion, describes a birding excursion during which *Not even a crow* is seen (81; italics in original). But the walk—another of McKay's favourite tropes—continues "through the hoary undergrowth near / the stream bank" (81), the speaker and his companions maintaining their desire to see (or hear) a bird while making the most of the experience and what the experience makes possible: a chance for introspection and companionship, an opportunity to reflect on such desires, a realization that there is more than one way of knowing, of being in the world. P. K. Page uses the glosa form to engage with McKay's avian poetics.

The glosa is a form particularly adept at dedication and address to another poet's work. Glosas take four lines from a poem as an epigraph and redeploy each line as the terminal line in each of its own ten-line stanzas, of which there are four. Page is the Canadian glosa poet par excellence. In *Coal and Roses: 21 Glosas* (2009), she includes "Improbable Concept" (48–49), which borrows a quatrain from McKay's "Edge of Night" (*SD* 69). The epigraph reads:

> Certainly the dead watch us, but not
> as opera, nor as the Great Grey Owl
> tunes in gophers underground.
> We are their daytime television.

McKay's poem—hardly a typical bird poem, despite the owl reference—advises against falling out of tune with the quotidian (occasionally exotic), bodily (occasionally bawdy) existence that is definitely not the purview of the dead, whose presence can sometimes be felt as "a lope / detached from the body" (*SD* 69). To acknowledge their presence and adjust our behaviour is to slip across the edge of night and to "fall in with [the dead's] radical bemusement," at which time we will cease being watched. This seems key, that humans—the living—remain alive when watched, an interesting reversal of McKay's preoccupation with birdwatching.

Page picks up on this reversal with the term "people-watching," which she suggests the dead accomplish perhaps with "Specially constructed binoculars." More pertinent, though, is the way McKay's avian poetics manifest in Page's glosa as an extension of the earlier poem's reference to a specific bird. In one of the poem's four stanzas, Page effectively out-McKays McKay; she becomes (or at least invokes) the birder-poet with field guide in hand and a little ornithological knowledge. Continuing from the quatrain's second line, Page writes:

> *Strix nebulosa*, the grey ghost
> or phantom owl, who sees through his ears
> or hears through his eyes or does
> whatever is required for finding food
> in the snow,
> who makes no sound
> beyond the whoooosh as he flies
> and the whooo-ooo-ooo as he calls
> and – unlike the yellow-eyed Great Horned –
> *tunes in gophers underground.* (49)

That Page can devoted a quarter of her poem—which is, like "Edge of Night," essentially a meditation on life and death—to a McKavian[4] exposition of owl ecology is a reassuring sign of McKay's place in English-language poetry. The multiple names—scientific, popular/regional—the descriptions of hunting/feeding, the transcription of the owl's call, the comparison to a similar species' behaviour—all are strategies that represent some elements of avian poetics that McKay has employed through his writing career. These poets who respond to McKay in their poems—Wheeler, Seymour, Page—are contributing to a lyric conversation with McKay and with a way of knowing and making, rather than simply mimicking a poetic style. The various strategies at work and play in the poems they have dedicated to McKay indicate to a large extent what I mean by avian poetics.

Writing about a living writer who has entered the most prolific phase of his career comes with some interesting challenges. The research and writing resemble less an archaeological dig than a field trip to study the habits of an elusive diving bird.[5] His underwater paths remain hidden during intermittent pauses in his poetic output; he returns from field trips with artefacts that accumulate and inspire: old tires, clumps of mud, feathers, bones, stories, songs—the flotsam and jetsam of the phenomenological world. Other scholars have written about birds in literature, and even more writers have interpreted birds in their work. "Few poets," writes Leonard Lutwack, author of a book on that subject, "fail to respond to birds" (xii); that is, nearly every poet in the English language has written about birds in some way.[6] As a result, a sustained critical analysis of this phenomenon might seem an obvious and easy project; and yet Lutwack's *Birds in Literature* (1994) remained the sole effort to record the various (mainly symbolic) roles of selected literary birds until Thomas Gannon published *Skylark Meets Meadowlark: Reimagining the Bird in British Romantic and Contemporary Native American Literature* (2009).

At times Lutwack, "a longtime and knowledgeable birder as well as literary critic, is content to ignore [a] bird's specific identity," or to resist pursuing an ornithological reading in favour of a symbolic one (Rowlett 635). Referring to Saint-John Perse's poem "The Bird" (198–99), for example, Lutwack is quick to offer an ornithological reading of Perse's observation that "most ardent for life of all our blood kin," "the bird is he who bears hidden in himself, to nourish his passion, the highest fever of the blood. His grace is that burning. Nothing symbolic about this: it is simple biological fact" (198). Lutwack explains that "[b]irds have twice the amount of sugar in their blood as mammals" (x–xi). Intermittently throughout his book, Lutwack offers ornithological qualifiers as explanations, as in the passage above, or as correctives, as in the following passage regarding Chaucer's *Parlement of Foulys*: "In the garden is a temple where the goddess of nature is holding a convocation of birds on Saint Valentine's Day, the occasion 'whan every foul cometh there to chese his make.' February is too early for some birds to mate in England," Lutwack observes, "but the poet is less interested in birds than the people they represent" (189). Birds for Chaucer are "a literary convenience for the poet to handle a serious subject freely and amusingly" (189). To pay attention to Chaucer's anthropocentric tendencies in a study of a contemporary Canadian poet is to acknowledge an avian literary history, to suggest that early poetry, replete with poetic licence and symbolism, maintains an important position in the development of literary ecology, even if such poems as *Parlement of Foulys* and *The Owl and the Nightingale* have little to do with actual birds. As Susan Fisher writes in her article about metaphor and homology in McKay's poetry, "[u]sing animals symbolically does not seem a terribly reprehensible activity, but perhaps it is a dangerous mental habit, a way of thinking that permits more overt forms of exploitation" (50). Chaucer has been established as an influential writer in a Western literary tradition, and his way of thinking, while not explicitly dangerous, has informed the way we think about the world, including about human–nonhuman relations. Chaucer and, by extension, the British Romantics represent a trajectory of thought that has contributed to Western instrumentalism, which as Mark Cochrane notes, McKay critiques in an attempt "to 'collaborate' with the ungraspable object, not possess it" (730). In the pages that follow, I trace this attempt in McKay's poems, especially those featuring birds and birding, positing it as a quintessentially ecocritical strategy.

In his anthropocentric tendencies, Chaucer is hardly alone. Others have written books that focus on the "use" (again mainly symbolic) of birds in the work of particular authors such as Chaucer and Shakespeare. Though parenthetical, "mainly symbolic" is the operative modifier in the previous sentence, and "use" the operative noun. The *use* of birds as symbols in poetry is interesting so far as it goes; I am more interested in how poets attend to and write about birds whose presence does not immediately and conventionally invoke common imagistic, allegorical readings (which is not to suggest all allegorical, symbolic readings are conventional). The pursuit of the birdness of poetical birds is not a simple undertaking; when Lutwack claims that "not all facts can be dealt with imaginatively; poets would be hard put to find in the articles of a professional ornithological journal much material that they could use in their writing" (19), he echoes late-eighteenth-century writer John Aikin, who argues, according to John Rowlett, that "the new [c. 1777] knowledge emerging from the study of natural history could serve descriptive poets admirably in achieving novelty in imagery and language," but "'every part of natural history does not seem equally capable of affording poetic imagery'" (625). I agree that poets would be hard put, but I want to emphasize that such a challenge should not in any way prevent poets from putting ornithological (or any scientific) fact to use in their poetry. The bird poem and the birder-critic extend logically from what are becoming orthodox discussions of ecopoetry by ecocritics.

In contrast to Lutwack's and Aikin's claims, then, and pursuing an ecocritical model open to various disciplines, I share Rowlett's desire to illuminate "literature by ornithological knowledge" (639). I base my discussion of ecocriticism on the premise that science and scientific literature can and do influence poetry and the reading of poetry. James Edmund Harting's *The Ornithology of Shakespeare*, first published in 1864 and subtitled *A critical examination and explanation of bird life in Elizabethan times as reflected in the works of Shakespeare*, is an example of a study informed "by ornithological knowledge" that relies on an older method of natural history, such as that practised by Gilbert White, than on contemporary biology as a basis for reading literature. Harting introduces his study with an overview of Shakespeare's credentials as "both a sportsman and a naturalist" (2) before arranging the literary birds "into certain natural groups, including the foreign and domesticated species" (viii).[7] Despite his claim that "it would be absurd to look for exactness in [such] trifles" as the green eyes Juliet's nurse attributes to eagles—a "supposition" that "must be regarded as poetic licence"—Harting grounds many of his observations in ornithological knowledge (25). "The awe," for example, "with which [the owl] is regarded by the superstitious, may be attributed in some measure to the fact of its flying by night" (85). While the fact of owls' nocturnal behaviour is based more in natural history than experimental science in the contemporary sense, such repeatable observations in nature represent an early scientific method. (Indeed, in *A Concise History of Ornithology*, Michael Walters claims that the scientific study of birds started with Aristotle, who "recognised" approximately 140 species of birds and offered close observations of their plumage, behaviour, and anatomy.) Harting also alludes to other observations (from amateur naturalists as well as ornithologists) in confirming the identity of birds in Shakespeare. He refers to such prominent British ornithologists as W. B. Tegetmeier, William Yarrell, and Francis Willughby, whose *Ornithologiae* (1676), translated into English as *Ornithology* in 1678, was a landmark—"the most comprehensive seventeenth-century handbook on birds, [it] contained the period's best avian classification system" (Battalio 27; cf. Walters 37–40). However, the lack of what today is considered scientific knowledge in the book (verifiable knowledge derived from manipulative and repeatable laboratory experiments) can be attributed to the ornithology of the time, which consisted mainly of natural histories (for example, Gilbert White's *The Natural History of Selborne* [1789] and Thomas Bewick's *A History of British Birds* [1826]) and field experiments.

Michael Jeneid's "gambit" in writing *Chaucer's Checklist* is similar to mine in putting forward an eco (avian) criticism with a difference: "that Chaucerians will gain a deeper appreciation of their preeminent medieval poet by paying close attention to his birds and seeing how effectively they have been used in some of the world's greatest literature" (3). My project differs from Jeneid's, though, in the way it seeks to develop an appreciation of the birds, minus the possessive ("his birds"), that Don McKay writes about, and birds' complex (inter)relations to an ecological knowledge, and an ecology of knowledge.[8]

A book-length study of McKay's poetry cannot avoid birds. But what is it about birds that compel poets in the first place? Rowlett offers a fairly typical set of reasons for humans' historical interest in birds and calls on ecocritics to elaborate:

> For anyone interested in ecological criticism and theory, the class *Aves* composes an especially rewarding group of natural creatures to inquire into since, like us, they are found in every waste and wilderness of every continent; they extend every ocean to the sky. They enliven every doorstep, and are known—to some extent—by all humans. Birds have always provided food for thought as well as for the table, and, as any birder of taste knows, they have inspired a range of aesthetic responses. For some time now, they have constituted a subject of study in their own right, serving as a pleasurable means of examining questions in ecology, ethology, biochemical systematics, and evolutionary biogeography—and as a rather less pleasurable means of measuring the health of our environment. (631)

As others have noted, humans have been observing and living with birds for centuries, and for well over a century literary critics have been teaching poems about birds. But how many lecturers consider the dynamics of soaring in "The Second Coming," or contemplate the physics of buckling in "The Windhover," or explore the evolutionary biology of birdsong in "To a Skylark"? How many have seriously considered literary birds as living, breathing creatures with interesting, and applicable, lessons to teach readers about poetry? Surprisingly few, I wager, even though Thomas Hardy has provided a model for just such a thing.[9]

Birds are often considered to be unequivocally "other" than humans, not to mention other than earth- or sea-bound creatures. Leonard Nathan, in *Diary of a Left-Handed Birdwatcher*, cites Donald Culross Peattie to explain why: "Man feels himself an infinity above those creatures who stand, zoölogically, only one step below him, but every human being looks up to the birds. They seem like emissaries of another world which exists about us and above us, but into which, earth-bound, we cannot penetrate" (11–12). In addition, Nathan tells a story, an origin story of sorts, to account for the particular affinity between poets and birds. He tells the story of Vālmīki, the great Indian sage who "utters a terrible curse" on a hunter whose arrow has killed a male krauncha—a demoiselle crane—in the midst of its mating ritual. The sage utters the curse, it seems, in the form of a "well-turned couplet" and, as a consequence, invents poetry; Vālmīki, in other words, is simultaneously the first poet and the first birdwatcher (15–16). Nathan's story follows his claim that "poetry and birds have been associated since the beginning of civilization, probably before.... [A]ncient poets put birds into their poems not just as symbols for human feelings but also as authentic forms of otherness.... Birds enter poems to mediate between us and the world" (15). Unfortunately, in this instance, Nathan implies that "we" and birds are not part of the world. Although birds often represent for McKay "authentic forms of otherness," he goes out of his way to check a human tendency of imagining our superior place in the world, despite the obvious differences among species.

And so, in the chapters and interchapters that follow, I posit a particularly McKavian way of thinking the relation between humans and the other-than-human world. By focusing on specific birds that McKay writes about in his poetry, and by attending to field guides as well as literary criticism, I demonstrate McKay's role in a tradition of Canadian nature writing and his influence on Canada's fledgling ecocriticism. The poems that McKay animates with flora and fauna living outside language refer the ecologically curious reader to the field guide in much the same way an unfamiliar bird or tree or rock does. Knowledge of species specificity in McKay's work is important for a number of reasons, which I explore in the chapters that follow.

part one

Chapter One

Nesting

> A thatched cottage is set on the ground like a nest in a field. And a wren's nest is a thatched cottage, because it is a covered, round nest.
> – Gaston Bachelard, *The Poetics of Space* (98)

> [W]e have a proverb according to which men can do everything except build a bird's nest.
> – Ambroise Paré, qtd. in *Bachelard* (92)

A wonderful tension resides in Don McKay's poetics between the domestic nest—often, but not always, the kitchen—and the urge to get outside where observations can be made. Two poems appearing together in McKay's breakthrough book *Birding, or desire* (1983)[1] get at this tension in different ways. Like the dog at the end of "Smash the Windows" (114), each of us will have had, by the time we die, a "brief / but action-packed career." McKay has a knack for reminding us of our species' youth in evolutionary (and geologic) terms. The poem that ends with a dog "crashing through the window" is—up to that slightly funny, slightly sad moment—a birthday poem for the speaker's daughter. While a thirteenth birthday is perhaps premature for empty-nest anxieties to take hold, crossing the threshold between child and teenager invites both nostalgia and a sense of mortality. After an evening celebrating "with scotch and old-time fiddle music," "smoke and / bawdy ancient English folksongs"—presumably the birthday girl did not partake of scotch and smoking and song—friends begin to leave. The final gift comes from time itself: memories of past significant events, including the moment ten minutes after her birth that the daughter first locked eyes with her father. Reminiscing thus aims to protect against the inevitable forward-looking reality that children grow up and leave the family home—insert the appropriate cliché about leaving the nest here. That she is only thirteen and unlikely to fly the coop just yet comforts the parents, to be sure; but that damn dog, "like the appendix of the party," shatters from without that comfort and any sense of domestic safety.

The window is a threshold apposite to the call in *Ornithologies of Desire* to pay attention to what's outside. From a parental perspective, the dog crashing through the window—shortening if not ending his life—augurs ill for a child on the verge of entering the wide world. The poem's title, however, anticipates the ending while offering a gloss on its metaphorical significance. The imperative to smash the windows issues a challenge to acknowledge wilderness as part of domestic space—its dangers as well as its potential—and to act on an animal desire to walk among grasses and trees and mammals and birds. Deliberate acts of breaking out of domesticated space to exist sensuously in the world beyond home prefigure the dog's inadvertent violence, which rends the speaker from his nostalgic reverie.

Movement between inside and outside occupies the speaker in "Simply Because Light" (115), too, though in a far less violent manner. The domestic scene, with the speaker "disparaging the dishes" his spouse is trying to wash, sets up a string of memories and desires for memories related to birth and children, the vagaries of marriage, and a dialectics of inside and outside, as Gaston Bachelard would put it. Light "falling a certain way through the dining room widow" provides a stimulus for the speaker to get outside and "lapse in speech on the balcony." That he wants "memories that germinate" and children who "wonder at the seed they were" reaffirms the extent to which home in much of McKay's work resembles a nest from which all must leave even as all require the basic protections nests and other domiciles offer. The window in this poem remains intact, yet the way it admits crepuscular light agitates the speaker in ways that recall the dog's agitation in "Smash the Windows." Similarly, by responding to the light's clarion call in "Simply Because Light" in a manner that affirms a middle-class domesticity—all the speaker wants is to "have a beer / on the balcony instead of" ruminating indoors and contemplating memories and memories-to-be—the speaker enacts a movement from inside to outside in a safe, comfortable manner. Still, the implicit violence of "Smash the Windows" followed by the complicit violence of domestic life—the speaker recalls a "fight in the hotel in Edinburgh" alongside "other fights and hotels we have known"—plants seeds of a different kind, which McKay explores throughout his corpus.

Take the imaginative act of "cabinning," for example, which McKay discusses briefly in "Approaching the Clearing" (*DW* 97–110), an essay published over two decades after *Birding, or desire* that invokes the office as one of many possible rooms of one's own in which to do the work of writing, some interior space that "ensure[s] seclusion and protect[s] the artist from routine busy-ness" (97). "Approaching the Clearing" engages domestication as the product of latent violence in relation to a desire for ownership, at best, and systemic colonialism, at worst. The moments a poet finds himself in a clearing that enables "mental openness, vulnerability and wordlessness" (99) cannot last forever, in part because such openness, for all its creative potential, is unsustainable. As an antidote, McKay suggests "an impulse" he calls cabinning, which despite its benign implications "projects us into the clearing in a way that alters all the relationships inside it" (99). To make a home, even to imagine making a home, requires alterations to a place and its inhabitants. These alterations are not necessarily for the worse, and the experience of encountering a clearing in the forest, as I discuss in more detail in Chapter Seven, offers important opportunities to consider humans' place in the world.

If McKay's writing about domestic space and nests/nesting—whether metaphorically, as I've been discussing so far, or ornithologically, as I discuss below—does anything, it provides a home base from which to consider the way humans relate to, and write about relations to, the other-than-human world. In other words, thinking about home-as-nest encourages thinking about nests as profoundly complex spaces for humans and birds alike. McKay articulates a desire to rethink our place in the world most clearly and concisely in the essay "Otherwise Than Place" (*DW* 15–31): "What interests me right now are the possibilities for reverse flow in a relationship that has been so thoroughly one-way. The saga of place has involved colonization, agriculture, exploitation, land use, resourcism, and development (sustainable and otherwise). 'What we make,' Helen Humphreys observes, 'doesn't recover from us'" (18). Without claiming to know precisely how to enact such a reversal in the unbalanced relations between humans and nonhumans, McKay offers "meditative medicine" (19), which includes ways of attempting the world[2] rather than ways of owning the world, ways of telling and listening to many voices, stories, songs, rather than ways of telling the same old story and enforcing the same old binaries: science/literature, nature/culture, baseland/hinterland, texts/lumps[3]—binaries that have helped determine unsustainable relations to place.

Place, landscape, nature—these have been the primary sites of ecocritical engagement even as literature of place, landscape painting, and nature poetry have been to varying degrees the subjects of books like this prior to the emergence of ecocriticism as a field of study in the 1990s. McKay occupies a central place in this philosophical development. McKay is a poet of place; he is attentive to particular landscapes; he is a nature poet. But while he is capable, like his Romantic predecessors, of evoking emotional responses to particular places and experiences in straightforward, albeit metaphorically complex, lyrics, McKay's central concern has long been the deteriorating health of the planet and its inhabitants. Over a decade before articulating his wilderness aesthetic and avian poetics in essay form, McKay wrote nature poetry with a pronounced difference. In "Nocturnal Animals" (*B* 49), for instance, the speaker inhabits a familiar domestic space from which to contemplate the world outside and his relation to it. Southern Ontario, the place of McKay's early poems, "surrounds [the] kitchen like well-fed flesh," while the speaker sips coffee and recounts the plight of wolves in Lobo Township (in Middlesex County, near London, Ontario):

> Two years ago the wolves took shape
> in Lobo Township, lifting the tombstone of its name
> to lope across these snowy fields
>   between the woodlots
>   spectral
>   legless as wind, their nostrils
> wide with news of an automated pig barn
> waiting for them like an all-night restaurant.
> Shot, their bodies wisped away, their eyes
> stubbed out.

McKay announces his wilderness aesthetic in "Nocturnal Animals" by centring on a species that is native to a particular area of southern Ontario but that remained present only through an act of nomination (*lobo* being Spanish for wolf). The speaker marks the wolves' return, sensitive to their lupine intelligence, which leads them (ironically, perversely) to prey on pigs that are cultivated and slaughtered for human consumption. The wolves' spectral presence as they "lope across these snowy fields / between the woodlots" describes their ability to inhabit the environment furtively—they are, after all, along with the restless speaker, the eponymous nocturnal animals—grey bodies against and across a white background at night. But it also describes how ephemeral they are in a landscape modified by, and for, humans, a landscape that has been ineluctably cabinned, as it were. As in other wolf stories, they will not be tolerated: the light in their eyes is "stubbed out," extinguished like so many cigarettes in an ashtray. The force of colliding cultures beyond domestic space—the wolf, the township, the man in the kitchen—recurs in McKay's work as a point of fruitful, if vexed, encounter. Most of McKay's nature poems invoke the human in, and human impact on, nature, both as an acknowledgement that human culture is natural and as a way of decrying the extent of our destructive talents and tendencies. In "Nocturnal Animals," McKay includes, in addition to the speaker and wolves and pigs, a truck moving along Highway 22 and an old Buick dreaming in the garage—nocturnal animals all.

These human-made, ultimately symbolic nests indicate a subtle entry into McKay's avian poetics. Inside our nests, McKay seems to suggest, we incubate ideas and (for some of us) we raise children. Inside their nests birds lay eggs, tiny packages of embryo, yolk, albumen, and various extra-embryonic membranes that eventually, if all goes well, transform from an oval mass into a living, breathing bird. Nestlings begin to learn vocalizations, to recognize food, and to recognize predator and prey before developing sufficiently to leave the nest. Despite his vast body of writing about birds and his interest, as essayist, in the nesting habits of bushtits, McKay does not seem to devote much of his birding time—or much of his writing—to the discovery of nests and eggs. Nevertheless, this opening chapter posits a relation between nests and McKay's status as Canada's foremost bird poet (and birder-poet).

In his revised review of *Birding, or desire*, "The Antithesis of Rape, Which Is Not Chastity: The Voice of Don McKay," Robert Bringhurst calls McKay "the English language's Halitherses," referring to a seer who appears in Homer's *Odyssey* (29). Halitherses was, according to Homer, the best "at understanding birds, and he had the skill of putting what they taught him into a language that less observant humans could understand" (29). The extent to which McKay attends to specific birds in the field certainly supports Bringhurst's comparison and, indeed, corroborates many of Bringhurst's own ideas regarding the poetical capacity of the more-than-human world. While I agree with Bringhurst's assessment of McKay as a modern-day Halitherses, I think a more recent comparison might be fitting. If we consider both his "intense engagement with the natural world, his respect for the local environment as an autonomous realm [that] constitutes the core of his originality as an ecological writer" (McKusick 236), and the extent to which "Birds are essential" to his poetry (Bate 156), John Clare might represent a more immediate, though hardly contemporary, poetic antecedent to McKay. Both Clare, a self-described peasant born in 1793, and McKay, born into a middle-class family in 1942, write out of a realization "that since the eighteenth century [humans] have radically changed the face of the earth in ways that may not be altogether desirable" and express, if indirectly, concern "that there has been a reduction of both the quality and quantity of natural biosphere resulting in the extinction of untold species of fauna and flora"

(Lutwack 233). Clare is often "regarded as the first ecological writer in the English tradition" (McKusick 227), while McKay, I argue, cultivates a contemporary version of ecopoetry informed by precise knowledge of specific birds and their ecologies.

Thomas Gannon's reading of Clare provides a basis from which to understand my pairing of him and McKay. Gannon's reasoned critique of British Romanticism's big-name poets, whose bird poetry manifests as "recuperative emblems for, above all, very human strivings and needs, as ultimately failed attempts to recuperate the Romantic self or 'I' through an avian Other" (60), meets some resistance when encountering Clare's work. According to Gannon, "Clare's peculiar, almost *egoless* empathy for [the] actual environment" exemplifies a poetry attuned to ecological dynamics. Moreover, Clare embodies, *pace* Coleridge, characteristics of "a clown and shepherd," a humble poet "who could only see the world in a grain of sand—or in the eggs of a particular Eurasian wryneck's nest" (179). Some comments about nests and nesting in Clare and McKay offer insights into (avian) ecopoetics and suggest compelling avenues for further comparative research.[4]

In "Easter 1981" (*B* 89), McKay asks readers to

> think of all the nests and
> nests in progress up there swaying twig by
> straw by string by bit of rag
>   and of our own
> coagulations from inside
> the manic voice of playoff hockey, close-shaved, naked,
> furred by the tuning up of fiddle and guitar
>   while underneath
> the kids are blowing eggs:
>   noises from our rich
> and slithy pre-existence.

This poem avoids specificity with regard to bird species or ecological relations—unlike, say, "A Toast to the Baltimore Oriole" (*B* 88), in which the speaker toasts the bird's "good looks and the neat way [it] shit[s]" and "dedicate[s] baseball" to "the sturdy fragile woven / scrotum of [its] nest"—but it effectively implies a human ecology that extends homologically, and domestically, to include bird nests, playoff hockey, and Easter eggs. Spring brings with it "natural" occurrences, such as nest-building, as well as such "cultural" events as the playoffs and Christian celebrations of Christ's resurrection. No peasant poet, McKay acknowledges in this poem humans' cultural and natural existence as "rich" with both middle-class activities associated with holidays and evolutionary connections to our "slithy pre-existence"—out of the fertile muck, as it were. "Easter 1981" succinctly posits the idea of home for McKay on a threshold between domesticity and wilderness, posits the birder-poet, as he writes in "The Bushtits' Nest" (*V* 83–106), as "a citizen of the frontier, a creature of words who will continue to use them to point" (87). "The Bushtits' Nest" is McKay's most sustained writing about nests, and thus represents a logical way into his avian poetics and a point of comparison with Clare's ornithological writing about nests.[5]

Since all birds are oviparous and thus unable to provide the sort of protection viviparous species, such as humans, provide up until the birth of their young, they need to find and/or produce suitable nesting sites (Bennett and Owens 68–69). The human search for home is wide ranging and often personal; the search can be literal, spiritual, metaphorical.[6] The avian search for home can be equally multiple. It is when observing bushtits that were—as McKay "inferred later with the help of reference books"—building a gourd-shaped nest while attempting "to summon something out of nothing" (*V* 102) that McKay realizes birds' ontological confidence, that they, unlike humans, "do not need a Lao-tzu to remind them of the non-being [air] their lives depend on" (104). Yet despite the bushtits' ability to "be next door to nothing," their idea of home seems to be "closer to a kitchen in Newfoundland than to a hermitage" (103, 104). The nest-building continues in spite of the car parked underneath it, in spite, that is, of humans' increasing presence in and pollution of natural spaces, and the birder-poet is left to stand, "mildly agog at the prospect of domestication occurring in the natural world" (106). McKay's description of the nest invokes domestication and human dwelling, thus courting the absurdity Bachelard suggests accompanies "images that attribute *human* qualities to a nest" (92). The inevitably anthropocentric metaphor, however, relies more on a sliding scale of domestic qualities than on the absurd claim that bushtit nests resemble Newfoundland kitchens. In other words, the bushtits' tolerance for neighbourly coming and going surprises the human observer, who likely assumes, given the birds' extreme otherness, that they would prefer hermit-like peace and quiet. Nests, for birds and for humans, need not be sanctuaries utterly free of noise.

A French philosopher of science, Bachelard recognized the potential for correlation between bird nests and human ideas of home when he wrote *The Poetics of Space* in 1958. Suggesting that the topic of his book might fittingly be called *topophilia*, Bachelard anticipates both E. O. Wilson's *Biophilia: The Human Bond with Other Species* (1984) and Yi-Fu Tuan's *Topophilia: A Study of Environmental Perception, Attitudes, and Values* (1990). Bachelard's work resonates with ecocritical studies, I think, because of the room he allows for phenomenology to inspire reflection on natural objects. Jonathan Bate ends his discussion of Bachelard's phenomenological affinity to Clare's poetry by rewording a key tenet: "'The cleverer I am at miniaturizing the world,' writes Bachelard, 'the better I possess it.' The thought is beautiful and true, but the associations of 'clever' and 'possess' are wrong because they are evocative of Cartesian man. Let us rephrase: the more attuned I am as I miniaturize the world, the better I dwell upon the earth" (161).

By miniaturizing, Bachelard means focusing on the small domestic spaces that protect us and our belongings—rooms and wardrobes—as well as their outdoor corollaries—shells and nests. One poet's attuned miniaturization—for Bate, that poet is John Clare—is another poet's attentive proximity. For me, that poet is Don McKay. The closer McKay brings readers to the birds and objects he writes about, the smaller and more precise they seem. The precision and accuracy of McKay's language invite attentive, respectful dwelling upon the earth, particularly as McKay reinvigorates a Bachelardian dialectic between inside and outside, a tension between domestic and wilderness spaces. But in McKay's poetics, wilderness often inheres in supposed domestic space and objects.

In his attention to nests, though, Bachelard is less concerned with the vagaries of ornithology than with his phenomenological relation to the world of objects. "For it is not the task of this phenomenology to describe the nests met with in nature, which is a quite positive task reserved for ornithologists," he declares (93)—just as most poets who write about birds are less interested in birds and more interested in the types of people they represent. Even so, Bate finds Bachelard's spatial poetics useful when searching for a lexicon with which to respond to Clare's poetry. As Scott Bryson suggests, much ecocriticism is interested in "alternatives that give us a more precise lexicon with which to describe our efforts at finding a home in nature while simultaneously respecting its ultimate unknowability" (*West* 43). Bachelard's phenomenology provides for Bate's inquiry into Clare's nest poems what field guides and patient observation provide for my inquiry into McKay's writing about bushtit nest architecture. McKay's encounter with the bushtits' nest offers rich material for the birder-critic; it also invites a broad ecological consideration of the nesting material, namely the lichens, which, in addition to spreading through spores, "rely on the transportation of bits of their thalluses (bodies) by birds" in order to reproduce (105). Attention to the unfamiliar birds leads to identification, which in turn leads to awareness of nesting habits that direct the careful observer toward the ecology of lichen. John Clare would be proud.

A contemporary of Wordsworth, Byron, and Keats, Clare has developed a "reputation as 'the finest poet of Britain's minor naturalists and the finest naturalist of all Britain's major poets'" (Robinson and Fitter vii). He kept copious field notes that have been reproduced as *John Clare's Birds*, edited by Eric Robinson and Richard Fitter, who note that, along with having been "something of a pioneer in his interest in bird song" (xiii), Clare "free[d] himself from those conventional poetical associations of birds where, for example, the nightingale is symbolic of ruined love and the cuckoo of marital treachery" (viii). Clare's observations were apparently detailed enough to enable identification in the field; a historian of Northamptonshire's flora, for example, "was able to identify 135 plant species from Clare's poems and found that no fewer than forty had not been recorded by earlier botanists" (xix). His field notes are not always so informative; the entry for pettichap (chiffchaff), for example, contains the briefest of references to the fact that "it makes a curious nest in low bushes" (50); however, these observations inform Clare's poem "The Pettichap's Nest," which is considerably more descriptive:

> – that snug entrance wins
> Scarcely admitting e'en two fingers in
> And lined with feathers warm as silken stole
> And soft as seats of down for painless ease
> And full of eggs scarce bigger e'en than peas. (183)

These lines are not without metaphor, but the poet's fingers feeling around inside the nest provide specific information which, in turn, enables Clare to make metaphor informed by accurate details. That same accuracy determines the proximity of the reader to the world, not while reading the poem but afterwards. If nothing else, the next time I ramble across a Northamptonshire field, I will be aware of the pettichap's nest because of "The Pettichap's Nest"—presumably I will have consulted a field guide to British birds (since neither pettichap nor chiffchaff is indexed in my copy of David Allen Sibley's guide to North American birds or my copy of *Roberts Birds of Southern Africa*), and I will have seen an image of the bird; and perhaps I will have learned whether pettichap eggs are as small as Clare indicates.

According to Bate, "In the poetry of John Clare, as in the vision of Bachelard, a nest is the small round thing which is the natural world's analogue of the human idea of home" (Bate 157). Following from Bachelard's interest in "miniaturizing the world" (150), we can think about the nest as a miniature human dwelling, or home. Such an interest in miniature, on such minutiae as a bird's name, the number of times per minute it beats its wings, what it eats, is a strikingly poetic parallel to scientific reductionism. At a time when his contemporaries were attempting to articulate the grandiloquent terror of the sublime landscape, Clare was intensely interested in recording how many eggs magpies lay (five to eight "of a watery green colour thickly freckled with brown spots" [10]) and in what they use to line their nests ("twitch and dried roots" [11]). For Bate, the value of Clare's interest, and of contemporary critics' interest in Clare, lies in how Clare's accuracies help us "to live fully but without profligacy upon our crowded earth" (161). It is surely no coincidence that birds are responsible for the first poem and the first poet, for humans' successful attempts at flying (if we believe the literature on the earliest flying machines), for human music, and also for what is widely considered to be the first work of environmental writing in North America (Rachel Carson's *Silent Spring*). The influence of birds on human life is reflected, too, in the value of all such bird poetry.

Nests are also, as we're reminded in McKay's collection *Paradoxides* (2012), sleeping places. In the poem of that name (*P* 31–32), based on a series of photographs by environmental artist Marlene Creates that document impressions she has left after lying on the ground, nests' ephemerality emerges as a key, and often overlooked, element of their nature. In these photographs,

> Something whispers here
> so softly it's dissolving
> even as the camera clicks:
> catch-and-release, it says, place
> is gesture, is delible, the rumple of a moose-bed,
> the bower left by lovers, the punched strike
> printed by a hunting owl in the snow – (31)

So it seems that what we make can occasionally recover from us in a way that admits "this memory is earth's / not ours" (31). Far from altering the landscape permanently, yet still within striking distance of cabinning, Creates's photographs document presence "in the pressed grass" and "bent-over reeds" while allowing for analogous acts of creation by other creatures, whether sleeping or hunting. Despite these places' finity, the photographic record maintains them as places from which to see the world, in much the way Tim Lilburn's project of sleeping in a root cellar positions the human-in-the-landscape as a watcher sensitive to the landscape's particularities. For Lilburn, the root cellar "was a place to wait," a "listening post a distance out in the unknown terrain, the land that baffled [him] and the other world beside that world" ("Going" 181). Unlike Creates's sleeping places, which dissolve yet remain captured as image, Lilburn's root cellar implies long-term functionality—if, indeed, it is ever used as a root cellar to store vegetables—even as he imagines "that it's disappeared entirely, back into the hill, fused" (181). Both Creates's and Lilburn's projects insinuate humans into places typically inhabited by nonhuman animals; McKay's writing about nests and domestic space continues the thought experiment.

An anecdote shared by Rosemary Sullivan confirms the significance of nests for McKay and goes some way to explaining, perhaps, why they make up so little of his poetical work. Recalling a workshop for writers in Saskatchewan, Sullivan marvels as much at the flora and fauna McKay was willing to point out as at a coyote warren that he chose not to share. "Each morning," Sullivan writes, "he'd tell us of their progress, but we knew instinctively not to ask to accompany him to the site. It would have been as absurd as asking to invade the nursery of a human stranger, as much a violation of the coyote's privacy" (16). Since nature is neither "tourism" nor "voyeurism" (16), the quiet attentiveness of a single human suffices to observe and record the coyotes' life in their den. By limiting exposure, the participants in this writer's retreat respectfully acknowledge an otherness that, given their work with McKay, will potentially enter their world view and their writing. Humans might be capable of building anything except a nest—we can fly! we can sing!—but we can construct homes that harken to both the safety and vulnerability of nests, that recapitulate both the comfort provided by nests and the inevitability that those raised in them will leave one day.

The last section of "As if Spirit, As if Soul" (*S/S* 57–59) reverses the violence and latent terror of "Smash the Windows," offering an all-too-familiar scene as an attempt to explain a vague "something" that "settles" and "accumulates" (58) following a sense of "lifting off, letting go" (57). The first two sections, referring to settling and lifting, correspond I think to spirit and soul, respectively (notions I discuss in more detail in Chapter Nine). The third section describes a scenario that renders the speaker's short essay on spirit and soul in material terms. "I don't know / how the house wren managed to get in," the speaker says, "but it was hard to get out" (59). Unlike the dog and the thirteen-year-old daughter from the earlier poem, the house wren occupies domestic space inadvertently, possibly having flown (or hopped) in through an open window or door. The speaker's nest, as it were, has been infiltrated by an outside presence, a biological entity typically residing in wilderness. The wren's presence complicates the speaker's relation to wilderness and implicates him in an act of confinement. Though the bird has not been captured intentionally, its very insideness seems to indicate a case of cabinning gone wrong. No matter the speaker's intentions, the wren "batter[s] / at the window as though trying to call this stiff air / back to life, its panic / fanned by my efforts to help" (59). That the tension between nesting and the urge to get outside here resides in the wren sets the speaker up as a watcher whose own desires confront one another as he contemplates what needs to be done: he simultaneously "wish[es] it would find the open door" and "hope[s] it never would" (59). The former scenario would result in a tiny bird returning to the open, not-stiff air, while the latter remains less clear. The one scenario the speaker does offer is as ridiculous as it is telling of a mind intent to observe the world with equal (or not) parts respect and desire for control (not unlike the aforementioned cabinning). The speaker imagines a "time out" with the bird "perched on the fridge to cock its slender tail, me asking / would it care for some granola as it / empties another waterfall of notes / into the indrawn air of the kitchen" (59). We find ourselves back in the kitchen, back with a creature aiming to get out through the window, except this time the creature lacks the ability to do so. That a bird, which is known for nest-building, wants unequivocally out of the kitchen's domestic nest hints at the kind of careful yet fraught thinking alive in McKay's poetics. With these and other nests in mind, I turn in the following sections to those master nest-builders, the birds, and the various ways their flying and singing get taken up by a poet whose attention to biological and ecological detail fuses with knowledge of a tradition of nature writing and poetry about birds.

Chapter Two

Naming

> "Must we study Roger [Tory] Peterson's bird books in order to read literature?" I am tempted to reply: Yes, that would be a very good thing indeed, and not just for nonfiction but for fictive genres as well.
> – Lawrence Buell, *The Environmental Imagination* (97)

> [O]ne should never construct sentences with "the animal" as the subject. [Oskar] Heinroth used to interrupt such sentences with the mild and friendly interjection: "Are you referring to an amoeba or a chimpanzee?"
> – Konrad Lorenz, *The Natural Science of the Human Species* (260)

A focus on naming serves to recognize the empirical scientific paradigm that has dominated Western cultures since the Enlightenment. Carolus Linnaeus is a key figure both in the history of ecology—he was a botanist whose system of binomial naming, devised three centuries ago, continues to serve "the field ecologist as a generally satisfactory system of organizing ecological information" (Keller and Golley 33)—and in McKay's avian poetics. Naming also enables a closer study of McKay's metaphorical language—his naming and renaming in pursuit of precision and proximity—alongside a consideration of the paradoxical role of language as straightforward, communicative, denotative medium and as problematic, metaphorical, connotative medium. While such a discussion of the dual role language plays acknowledges differences between scientific and poetic writing, it also informs the ornithological desires of my title. When language breaks down in its attempts to name the world—as when a car breaks down or a computer's hard drive fails—we often, according to McKay, "sense the enormous, unnameable wilderness beyond" the breakdown, "a wilderness we both long for and fear" (*V* 64). Like all desire, this species of longing requires the potential for unattainability in order to qualify as desire. The desire to attain knowledge of the world inheres in the human practice of naming. Naming simultaneously succeeds in providing common frames of reference for communities of like-minded people and fails, often, to describe or define satisfactorily what is named. Though neither scientists nor poets are capable of naming with complete accuracy, I argue that attention to species specificity and ecological accuracy—which reflects the desire for a common frame of reference, for creating a community of science and literature scholars—compels readers and critics to get closer to the birds about which McKay writes. Knowing the names for things does not replace other, more intimate, ways of knowing,[1] nor does it constitute scientific knowing in and of itself. But knowing names "embeds uncommon courtesy and an alertness for the store of information in an inanimate source" (Ricou *Salal* 32). In the absence of (and/or alongside) experience, oral histories, and stories that name the world and its relations, science has become the largest, most accessible "store of information" we can look to. Challenges arise once ecocritics begin examining the ways in which such information is produced, disseminated, and interpreted.

To continue naming in the face of our limitations is to grasp at specificity on the verge of inaccuracy: no name can express the totality of a thing. But naming can express relations between things named, and McKay often employs naming in his poetry to engage an ecological view that includes cultural as well as natural phenomena. In "Twinflower" (*A* 4–5), McKay provides a more concise version of Adam's task reimagined than appears in the essay "The Bushtits' Nest" (*V* 79–106). The moment sees Adam pause in the midst of fulfilling his father's request of getting "some names / stuck on these critters" (4). The character of Adam resembles the McKavian speaker who names skeptically, who gets easily engrossed in the gestures of nonhuman beings. Recognizing the damaging set of cultural values inspired by historical divisions between pre- and post-lapsarian worlds, McKay postulates a pre-lapsarian world full of post-lapsarian anxieties. For McKay, labelling the world has always been an unsettling project.[2] After recounting Adam's thoughtful pause, McKay's speaker in "Twinflower" walks "accompanied by [his] binoculars and field guides," able to identify the flower when he sees it, which he does when he least expects to; suddenly, "there they are, and maybe have been / all along, covering the forest floor: a creeper, a shy / hoister of flags, a tiny lamp to read by, one / word at a time" (5). The litany of names the speaker attaches to the twinflower upon seeing it points both to the power of metaphor to give "multiple names to each thing" (Leckie 143) and to the limitations of human linguistic response. The metaphorical naming contrasts sharply with the twinflower's Latin binomial, which we learn from the speaker is *Linnaea borealis*, after Carolus Linnaeus, deviser of the most influential system of scientific naming. McKay's metaphors, though desirous of achieving precision, highlight the narcissism with which Linnaeus appropriated the tiny flower and asked it "to join him in his portrait / [...] / to branch and nod beside him / as he placed himself in that important / airless room" (5). But if the list of metaphorical names functions as a "critique only of a certain kind of systematizing arrogance" (Leckie 136), it also serves to recognize the speaker's complicity in longing "to find them in the field guide," after which "the bright / reticulated snaps of system will occur / as the plant is placed" within a category that includes other, similar plants (5). "Twinflower" articulates one aspect of the difficult-to-know world, offers ways of knowing that simultaneously impose human systems on the natural world and that acknowledge the problems of doing so. The flower might remain, as Leckie suggests, "itself, a flower encountered on a walk in the woods" (144), despite attempts to appropriate it—via Linnean taxonomy and McKavian metaphor—but it also represents a human desire to uncover the unknown and the ecopoetical impulse to get outside.

This impulse to get out of the office and into the field, as I demonstrate, is an integral component of the type of ecocriticism I would like to see practised. It's not a new impulse. Over a century before ecocriticism consolidated into a relevant critical idiom, Wordsworth urged readers to get "Up! Up!" and "quit your books" in "The Tables Turned: An Evening Scene":

> Books! 'tis a dull and endless strife,
> Come, hear the woodland linnet,
> How sweet his music; on my life
> There's more of wisdom in it.
>
> And hark! how blithe the throstle sings!
> And he is no mean preacher;
> Come forth into the light of things,
> Let Nature be your teacher. (166)

I have chosen two stanzas that use particular birds to entice the speaker's "friend" outdoors because they nicely correspond to the avian poetics I wish to highlight in environmental literature; they also enact a correlation between birds—in this case birdsong, which I discuss in more detail in Part Three—and extra-textual wondering/wandering. Granted, Wordsworth's reasons for deferring to the linnet (*Fringilla linota* Linn.), whose song according to Thomas Bewick "is lively and sweetly varied" (119), and the throstle (or song thrush, *Turdus philomelos*), which is according to John Clare "the Thrush celebrated for its fine song" (Robinson and Fritter 26), have more to do with a belief in a transcendental nature to which the lyric "I" reaches than confidence in scientific observation. In his posthumously published book, *The Hedgehog, the Fox, and the Magister's Pox: Mending the Gap between Science and the Humanities* (2003), Stephen Jay Gould picks up on this very tendency of Wordsworth's "beautiful, but tragically flawed verse" (106). Isolating the penultimate stanza—"Sweet is the lore which nature brings, / Our meddling intellect / Distorts the beauteous forms of things. / We murder to dissect"—Gould counters with a defence of the scientific method: "I would only say to the poets that science must dissect as one path to understanding, but never to destroy the beauty and joy of wholeness" (106). Nevertheless, the poem's central thesis supports a readerly agency "That watches and receives" and offers critiques of biology and poetry in equal measure. "Enough of science and of art," Wordsworth writes; put the books away for a while and work to develop an attentive discourse with the physical world.

The desire for scientific or taxonomic accuracy will not always reward the ecocritic with an entirely valid reading; the poem or book itself is likely to invite such investigation while determining the degree of ornithological perspicacity beyond which the ecocritic risks the rather uncritical, derivative act of merely applying a different species of theory. The outward expression of scientific curiosity, or of a willingness to attend to the world via the distinctive perspectives offered by sciences, literatures, and direct experiences, which compels the critic to get out of the office and into the field and/or field guide is theory enough. Far from turning poetry, or the study of poetry, into a science, more accurate knowledge of bird names, behaviours, habitat—of avian ecologies, in short—enables more accurate metaphors, more precise attempts at thinking about what it means to be human, about how to live carefully and humbly in the world we share with others. An early poem by McKay, "'The Bellies of Fallen Breathing Sparrows'" (*B* 93),[3] effectively and humorously examines the results of too much book learning. Addressing his lover, the speaker begins:

> Some things can't be praised enough, among them
> breasts and birds
> who have cohabited so long in metaphor
> most folks think of them as married

As a tacit acknowledgement that birds traditionally inhabit poetry for purely symbolic—and in this case mainly sexualized—reasons, the poem's opening makes no pretension to ornithological specificity. This poem is less a nature poem than one about nature poetry. Instead of offering observations of birds in situ, the speaker brings recollections from the field into the bedroom. When he witnesses his lover remove her shirt, he claims that the inside of his head "is lined with down / like a Blackburnian warbler's nest, / the exterior of which is often rough and twiggy / in appearance." Here the specificity with which McKay names a bird simultaneously acts as self-deprecating gesture—if the exterior of the nest is rough and twiggy so, by analogy, is the exterior of the speaker's head—and shifts the traditional sexist link between birds and women (more accurately, girls) to align birdness with a man. This poem stands up as an early manifesto for the precise application of metaphor. In closing, McKay reflects on the history of a specific erotic comparison:

> The man who wrote "twin alabaster mounds"
> should have spent more time outdoors
> instead of browsing in that musty old museum where
> he pissed away his youth.

Poets make metaphors out of materials and experiences that are near to hand, familiar, knowable. When writing about something as personal and sensuous as love and companionship, the material offered by museums and sculptures might not provide the most accurate metaphors. The difference is one of degree and not of kind—the living world offers more intimate (personal) metaphors than the world of art.

While McKay exhibits highly practised skills with metaphor[4] and his images are well chosen from a birder's repertoire of names and field knowledge, he also cultivates a distrust of metaphor. In essays he has written about the impossibility of full congruence between word and world, as well as in his poetry, he occasionally resists metaphor. In "Night Field" (*NF* 38–41), for example, a three-part poem about the destructive rituals associated with clearing house and moving, the middle section recounts a peculiar narrative. McKay writes in the second part about an ominous painting "given to him [the nameless main character] by his godparents a few years / before his godmother died." The gesture of the gift itself is "so loaded it occupied his / mind like a cathedral" (*NF* 39). Though he spends countless hours "gazing into the field" depicted by the painting's black "spectrum of purples / and bronzes" with "a tuft or / tussock of straw in its lower middle," "tilting his head this way and that way, trying this combination of straws and blackness," he is unable to see a "monster" or "a field with a monster in it," which everyone else claims to see. After considering the possibility that the painting is an outsize "Rorschach test" (thus associating what is seen or not seen with the viewer's subconscious), we eventually read that "the old woman is an old woman, the dog is a dog, the field is a / field, and the monster who will laugh and steal the silver thread / of meaning from a life is never there when he's looking" (40). By deviating from his litany of equations when he gets to the monster, McKay effectively returns to the notion introduced at the beginning of the poem's second part: gestures are themselves loaded with meaning, and life is the ultimate gesture (in this case the life of his godmother, whose death, others in the poem believe, "the monster" portends and mocks). Perhaps the poet is trying on things' names for a change, testing the accuracy of nomination, rather than demonstrating a simple distrust of metaphor, although I am not convinced they can be separated. Merely knowing a name and choosing persistently to rely on its inherent accuracy prevents metaphor, which in turn prevents understandings of the way humans construct through language, and of the ways nonhuman biota (and abiota) make meaning, too.

Leslie Marmon Silko provides compelling evidence for the capacity of nonhuman nature to create multiple layers of meaning. She writes about how in Pueblo culture "The squash blossom is *one thing*: itself" and "a bolt of lightning is itself, but at the same time it may mean much more" (28). Adam Dickinson offers a similar version of this simultaneity of meaning when he writes of metaphoricity as both the *is* and *is not* of a thing: "metaphor, as the crossing of contexts, as the site of an ecological complex, depends on non-metaphor, it depends on the distinctness of things in their language-games" (diss. 30). Thus, when "[r]epresented only in its intrinsic form, the squash flower," for example, "is released from a limited meaning or restricted identity. Even in the most sophisticated abstract form, a squash flower or a cloud or a lightning bolt [becomes] intricately connected with a complex system of relationships" between ancient Pueblo people and "the populous natural world" (Silko 28). Though we should "know the names for things as a minimum" (Lilburn "Going" 184), we must also be aware that such knowledge has the potential to congeal into mere self-knowledge. We humans are the ones, after all, who have chosen the names. It becomes important, then, for the ecopoet and the ecocritic to acknowledge their own epistemological limitations, to realize that, as Lilburn writes in the essay "How to Be Here?": "The world is its names plus their cancellations, what we call it and the undermining of our identifications by an ungraspable residue in objects. To see it otherwise, to imagine it caught in our phrases, is to know it without courtesy, and this perhaps is not to know it at all" (5). Knowing is always inflected by what we do not know, things by what they are not. The same goes for things as symbolic entities. In "Dark of the Moon," McKay encounters moon as metaphor and writes of a moment when the speaker, the supposedly "monolithic, anthropocentric lyrical 'I'" (Dickinson diss. 33), somehow misses the moon's metaphorical significance:

> Once past the street lights I miss it,
> "poised" at the spruce tip, "floating"
> in the pond, the way it gathered longing into moths
> and kept reality from overdosing on its own sane
> self. It seems the dead,
> who would otherwise be dressing up in moonstuff, blending
> with the birch to be both here
> and not here, lose interest in us and descend
> below the reach of roots. The hydro wires
> are hydro wires, the streets are streets, the houses
> full of television. (*AG* 7)

Here is a lyrical "I" aware of the potential for metaphor to lapse into cliché; the scare quotes around participles imply an easy, self-conscious simultaneity. More importantly, this poem acknowledges a relation between the physical world and the world of metaphor. Its title refers to the last three days of the lunar cycle, just prior to a new moon—"that no moon we call new," as McKay eloquently puts it at the end of "On Leaving" (*AG* 70)—when the sky is darker than usual because of the moon's near complete absence from view. Without the moon, the symbolically absent—"the dead"—have no "moonstuff" in which to dress up, no borrowed light with which to insinuate presence where absence persists. In this case, "miss" also suggests nostalgia for metaphor. Without the moon casting its reflected light upon the world, things remain what we have named them, and other sources of light, namely televisions, command more attention than they would under normal circumstances.

McKay's persistent uneasiness with the supposed authority of human language to produce uninflected knowledge speaks to a desire for a responsible thinking, especially with respect to humans' relations with the nonhuman world, which I argue ecocriticism has the capacity to support. Such an ecocriticism would manoeuvre necessarily between and among various disciplinary approaches to the physical world while accommodating a complex set of challenges to anthropocentric conceptual models of the universe.

One of the ultimate goals of this approach is to impel literary critics to spend more time listening to what the sciences have to say about natural phenomena, to be sure; but attempting an ecocriticism open to interdisciplinary and interspecies voices invites charges of, at best, academic dilettantism and, at worst, disciplinary ineptitude; it might lead unwittingly to "the death of distance and its children" (McKay *NF* 22). In other words, the specificity an ornithology textbook provides regarding, say, the skeletal structure of the indigo bunting—the subject of McKay's poem "Meditation on a Small Bird's Skull" (*NF* 22)—represents at once a multiplicity of interpretive possibilities and a set of risky propositions. Even though ecocriticism has more or less arrived as a valid and vital subdiscipline within, predominantly, English departments, the application of scientific knowledge to the reading of poetry remains, for some, a fringe activity.

There might be good reason for such suspicion of cross-disciplinary work. In "Meditation on a Small Bird's Skull," McKay offers a warning to the literary-minded critic who decides to cross disciplinary and phenomenal distances to get closer to the world outside text, to pick up and hold, as it were, a small bird's skull:

> If, like me,
> you feel the urge to stick the sharp end
> in your ear
> (hoping for some
> secret of the air)
> be careful.
> We are big and blunt and easily fooled and know few
> of the fine points of translation.

In a few brief lines, McKay anticipates the respectful decision in "Load" not to touch a white-throated sparrow recovering on the shore of Lake Erie. He manages to turn the warning into one against human foolishness, effectively maintaining a sustained metacritique of language, poetry, and metaphor. The gesture of "stick[ing] the sharp end" of a bird's skull into his ear is as "loaded" as the gift of the painting in "Night Field," but the reminder here to check the symbolism with a modicum of humility (itself tempered by equal doses of ornithological and experiential knowledge) is also a reminder that we humans have a lot to learn from the material world. McKay's self-deprecating voice here implicates his readers. He challenges us to identify as big, blunt instruments that are fooled easily. One response to his challenge is to turn to ornithological literature for assistance with learning some of the "fine points."

Ecocritics typically, though not always, feel as comfortable including field guides and science textbooks (not to mention the occasional bit of fieldwork) into their research and writing as they do dictionaries and literary journals. Those poems of McKay's that seek out a proximal relation to the world do so by scrutinizing the word/world relation, but they also, unlike much in postmodern thought, affirm a world that exists beyond language.[5] According to Alanna F. Bondar, "McKay uses birds and birding as a means of examining the desire for movement and for exploration into the unknown in the hope of satiating curiosity and intellect" ("Every" 17); Nicholas Bradley claims that McKay "uses birds in order to contemplate the individual's relation to home" ("Ecology" 156). I prefer to think that McKay does not "use" birds, but rather that he uses his faulty words, field guides, and patient "attention to detailed observation and acutely precise comparisons" (Elmslie 89) to get closer to the world that persists without his words. Proximity inflects specificity; specificity inflects the poet's, and the ecocritic's, relation to the more-than-human world.

A poem by Margaret Avison—a favourite of McKay's—illustrates the extent to which getting the name wrong constitutes, at best, a lack of engagement with supplementary material. In her Governor General's Award–winning collection *No Time* (1989), she footnotes "The Butterfly" to explain a revision she made to an earlier version. She made the revision, she says, because she "ha[d] learned that 'moth' and 'butterfly' are not interchangeable terms (as [she] had written them in ignorance in the earlier version)" (*No Time* 66).[6] In the original version of the "The Butterfly"—written in 1943 and published in 1960—Avison concludes with the following stanza, in an attempt to describe the effect of the butterfly, which the narrator sees "suddenly" amidst a storm:

> The meaning of the moth, even the smashed moth, the
>   meaning of the moth—
> can't we stab that one angle into the curve of space
> that sweeps so unrelenting, far above,
> towards the subhuman swamp of under-dark? (1960: 354)

In the revised version, Avison changes the final stanza to reflect her newfound knowledge of the difference between a butterfly and a moth:

> The butterfly's meaning, even though smashed.
> Imprisoned in endless cycle? No. The meaning!
> Can't we stab that one angle

> into the curve of space that sweeps beyond
> our farthest knowing, out into light's
> place of invisibility? (1989: 66)

Whereas in the first version—inaccurate naming notwithstanding—the repetition of the monosyllabic "moth" in the first two lines creates an undesirable aural effect, the latter version's singular "butterfly," followed by a question, a negation, and a resounding imperative, emphasizes a meaningful relation between speaker and butterfly.

Avison, a poet presumably more devoted to Christian-based religiosity than to environmental concerns and details, nevertheless feels compelled to make the terms of her metaphor more biologically accurate.[7] Despite the anthropocentrism inherent in her language-centred vocation, Avison insists on acknowledging a correlation and contiguity between her words and the physical world, in this case the world of butterflies and moths. That she should go so far as to revise—and call attention to the revision of—a published poem strikes me as significant. The shrinking distance between metaphorical and biological knowing enables an environmental criticism aware of the value of taxonomic accuracy and the importance of knowing—physical laws, the names of things, ecological dynamics. Despite having gained some knowledge about the identification of moths and butterflies, Avison stops short of engaging lepidoptery as fully as she might have.[8] The species of butterfly (of which there are approximately 15,000 worldwide and 700 in North America) she writes about appears to be irrelevant to a reading of the poem; such irrelevance inflects a reading of the poem in terms of the attention it pays to the natural world. The *metaphor* might be more precise, but the lack of specificity prevents "The Butterfly" from achieving the degree of accuracy—taxonomical, biological, ecological—that McKay's poems often do.

In a review of *Birding, or desire* (1983),[9] Robert Bringhurst identifies in McKay's writing a "precision of observation" that distinguishes it from McKay's Romantic and Canadian lyrical antecedents ("Antithesis" 30). Referring to Wordsworth as a poet whose "vision of the natural world was full of rapture instead of detail," Bringhurst articulates what has become a characteristic of McKay's poetry since the publication of *Birding, or desire*, namely taxonomic specificity (30). In a dialogue between Bringhurst and Laurie Ricou, Ricou picks up on Bringhurst's earlier assessment and uses it to mark a significant distinction between different types of contemporary poets. The dialogue, taking as its subject Bringhurst's poem "Sunday Morning," is not conventional literary criticism but a discussion of, among other things, trees and birds, specifically bristlecone pine, ravens, and white pelicans. Ricou aligns Bringhurst—the Bringhurst of "Sunday Morning," at least—with other poets "who, like Don McKay, don't say 'tree' and 'bird,' but white pine, red pine, loon, or Blackburnian warbler" (96). The significance of such specificity rests neither in the intrinsic power of nomination and taxonomy nor in a careless deference to the conventions of scientifically objective, reductionist discourse. Unlike Avison's footnoted corrective, Bringhurst's attention to a specific tree—bristlecone pine[10]—enables readers to "discover a story" by "show[ing] a way to think about things" that requires intimate and accurate knowledge (97). The astute reader, Ricou implies, takes "time, outside the reading of the poem itself, to find out about" its subject. The extra-textual, often extracurricular effort reveals, in turn, "some of the implicit patterns in the poem" (97): if the poet has stepped outside, the search for pattern *inside* the poem requires the literary critic to pay attention to more than language and linguistic conventions by following the poet outside the poem.

Ecocritical concern for environmental issues can gain credence and imaginative power from specific scientific knowledge (ecological, botanical, evolutionary)[11] that helps make such concern meaningful in the long term: by providing readers with a specialized critical vocabulary and theoretical contexts to make collaborative discourse and research possible. Knowledge of the science of ecology is useful, since as Barry Lopez argues in "Landscape and Narrative," "[o]ne learns a landscape finally not by knowing the name or identity of everything in it, but by perceiving the relationships in it—like that between the sparrow and the twig" (*Crossing* 61). The emphasis on relationality supports ecologist Charles Krebs's definition of ecology as "the scientific study of the *interactions* that determine the distribution and abundance of organisms" (3; emphasis added). Even in its more popular usage, which is only vestigially related to the scientific term, ecology implies a world view that privileges interaction and interconnectedness (Keller and Golley 2). Vocabulary might not be all; or, as Phyllis Webb puts it in "Imperfect Sestina," "there may be more to a bird than its name" (72). But strategies for naming and knowing are essential aspects for any ecological, and hence ecocritical, project. Lopez's sparrow, though it could be any number of sparrow species, is significantly not a chickadee, or a junco, or a crested myna—or a butterfly. To notice "relationships" requires some knowledge of identities and behaviours; for the non-scientist, it requires some knowledge of science. But as Dana Phillips argues in his preface to *The Truth of Ecology*, "ecocriticism has been lamentably under-informed by science studies, philosophy of science, environmental history, and ecology," despite frequent claims by ecocritics to interdisciplinarity (ix). Patrick D. Murphy provides some context for Phillips's critique when he claimed, three years earlier, that "[m]any ecocritical essays and analyses … display little working knowledge of contemporary critical and literary theories and tend to downplay the degree to which literary criticism constitutes a theoretical discourse" (17–18).[12] Murphy goes on, effectively anticipating Phillips's desire "to cure ecocriticism of its fundamentalist fixation on literal representation" (*Truth* 7), to suggest that ecocritics "represent themselves as being antitheoretical because they oppose abstraction" (18). For all that Murphy purports to further the study of "nature-oriented literature," though, he does little to advance ecocriticism as an interdisciplinary endeavour. Phillips likewise, for all that he calls upon ecocriticism to inform itself with the science of ecology, undermines the possibility by shifting his critique from ecocriticism to ecology proper.

The ecocriticism developed in this book comprises both awareness of the paradoxical limitations and necessity of language, which McKay refers to as its "abject thinness" (*V* 64), and "belief," as Albert Einstein has it, "in an external world independent of the perceiving subject [which] is the basis of natural science" (60). The belief to which Einstein refers is a controversial one, to say the least, and one that has provoked a good deal of debate so far as the possibility—and value—of realism in literature is concerned. Critiquing Lawrence Buell's *The Environmental Imagination*, for example, Phillips questions the practicality—and the sanity—of Buell's desire for a redirection of the academic gaze outward from the text. Making reference to a "grove of second-growth white pines" that Buell claims "can be found in the pages of American literature" (5), Phillips says that "textual functions … is [sic] surely what the trees must be, and can only be…. It seems not so much naïve as occult to suppose otherwise" (6). Perhaps. And so the questions remain: How does one write or read about something (a white pine, a white whale, a white-throated sparrow) without defaulting to a symbolic, metaphoric, allegorical version and thereby attracting criticism for an anti-imaginary punctiliousness? How can a literary critic not take seriously J. M. Coetzee's alter ego, Elizabeth Costello, who says in *The Lives of Animals* (1999): "'When Kafka writes about an ape, I take him to be talking in the first place about an ape; when [Thomas] Nagel writes about a bat, I take him to be writing, in the first place, about a bat'" (32)?[13]

Or perhaps not. One critic Phillips leaves out of his discussion is Joseph Carroll, whose *Evolution and Literary Theory* influences Glen Love's *Practical Ecocriticism*, mainly for its "support of the tradition of interdisciplinary study, which recognizes the influence of an external world on the mind of the writer" (7).[14] Arguing for "the relevance of biology to literary theory" by way of Darwinian evolutionary theory (1), Carroll recalls proponents of the New Criticism who, like Einstein, do "not deny that literature is influenced by and refers to a world that exists independently of the literary text" (55). Clearly, a return to New Criticism, with its tendency to ignore extra-textual context, is not the answer: both Buell and Phillips decry such a move (albeit for different reasons: Buell, according to Phillips, wants nothing to do with theory while Phillips feels ecocriticism should embrace contemporary literary theory).[15] Because the life sciences specialize in studying aspects of the world that exist independently of human language and literature, I suggest much of what has been done in the area of science and literature provides a useful starting point from which to consider how scientific knowledge or the scientific method can inform ecocritical theory.

But I am not overly concerned with the mimetic function of McKay's poetic language. While one might usefully debate how realistic the description of a western redcedar is, for example, by considering its size and geographical distribution, no amount of physical description can reproduce, mimetically, the ecological interactions between western redcedar and western hemlock, northern flickers, and Coast Salish people who build totems and canoes. I do not go so far in my ecocriticism as nineteenth-century American naturalist John Burroughs, who "credit[s] the true poet with greater insight into nature than naturalists" and who "seeks to expose poetry's lapses of accuracy" by correcting "factical"—primarily "ornithological and botanical"—mistakes "committed [by poets] for the sake of melodic or imagistic euphony" (Buell *Environmental* 88). If I do point out errors or inaccuracies, as I do in Avison's poem, it is to provide a set of practices against which McKay's species-specific poetry works. But as Page's McKavian glosa attests, even the poet whose work stands as representative of avian poetics can stop well short of taxonomical accuracy. I am less interested in correcting supposed lapses in accuracy than I am in poets' attention to and attempts at accuracy by way of proximal knowing informed by field guides, textbooks, and experience. The choice of "an obscure poet from Kansas" to "imagin[e] yews and nightingales" as part of the Kansas landscape (Buell *Environmental* 88)—whether intentionally or not—does not in itself make bad poetry, despite the ecological inaccuracy. But it does not make ecologically sound poetry either; it does not make poetry that invites readers into a knowledgeable relation with the environment. That Don McKay gets so many things ecologically and biologically right raises important questions about the roles of literature and literary criticism in thinking about the environment and how humans interact with it: Will the imagination become a diminished requirement for good—that is, environmentally sound—writing? If field guides and science textbooks explain ecological and taxonomical relationships and details, does it ultimately matter whether a poet has spent time in a particular place before she writes about it? How can poetry that achieves a high degree of ecological accuracy impel readers to drop the book and get outside? How can recognizing names of birds, trees, rivers, peoples, represent anything other than acts of linguistic imperialism?

In "Going Home," Tim Lilburn suggests that, as humans, "[w]e should learn the names for things as a minimum—not to fulfill taxonomies but as acts of courtesy, for musical reasons" (184). According to Neil Evernden, "The act of naming may itself be a part of the process of establishing a sense of place" (101); this process, though, is problematic for "creatures [who are] in a state of sensory deprivation" such as humans in urban, globalized environments seem to be, bombarded by "the advertisers who promise an easy surrogate, a commercial sop to [our] need for place" (100–101). Concerned with Western culture's reductive construction of natural space as commodity, Evernden allows for the possible coexistence of natural and urban spaces through metaphoric association; he also recognizes the crossing of "the mind's appropriations" (McKay *V* 21) with what exists beyond, even prior to, cultural acquisitions. He cites Northrop Frye's famous essay: "the motive for metaphor ... is a desire to associate, and finally to identify, the human mind with what goes on outside it" (Frye *Educated* 11, qtd. in Evernden 101). While Evernden wants to use Frye's claim to support an ecological literary criticism that recognizes the importance of the world as it exists outside human language, his ellipsis elides Frye's reference to Wallace Stevens, whose poem "The Motive for Metaphor" provides the title for Frye's essay. Frye's point, it seems to me, is to warn his fellow critics to be "careful of associative language" that attempts to "describe this world"—"the objective world, the world set against us"—without "logic and reason" (10–11). Contrary to Evernden's ecocritical world view, Frye argues that "literature belongs to the world man constructs, not to the world he sees; to his home, not his environment" (8), effectively enacting a separation between what Linda Hutcheon identifies as "the world that we construct" and "the world of nature" ("Eruptions" 154). In other words, to say my environment is my home is to use a metaphor, since environment is the world we experience, and we cannot construct it, and home is the *literary* or *imaginative* world we construct. Frye seems to be supporting a disjunctive world view that reinforces such typical binaries as human/animal, culture/nature.

But, as McKay argues in *Vis à Vis: Field Notes on Poetry & Wilderness*, "it is as dangerous to act as though we were not a part of nature as it is to act as though we were not a part of culture" (30–31). Humans are namers, and we are named. Humans are complicit in linguistic imperialism even as we are implicated in a natural system: *Homo sapiens sapiens*.[16] To learn the names of things, McKay recommends looking to field guides and textbooks in addition to seeking experience along figurative and actual trails (*V* 27). The trail that leads through typical wilderness to a familiar notion of home—a log cabin by the river, a sport-utility vehicle in a parking lot, an outhouse among a grove of birch trees—moves us, back and forth, along the edges of disparate worlds and ideas.

To speak of nature poetry that is not, as American poet Galway Kinnell suggests in an interview, simply "a matter of English gardens, of hedgerows and flowers" but that "include[s] the city too" (Packard 107) is to speak of an ecopoetry that recognizes naming's artifice, a recognition McKay desires and that is in part "governed by ... an attempt to preserve, in the physique of language, a vestige of wilderness" (*V* 63). In support of Kinnell's notion of an inclusive nature poetry, McKay's idea of wilderness is an openly transgressive one by which he "want[s] to mean, not just a set of endangered spaces, but the capacity of all things to elude the mind's appropriations" (*V* 21). That is, any thing viewed out of its traditional context—usually in relation to its usefulness to us—retains traces of wilderness: "a coat hanger asks a question," says McKay, "the armchair is suddenly crouched" (21). Wilderness is not, as some critics suggest, a synonym for the wild or wildness; the stories McKay tells, and to which he listens, are not simple analogues for Western canonical stories "immersed in the sensuous, creaturely, and indeterminate realm of wildness" (Herriot 218). Wilderness is place made personal and public all at once—and then unmade again in an instant through the breakdown of utility. The word "wilderness" preserves a tentative uncertainty, as though McKay is reluctant to articulate a common term—wildness—with links to primitivism, a term that thus occupies one side of a simple dichotomy: wild, er, ness. Such defamiliarizing tactics—not unlike the coat hanger and armchair—seek to bridge ideological gaps between humans and nonhumans, and epistemological gaps between what early Canadian (eco)critics would have called baseland and hinterland,[17] effectively positioning *us* alongside and within a "natural" pattern of existence while at the same time positioning nature within a "cultural" one.

To name is not necessarily to tame, then. Wilderness persists in the act of naming because language is not capable of telling the whole story. McKay addresses the wilderness inherent in names in the prose piece "A Small Fable," in which he reimagines the biblical tale of Adam naming the world. McKay's Adam resembles the speaker of "Nocturnal Animals," awake in the middle of the night to work through a prevailing mood of doubt. Though he goes to bed after naming all day, content with a "sense of an inexorable order inexorably ordering" (*V* 89), Adam wakes up conscious of a potential "slippage in the belts and snaps, a little play between 'Cooper's hawk' and the bird with the fierce orange eye and the talons like sharpened knitting needles" (90). The doubt pervading Adam's sleep stems from the realization that each name inadequately, incompletely, describes its concomitant creature. Screech owl, in particular, gives Adam crepuscular pause: "*Screech owl?* What had he been thinking? … Anyone could tell you that a screech was an *ascending* scream… . But the owl's voice fluttered down, a heart sinking" (90). Spurred by this realization, Adam considers other names, recalling them now "with a new critical eye and ear, feeling their clunkiness, their prefab quality: ring-necked duck, common loon: they lay there like shucked cocoons," particularly when viewed in the dark of night (91). If by confronting the arbitrariness of naming within a Western Judeo-Christian paradigm McKay questions the assumed power of an entire epistemology, he also implicates himself in the practice of inaccurate nomination and, worse, the whitewashing of ecological devastation and human displacement.[18] Language, whether poetical or scientific, decorative or instrumental, reflects a residual human desire to fix in place, to imbue with properties sufficient to inspire nostalgia, memories meant to recollect—in tranquility, natch—what is no longer present, familiar, or useful.

ecotone one

Poetry's landscape is an ecotone where human and natural orders meet.
– John Elder, *Imagining the Earth* (210)

FIELD MARKS

Knowing, not owning:
being, not having,
the rags and the blisters
of knowledge we have:
– Robert Bringhurst, "Gloria Credo Sanctus et Oreamnos Deorum" (154)

During the following half century [between 1934 and 1990] the binocular and the spotting scope have replaced the shotgun.
– Roger Tory Peterson, *A Field Guide to Western Birds* (5)

It has become a characteristic way for him to begin the day: black coffee and a newspaper. A quietly patient routine he hopes will translate effortlessly to time spent in the field: quietly patient routine as metaphor—no, not just metaphor, but strategy—for living every day in the world. As a lifelong student of literature, a scholar, he (the birder-critic; let's call him BC) understands that fieldwork inheres metaphorically in the process of close reading, a process distinct from the act of theorizing critical strategies of approach and analysis. The difference between close reading and theorizing is, he will admit if asked, a difference in degree and not in kind; he is all the more aware of this distinction for having years ago shifted his research focus from the postmodern implications of Canadian historiographic metafiction to the ecological implications of Canadian poetry and poetics. The latter interest has, almost by necessity, become a compulsion to resist categorizing himself as a particular kind of scholar—to being categorized, labelled, lumped in with a group of like-minded academics—by insisting on the permeability of disciplinary and epistemological boundaries. Over time, BC has come to realize the boundaries more closely resemble, not permeable cell walls, but intertidal zones, riparian buffer strips, forest-clearcut edges: what ecologists call ecotones, areas where two ecosystems meet at their edges and create a third ecosystem with both shared and distinct characteristics. Literary criticism, then, resembles fieldwork.

Northrop Frye understood fieldwork's metaphorical power when he wrote the preface to his collection of "essays on the Canadian imagination," *The Bush Garden*, in 1971. For Frye, who built a reputation writing about "world literature" and addressing "an international reading public," the annual-review essays he wrote for *The University of Toronto Quarterly* during the 1950s were "an essential piece of 'field work' to be carried on while [he] was working out a comprehensive critical theory," namely his *Anatomy of Criticism* (*Bush* xxviii). The poetry being written in Canada while Frye was teaching at the University of Toronto became a field through which Frye could, as it were, walk; his proximity to that field, his closeness to living poets and a specific, albeit geographically diverse, place—the relatively young political entity called Canada—inflected the drift of his critical works, not to mention his reputation, thereafter.

BC likes to think that Canadian poetry is to Frye's criticism as birds are to BC's ecocriticism: "it is with human beings as it is with birds: the creative instinct has a great deal to do with the assertion of territorial rights" (Frye *Bush* xxi). Moreover, it is with the study of patterns in poetry as it is with the recognition of patterns in the field: "There is order in the universe, and birds are no exception. All the minutiae of variation (appearance, behavior, occurrence, etc.) fit into predictable patterns [which with experience] coalesce into a framework of knowledge" (Sibley 10). Margaret Atwood recapitulates both Frye's avian metaphor and the field guide author's emphasis on pattern recognition in her foundational and controversial *Survival: A Thematic Guide to Canadian Literature* (1970), which "attempts one simple thing. It outlines a number of key patterns which [Atwood] hope[s] will function like the field markings in bird-books [such as beak shape, crown stripes, and throat patches]: they will help you distinguish this species from all others, Canadian literature from the other literatures with which it is often compared or confused" (19). Pattern recognition is an important step in identifying and then talking about birds and literature. As much as BC appreciates Frye's and Atwood's avian references, he recognizes in them the beginnings of a pattern that literary critics in Canada were quick to dismiss as simplistic and reductive. If he is going to accomplish anything useful with his research, he will have to avoid the pitfalls of thematic criticism without dismissing it outright and engage an experiential criticism that flourishes in the space between thematics and theory, words and worlds.

In order to understand how a poet's proximal relation to birds inflects his poetry about birds, BC decides one day to take up his binoculars, find a field guide, and spend some time outdoors. Reading Northrop Frye and Margaret Atwood is all well and good—and necessary—but an extra-literary approach to contemporary Canadian poetry is necessary to attempt an ecological literary criticism that recognizes ecology as both a science and a metaphor. On one hand, poets privileged enough to spend time birding (and to write about birds and/or birding) tend to acknowledge in their very language their own linguistic, and therefore human, limitations. On the other hand, birding might be one of the most democratic of outdoor activities. Everyone is a birder, whether one lives in country or city, farmland or suburbs. One of the stranger examples of this tenet is the collection of observations made by American soldier Jonathan Trouern-Trend while he was on a tour of duty in Iraq, called *Birding Babylon: A Soldier's Journal from Iraq*. An early entry provides a glimpse into the strangeness: "Birding was limited due to being surrounded by thousands of coalition troops coming from or going to Iraq." A month later, Trouern-Trend recounts having "to go everywhere in body armor and helmet, so Saturday was a day for birding in 'full battle rattle,' weapon included, of course." Thinking about the incongruity of these images while trying to identify which species of warbler has landed in the cedars along the pond's south edge, BC is thankful the only "battle rattle" he sports consists of binoculars, camera, pen, and paper.

Back home, BC picks up Beryl Rowland's *Birds with Human Souls: A Guide to Bird Symbolism* and flips to the preface while his photos upload from the camera. "Emily Dickinson," he reads, "was able to confront a bobolink or robin at eye level as it happened along the path in her Amherst garden, and appreciate both symbol and fact simultaneously" (vii). Despite living in an apartment without access to a garden, BC desires precisely that simultaneity Dickinson was able to appreciate and translate into poetry. The simultaneity of "symbol and fact" suffuses his research about birds in Don McKay's writing, while BC struggles to articulate the significance of such avian tension. Because, as Rowland suggests, "we rely more and more [for our delight in birds] on memories and traditions derived not from life but from books" (viii), BC intends to rely less on books than he would have before he began reading McKay's poetry with eyes and ears attuned to specific birds.

By combining the literary with the extra-literary, he feels he can get closer to the birds, trees, and rivers he reads about, in much the same way biographies help readers get closer to their subjects and historical context brings readers into proximity with a literary time. But, as Leonard Nathan has noted, "Field study requires hard labor, a willingness to sit a whole bitterly cold day on some icy ridge waiting for something to happen" (127); BC is used to sitting all day—but usually in climate-controlled offices and libraries. With fieldwork, you hope "the willingness and waiting sometimes pay off with a special thrill. You feel it when you see knowledge—even small bits of it—fill in the empty slots of your ignorance, when data begin to assemble themselves into a pattern" (Nathan 127). Patterns interest BC immensely; he has been thinking a lot about how the literature he's been reading is concerned with patterns, with recording them rather than solving them. BC has recently read a novel set in late-nineteenth-century England; one of the characters, George, is urged by his sister, Maud, to take up birdwatching, and he measures the benefits against the "hard labor" noted elsewhere:

> He stuck at it dutifully for a few months, but in truth he had trouble following a bird in flight, and the ones at rest seemed to take pleasure in being camouflaged. Additionally and alternatively, many of the places from which it was deemed best to watch birds struck him as cold and damp. If you had spent three years in prison, you did not need any more cold and damp in your life until you were placed in your coffin and lowered into the coldest and dampest place of all. That had been George's considered view of birdwatching. (Barnes 329)

Prison has not been part of BC's life thus far, so while the comparison might be apt it wasn't enough to deter him from undertaking to bird. And though Vancouver can hardly be said to threaten with bitter cold and icy ridges, it has its share of cold, rainy days that might give even the most ardent birder pause. But birding has the capacity to bring readers into closer contact with the world and its inhabitants. In a published dialogue with British Columbia writer Robert Bringhurst about Bringhurst's poem "Sunday Morning," Laurie Ricou argues convincingly "that the poem is to the critic as the bird is to the ornithologist.... The birder-critic, who must pay close attention to the nuances of marking, has first to be quietly patient" (Bringhurst and Ricou 93). BC hopes to progress, stepping away from the text and into various fields, from recognizing field marks and using field guides to eventually becoming a writer himself and making field notes.

Back in his living room with his coffee and paper, something catches BC's attention. Maybe it's because that morning, Thursday, 28 September 2006, he was planning to step out of the office and into an actual field to observe birds instead of just reading about them. A headline in *The Globe and Mail*'s Review section—"Birdman of B.C."—initiates a process he hadn't planned to undertake. The article, a fairly straightforward Q&A with Vancouver author and artist Douglas Coupland, wasn't really about birds. But something in the interviewer's final question, the only question that included any mention of birds, resonates. Leah McLaren recounts the last time she met Coupland, when he was "taking a case of peanuts home to feed the blue jays" (R2). That morning, he—the birder-critic—accomplishes a task of epiphanic proportions. He recognizes an error in nomination, a failure in taxonomy. Douglas Coupland, you see, lives on British Columbia's west coast. Blue jays (*Cyanocitta cristata*) do not. According to the Cornell Lab of Ornithology, "The western edge of the range stops abruptly where the arid pine forest and scrub habitat of the closely related Steller's jay (*Cyanocitta stelleri*) begins" ("Blue Jay" n.p.). Coupland feeds Steller's jays, not blue jays. Is the mistake McLaren's, BC wonders, or Coupland's?

The Steller's jay was the first west-of-the Prairies species BC came to recognize. Because he grew up in southern Ontario, the birds of his childhood and his imagination were mourning doves, grackles, cardinals, and blue jays. Once in Vancouver, though, those birds came to occupy a portion of his consciousness reserved for nostalgia, at best, and narrow-minded assumptions regarding the primacy of originary experience, at worst. He recalls some favourite lines from one of John Thompson's ghazals: "Absence makes what / presence, presence" (135). Mourning doves gave way to rock doves (pigeons), grackles to northwestern crows, cardinals to starlings,[1] and blue jays to Steller's jays. Of the four new species in BC's expanding world view, only the crows and Steller's jays were native to British Columbia; only the Steller's jays were not a ubiquitous presence. Perhaps it was this refusal to be ever-present that drew BC to these crafty, loud versions of blue jays. Crows and jays belong to one of the most common of bird families, the Corvidae, which also includes ravens, magpies, and other jays; they are found worldwide, except for South America, Antarctica, and some islands (Peterson 252). Northwestern crows (*Corvus caurinus*) differ from American crows

(*Corvus brachyrhynchos*) in at least three ways: they are slightly smaller, have faster wingbeats, and, as their common name suggests, occur along "the narrow northwestern coast strip" of North America (252).

BC understands, without much in the way of research or fieldwork, why pigeons, starlings, and crows are so successful and so, well, *present*. Crows, pigeons, and starlings have demonstrated certain intellectual capacities previously thought to belong only to primates. New Caledonian crows can actually make tools (see Weir, Chappell, and Kacelnik), pigeons have been shown to differentiate between paintings by Chagall and Van Gogh (see Watanabe), and starlings have the capacity to recognize recursive linguistic structures (see Gentner et al.). Steller's jays complement their cognitive abilities with aesthetic ones, even if their "harsh 'shaar,' and rapid rattling 'shek, shek, shek, shek'" ("Steller's" n.p.) are unlikely to inspire the next Mozart. But Steller's jays exhibit a *jouissance* possibly a third of the way toward ravenhood, an indication of playfulness that, in concert with their intelligence and vocal range, should make them as notorious as other corvids for their affinities with humans. Steller's jays even *look* like they're wearing a hood of raven (or crow) feathers.

Around the time BC arrived in British Columbia and began enriching his memories of eastern birds with experiences of western ones, Don McKay was publishing essays about his experiences as a transplanted birder-poet. For McKay, "bushtits were one of the first west-of-the-Rockies species" he encountered (*V* 83). The encounter was significant enough to inspire an essay, "The Bushtits' Nest," about the relations among metaphor, wilderness, and poetry, because McKay, a well-known birder, was unable to identify the birds when first asked to—"which was socially embarrassing, but at the same time exciting, since the details of their presence … could occur without the centralizing and reductive influence of the name, which so often signals the terminal point of our interest" (*V* 83–84). In McKay's poetics, each of these familiar words—metaphor, wilderness, poetry—means differently; each word, newly understood, enables an engagement with the world that neither recapitulates nor reaffirms a colonial relation to the world through language: metaphor is "the place where words put their authority at risk, implicitly confessing their inadequacy to the task of re-presenting the world" (85); wilderness is "the placeless place beyond the mind's appropriations" (87); and "a poem, or poem-in-waiting, contemplates what language can't do: then it does something with language—in homage, or grief, or anger, or praise" (87). BC likes that McKay simultaneously loves and distrusts language, admires the way he finds comfort in the inevitable failure of his, and all, naming.

BC's quiet patience includes a willingness to fail, a willingness to get lost in the literal as well as the figurative sense. He is not truly a birder, you see; he has been trained as a literary critic. The poem, or the novel, has been his field, not the forest, or the riparian buffer zone. All this has changed, however, as BC has begun working at the intersections of literature and ecology. Reluctant simply to enter the realm of "pure spondaic" theory (*D* 88), BC decides to take seriously American ecocritic Lawrence Buell's call for a literature, and a criticism, that leads readers back to the physical world rather than away from it (*Environmental* 11). The birder-critic is willing to acknowledge and to embrace the limitations of language, of knowledge, of naming. The west coast invites an especially rigorous introspection, in part because "*there is nowhere on the planet left to go*" (Gaston 37). With no more continent to the west of what has already been claimed and/or embroiled in legal battles for ownership, and with the current state of global environmental crises, perhaps the west-coast poet is turning his gaze to the local, the familiar, the edge of known geography and ecology—and literary criticism. The North Pacific Coast, like all coastal regions BC can think of, provides rich metaphorical possibilities for poetry; its landscape, as John Elder has written, "is an ecotone where human and natural orders meet" (*Imagining* 210).

The quiet patience BC is cultivating, which is characterized by the poet who pays "close attention" to his surroundings—birds, rocks, trees—seems at odds with much of what constitutes contemporary global culture, aesthetically and ideologically. Polish poet Czesław Miłosz "finds that the boundary between categories and reality is more complicated than he previously thought" (Morris 50). He didn't come to this conclusion—this epiphany—in the inner world of his poetry, or while travelling throughout Europe, the Old World. He reached this epiphany after having moved "to the shores of California in middle age," into a "strange, new intoxicating environment [that] leads him back to close observation of natural life forms" (Morris 50). More specifically, "he is struck by the similarity of the Steller's jay of the [North] American west coast to the species of jay in his native Poland" (50) after hearing "Jays screech outside the window" and recognizing "the cries, the thievishness, the audacity" common to all jays (Miłosz 20). "Jayness is a human construct, but it also exists": so writes David Copland Morris (50) in response to Miłosz's reflections on the "amazing," paradoxical ontology of being a jay by not being aware of being a jay. *I think not about myself, therefore I am.*

BC is reminded by this discussion of avian ontology of similar ruminations by McKay, albeit in a more sweeping statement about birds in general, about birdness. Reflecting on bushtits' gourd-shaped nest hanging precariously over his driveway, McKay notes their status as "'creatures of the air' not only because they fly through it but because it comprises so much of their bodily presence" (*V* 104). Don Stap refers to avian physiology to explain birds' ethereal existence and describes a Bewick's wren that was in the midst of repeating "a complex series of notes with precision and force": "Each time he sang, the wren expelled air from his respiratory system with extraordinary efficiency. Nearly 100 percent of the air passing through a bird's vocal cords is used to make sound. Humans use only about 2 percent" (73–74). In his statement about the non-being of avian existence, McKay both acknowledges a human need for textualized meaning and an avian proclivity to *mean textually*. Bushtits become a living, breathing Lao-tzu from which BC might learn a little something about the world and his place in it. Identifying a bird—"'Ah, bushtits': check, snap. Next topic" (*V* 84)—tells BC as much about himself as it does about the bird. *I think about birds, therefore I am.* Field marks place BC in relation to an invented system of knowledge and the objects of that system.

But what is the relationship between identifying features—field marks—and the words we use to name birds? "The bird 'student,' too," writes Thomas Gannon, "indoctrinated into Peterson's 'field mark' revolution, is thus armed with a set of visual and verbal signifiers that determine the scope of his/her interpretations of these new-world 'aborigines' with feathers and wings" (Gannon n.pag.). BC is not terribly interested in participating carelessly in a Foucauldian narrative of order; as much as they exist as parts of individual birds, field marks are tools for identifying avian species. They are but one tool of many that birders have to employ in the field or in the office.

The tool is far from perfect. Even when applied to domestic animals, like dogs, which weigh appreciably more than twenty grams and sport characteristics selected by breeders, identification based on visible markings is an inexact science. BC ponders this example while walking with the dog he and his partner rescued from the SPCA in Toronto. She had been found wandering downtown alleys and been identified by the SPCA as a spaniel-dalmation mix. BC was in British Columbia at the time, so he had only a vague idea of what this dog looked like (this was just before the digital-camera revolution). Medium-sized (maybe fifteen kilograms), white with black spots, long hair on tail and ears, a bit of brown on the face—this was how she was described over the phone. Nevertheless, BC was asked to name the dog (which had been christened

Sara upon arrival at the SPCA) as a sort of invitation into this new relationship between woman and dog.

Naming a pet differs in many ways from identifying a bird species that has already been named (notwithstanding dogs' Linnaean identity, since 1758, as *Canis familiaris*). Recognizing birds in the field adds a layer to the already-named species—at least in those cases when it can be determined. It would be a few years before BC realized, after noticing a familiar-looking dog on a magazine cover, that the spaniel-dalmation—the mixed breed, the mutt, the Heinz 57: the no-names of naming—was in fact a Llewellyn setter. A pure breed, according to some breeders who follow the Field Dog Stud Book, which requires a specific type of bloodline. More accurately, Llewellyns are a strain of the more commonly recognized English setter. Because pets share space in our homes and because our relationship with them is fundamentally one based on companionship, personalized names become necessary. Acknowledging this simple fact, BC chuckles to himself, imaging a walk through the neighbourhood with the purpose of bestowing names on individual birds. Do people do this? he wonders. A film called *The Wild Parrots of Telegraph Hill* (2005) documents the relationship between a San Francisco man and the feral parrots that occasionally visit him. He named them, fed them, cared for them if they were ill. Despite the parrots' wildness, they established companionship with him. He knew them well enough, or so it seemed, to give them names: Mingus, Connor, Picasso, Sophie, Olive, Pushkin. The names likely say more about the man than the individual parrots.

When wild animals—raccoons, deer, crows—insinuate themselves into our backyard worlds by visiting on a recurring basis, they become, for many people, like pets. Perhaps sharing stories about such encounters becomes easier without having to refer time and again to "the raccoon" or "that deer, the one I told you about last week" or "the crow with the white wing feather." Perhaps. But what do the alternatives imply when more often than not they become "Ricky" or "Bambi" or "Spot"? BC shakes his head at this, at the sheer unimaginative effort such easy naming betrays. Such naming could just as accurately be seen as gestures of ownership. That raccoon is mine. That deer belongs to me. To all of us. But those descriptive, ridiculously popular names gather each creature into a comprehensible, anthropomorphic group; they're merely shorthand tags that reinforce the assumed hierarchical structure that puts humans at the top. Does the same apply to the descriptive naming of domestic pets? Boots the tabby? Spot the dalmation? Are such names better or worse than human names? Annabelle the shorthair? Max the terrier? Does it depend on how much irony the namer intends? Once, because he had been reading Michael Ondaatje's *In the Skin of a Lion*, BC gave the name Caravaggio to a stray cat that some friends had unofficially adopted. If you're going to use a human name, he thought, you might as well aim high. Mozart the cat? Woolf the dog?

All this anxiety about the act of naming a dog he hasn't met is likely as connected to his and his partner's long-distance relationship as it is to a phenomenological conundrum. No name, he realizes, will be perfectly adequate. The dog is there, and a name is needed for pragmatic reasons, at the very least. But he knows the name he suggests will reveal something essential about himself. Or it should.

Undecided, BC turns again to McKay for a reassuring dose of uncertainty: "The small measure of congruence evident with the onomatopoeic chickadee disappears entirely with ring-necked duck, a beautiful diving duck whose neck ring is all but invisible unless you're holding the bird in your hands" (McKay V 64). While BC was hiking around Sasamat Lake in Port Moody, B.C., one Sunday morning, other hikers huddled on a footbridge, clambering to identify a small gathering of black-and-white ducks in the middle distance. Most wanted to name them ring-necked (*Aythya collaris*), but no one could see, really, even with high-powered binoculars, a copper-coloured ring around its neck (a seldom-seen field mark used in identifying the species). Proximity inflects specificity, sometimes to a degree that is not particularly useful. American critic Dana Phillips complicates the congruence evident in the chickdee's onomatopoeic name by imagining a novice birder attempting to identify a particular species of chickadee. Phillips notes that "establishing the identity of black-capped as opposed to Carolina chickadees can be surprisingly complicated" (178) in spite of the illustrations and descriptions—including field marks—Roger Tory Peterson's field guides provide. In the end, "the birder is confronted with a variety of interpretive options" (178); in the end, Peterson's (or Audubon's or Sibley's) "stylized images" cannot enable, in each instance, the proper identification of a bird: "the birder will have to engage in a lot of back-and-forth between text and world, and world and text, and between stylized image and bird, and bird and stylized image, if she really wants to know what kind of chickadee she saw" (179). If the desire to know is strong enough. Phillips also refers to the green-backed heron, which used to be called the little green heron, even though it is neither little nor "green all over, as the name implied" (180). The new name, while it is not "especially descriptive," is both arbitrary and "perfectly accurate" precisely because the bird does have a green back and other characteristics not included in the name (180).

With all the uncertainty, inaccuracy, and, BC reckons, whimsy surrounding the act of naming—especially in light of the fact that birds, like most species, have both a common name and a scientific, or Latin, name—why does it remain such an important aspect of birding and of poetry? After reading McKay and considering the differences between blue and Steller's jays, BC finds the act of naming itself less compelling than contemplating the implications of a human desire to name and to know. But to arrive at such a position, one must first establish a useful repertoire of names and be able to identify field marks. It's like Francis Ford Coppola directing Dennis Hopper, who hadn't learned his lines (but had apparently done a few in his trailer) prior to shooting *Apocalypse Now*: if you know your lines, then you can forget them. For poets, the analogous steps are to master grammar so as to create meaning at the edges of linguistic order; for ecopoets, to undermine the unquestioned authority of anthropocentric language and knowledge in order to elevate the standing, in ethical terms, of other-than-human beings. Scott Bryson illuminates the paradox a little, claiming that for ecopoets "Ignorance is exalted over conventional knowledge, which is usually connected with the *acquisition of wisdom*," with the collection of empirical data at the expense of other ways of knowing (*West* 105). Bryson's "ignorance," thinks BC, informs a humility that encourages an understanding of the world *qua* the world. But humility with McKay is not prizing ignorance so much as following a trail of ecological referents to get closer, maybe getting lost in the meantime because of a lack of knowledge (perhaps an ignorance) that is inevitable, though not necessarily "prized." We can know via biology, ecology, and ornithology. The question remains: So what? What will we do with such knowledge, knowing? Folding the paper and putting his mug in the sink with the rest of the breakfast dishes and grabbing the leash by the door, BC sets out with Mackenzie for a walk. So, he thinks, let's find out.

part two

Wherever they were—at the bar, in the relative's shack, or in Sumner's parlour—they would eventually find themselves plotting the next stage in their plans to build a flying machine.
– Jack Hodgins, *Innocent Cities* (105)

It might seem that home is the moment of passage from ontological to epistemological dwelling, the place where knowledge as power begins.
– Don McKay, "Baler Twine: Thoughts on Ravens, Home & Nature Poetry" (*V* 23)

Chapter Three

Homologies

> That birds and crocodiles are each other's closest living relatives was a consensus view long before the advent of DNA sequencing, as [was] the conclusion that reptiles (including birds) are more closely related to mammals than they are to amphibians.
> – Harry W. Greene, "Improving Taxonomy for Us and the Other Fishes" (738)

Don McKay writes flight as both biological phenomenon and literary metaphor while acknowledging the value of attending to place and its inhabitants. The resistance to "nature" has in many ways led criticism and theory of the past thirty years or so to misplace, misunderstand, and misrepresent much literature being published in Canada. A study with a strong focus on birds and birding in the poetry of Don McKay, for example, might be construed as thematic, and thematic criticism is precisely what faced the most resistance, in Canadian literature circles, in the wake of Frank Davey's "Surviving the Paraphrase." Bound up in Davey's position, though, is another term meant to reinforce the notion that Canadian literature and criticism were disproportionately concerned with nature. Focusing on D. G. Jones and his critical study of "themes and images in Canadian literature," *Butterfly on Rock* (1970), Davey identifies a "fallacy of literary determinism" and calls into question the extent to which an author's work can—and should—be explained by "reference to the geography and climate of the country, to western intellectual history, to his culture's religious heritage" (6); one might reasonably add ecology and botany to this list of influences. While I share Davey's distrust of reducing literary meaning to determinism, literary and otherwise, I remain unconvinced that literature can escape it altogether. Davey posits Frye's "reference to the 'bleak northern sky' and to the St. Lawrence River's swallowing of travellers into 'an alien continent'" as geographic determinism, which ignores authors' freedom to select influences ("Surviving" 6). As regards characterizing and analyzing national literatures, I agree that geographic considerations alone limit more than they enable. But I disagree with Davey's suggestion that place—and by extension specific considerations of biotic and abiotic inhabitants of place—does not influence the production of a text in some way(s). And not only rural, wild places, but urban, suburban, cosmopolitan places shape authors' world views, aesthetic choices, and, dare I say it, themes. As I demonstrate in my reading of McKay's species specificity, knowledge of place provides precise language for making precise metaphors, even metaphors that enact anthropocentrism with varying degrees of sophistication. Influence, as a sub-branch of determinism, takes many forms, including historical and contemporary literature, geographic location, and local species of flora and fauna.

In his study of the Confederation group of Canadian poets, D. M. R. Bentley argues for American naturalist John Burroughs's influence on the group, particularly on Charles G. D. Roberts, Archibald Lampman, and Bliss Carman. Bentley credits "a synchronicity born of both environmental similarities [between New England and New Brunswick] and of Burroughs's influence on the Confederation group" as causing "a great many flora and fauna of New England"—which Burroughs himself describes in such pieces as "Nature and the Poets" and "Birds and Poets"—to appear as potentially rich materials in the Canadian poets' work (148). Bentley finds much support for his thesis in *At the Mermaid Inn*, a weekly column Wilfred Campbell, D. C. Scott, and Lampman wrote for the Toronto *Globe* (1892–93). If the synchronicity Bentley refers to suggests that the Confederation Poets were influenced more by American writing than by other Canadian writing[1]— Campbell's column for 16 July 1892, for example, fails to mention any Canadian writers—it also points to an early instance of a bioregion taking precedence, even if unconsciously, over political regions. Indeed, as Bentley notes in introducing Burroughs as a key influence, the commingling of political and bioregional forces is in keeping with the commonalities "of … scenery, climate, atmosphere, flora, and fauna" between "the northeastern states, the Maritime provinces, and the southeastern portions of central Canada" (147). Despite the way this part of Bentley's argument avoids clarifying the problem of the group's "geographical diversity" (5), in Bentley's estimation,[2] the Confederation group's turn to the specific, local environment as material for their poetry enables an outward-reaching engagement with literature and thought beyond the local. Considering the dearth of Canadian guide books on birds[3] in the nineteenth century, such outward gazing is hardly surprising; I am not sure, however, why such Canadian texts as Susanna Moodie's *Roughing It in the Bush*, Catharine Parr Traill's *The Backwoods of Canada*, or even Alexander Mackenzie's *Voyage through Montreal* would not have been consulted.[4] Perhaps the Confederation Poets did consult such texts, but I have yet to find proof.

For McKay and many ecopoets, place and its multiplicitous inhabitants, that is "the nonhuman environment," function "not merely as a framing device but as an active presence, suggesting human history's implication in natural history" (Buell *Future* 25). Lawrence Buell and Robert Kern both consider some degree of "environmentality as a property of any text" (Buell *Future* 25) and operate under "the assumption that all texts are at least potentially environmental ... in the sense that all texts are literally or imaginatively situated in a place, and in the sense that their authors, consciously or not, inscribe within them a certain relation to their place" (Kern 259). These claims are not made in support of literary or geographic determinism, but they express the primacy of thinking the relations between author/text and place/nonhumans.[5] In the case of those texts more obviously attuned to ecological poetics, I would change Kern's phrasing to "literally *and* imaginatively," so as to encourage flexible complexity of both literal and metaphorical readings. In order to avoid an ecological universalism that might result from the reading of every text as (potentially) environmental, though, I stress the importance in my reading of McKay's poetry of ecological and species *specificity*, which impels readers along a trail of scientific and experiential referents. Any literary or critical responses to locally specific birds returning to breed, for example, succeed as ecocriticism when they emerge from interdisciplinary encounters with biological and ecological information.

Such encounters with ideas and language from scientific disciplines become catalysts for making (and understanding) metaphors. In his contribution to *The Third Culture: Literature and Science* (1997), William van Peer argues in favour of critics (and, presumably, poets) familiarizing themselves with scientific knowledge, claiming that "[t]here is no point at all in talking about quantum mechanics 'as if' its insights could be applied to our everyday macro world. Making analogies in this respect is not only to profoundly misunderstand such theories, it is also highly misleading and therefore confusing, and potentially undermining to a rational approach to the world" (41). Although I concur with van Peer's desire for *precision* when making analogies/metaphors, it is useful to remember that scientists (including and perhaps especially physicists) often talk in metaphor and that all "metaphor, and its related figures" make "a claim for sameness which is clearly, according to common linguistic sense, false" (McKay *V* 68).

Thus when physicists explain patterns of sound and light as "waves," they radically challenge what van Peer considers a "rational approach to the world." As Frieda Stahl notes, physicists "infer wave behavior from interference or diffraction patterns" rather than observe sound and light waving, as they can when watching water surfaces or stretched strings (59).[6] Even van Peer's language betrays his argument: What does an approach modified by reason consist of, exactly? And how does one approach the world in its entirety? I might consider "approach" teleologically to imply a hierarchical conception of humans in evolutionary terms, or the metonymy of "the world" too inclusive to comprehend fully. I might say van Peer's claim, full as it is of metaphoric language, is confusing. But it isn't, of course. Because most language users have developed the capacity to make the irrational leaps required by language, particularly by metaphor. As Jan Zwicky puts it in *Wisdom & Metaphor* (on a page facing the *Oxford English Dictionary*'s entries for "analogy" and "analogon"): "To understand a metaphor is to recognize that if one context or conceptual constellation is laid over another, just so, aspects or outlines will spring into focus, a common pattern will be discernible—one that makes a difference to our grasp of the individual constellations or contexts separately" (Left 24). Zwicky argues to value the risk of imprecision or irrationality when making analogies, but urges taking the risk in a thoroughly self-conscious manner—"just so," as it were—to open the possibility of congruence, commensurability, consilience between two seemingly dichotomous ideas, images, disciplines.

Consilience is sociobiologist E. O. Wilson's notion of a unity of knowledge regarding the natural world, a notion related to his earlier theory of biophilia, which is humans' intrinsic affinity with living beings. Wilson has been a key scientific figure in the debate about the supposed differences between the "two cultures": "The role of science, like that of art, is to blend exact imagery with more distant meaning, the parts we already understand with those given as new into larger patterns that are coherent enough to be acceptable as truth. The biologist knows this relation by intuition during the course of field work, as he struggles to make order out of the infinitely varying patterns of nature" (*Biophilia* 51).

If the biologist recognizes the relations between old and new patterns of meaning—even if the meaning itself remains uncertain—and employs the scientific method (hypothesis) in his struggle, perhaps the poet (and in her small way, the ecocritic) employs metaphor in an analogous way to test the limits of relational thinking, meaning, and living.[7] This analogy helps to explain how McKay's substantial "gift for metaphor" (Coles 42) has developed alongside his preference for species specificity; moreover, as

Kevin Bushell reminds in his essay on McKavian metaphor, meaning "generates from relationships, both in the world (experience) and in language (metaphor)" (38). To modify and extend Wilson's phrase, then, the role of the ecocritic (interested in following scientific and experiential trails of referents)[8] is to extrapolate how more precise metaphors and more accurate naming elicit a complex and proximal relation between humans and the nonhuman subjects of poetry. In the case of McKay's poems about flight, which are just as likely to acknowledge flight's metaphorical transcendence as they are its physics, the relation provokes contrary images of domesticity and wilderness. It is a contrariness into which Harry Greene, in this chapter's epigraph, provides insight: if birds' reptilian ancestry places humans (as mammals) closer to avifauna than reptiles are, it also reaffirms the wild distance between the current epoch and the age of the dinosaurs.

Home and flight seem at first glance to be opposite human desires. The desire for home is a desire for safety, for a comfortable dwelling that McKay claims, among other things, "makes possible the possession of the world" outside (*V* 23). Home, according to McKay, "is the action of the inner life finding outer form; it is the settling of self into the world" (22) and "the place where knowledge as power begins" (23). A space in which to feel safe, then, offers a space to make the self familiar by positioning it, via knowledge, within the world outside. The desire for flight, on the other hand, is a desire for no place and all places, for the ability to leave home—the earth—and the freedom to return when necessary, a duality present most obviously in homing pigeons. As McKay's idea about the possession of the world implies, both desires have the potential to manifest humans' worst pathologies regarding our place in the world. Although I devote this and the following two chapters to McKay's poems about bird (and human attempts at) flight, I recognize a concomitant interest in notions of home as a perhaps unattainable "existence apart from wilderness" (25). Unattainability, in part, sparks the desire that bonds homemaking and flight in McKay's poetry and poetics.

In *Another Gravity*, "Homing" (19–20) offers bird migration as a subtle indication of the twin desires for flight and home. The speaker remembers home before it settles pragmatically into "real estate and its innumerable / Kodak moments," and he identifies home as "the first cliché" (19). Cliché in this case connects home both to the process of writing (following from the term's original meaning as a stereotype, or copied block used in printing) and to the repetition of events in memory such that "things should happen / twice, and place / share the burden of remembering" (19). The speaker succinctly articulates the paradox of home—the impulse to stay until ready to leave followed by the desire to return—while implying a historicity of home with the lines, "Abide, / Abode" (19).[9] Following this paradox, the speaker recalls a plate his parents bought on their honeymoon; it depicts a "hand-painted *habitant* / sitting on a log," having "paused to smoke his pipe, the tree / half cut and leaning," and a "bird, / or something" hanging overhead (19). Then, reminiscent of Keats's speaker in "Ode on a Grecian Urn," he offers an interpretation of the scene, which ignores the habitant and focuses on the leaning tree pointing, the speaker avers, toward home (and beyond) and "the smudged bird" (19–20). What kind of bird? Perhaps

> it's a Yellow Warbler who has flown
> from winter habitat in South America to nest here
> in the clearing. If we catch it, band it,
> let it go a thousand miles away it will be back
> within a week. How?
> Home is what we know
> and know we know, the intricately
> feathered nest. Homing
> asks the question. (20)

The question posed by the act of homing—How?—seems more important than the answer, especially when we consider the convoluted response McKay provides in the poem's final strophe.[10] The response is convoluted, though, because the complexities of migratory behaviour, which he is talking about without naming, itself remain largely unexplained by ornithologists. Although birds are not the only organisms that migrate—whales, butterflies, and caribou are notable others—many avian migrations defy simple explanation, and the vast physical differences among birds that migrate make any one theory difficult to assert.

The ability to fly plays a significant role in humans' fascination with bird (and monarch butterfly) migration, because of the immense distances some birds can travel only to return home to mate, build a nest, and raise their young. Over millennia, migrant birds have developed efficient strategies for optimizing fuel consumption while maintaining appropriate speed (to ensure timely arrival at breeding grounds). Adaptations selected for migration include "flexible organs that grow and shrink in relation to the requirements of fueling and transportation," that is, "to boost their food-precessing capacity [and] grow larger [flight muscles] to lift increasing fuel loads" (Åkesson and Hedenström 124), and the ability to orient themselves and navigate long distances (often around or over ecological barriers).[11] Without benefit of calculus or a scale to determine their own weights, individual birds must estimate when and how much to eat in order to accomplish physical feats humans can barely imagine.[12] The arctic tern (*Sterna paridisaea*), to use an example of a bird that covers extreme distances in migration, travels south from Canada's Arctic Circle "at the end of summer, crosses the Atlantic, turns south along the coasts of Europe and Africa, to reach the Antarctic two months later. All told, it is a 15,000-mile (25,000 km) return trip" (Gingras 149). Although a week is a relatively short time for yellow warblers (*Dendroica petechia*) to travel a thousand miles, this species does travel extensive distances from South America to North America in spring (Lowther et al. n.p.). That McKay thinks and writes an idea of home, including the desire to return, through migratory bird behaviour suggests a connection between the desire for home and the desire for flight, the latter of which he contemplates in more detail elsewhere in *Another Gravity* and other collections. The connection itself, as it manifests in another west-coast writer's work, is worth considering in more detail, not least because as a work of prose fiction it thinks narratively rather than lyrically.

In *Innocent Cities* (1990), Vancouver Island-based writer Jack Hodgins, too, combines a concern for problems of home and homemaking with the human desire to achieve flight. His narrative treatment of the tensions between home and flight reflects many of the ideas McKay develops in his poetry. Logan Sumner, the novel's protagonist and inventor of a flying machine, is "one of the few who'd been born" in mid-nineteenth-century, and hence "innocent," Victoria, B.C., yet he rarely feels at home there (286). As an adult, Sumner finds himself in the ironic position of having to construct home in a space that is reconfigured on all sides by inhabitants from elsewhere who, seeking the comforts of home, inscribe bits of their remembered pasts and imitations of the places from which they arrive on British Columbia's coastal landscape. The narrator, by way of recognizing Sumner's position relative to the newcomers around him, writes that,

> because he had grown up here when the island was still a colony and the city not much more than a palisaded fortress of exaggerated dreams, he moved through the landscape as though it did not even register itself upon his sight. In this way he was unlike most of the population of newcomers who still regarded the crashing waves and the giant coniferous trees and the wild green forest undergrowth with expressions of alarm, amazed that the monstrous elements of their adopted home had not yet been reorganized into tidy European gardens or reduced to familiar stretches of horizontal California desert. (xiii)

From an ecocritical perspective, Sumner's affection for the uncultivated landscape of Vancouver Island seems consciously to resist a Frygian garrison mentality. The word "palisade" might not be diametrically opposed to "garrison," but I have difficulty thinking of another word that so readily invokes Frye's term while simultaneously, and subtly, posing a challenge to its validity in constructions of Canadian identity, literary and otherwise.[13] While "palisade" refers to a fenced enclosure made of wood (and, later, of metal railings), it also suggests in horticultural terms, according to the *Oxford English Dictionary*, "an espalier; a row of trees or shrubs clipped to form an ornamental hedge."[14] The "colony" of Sumner's youth, far from building defences against the "wilderness," was safely ensconced behind a living forest wall, ostensibly safe from other Europeans. Hodgins reinforces this notion in two ways: by setting the novel in 1881, approximately a decade prior to the construction of Fort Rodd Hill—a military structure ostensibly more in keeping with Frye's "garrison"—and by introducing Sumner's tendency to "lift a forearm to his nose and inhale the scent: western red cedar, hemlock, Douglas fir" (xiii). The specificity with which Hodgins writes Sumner's relation to Victoria reveals a familiarity and a connection to home that is unique to one of the only characters, other than First Nations inhabitants, to have been born in that city.

Highlighting the importance of landscape in constructions of home and Sumner's comfort with "giant coniferous trees" (indicated by his ability to move through them without necessarily being conscious of them), the narrator introduces one of the paradoxes of home that plagues Sumner. Convinced that the only way to construct home is to inhabit a space that is away from home—embracing the creativity that is inspired by absence[15]—he desires to go elsewhere. This desire, while not strictly speaking ornithological, involves at least two attempts by Sumner to distance himself from Victoria by distancing himself from the earth. In the first instance, he decides to purchase a headstone next to his late wife's and engrave it with a running commentary on his opinions of life. Sumner's "purchase of the second stone was considered by some to be an eccentric and even morbid act," but not so eccentric and curious as his discovery that "[w]ithin six months of the funeral ... the original words were inadequate" (4). In order for him to feel comfortable in his world, Sumner revises the words on the granite face as often as he changes his opinions and understanding of the world around him. The only way for Sumner to resist the permanence of history is to change it, to keep moving, essentially making a personal history as he records it. Because his medium is stone, though, the changes consist primarily of physical additions resulting in a towering manifestation—part memorial register, part advice-to-self, part collected aphorisms[16]—that reaches farther from ground and closer to sky.

In his second attempt to distance himself from Victoria, and the one more pertinent to a reading of McKay's avian poetics, Sumner repeatedly attempts to invent a flying machine. The flying machine functions both as a connector of land and sky (as well as sea and sky), much as his gravestone does, and theriomorphically as a representation of a bird, which the machine resembles in the majority of its manifestations. The bird as symbol, connecting earth and sky, flies often in both Victorias—the innocent cities of the title are Victoria, British Columbia, Canada, and Ballarat, Victoria, Australia. In fact, birds populate the novel, each instance tending to suggest betweenness, impermanence. (Mr. Horncastle's hotel is called The Great Blue Heron. "Why was the hotel named for this great awkward bird? Simple. 'You've seen him. Stands at the side of the water. Waits for his dinner to come to him.' What else were any of them doing here, he challenged his listeners to tell him. Waiting for the next boom" [34]. A drifter who builds a shack in the hollow of a tree is called Mr. Hawks. Kate Jordan, before leaving Ballarat, fed up with the hordes of cockatoos "laughing" at her from eucalyptus and blue gum trees, fires a musket at the birds from her verandah, forcing those not willing to "risk the alternatives" to choose "immediate ascension into some other sphere" [83–84]). The birds in Hodgins's novel function less ecologically than symbolically; despite the accuracy with which Hodgins names them, they tend to represent ontological liminality inherent in their ability to fly.

Intermittently Hodgins provides glimpses of the flying machine's progress. Sumner himself has little to do with its construction beyond financing it; Zak, his Native friend, is the one charged with designing the machine, which goes through myriad versions before it finally succeeds—and fails. Zak studies the designs of George Cayley, whose Old Flyer reportedly lifted a ten-year-old boy in 1849 (Gibbs-Smith 47), and da Vinci, whose design problems Zak discovers after "closely examining the feathers, the bones, the joints of a dead willow grouse's wing, looking for its secret" (107). As successive attempts to become the first to build a flying machine able to stay aloft "for more than just a few seconds" fail (332), Sumner eventually relents in his desire to study more books while Zak figures it out for himself (181). While the first few versions of the machine resemble a dragonfly, the final version, the successful one, is christened the *Blue Heron*—not that it necessarily looks like a heron. To make a successful flying machine, Zak "ignored the impossibly intricate plans drawn up by" Sumner, "who had studied too many European failures in books and magazines"; instead, Zak takes "the lead from his own people," constructing "the frame for his great raven" out of wooden strips from a tree he had found and split himself (329). Historically, "[t]he key innovation of the Wrights' [successful] design," according to David Alexander, "was inspired by birds: the Wrights observed that gliding birds turned by twisting their wings lengthwise" and "were the first inventors to realize that aerial banking is not a byproduct of a turn (as in ships) but rather what *causes* the turn" (290). In other words, attention to avian biology informs the history of aerodynamics and aviation as much as it inflects McKay's poems about flight.

In the end, Zak's machine does fly; it carries Chu Lee—along with the opium he is planning to sell for his uncle—across the ocean toward the American side. Before he can land or turn around, however, American police, acting on a tip, shoot the machine out of the sky, cutting short Sumner and Zak's brief achievement. Hodgins implies that to fly means risking a crash under the weight of the technology developed to satisfy the human desire to fly; paradoxically, he implies that the desire for home outweighs the desire for flight. Perhaps it takes the narrative space of a novel to reach such a conclusion, while it takes the concise lyricism of poetry to explore the desire to fly, by way of close attention to the physics of flight and avian movement, without crashing to the sea like Icarus (whom I discuss in Chapter Five).

As Battalio and others note, ornithology has, more than most areas of biological study, a history informed by both professional biologists and interested, devoted amateurs whose field notes and participation in bird counts and banding studies "have greatly increased our understanding of bird biology" (Perrins and Birkhead 1). Such a historical development accords nicely with E. O. Wilson's claim that "[s]cience is not just analytic; it is also synthetic." "It uses artlike intuition and imagery" in the process of thinking about the world and humans' relations to the world (*Biophilia* 54). In developing his theory of biophilia, Wilson goes so far as to suggest that, eventually, "[t]he excitement of the scientist's search for the true material nature of the species recedes, to be replaced in part by the more enduring responses of the hunter and poet" (55). I would like to pause for a moment and consider the multiplicity of Wilson's "and," both as it functions to join two seemingly irreconcilable designators ("hunter" and "poet") and as it problematizes a relation (hunter "and" poet) within my ecocritical project.[17]

In his "Introduction" to *One Culture: Essays on Science and Literature*, George Levine[18] complicates the divisiveness of "science and literature" by devoting considerable space to the difference "announce[d], through the 'and'" (6). Building, it would seem, upon G. S. Rousseau's notion—in "Literature and Science: The State of the Field"—that the "and" conjoins far more than it separates, Levine writes: "'And' implies relationship, of course, but (para)tactically refuses to define it. The 'and' also intimates the oddity of the relationship: what can the two have to do with each other? It implies, moreover, that in spite of the conventions of literary hostility to science, and of scientific indifference to literature, the relationship matters" (6). Levine's doubling of "and" into both tactic (strategy)[19] and parataxis is interesting for the space it leaves readers to engage the relation *between*—in this case, the relation between science and literature, writ large. The implication of Levine's parenthetical compounding is that "science" and "literature"—as they are typically conceived of in these debates—are analogous to related but dissimilar clauses in a sentence, and that the "and" simultaneously connects and divides in ways it would *not* under normal grammatical conditions. It acts, that is, as parataxis, as a semicolon or a full stop rather than as a conjunction. In his dictionary of literary terms, Chris Baldick offers an example of parataxis in literature—where "the relationship between one statement and the next is not made explicit" (161)—from Henry David Thoreau's influential *Walden*.[20] That Baldick chooses one of the foundational texts of nature writing—that strange amalgamation of non-fictional memoir and natural history—is fitting when one considers Levine's meditation on the edge of "and" alongside Wilson's (para)tactical insinuation regarding the environmental impact of hunters and poets. If the interdisciplinarity of ecocriticism is perpetually in question, the relation among hunters, birders, and poets is more so.[21]

Like birding, the practice of poetry is in many ways the most amateur of activities. John Burroughs argues that "poets are the best natural historians, only you must know how to read them. They translate the facts largely and freely" (22). Louis Halle makes a similar argument when he ends *The Appreciation of Birds* with the claim that "in the flight of a bird is a whole philosophy, if only we could read it right" (125). And, in his Foreword to David Alexander's *Nature's Flyers*, biologist Steven Vogel proposes that in flight birds "are telling us something, but they give only the text and leave to us the deciphering of the subtext, the mechanisms beneath the phenomenon" (xiii). An ecocriticism open to crossing disciplinary borders and experiencing phenomena beyond the text requires that ecocritics learn how to read in new ways. The capacity to read across disciplines often seems anathema to the institutionalized imperative to specialize and professionalize. In the Afterword to *Fiddlehead Gold: 50 Years of The Fiddlehead Magazine*, McKay, a former editor of the journal, writes of poets like himself: "We can get so hooked on being 'professional' (don't forget your SASE) we can forget that being *amateur*, in the deep sense, is what it's all about" ("Common Sense" 235;

author's emphasis). The deep sense McKay refers to is the meaning that is often eclipsed by the more common one, which is "not professional." McKay refers to a person who practises something out of love for it, someone whose *in*expertise contains, alongside the risk of failure, the potential for genuine insight. For this reason alone, it is not surprising that birds and poetry are as historically connected as they are and that birdwatching and poetry are related activities.

In *Lifebirds* (1995), George Levine traces this connection in a personal memoir. The book is interesting for what Levine has to say about the bird–poet connection and for the book's status within a particular nascent genre of the personal essay, namely the poet-academic writing of his (he is invariably male) limitations as a birder, of his role as perpetual amateur. Moreover, this genre—call it "humblebumblingbirderlit," to which I would add Leonard Nathan's *Diary of a Left-Handed Birdwatcher*, McKay's *Vis à Vis*, and Chris Cokinos's *Hope Is the Thing with Feathers*[22]—reconsiders birds *on* the page even as it gestures toward their existence *off* the page:

> Making birds primarily a means to an end would be a betrayal of the birds, of how I experience them, and of my sense of what birding is about. I hope and more than hope that what I am writing affirms the importance of birds as birds, of birds as part of an enormous non-human world which we cannot afford not to engage, about which we cannot afford not to think and imagine, from which we cannot afford not to take pleasure, which means taking risks. (Levine 6)

Even if the risk entails nothing more than being ridiculed or scorned for emphasizing "the importance of birds as birds" in addition to birds as symbols, its worth as a relatively small risk extends to ecocritics' questioning what has become a default mode of reading symbolically, as J. M. Coetzee's alter ego, Elizabeth Costello, might say, in the first and only instance.

Even though ornithologists have clarified many of the mechanisms of bird flight that remained unexplained for, and thus unavailable to, earlier poets, "the wonder continues everlasting" for scientists and poets alike (Halle 123). All flight, not only avian, is a seemingly impossible accomplishment that depends on fundamental contradictions of ratios, namely weight to lift and thrust to drag. To render the evolutionary biology of the matter simply, birds' wings are airfoils. According to Bernoulli's principle, pressure is lowest where velocity is greatest: the shape of a bird's wing (an airfoil) forces air that flows over it to travel farther than the air that flows under it, which causes the upper-surface air to speed up, or increase in velocity, thereby creating differing pressure levels above and below the wing. Therefore, the lower pressure over the top of the wing creates lift to counteract gravity. For level flight, lift must be equal to the bird's weight (Gill *Ornithology* 98), and to achieve altitude and distance birds must either expend energy by flapping (to produce enough thrust to help produce lift) or locate vertical airflow—"currents that can minimise the effects of gravity," such as convection, orographic lift,[23] and turbulence (Elkins 43–51)—in order to maintain or increase lift. In order to exploit these air currents, birds have had to develop specialized skeletal and wing structures: lightweight, hollow bones;[24] a keeled sternum; the form of wings in relation to individual feathers; and the ability to control direction, speed, and altitude by way of specialized tendons and muscles—all are examples of evolutionary adaptations for flight in birds. To render avian wings as airfoils, however, is a necessarily reductive move in the history of aerodynamic theory. As Louis Halle writes, the shape of birds' wings in flight is not fixed but "constantly changing in response to the constantly changing pressures of the air through which it moves, or to suit changes in course or speed.... No one shape is quite retained for more than a moment" (108). Such dynamic movement translates well into the poet's repertoire of "fancy linguistic figure[s]" (*V* 85)—metaphor, cadence, onomatopoeia—even as he struggles to write birds that "are complete in themselves, free of apparent ambitions beyond flying, eating, reproducing, protecting territory, and singing" (Oughton 36). Airplane wings, like printed poetry, might remain visibly rigid—unflappable—but just as airplane wings must "give" a little,[25] the shapes and rhythms of McKay's verse warp and dip in response to the vagaries of voice.

Despite the obvious biological differences between humans and birds, some similarities do exist, at least from an evolutionary perspective. Margaret Morse Nice has recorded developmental characteristics of baby birds at hatching. From her field observations, Nice posited a number of conditions on the continuum between superprecocial and altricial. These included down (present or absent), eyes (open or closed), mobility (ambulatory or nestbound), parental nourishment (no or yes), and parental attendance (minimal or essential). Like human babies, "[a]ltricial birds are naked, blind, and virtually immobile when they hatch and thus are completely dependent on their parents" (Gill *Ornithology* 432); the the greater the number of altricial characteristics a bird exhibits, the more likely it seems to "get noticed in literature," according to Lutwack's claim that, of the many thousands of birds, "only a few" tend to get written about with any regularity: "large birds that are conspicuous on land or in flight and only those small birds that can be heard or seen near human dwellings and workplaces" (18). While the notion that an evolutionary affinity determines which birds McKay writes about is admittedly far-fetched, I cite Nice's observations as a way of introducing Susan Fisher's argument that McKay writes beyond metaphorical relations to compare humans and birds via homology. The biological evidence provided by Nice might not explain the symbolism of certain birds, but it suggests an affinity with humans that provides an extra-literary reason for poets' fascination. Fisher cites a number of McKay's poems in which she identifies a comparison based on Neil Campbell and Jane Reece's definition of homology as "similarity resulting from common ancestry," which includes mammalian bone structure and, in the broadest sense, DNA (448). Though homology is a term from biology, Fisher appropriates it "as a literary term in order to describe comparisons that exist not by virtue of poetic invention but because of biological connection" (57).[26] Despite the characteristics that humans share at birth with recently hatched altricial birds, the homologous aspects of McKay's poetry relevant to my discussion of bird flight have more to do with the *desire* to fly than with biological or evolutionary similarities between people and birds, since humans are physiologically incapable of flying. Fisher argues that "McKay's knowledge of evolution and phylogeny enables him to write about other creatures homologically" as a strategy to circumvent "the distancing tropes of analogy and metaphor, or simile" (57). While I agree with Fisher's reading, I maintain that the efficiency of McKay's metaphorical precision in concert with his extra-literary specificity achieves the same goal of inviting readers into closer proximity to the more-than-human world.[27]

My interest in the trails of referents that bring readers and the physical world into closer proximity is partly a reaction to critics' primary focus on McKay's metaphorical acuity. Flight for McKay sometimes means flight; in some poems about raptors—birds whose size and frequent use of thermals make them relatively easy to view on the wing compared to, say, warblers and bushtits—neither metaphor nor homology alone suffice to articulate the poet's awe in the face of the birds' aerial achievements. Sometimes a meditation on birds' aerial capabilities, though expressed in human language and therefore necessarily anthropocentric in some sense, is necessary to write poetry about birds' aerial capabilities. George Levine makes a salient point that is helpful in contemplating raptors in, and outside of, poetry. Referring to the sharp-shinned hawk, "common enough in most places [but] not everyday occurrences for" non-birders, Levine meditates on his experience with hawks in general: "Hawks continue to feel to me like birds that mark a radical distinction between the domestic, the urban or suburban, and the 'natural'" (*Lifebirds* 74). Levine's observation suggests that hawks elicit a mixture of familiarity (which they share with more "urban" birds) and a particular sort of awe (which tends to be reserved for birds of prey).[28] Levine reinforces the different awe-inspired reactions to different birds: "I love hummingbirds almost as much as I do hawks, but hawks in their size and power and apparent calm, as they soar or hover or gyre into an ultimately invisible distance, inspire an awe and envy that smaller birds can't" (71). The difference is attributable as much to the fact that larger birds are typically easier to spot, whether roosting, soaring, or feeding, as to a human "delight in casual brutality and long-distance death" (McKay V 19). McKay's observation implies a homologous relation based not on physiognomy but on behaviour, or psychology. The appearance of power and calm, in other words, draws humans to birds of prey as symbols of strength. More often than not, we want to be them.

Others, too, have afforded birds of prey a special status in their observations and poetry. According to David Quammen, "birds appear frequently throughout [Robert Penn Warren's] early and late poems. Herons, owls, geese, gulls, crows. These birds are not decorations. They are not merely symbolic" (186). Like most birds appearing in McKay's poetry, they are symbols with real-world counterparts whose biological attributes provide ecological information both within their habitats (outside the text) and among ecocritical discussions (inside the text). Warren's poetic "attention," though, "was especially captured by hawks," so much so that "one critic [probably Harold Bloom] discussed the fact in a review" (186). In *Reading the Mountains of Home* (1998), John Elder brings the awe Levine mentions into close contact with the written word, acknowledging the impact of W. B. Yeats's "The Second Coming" on Elder's own relation to the Green Mountains of Vermont. "I always like remembering Yeats's term 'gyre' when I watch falcons wheeling above this ridge of the Green Mountains," Elder writes. "It's a sharply angled word, conveying the tilts and accelerations within their circling flight. A slow, floating curve can suddenly warp downward at Mach speed when a falcon glimpses prey" (153). Unlike the "mere anarchy" Yeats alludes to in his poem, however, the falcon's shift to mach speed suggests a degree of control—mere degrees from chaos—to which humans can only aspire: falcons that "lack all conviction" (Yeats 294) will not survive long enough to produce offspring, since lack of conviction is a trait unlikely to confer an evolutionary advantage. While this reading does not remove the possibility that Yeats's falcon is symbolic of a world moving closer and closer to anarchy, it does emphasize the importance of precision in the metaphor. The poem would not likely have the same impact if the falcon were "flapping and flapping in the widening gyre." Or if the falcon were a gull.

With all flight, necessary contradictions must be achieved, as when another species of diurnal raptor, the osprey (*Pandion haliaetus*), demonstrates its aerial hunting technique in McKay's "Migratory Patterns" (*B* 69–72):

> the osprey in full scalloped stretch above the creek that
> buckled, folded in his flight becoming
> plummet, turned into the very gravity
> each feather is the delicate
> repudiation of: (71)

Slightly larger than North America's largest falcon (gyrfalcon, *Falco rusticolus*), osprey are agile and dextrous; they hunt fish by hovering over rivers or lakes before plummeting, feet first, into the water to capture their prey. McKay's observation that the osprey "becom[es] / plummet [and] turn[s] into" gravity, while echoing the cliché that what goes up must come down, simultaneously invites metaphysical contemplation of seeming (ontological) metamorphosis and alludes convincingly, if metaphorically, to at least one ecological (and evolutionary) relation—between fish and raptors—resulting from the osprey's flight capabilities. His description of feathers as "delicate repudiation[s]" of gravity likewise impels me to consult my field guide's section on bird topography to learn more about feathers, about their architecture; once I realize that Sibley's topography, which details individual head, body, and wing feathers, reveals little of feathers' structure, I turn to Frank Gill's *Ornithology* textbook and learn that "Feathers consist mainly of keratin, an inert substance of insoluble microscopic filaments embedded in an amorphous protein matrix" (65). In other words, barbs ("filaments") branch laterally from the rachis (the portion of shaft distal to the body) to create the "flat vane" we recognize as a feather; the hollow base of the shaft (that "amorphous protein matrix"), sometimes called the quill, "anchors the feather below the surface of the skin" (Gill 66). Feathers represent an important evolutionary adaptation insofar as they are, in addition to a bird's specialized muscles, tendons, and bones, necessary for flight; insofar as human hair and nails consist of a type of keratin, feathers have been used to symbolize human contact with the Divine because feathers play a crucial role in flight and, like hair and nails, they "endure after the bird's death and therefore often stand for the continuity of life" (Lawrence 9).

According to Bernd Heinrich, "Birds' feathers ... may have originally evolved from scales as a sun shield or as insulation from either heat or cold. It was then possible for them to be further modified as structures for flight, for tools in sexual and other signalling, and—in sand grouse and ravens—for transporting water to the young" (*Ravens* 78). From an evolutionary perspective, then, feathers may indeed represent a "continuity of life," while from an ecological perspective they confer numerous advantages to enable such continuity (through reproduction).

In *Diary of a Left-Handed Birdwatcher*, Nathan tells of an encounter he has with Lewis, his ornithologist/friend. Nathan offers this encounter as a way of insinuating himself, and his poetical tendencies, into a conversation about the seeming physical impossibility of flight. After picking up a feather, Lewis gives it to his friend and tells him he holds in his hand a natural miracle. "So light is it that, if I turn my eyes away," Nathan writes,

> I will know it's there only because of a sensation of softness. It's all grace in and of itself. But the license I permit myself I won't permit Lewis, and I say, 'If you mean by miracle the suspension of natural law, isn't that a contradiction?'
>
> Lewis shrugs and says, rather brusquely, 'Forget that. That's small potatoes. The serious miracle is that there is any law at all.' (122)

Science might not be the study of miracles, and memory might not be, as McKay writes in the poem "Drag" (*AG* 11), "heavier than air." "But," as McKay writes in the same poem, "however, / on the other hand." Drag, it would seem, wants to impede forward momentum; and yet without drag, flight would be impossible. It reminds me of another natural law that might be a miracle, or might be a poem—namely Isaac Newton's contention that for every action there is an equal and opposite reaction.

Lewis and other ornithologists tend to agree about the evolutionary significance of flight to birds, acknowledging that "the ability to fly is the key adaptation that has made birds [as] successful [as they are]" (Hedenström 415).[29] Literary critics tend to agree about the significance of flight to humans, more specifically to poets. Recapitulating the evolutionary explanation for poets' interest in flight, but with a more socio-cultural bias, Leonard Lutwack claims that flight and song are "the qualities [poets] most admire in birds, for it is to these powers that birds owe their remarkable survival in the vast and varied environment[s] they inhabit" (*Birds* 45). Discussing contemporary American poet Jorie Graham's "ongoing negotiations with the world and with poetry," Willard Spiegelman likewise argues that "the appeal of birds to poets needs little explaining. Both as metaphor—bird as idealized natural singer, unfreighted by language and consciousness—and as metonymy—bird as substitute for the soul and its wish for flight—members of the avian kingdom [*sic*]³⁰ could sustain a poetic taxonomy equivalent to one devoted to flowers" (219, 222). Lutwack, more aware than Spiegelman seems to be of ornithology's place in literary studies (or aware at least of the value of natural history and science to literary studies), nevertheless maintains a dichotomous view of the ways poets and scientists think about flight: "The ability of birds to fly has inspired both scientists and poets, scientists esteeming flight a physical triumph of the first order and poets seeing in flight a powerful symbol of the transcendence they wish to achieve in their writing" (Lutwack 45–46). Neither Lutwack, in his comprehensive study of literature in English, nor Spiegelman, in his focused critique of a contemporary American poet, worries about the ease with which birds, generally speaking, have been "treated." The language of avian "powers," of animals "unfreighted by language and consciousness," and of surrogate "souls" for poets existentially bereft of meaning betrays a Romanticism they do not address candidly in their criticism.

Chapter Four

Flight

> The expansiveness gained by poetry's incorporation of scientific insight propels the human perspective beyond earth's gravity. But from the vantage of space, earth itself becomes a radiant particular of decay—a crystal, a seed. Poetry and science, nature and culture, all are included within such an oscillation.
> – John Elder, *Imagining the Earth* (207)

Flight fascinates humans, I think, because from an evolutionary perspective we have been selected for traits amenable to walking, not flying. Somewhere along the myriad lines of potential adaptations and chance mutations we lost our chance to fly. Bird flight represents the locomotive equivalent of what humans have not achieved and, as such, introduces an ancient nostalgia for, or distant memory of, what might have been: "It must have seemed to early man [*sic*], earth-bound and leaden-footed, that these graceful passages through an element he could not master were the epitome of all he could never be, the incarnation of that finer part of himself which he felt to exist yet could never define" (Brown *Gods* 4). W. J. Brown implies that humans' inability to fly exists alongside a desire to fly. The earliest humans, he speculates, would not have had the capacity to recognize their desire for what it was; they would have known only a feeling—or felt a feeling—of lightness upon witnessing birds in flight. Their bodily heaviness would have made them aware only that they could not join the birds—but it could not, prior to scientific explanations of gravity and physics, explain the twinge they felt as they stood and watched the busy skies. Mircea Eliade identifies such a "nostalgia for flight" (480) as "an essential element in human consciousness" (Lawrence 156). Whether that aspect of human consciousness serves more or less as punishment for something beyond our control, it nevertheless remains.

Rebecca Solnit examines the flip side of the evolutionary story: "The list of what we eventually got from bipedalism is long and alluring, full of all the gothic arches and elongations of the body. Start with the straight row of toes and high arch of the foot. Go up the long straight walker's legs to the buttocks, round and protuberant thanks to the massively developed gluteus maximus of walkers, a minor muscle in apes [and absent entirely in birds] but the largest muscle in the human body" (35). Alluring though this list is, complex human musculature ensures that we remain as earthbound as our oldest ancestors (some of whom might, admittedly, have been arboreal). We are quite simply too heavy to fly; our sternum and pectoral muscles too underdeveloped. But our brains, as Eliade has it, have capacity enough to imagine flight, to recognize our physical limitations, and to express a desire to achieve and experience flight (never mind the wherewithal to calculate formulas and construct machines that make the dream of flight come true). McKay writes more about pectoralis in his avian poetics than he does about gluteus, but the latter does have its place, usually accompanied by an unexplained sadness. At the beginning of *Night Field* (1991), McKay portrays a hike that is both emblematic—of the poet's moving through the world, of the cadences of human locomotion in concert with his immediate environment—and pragmatic. Birders must get to the field (usually by car) and, once there, be able to get around quietly and efficiently. The act of birding requires an act, sometimes many acts, of walking.

The act of birding is implicit throughout much of McKay's poetry, and the act of hiking is often explicitly presented in his books as a way to birding. An early poem in *Night Field*, "Black Spruce" (7–13), offers a short journal account of the speaker's hike near rocky Lake Superior. Anticipating the flight poems of *Another Gravity* in the way a camel anticipates water on the third day of travel, McKay writes:

> Eventually the pack becomes
> your hump, the weight of your food
> and the weight of your clothing
> and the weight of your shelter
> and the weight of your forgetfulness of all
> of the above.
>   Added to the sad
> dumb sadness of your ass as it tries
> to reconstrue itself as muscle,
> lift your life up,
> over another ridge. (*NF* 7)

The hiker's ass, having yet to "reconstrue itself as muscle" for the walk, doesn't deserve the Latin "gluteus maximus" the way the sparrow's breast muscles in "Load" are named pectoralis major and minor.[1] The sadness attached to the hiker's ass compounds as the weight of survival gear conspires with gravity to keep the hiker on firm ground, inclining—in both senses of the word—toward a ridge, a "belly-smooth red-brown rock," from which to take in Lake Superior "in a single glance" (12). In addition to drawing attention to the human need to carry extra weight in the form of a pack full of survival gear,[2] the repetition of the phrase "and the weight" adds a further sense of gravity, of gravitas, to the proceedings, while looking ahead to the other gravity McKay explores nearly a decade later in *Another Gravity*.

McKay recognizes gravity as the main physical impediment to flight while simultaneously acknowledging how gravity functions in important biophysical and mythological ways, including in the act of flying. The poems in *Another Gravity* reflect ecological relations between sanderlings and intertidal zones; horned larks and memory; sharp-shinned hawks and Robert Creeley. These interconnections support Ricou's observation, which he makes after reading Roger Tory Peterson's field guide, that in addition to providing access to specific birds "birding is also a way to know trees and rocks and seas and all that weaves itself into habitat" ("Field Notes" 93). *Another Gravity* demonstrates McKay's understanding of the physics of bird flight and indicates a linguistic precision interested as much in naming specific birds as in naming the processes and mechanics involved in achieving flight, as in the poems "Lift," "Drag," "Load," "Angle of Attack," "Camber," "Glide," "Hover," "Feather," "Hang Time," "Plummet," and "Turbulence." While individually McKay's poems "about" flight in *Another Gravity* make only passing references to the scientific literature—there is a keen amateur's take on the complexities of physics and aerodynamics—together they imply a sophisticated ecological poetics in which the language of image and metaphor is as welcome, and as powerful, as the language of avian aerodynamics. Just as lift alone is not capable of making a bird achieve flight, the poem "Lift" on its own does not fulfill an ecocritical desire for interdisciplinary, extra-textual meaning. Similarly, the poem "Camber," with its opening lines invoking "That rising curve, the fine line / between craft and magic where we / travel uphill without effort" might do little to mimic, even in poetic form, the upward convexity of an airfoil. The collection as a whole requires opposing forces—in the guise of poems—in order to achieve metaphoric flight and articulate an accurate discussion of the physics of flight.

"Lift" and "Drag" demonstrate this interrelation. As companion poems, they both complement and complicate each other. On the page, the poems face away from each other—atypical for companion poems—which forces me to flip the single leaf forward and back to compare their complementary elements. The book moves forward after "Lift," but reading "Drag" sends me back to check the degree of connection between the two poems.[3] In aerodynamic terms, lift and drag are not directly opposing forces (lift is opposed by gravity; drag is opposed by thrust); though lift helps birds get off the ground and drag acts against their forward momentum, sustained flight is not possible without both. "Lift" begins with a moment just prior to flight, that moment when a bird is just about to push off from the top corner of a building:

> To stand with mind akimbo where the wind
> riffles the ridge. Slow,
> slow jazz: it must begin
> before the instrument with bones
> dreaming themselves hollow and the dusk
> rising in them like a sloth
> ascending. (*AG* 5)

In part because McKay tends to name accurately, the pronoun "it," with no clear antecedent, emerges from these opening lines as the most compelling word. It is lift; it begins before the performance (to extend McKay's jazz analogy: the moistening of the sax's reed; the oiling of the trumpet's valves); it dreams of bones that are, like most bird bones, hollow. The rising dusk is embodied by the moon, which rehearses nightly "shades of pause / and spill." The moon, reflector of light, also has a relationship with gravity that plays out in the tides. Held in orbit by earth's gravity, the moon acts as a reminder of what resists lift. In "Drag," McKay names gravity "that irresistible embrace," at once necessary and inevitable. Gravity occurs through *Another Gravity* as an idea—a force—that holds individual poems in its orbit, while thrust occurs similarly, as it were, naturally in the form of forward momentum (assuming one reads the book front to back). Because they occur more or less constantly, neither gravity nor thrust appears as a poem of its own as lift and drag do.

"Drag" begins, fittingly, with a conjunction that suggests connection and resistance. "But, however, / on the other hand" effectively communicates the force—drag—parallel to but opposite to the direction of movement—thrust (6). Unlike gravity's embrace, which counters lift, "Drag / wants to dress the nakedness of speed, to hold clothes / in the slipstream until body reincarnates." Clothed, the pure speed of air/wind is forced to subside; if the clothes are light enough they might, puffed with air (a body reincarnate), achieve lift and float a little while. Filled with a human body, they will achieve no such thing. "Lift" ends with the speaker, mind presumably akimbo, waiting for something—"Something quick. / Something helpful to the air." Something akin to a force perpendicular to a wing's motion in the air, perhaps, in concert with other forces. In "Drag," the speaker is still waiting; he returns to what might be the same ridge from the beginning of the previous poem:

> When I approached the edge
> it seemed one gentle waft
> would carry me across, the brief lilt
> of a Horned Lark up from the roadside gravel
> into the adjacent field.
> However,
> on the other hand. It occurred to me that,
> unlike Horned Larks, who are imagination,
> I was mostly memory, which,
> though photogenic and nutritious, rich
> with old-time goodness, is notoriously
> heavier than air.

The image of the speaker approaching the edge drags me back to the riffling wind at the beginning of "Lift" and, even further, to the collection's opening poem, "Sometimes a Voice (1)" (3–4). The speaker of the companion poems might very well be the subject of the opening poem (which I discuss in Chapter Five as an Icarus figure). The odd juxtaposition of horned larks (*Eremophila alpestris*) (imagination) and the speaker (memory) in "Drag" supports this reading, since the subject of "Sometimes a Voice (1)" has, by the end of the poem, "run off into sky" (4) and become a memory. There is perhaps a residue in these poems of Eliade's "nostalgia for flight," albeit one tinged with a complex understanding of the physics of flight. What remains regards the short, pragmatic flight of horned larks—described by Sibley as "buoyant and flowing" (363)—as imagination, which knows no limits. The lark itself, though, despite the ease with which it accomplishes that "brief lilt," depends upon multiple physical forces acting in concert to reach the field.

In combination these poems communicate an attention to the natural world and an engagement with a discourse about the natural world. The connections between poems metonymically reflect aerodynamic relations between a wing's angle of attack—the angle a wing makes with its range of motion—and lift: as the angle of attack increases, so, too, does lift (at least up to a point beyond which the bird will stall). However, cambered wings, much more common among birds than symmetrical wings, produce lift at zero angle of attack. In the poem "Angle of Attack" (*AG* 16), McKay writes of the need for both the physiological suitability offered by the "rising curve" of wings and the learning curve necessary to develop an understanding of how to create lift, how to "live / next door to nothing, / and with art":

> You may openly
> endorse the air, but if you can't
> be canny, and, come to that, apt,
> chances are you won't
> get off the ground.

"You" in this context succeeds both as address to a bird as subject and as rhetorical gesture to bring readers closer to the physical world. Both the canniness and the aptness, moreover, that the speaker identifies as necessary to "get off the ground" recapitulate the familiarity and accuracy that come with a poetry attuned to species specificity and precise ecological knowing. One species of bird that McKay seems to think supremely apt for, and canny in regard to, flight, is the swallow. Indeed, as swallows spend the majority of their lives on the wing, they demonstrate little difficulty in getting off the ground.

Long celebrated for their aerial agility, swallows in particular have presented poets with a way to pay homage to avian acrobatics as symbols of Transcendence or Truth. W. J. Brown cites the naturalist Sir William Beach Thomas, who claims that "[o]ne of the sights that never grows stale, flat, or unprofitable is the flight of the bird: the slow sail of a gull, the muscular dash of a pigeon, the smooth speed of the swallow's circles" (3). In "The Blue Swallows," Howard Nemerov has "the mind in its brain" consider swallows' smooth speed and witness "the swallows' tails as nibs / Dipped in invisible ink, writing …" (397; ellipsis in original); but the speaker wants to resist the modernized augury by which the mind systematically interprets the swallows' flight patterns. "Poor mind," the speaker asks sympathetically, "what would you have them write? / Some cabalistic history / Whose authorship you might ascribe / to God? to Nature? Ah, poor ghost, / You've capitalized your Self enough" (397). Such capitalization represents an egoistic poetic tradition that ascribes authority to humans and human-made entities/deities. Nemerov comes close to undermining his commentary with the near-apostrophe "Ah, poor ghost," but his use Ah instead of Oh retains enough residual apostrophe to be effective as critique while simultaneously signalling the mind's (in its brain) moment of recognition, as expressed in "Ah, yes, but...." McKay employs the same interjection in "The Bushtits' Nest" when discussing "the centralizing and reductive influence of the name, which so often signals the terminal point of our interest. 'Ah, bushtits': check, snap. Next topic" (*V* 84). Lyric Os and Ahs mete distance between subject and object by addressing a gap—epistemological, evolutionary—and filling it with a sound. Not with a word, so bereft of consilience does language seem to be, but with a soft, aspirant sound.

In "Remembering Apparatus: Poetry and the Visibility of Tools" (*V* 51–78), McKay distinguishes between language and poetry, arguing that the latter "comes about because language is not able to represent raw experience, yet it must" (65). Whereas language is a naming that confers a knowable sense of identity (think of Adam's task), poetry as McKay has it "is only a listening," which "introduces the unnameable (that is, wilderness under the sign of language) into nomination" (66). The paradox is not easily negotiated, to be sure, but one way to understand it, perhaps, is to think of how much walking poets do while composing poems, and consequently how many poems include a speaker on a walk: walking becomes, in a McKavian sense, "both a recognition of the spiritual [and, I would add, ecological] importance of connection with the earth and the political importance of *being* open, of being on foot" where "we are able to imagine an accord between poetry and ecology" (Burnside 100, 105). The act of walking, in other words, contributes to the process of composing poetry by bringing phenomena into close proximity and subjecting them to perspectival shifts, which reveal the limitations of language and naming. The closer we get to a tree or a bird or a fungus, the more potential names become evident. Within the poem that seeks to record an engagement with the earth, the figure of apostrophe becomes an "address to the subject which returns to Adam's task in a wholly different frame of mind. The 'o' which sometimes precedes apostrophe, and is always implicit in the gesture, might be described as the gawk of unknowing.... In poetry it is the gesture loaded with lightness, an opening into awe. It says 'this is for you, not just about you'" (McKay *V* 66). The lightness with which McKay imbues apostrophe refers simultaneously to the opposite of an earnest human desire to own the world and to an avian lightness that enables birds to fly, to imagination rather than memory.

McKay invokes God to create awareness of the *ecological* significance of swallows' aerodynamics. In the second section of "Swallowings" (*B* 83–87), McKay imagines that

> After God invented the swallow he sat back
> satisfied.

> At last,
> the aeronautical bird.
> This, he thought, is going to be one hell of a surprise
> for them mosquitoes. (84)

Aero·nautics: The science, art, or practice of sailing in the air; aerial navigation. Other birds might fly greater distances, or reach higher speeds, but swallows are the first to sail the air. With a single, albeit compound, modifier, McKay addresses the interdisciplinary, ecocritical potential of birds and poetry, and in these six lines he accommodates, if not exactly an evolutionary poetics, an ecological poetics. As primarily linguistic, intellectual creatures obsessed with meaning-making, humans have often focused on what bird flight means to humans socially, culturally, and personally. While part two of "Swallowings" emphasizes the impact of swallow behaviour on mosquitoes, one does not need to have portaged in Algonquin Park in mid-August to appreciate how swallow behaviour might affect human life, too, by keeping mosquito populations in check.

Nemerov's poem deals more explicitly than McKay's short sequence with a particular human response to the flight of swallows. In "The Blue Swallows," the mind has yet to realize that the time has come

> To waken, yawn and stretch, to see
> With opened eyes emptied of speech
> The real world where the spelling mind
> Imposes with its grammar book
> Unreal relations on the blue
> Swallows. (397)

The mind's eye, synesthetically bereft of speech, gains the capacity to observe the real world and the relations at work (and at play) in the world. That swallows help control mosquito populations constitutes one example of a real-world relation in stark contrast to—though neither mutually nor necessarily exclusive of—the "Unreal relations" imposed by the grammatical mind searching the sky for auguries. If Western culture has largely moved away from the wisdom imparted by augurs, the figure of the poet has, since the beginning of the current era, adopted a similar role, albeit in print.[4] Nemerov, aware of this barely perceptible shift in symbolic observation, dispenses with the barely perceptible irony of the near-apostrophe in the poem's final strophe: "O swallows, swallows, poems are not / The point. Finding again the world, / That is the point" (398). Despite the blatantly conventional apostrophe in the first line, Nemerov successfully uses the Romantic convention against itself by carefully ending the line after the negative "poems are not," which follows the doubly named "swallows, swallows." In order to find the world again, to get closer to it, the poet implies paradoxically that he must eschew poetic conventions and the "unreal relations" imposed upon them by language.

And if finding the world—ostensibly the "real world" mentioned earlier—really is the point, that is not to say poetry has no role to play in the finding. Rather, some combination of real and unreal relational strategies—akin perhaps to Wordsworth's extra-textual project in "The Tables Turned"—presents ample opportunity for ecocritical attempts of the world. Consider Part Four of "Swallowings"—a title that invokes a gastronomical act integral to both mammals and birds—in which the poet observes that "Under a Red tail's wing, we are all / on the same plate / slowly rotating," prone in our slowness, our terrestrial life, to be swallowed. The swallows, on the other hand, are more apt to escape the same fate: their (not always successful) defence is flight, their wings "snickersnacks"[5] that "cut and thrust carving smaller" spaces in air.[6]

Nemerov's and McKay's swallow poems are hardly scientific treatises, yet each invokes images or ideas of swallows that can be checked against ornithological literature while drawing attention to poetic conventions traditionally used to elevate the poet-speaker over the heavily symbolized bird. John Burroughs's comment on Walt Whitman's "Out of the Cradle Endlessly Rocking" gets, I think, to the heart of my motivations for examining McKay's avian poetics. "The poet's treatment of the bird," Burroughs observes, "is entirely ideal and eminently characteristic. That is to say, it is altogether poetical and not at all ornithological" (20). In treating the bird, a mockingbird, "entirely and eminently" in terms that are "not at all ornithological," Whitman essentially uses an imagined instance of seeing a bird to relate the moment a young boy's poetic inspiration is born. In his reading of the poem, Leonard Lutwack allows that Whitman's description of the "nest, and four light-green eggs spotted with brown" is "ornithologically sound" (67), contrary to Burroughs' criticism; however, Lutwack also claims that "sighting a pair of breeding mockingbirds on Long Island would have been a very special event, since that species rarely nested north of Maryland in 1859 when Whitman wrote the poem" (67). Whitman's poem, though, as Burroughs implies, is more about a boy learning "that he is capable of 'translating the notes' of the mockingbird" (Lutwack 71) than it is about the nesting behaviour of mockingbirds; indeed, the specificity Whitman employs in this poem seems out of keeping with "a bard who," according to

Burroughs, "habitually bends his ear only to the musical surge and rhythmus [sic] of total nature, and is as wont to turn aside for any special beauties or points as the most austere of the ancient masters" (17). Not only do I argue that McKay habitually bends his ear to specific rhythms in nature—more on listening in Part Three—but that he incorporates in much of his verse a critique of the "ancient masters" whose responses to "total nature" Whitman seems to have adopted and perpetuated.

"Close-up on a Sharp-shinned Hawk" (*B* 22) exemplifies an early attempt by a young poet to acknowledge a tradition of nature poetry while avoiding simplistic recapitulations of Romantic form. Weighing a scant 140 g, the sharp-shinned hawk (*Accipiter striatus*) is North America's smallest accipiter.[7] I read "Close-up on a Sharp-shinned Hawk" as a sonnet that actively resists its form, albeit less self-consciously and less evidently than a later poem ("'Stress, Shear, Strain Theories of Failure,'" which I discuss in the concluding chapter). With fifteen lines instead of fourteen, irregular rhyming, and unconventional metre, "Close-up" does not immediately reveal itself as a sonnet. By approaching it as one, though, and considering the trochee as an inverted iamb, I want to suggest the opening line's trochaic pentameter introduces a sonnet with a difference. Even this reading of the opening line requires a bit of a stretch, however, as strictly speaking it contains only four feet instead of five: "Cón-cen | tráte up- | ón her | áttri | bútes:" I argue that the colon, syntactically meant to introduce a list of field marks, a measure of the raptor's identity, functions as the line's final syllable, a pause or breath before the lines that follow. This visual tag at the end of line one foreshadows the extraneous fifteenth line, which fills in what the missing syllable/breath makes possible. The colon also enacts one of the hawk's attributes, namely its ability to "impose / silence." The entire poem is worth quoting so that we may, as it were, consider its attributes:

> Concentrate upon her attributes:
> the accipiter's short
> roundish wings, streaked breast, talons fine
> and slender as the x-ray of a baby's hand.
> The eyes (yellow in this hatchling
> later deepening to orange then
> blood red) can spot
> a sparrow at four hundred metres and impose
> silence like an overwhelming noise
> to which you must not listen.
> Suddenly, if you're not careful, everything
> goes celluloid and slow

and threatens to burn through and you
must focus quickly on the simple metal band around her leg
by which she's married to our need to know.

Once the sonnet form is evoked in the opening line, what follows is a sequence of knowing exercises in poetic style that results in a McKavian unsonnet. McKay demonstrates a capacity to write trochees, anapests, Alexandrines, and even an iambic octameter, as if to show he can do it without capitulating to the traditional protocol. In fact, the only line that McKay writes in iambic pentameter, the standard sonnet metre, is the extraneous fifteenth line. Contrary to Richard Greene's claim, in a review for *Books in Canada*, that McKay is merely "a poet of considerable gifts, which are, in general, badly deployed" (27), McKay develops a poetic style that attends in equal measure to rhythm and cadence—of human language and avian ecology—and the dangers of a human desire to know. In the process, he reveals a valid reason for his persistent distrust of rigidly structured verse by drawing a direct connection between the strictures of the English sonnet and a human "need to know." The poem would have made sense had it ended at line fourteen; most readers understand the implications of a metal band on a hawk's leg. By conforming to the sonnet's metrical requirements in that final line, McKay does more than connect a human thirst for knowledge with a desire to control nature. He also draws a subtle link between desire to control the hawk and poetic control of language. The fifteenth line's iambic pentameter, in other words, pushes against conventional parameters of the sonnet form, which the poem simultaneously evokes and critiques.

Of utmost importance to a McKavian exercise in un-sonnetting the sonnet is the simultaneous homage to the form and to the bird specified in the title. Not "Shall I compare thee to a summer's day," then, but "Shall I compare thee to a baby's x-ray." To be sure, roundish wings and streaked breast are field marks that aid in identifying sharp-shinned hawks, and yellow eyes are characteristic of juveniles. This list of attributes introduces the theme of ownership residing in that final, regularly metred line. The verb "married," describing the relationship between hawk and human, modifies our reading of the "simple metal band around her leg" to suggest a wedding band, effectively reaffirming the poem as sonnet, a form traditionally associated with protestations of love. The end-rhyming of "slow" and "know" in the poem's second part—the caesura following the period in line ten implies a turn in the sonnet which the word "Suddenly" reinforces—presents a complicated relation between the speed and knowing. One attribute of the hawk that McKay does not name here but associates with the osprey in "Migratory Patterns," nevertheless occurs in the poem's opening lines: its speed. The anapestic feet of "the accipiter's short / roundish wings, streaked breast, talons fine," in addition to drawing attention to the form's unnatural requirements by forcing two syllables out of "streaked," enacts the accipiter's sudden plunge as if it were diving for "a sparrow [it spotted] at four hundred metres," as surely as the spondaic "blood red) can spot" echoes the harsh reality of the raptor's need to kill. The paradoxical turn in the poem from speed to everything suddenly going "celluloid and slow," as in a nature documentary, resonates with Bartlett's observation that in general a tension between quickness and slowness measures McKay's lines, that "in McKay's world ... on-the-go speeds alternate with slow momentum" ("A Dog's Nose" 154). The subject of "Close-up on a Sharp-shinned Hawk" determines this productive, suggestive tension in the poem: if birding means watching creatures that are apt to move before birders have a chance to get a satisfying glimpse, it stands to reason that some combination of quickness and patience will enable the most satisfactory encounters. According to *The Sibley Guide to Birds*, "[s]ightings of accipiters are often very distant or very brief, and many birds must go unidentified" (113). "Close-up on a Sharp-shinned Hawk" shows the potential violence and danger in the ongoing practice of identifying birds; but it also demonstrates two stylistic qualities that Bartlett identifies as "exactitude" and "quickness." This McKavian unsonnet, in its precise account of a specific bird, shows "what it means to be at once attentive and energetic, provoking and exhilarating" (Bartlett "Dog's" 155).

In poems such as "Close-up on a Sharp-shinned Hawk," in which McKay demonstrates a simultaneous capacity for and suspicion of a dominant tradition in Western verse, McKay risks accusations from reviewers such as Greene that he writes "rambling and incremental" poetry in glib opposition to canonical masterworks (27). Glen A. Love argues that "[m]uch of what it means to be a western writer is to risk the contemptuous epithet, nature-lover" ("Revaluing" 233). While Love's reference to "western writers"—primarily American writers living in the western United States—necessarily considers certain elements of frontierism and biogeography key to writing about place and humans' relations in and with place, I extend the meaning to include all writers who write what is likely to be labelled "nature writing," since many English-language poets would suit the "contemptuous epithet, nature-lover." "The risk" Love alludes to, moreover, "is worth taking ... if it focuses attention on what appears to be nothing less than an ecologically suicidal path by the rest of culture" (233). The risk is worth taking if for no other reason than to play the fool in attempting to assuage by way of close attention any form of environmental degradation. McKay, who incidentally moved to the west coast in the mid-1990s, puts it this way in *Vis à Vis*:

> Admitting that you are a nature poet, nowadays, may make you seem something of a fool, as though you'd owned up to being a Sunday painter at, say, the Nova Scotia College of Art and Design. There are some valid reasons for this. At present, "nature" has been so lavishly oversold that the word immediately invokes several kinds of vacuous piety, ranging from Rin-tin-tinism to knee-jerk environmental concerns. […] It has been […] Lorne Greened. (25–26)

One response to "nature" that does not invoke "vacuous piety" is on display in Munro Beattie's critique of Canadian poetry from 1920 to 1935 in Carl Klinck's *Literary History of Canada* (1976). Clearly unmoved by Canada's poetic accomplishments during this period, Beattie complains that "[w]orst of all, the versifiers of this arid period, having nothing to say, kept up a constant jejune chatter about infinity, licit love, devotion to the Empire, death, Beauty, God, and Nature. Sweet singers of the Canadian out-of-doors, they peered into flowers, reported on the flitting of the birds, discerned mystic voices in the wind, descried elves among the poplars" (235). Although such obvious scorn for nature poets is less common in print today—I admit ignorance regarding contemporary views of elves—the difficulty ecocriticism has faced establishing itself as a bona fide subdiscipline attests to an undercurrent of disdain for the "jejune chatter" of such poets as Don McKay and the critics who devote a lot of space to "the flitting of birds" instead of to the flitting of words. My own ecocritical work has been described variously, if unimaginatively, as "for the birds" and "jejune and shallow," and I have heard more than one postmodern critic refer disparagingly to ecocritics, or critics interested in the health of the earth, as Earth Critters. Perhaps in the spirit of the birder-poet's humility, ecocritics should claim this label. What are we, after all, if not critters of the earth?

The truth of humans' animality, which differs from the Truth many Romantic and Transcendentalist poets gestured toward with metaphors about flight, reminds that everything we do in some way emerges from evolutionary adaptations, including language. Our animality also grounds us, causes the desire (and nostalgia) for flight about which McKay writes. When our language—grounded, inadequate—fails to describe a scene or represent a feeling, it fails to convince some critics that the world, the material, toward which the words point exists meaningfully. If nature poetry strikes such critics as a naive attempt to reproduce the world on the page, it does so by embracing aesthetics anathema to the concerns of overtly political responses to the world. McKay's precisely metaphorical poems resist critiques aimed at "nature poetry" in general precisely because they bring readers closer to the physical world by looking to science for accurate language and embodying experiential engagement.

McKay's nature poetry has not always demonstrated precise and consistent attention to birds and the rest of the natural world. His first book, *Air Occupies Space* (1973), is a fairly conventional collection of brief lyric poems that, although not informed by the ornithological or ecological precision of his later books, exhibits a predilection for nature poetry. His next two books experiment with the long poem and often deploy language in postmodern fashion. Though both *Long Sault* (1975) and *Lependu* (1978) contain poems that demonstrate McKavian attention and hint at the birder-poet to come, McKay hadn't yet found a way to be both grounded (in natural history) and aloft (in language). As a result, his reception among Canadian critics was uneven. *Air Occupies Space* was published the same year as Frank Davey's *From There to Here* (1973).[8] Davey claims with the publication of this book to have "helped begin the history of the word 'postmodern' in Canadian literature" (*Canadian* 245). *Long Sault* and *Lependu* mark a shift from a conventional nature poetry to what Davey calls in *Reading Canadian Reading* "the textual violences of surrealism and Dada" expressed in McKay's long poems (134). While Davey does not explicitly denounce the poetry McKay writes after 1980—after, that is, what Davey identifies as his surrealist long poems[9]—I find it telling that he continues to refer to *Long Sault*, published in 1975, when citing McKay in *Reading Canadian Reading* (1988). Granted, Davey refers to McKay only in the chapter called "Recontextualization in the Long Poem" (123–36), so the lack of reference to *Lightning Ball Bait* (1980), *Birding, or desire* (1983), and *Sanding Down This Rocking Chair on a Windy Night* (1987) is understandable, given Davey's critical interests; however, Davey leaves McKay entirely out of his book *Canadian Literary Power* (1994), despite the recent publication of the award-winning *Night Field* (1991). By contrast, D. M. R. Bentley mentions McKay, albeit briefly, in his 1992 study of ecological poetry in Canada, *The Gay]Grey Moose*, noting that the postmodernism Davey associates with demonstrates an awareness "of the ideological implications of critical theory" as it relates to "the ecological thrust of much of the original *Tish* work" (284). Critics should not find it surprising, observes Bentley, "that such poets as Don McKay, Andrew Suknaski, Anne Szumigalski, and Brian Dedora, whose roots lie in the same Black Mountain soil as *Tish*, are responsible for some of the most ecologically sound poetry being written in Canada today" (284). Ecologically sound poetry did not interest the majority of critics writing about poetry in Canada following Davey's "Surviving the Paraphrase."[10] Ironically, McKay had distanced himself from whatever influence the Black Mountain movement might have had on his development by the time Bentley published his book.

I suspect McKay's "reasons for failing to postmodernize," which he attributes to an empirical "state of mind" he calls "poetic attention" (*V* 26), stems partly from his increasing proximity to the natural world. He admits in his interview with Ken Babstock that he experienced "a definite breakthrough ... with the love of landscape. In terms of recognizing [himself] as a linguistic creature.... And then the birdwatching, that was the major heave, acknowledging that [he] was hooked" (49). If McKay apprenticed with a postmodern poetic style that was in fashion at the time he began publishing and teaching, a time that coincided with a sea change in the way Canadian literature was perceived and studied in the years following Frye's Conclusion and Atwood's *Survival*, his ecological voice, the voice that has been developing steadily since 1980, continues to enact a movement away from the postmodern, poststructuralist notion that the world matters only when humans speak of it or speak it into existence.

While McKay's evaluation of the current tropic overuse and subsequent vacuity of the term "nature" does not reflect risk in the sense that Love proffers, McKay in *Vis à Vis* concerns himself with envisaging the edge "between poetic attention and romantic inspiration" (27). Risk is inherent in McKay's formulation of nature poetry precisely because he calls for a recognition—a re-cognition—of the role language *plays*: "as nature poet ... one does not invoke language right off when talking about poetry, but acknowledges some extra-linguistic condition as the poem's input, output, or both" (26). Though he is well aware of being "locked inside words," McKay keeps "returning to a ... point of permeability between [himself] and the non-human others with whom [he] share[s] the world" (Dragland 882). The extra-linguistic condition McKay refers to is a physical, material world that exists without the need of human awareness or articulation. That is, neither the Douglas fir growing outside my window nor the golden-crowned kinglets flitting through its branches require my imagination or my pen to exist meaningfully.[11] This is a risky statement to make for one invested in studying the language arts because it seems to privilege realistic depictions of the natural world over symbolic ones. I argue, however, that the risk is worth taking because the preference for symbolic (linguistic) constructions of the world contributes to an egotism and anthropocentrism that are systematically denying humans' complicity in environmental degradation. That the earth system would continue to exist even if humans become extinct is a matter of scientific consensus (though precisely what the world would look like is impossible to know). Humans depend upon a diverse matrix of life to survive; without that diversity—biodiversity, to use the popular term—a series of positive feedbacks will quicken global warming and life on this planet will likely consist of what can survive at the edge of continents, away from too-warm ocean deserts (Lovelock 80–81).

Bentley's position in his Preamble to *The Gay]Grey Moose* reinforces the need to take such scholarly, pedagogical risks—which at this point shouldn't be considered risks at all. As he reports, "little attention has been paid of late [as of 1992, that is] to the equivalences between Canadian poems and the external world of which they are in their very nature as analogous representations, [as] cultural artifacts, and [as] human productions, an integral and inescapable part" (10). If "poems are not possible without matter: the matter of which they treat, the matter upon which they are inscribed, the human matter that creates and apprehends them" (10), then matter—the material of imaginative, symbolical thinking—should rightly be a valid and compelling source of inquiry. The debate between Lawrence Buell and Dana Phillips, which I discuss in Chapter Two, deals with some of the problems that arise once poets and critics start looking to the extradictionary, to the real/material world for insight into poetic ideas. In his dissertation examining "the matter and time of ecopoetry," critic and poet Adam Dickinson continues to tread lightly upon this risky proposition: "A significant problem with realism in ecocriticism is that it presumes an unquestioned association with materialism. The materiality of the referential world is literally assumed in the reality of the 'ecopoem' (indeed, it is asserted as the proper focus of our attention, according to ecocritics)" (Dickinson "Lyric" 41). Not so much the proper focus as a legitimate one, the material world's association with realism need not, it seems to me, be questioned. Realism in (eco)poetry might, though, comprise more than the material world. Realism can also include human psychology and behaviour, responses to external stimuli that might not be "material" in the strictest, physical sense. The speaker's response to the painting—and to others' interpretation of the painting—in McKay's "Night Field" is a case in point. The suspicion of metaphor expressed in that poem and the litany of equations—"the dog is a dog, the field is a / field" (*NF* 40)—supports at first glance the ecocritical assumption that realistic portrayals of phenomena are possible. But it is the speaker's inability to read the painting—to interpret the metaphoricity of colours and shapes that suggest, to most viewers, emotions and ideas in addition to objects—that stands out in my reading of the poem. The question of realism in painting, of course, differs from that of writing, since the grammar of each medium differs.

Dickinson goes on, making language itself the source of his concerns about realism:

> The claim that the realist text is able to point outside of language and that its primary concern is this outside assumes and reinforces the material link between reference and object within language itself—it makes of non-language, or the extra-linguistic, a knowable and presentable object in literal language. Lyrical approaches to materiality, however, in their very dependence on figures and metaphoricity, emphasize the insufficiency of language to fully present matter, or to discretely distinguish a Wittgensteinian "language-game" (a specific context of linguistic interaction) that escapes language. Metaphor does not make the thing literally present, but it gives us a way to stand in relation to a substantiality that is not measurably accessible. (41–42)

Pitting lyric (or lyrical metaphoricity) against realism, Dickinson shrewdly positions ecocriticism alongside poststructuralist theories of language and the referential world—skeptical of semantic objectivity yet comfortable "with the notion that corporeal processes exist independently of human perception" (Keller and Golley 13). I agree with Dickinson's suspicion of claims that realist texts can faithfully represent objects in language. But the facility "to point outside of language" strikes me as a basic requirement for any text that wants to evoke the referential world of beings and objects. Pointing is not the same as grasping. Pointing allows that some things are ungraspable, unknowable, and that language has its limits. Whereas home "makes possible the possession of the world" as the place where we establish intimate connections with graspable objects—"the place where knowledge as power begins" (*V* 23)—some places provide no such comfort. In "Finger Pointing at the Moon" (*AG* 61–62), McKay writes that such places are desirable precisely because they are places where "our words / can fail us" (62). By pointing outside of language—at the moon, say, as a Zen Buddhist analogy teaches, or at a horde of crows flying to their roost at dusk—the birder-poet admits humility by turning his attention away from himself (and his finger) and toward something else. Writing about it does not recreate it, but the experience can occur because the material object exists independent of human language.

My response to Dickinson's convincing dissertation on lyrical metaphoricity focuses on an intriguing metaphorical turn, which begs the question Does the "way of stand[ing] in relation" of which he writes not require an actual place in which, literally, to stand? Ultimately, the relationality

Dickinson is speaking of, which rightly becomes articulated by way of metaphor, requires actual things to which poets and critics can "stand in relation." Clear-cutting forests impacts ecological dynamics at a rate with which most nonhuman species cannot keep up. Poetry and language have nothing to do with it. But they can have something to do with how we literally stand in relation to trees, birds, and, yes, even clear-cuts.

Chapter Five

Gravity

> step outside and let the earth turn
> underneath, trapdoors, new lungs, missing bits
> of time, plump familiar pods go
> pop in your mind you learn not
> principles of flight but how to fall.
> – Don McKay, "Kestrels" (*B* 99)

> Migration is a widespread biological phenomenon, not simply a trait characteristic of a particular taxon.
> – Bairlein and Coppack, "Migration in the Life-History of Birds" (121)

McKay's response to the assumption that language constitutes the matter of reality comes prior to Dickinson's argument, and it comes as a reimagining of traditional, namely Romantic, nature poetry, as my reading of "Close-up on a Sharp-shinned Hawk" attests. Not surprisingly, McKay's poetic critiques of Romantic verse often respond directly to some of the most famous poems about birds in flight, of which there are many. Shelley, in "To a Skylark," has the bird flying "Higher still and higher" "In the golden lightning / Of the sunken sun / O'er which the clouds are bright'ning" (ll. 6, 11–13), while Keats, in "Ode to a Nightingale," imagines his bird a "light-winged Dryad of the trees" (l. 7) in sharp contrast to the poet trapped in "embalmed darkness" (l. 43). But these poems, like Avison's "The Butterfly," are more about what the nonhuman means to the human—indeed, what it means to be human at all. Sir Edward Grey acknowledges as much in his assessment of Keats's avian ode, which he rates second only to his "Ode to Autumn." "Ode to a Nightingale," Grey writes, "touches heights of poetry that the lines of Wordsworth on the nightingale [in "O Nightingale, Thou Surely Art"] do not attempt; but the ode is less close to the bird" (71).

In other words, Keats's ode is fine poetry but poor natural history. Like so many other poems, its distance from the bird itself—a result, in part, of the conventionally formal address/language of the ode[1]—reinforces a conventional set of avian metaphors.

"Poets," according to Beryl Rowland, "have always envied the divine power of the bird, and some, such as the Romantics, believed they could acquire it for themselves" (xv). Critics, by extension, often identify flight with poetry's capacity—or power—to discover truth, a Platonic argument that follows from what Lutwack calls a "shamanistic identification with flying birds that enables human beings to make their escape from earth and move through space and time like gods" (52). I do not wish with my reading of McKay's avian poetics to set aside the rich tradition of avian symbolism and metaphor that continues in poetry to this day, or to stifle the ability of poets and critics to imagine. I do, however, want to highlight the critic's *in*ability at times simply to listen to certain poems "and be satisfied" because he feels compelled "to find out about persons, places, and things" evoked by the poet (Bringhurst and Ricou 95). This strikes me as a useful inability, one that is likely responsible, at least in part, for the development of ecocriticism and that is necessary for ecocriticism to remain relevant within increasingly interdisciplinary and political and social contexts. Lutwack also effectively dampens the dream of the speaker in Keats's ode by referring to Daedalus and Icarus, who have proven, ostensibly, "that the exercise of the imagination is not free like the flight of a bird, but uncertain and full of perils" (53). A sharp-shinned hawk's wings will not, having flown too close to the sun, fall off because the wax holding them together melts, but bird flight is not particularly free; it frees birds (that can fly) from earth, though they are still restricted by gravity; and it is also full of such real perils as hunters (avian and human), poor weather conditions, airplanes, and lighted windows along migration routes.

McKay addresses many of these concerns in *Another Gravity* (2000), a collection that develops a sustained avian poetic of flight. The book begins with a poem that is not about birds at all. In fact, of the thirty-two poems included in *Another Gravity*, only sixteen mention specific birds. The opening poem, "Sometimes a Voice (1)" (3–4), begins in contradiction, which, true to the necessarily opposing forces required to achieve flight (and which I've discussed in Chapter Four), recurs throughout the collection:

> Sometimes a voice – have you heard this? –
> wants not to be voice any longer, wants something
> whispering between the words, some

> rumour of its former life. Sometimes, even
> in the midst of making sense or conversation, it will
> hearken back to breath, or even farther,
> to the wind, and recognize itself
> as troubled air, a flight path still
> looking for its bird. (3)

This voice begins as a whisper between the modifier "sometimes" and its verb "to want" and transforms into what McKay identifies elsewhere as the aeolian harp, which he describes as "the larynx of natural phenomena" (*V* 27). Aeolian harpism "converts natural energy into imaginative power, so that Romanticism, which begins in the contemplation of nature, ends in the celebration of the creative imagination in and of itself. [...]: it speaks directly to a deep and almost irresistible desire for unity" (27). This is a lyric voice desiring its antithesis even as it longs to retrace its Romantic lineage and return to a prelinguistic time when it inspired lift instead of verse: another gravity. This voice wants to find "its bird," not its bard. Such subtle distinctions within the poem's erotic framework are fully in keeping with McKay's project of unsettling the lyric "I" cultivated by Wordsworth, Coleridge, Byron, Shelley, and Keats (in Chapter Eight I argue for such change on the level of phonemes and syllables, as between "bird" and "bard," for example, as a particularly McKavian rhetorical trope). But the poem shifts following this rather abstract preface to a more narrativistic version of the voice "as troubled air, a flight path still / looking for its bird." The speaker recalls a time when he and some friends were "shingling the boathouse roof," a job that was "all / off balance – squat, hammer, body skewed / against the incline, heft the bundle, / daub the tar, squat." The talk during the tedious hours on the boathouse roof turns to adulthood's "labyrinthine perils," which the speaker and his friends are content to avoid for as long as possible, comforted by a false sense of youthful vigour and immortality. After noticing that "The roof / sloped upward like a take-off ramp / waiting for Evel Knievel," Danny, one of the friends, boasts he can easily clear the "twenty feet or so of concrete wharf" between the boathouse and "the blue-black water of the lake." The boast results in more masculine palaver before everyone gets back to work. Then suddenly, "amid the squat, / hammer, heft, no one [sees] him go." Danny disappears. The "short flight between the roof / and the rest of his natural life" resembles the brief flight Zak and Sumner's flying machine makes with Chu at the helm, except McKay's poem contains more *gravitas*. Danny never returns, except perhaps as memory (see the discussion of "Lift" and "Drag," the two poems that follow "Sometimes a Voice (1)," in Chapter Four).

Despite the lighthearted banter deployed "to fray / the tedium of work" that encapsulates Danny's boast, the gravity of the situation—the disturbing death or disappearance of a friend—is reinforced by the image of Danny's "boots / with his hammer stuck inside one like a heavy-headed / flower." Though McKay has demonstrated his facility for humour in other poems, here he acknowledges with all the gravity the situation deserves that fatal consequences await those of us arrogant enough to think we have conquered the air. Flight, then, while clearly operating metaphorically in a poem such as "Sometimes a Voice (1)," also functions as a real achievement toward which humans strive. As such, I cannot quite follow Méira Cook's observation, in "Song for the Song of the Dogged Birdwatcher," her introduction to a selection of McKay's poetry, that "[i]f gravity refers to what is *material* in language then flight is all metaphor, all leap and longing, all air and stare and star" (xi). First, gravity, as Cook herself notes, "is title and technique, the coefficiency[2] of drag, the slow gagged pull of solemnity," which includes the ability—or not—of bodies to bear both physical and "moral weight, gravity and gravitas" (xi). Gravity is no more the sole material purview of language than Nature/nature is the sole purview of the Romantics; nor does flight, as I have demonstrated, occupy a wholly metaphorical realm within McKay's avian poetics. The poet's recognition of the biological and ecological dynamics responsible for flight combined with a tradition of flight-as-Truth metaphors ensures an interrogative, observational poetry literally in awe of avian aeronautical achievements.

It takes little effort to see "Sometimes a Voice (1)" as a version of the Greek myth of Icarus, the boy who, having been given a set of wings to escape the labyrinth on Minos with his father, gets cocky and flies too close to the sun, which melts the wax securing his makeshift wings.[3] But McKay offers a more explicit commentary on the myth: "Icarus" (*AG* 43–46) begins *Another Gravity*'s fourth section, which includes "Hang Time" (49) and "Turbulence" (50) and ends, fittingly, with "Plummet" (56). With "Icarus," McKay takes his place in a conversation among other notable poets who have addressed this particular myth, including W. H. Auden, whose "Musée des Beaux Arts" (179) deals ekphrastically with Pieter Bruegel's painting *Landscape with the Fall of Icarus*, and Al Purdy, whose "Bruegel's *Icarus*" (530–32) deals with the painting and with Auden's reading of it. If, for Auden, Bruegel's painting represents how suffering "takes place / While someone else is eating or opening a window or just walking dully / along," for Purdy it represents multiple instances of anonymous death. Though he begins and ends the poem with Icarus, "a scared little boy / a long way from home," Purdy focuses on the "dead body in nearby woods" "off to one side of the painting," which is also ignored by the other figures in the pastoral scene. In short, neither poet writes about flying; McKay, not surprisingly, makes flight the focus of his poem.

Since Icarus is a mythical character who lives on in story and painting, McKay has him endlessly repeating the moment for which he has been immortalized: "Over and over he rehearses flight / and fall, tuning his moves" (43). Falling follows flight, for man or boy, in an endless recapitulation of the myth; similarly, story follows physics as McKay imagines Icarus's feeling at achieving liftoff only to tumble inexorably "into freefall." Icarus "feels resistance gather in his stiff / strange wings, angles his arms to shuck the sweet lift / from the drag" and flies toward the sun before stopping "At the melting point of wax, which now he knows / the way Doug Harvey knows the blue line" (43). Even though Icarus is trapped in an endless cycle of failure not unlike the failure experienced by Sumner and Zak in *Innocent Cities*, McKay seems uninterested in using his version of the story to proselytize about human arrogance and egoism in the quest to fly. While the farmer in Bruegel's painting ploughs the field, the ship sails off and "the poets moralize about our / unsignificance," writes McKay. "Icarus is thinking tremolo and / backflip" and refuses to apologize (44). Icarus's success as a flyer exists concomitant with his failure to maintain altitude, a state of existence similar to McKay's birder-poet. The practice is what's important, the sense of repetition, "Repertoire, technique," and style: process instead of product and a willingness to risk learning from failure.

In the process of learning to fly, McKay's Icarus realizes the value of watching how real birds do it. He finds a spot to watch hawks and other raptors during fall migration: "Merlins slice the air with / wings that say crisp, crisp, precise as sushi chefs, while Sharp-shins / alternately glide and flap, hunting as they go," and "Icarus / notices how the Red-tails and Broadwings separate their primaries / to spill a little air, giving up just enough lift to break their drag up / into smaller trailing vortices" (44). Watching is an integral part of his practice because each bird has its own particular style that functions, in concert with physical attributes, as but one variation on the theme of flight. I can see how McKay's lyric style edges its way unapologetically into content, how the observed subject often informs stylistic and formal concerns, how watching can be articulated on the page as listening folded into speech: "O yellow warblers" (*V* 66–67). O broadwings. O Icarus. The gift of poetry—sometimes articulated as apostrophe—is often for McKay a "gift of failure" (*AG* 45); the same is true of the gift of flight for Icarus, who recognizes failure as a gift only after having found a place to sit and watch the spring migration and "let the marsh- / mind claim his thinking" (45). Like McKay's birder-poet,

Icarus's "watching is humbler, less appropriative, a thoughtless think- / ing" (45). The paradox can surely never be solved which, paradoxically, ensures that willing observers—poets, walkers, birders—will keep trying, "boosting / and balancing each other until they fall off" (46). Because the contrary forces enable post-failure thinking about what comes next, they offer good metaphors for the practice of flight and of poetics attuned to what has come before. As his unsonnets suggest, McKay's poetic repertoire includes traditional metrics deployed with reflexive suspicion and homage—lyric loop-the-loops fuelled by aeolian harp winds. The allusiveness of McKay's writing exemplifies this tendency to borrow and modify and, at times, fall.

The first of five poems that make up "Styles of Fall" (67–71), the fifth section of McKay's *Sanding Down This Rocking Chair on a Windy Night*, focuses on the dangers of gravity while alluding to a well-known poet. "Buckling" (67) evokes "The Windhover," Hopkins's famous poem about a kestrel whose aerial achievements represent Christ's divinity on earth. "Even the windhover makes mistakes," McKay's poem begins: "some slight / miscalculation and he's prey / to ordinary cats, trailing a slate blue wounded wing / beside the porch" (67). The birder-poet wonders how to reconcile Hopkins's unflagging appreciation of "morning's minion," the "dapple-dawn-drawn Falcon" identified by critics and birders alike as a kestrel (likely *Falco tinnunculus*, though possibly an American kestrel, *Falco sparverius*). Leonard Nathan refers to Hopkins's poem when trying to determine what to name the experience he feels while birding and identifying species, an experience he eventually comes to name, not without hesitation, "epiphany" (11). The scene in Nathan's book is brief. He prefaces a reading of the sonnet's octave by acknowledging his "stubborn, inveterate habit" of "going to books first in search of answers," in this case of "going to a poem where a bird is gorgeously celebrated" (9). After stopping at—or rather having been "brought to a hard stop" by—the octave's closing lines, "My heart in hiding / Stirred for a bird," and their seeming fidelity to Nathan's conception of ornithological epiphany, Nathan dismisses the poem's Christian overtones and claims not to have any "license to suit its meaning to [his] own faith," namely a faith in secular attempts at poetic truth (10). While Hopkins's natural theology remains integral to understanding how his sprung rhythm functions to move the poet—and ostensibly the reader—closer to God, one does not have to be a Jesuit priest to appropriate meaning, whether spiritual, poetical, or ornithological, from Hopkins's poetry.

McKay introduces this very difficulty in "Buckling" when he wonders, "How can we call up Hopkins and / reverse the charges" (67). In other words, how can the poet uninterested in the Christian overtones of Hopkins' verse—in the fact that Hopkins dedicated the poem "To Christ Our Lord"—isolate and magnify Hopkins's enviable style of species specificity, a style most noticeable in the micro-precision of his compound adjectives? Reading "The Windhover" as a sonnet—some critics consider it a great poem rather than a great sonnet; I wonder if it might be an unsonnet—requires the reader to identify the turn, the point in the poem when the problem set up in the opening lines is addressed, if not resolved. In conventional sonnets, the turn typically either follows the opening octave (as in the Italian form) or precedes the closing couplet (as in the English form); in "The Windhover" (neither an Italian nor an English, but what Hopkins termed a curtal-sonnet), the turn occurs in line ten, signalled by the capitalized "AND" following an emphatic "Buckle!" By echoing this turn in the title "Buckling," McKay draws attention to the eleven previous lines and their hyper-specific description of the falcon in flight, effectively de-emphasizing the Christian metaphor: prior to the turn the falcon is noticeably itself,[4] a "thing" that nevertheless represents "Brute beauty and valour and act," while after the turn the falcon becomes the speaker's "chevalier," addressed in the second-person "thee," which reminds that the poem is dedicated to Christ. Like the swallows in "Swallowings" that are "real" swallows, the kestrel in McKay's "Buckling" is real in the sense that he, as the speaker refers to the bird, is fallible and "fading" toward death; the only thing he can do is "feed him stale coke" so that the "quick lift of caffeine revives him   briefly" (notice how the extra spaces in this line emphasize the kestrel's mortality, the adverb specifying, after a hopeful pause, the extent to which the caffeine helps). McKay's poem, no less than Hopkins's, is about relationship; but in the former the relation is more directly between human and kestrel—the bird does not act as intermediary. This fundamental difference between the two poems implies an important stylistic choice in the birder-poet's quest to get closer to the physical world by way of language. Nathan concludes that time in the field can replace religious faith for the secular reader who dismisses the ecumenical overtones of "The Windhover" because he realizes that the poem's explicit Christianity prevents him from fully engaging with it. "Perhaps," Nathan writes, attempting to understand how to reconcile his near-ecstatic devotion to Hopkins's poem with his own professed secularism, "I need to be out in the field." The field offers myriad ways into such species-specific poems as "The Windhover," "Buckling," and "Close-up on a Sharp-shinned Hawk."

In the poem preceding "Styles of Fall," "Without a Song" (*SD* 61–63), the poet intones that "once / lyric poetry was naturalism," implying that a less problematic relation between word and world once existed:

> Unembodied tongues –
>
> > simoon
> > chinook
> > sirocco
> > pindar
> > harmattan
> > mistral
>
> > > and others we only know as
>
> sad abandoned vowels –
> expressed the planet's intricate
> ecologies
> > made wing
> of heavy objects, lifting gravity
> and eating it. (62–63)

McKay's commentary on the Romantic connection between flight and Truth in these lines simultaneously bypasses the Romantic tradition by parenthetically glossing "Unembodied tongues" to suggest not the voices of poets but the voices of the earth's atmosphere. Simoon, chinook, sirocco, harmattan, and mistral are all types of wind from around the globe, while pindar appears to be McKay's sly reference to the Greek poet, whose classical odes—irregular in length of line and stanza, in prosody, and in rhyme patterns, and indicative of a series of movements back and forth across a stage—would also seem to be under scrutiny in McKay's avian poetics. McKay writes a meteorological specificity, incorporating a critique of Shakespeare's rhyming scheme and generalization from Amiens' song in *As You Like It* (2.7 174–93): "Blow, blow, thou winter wind," quotes McKay's speaker before adding "(with a long i) not / unkind, but / dangerous as an alien" (61). The naming of winds (with a short i) enables a more inclusive (one might say more global) understanding of weather, especially as it affects bird flight and migration. A winter wind for residents of Côte d'Ivoire, Ghana, Togo, Nigeria, and Cameroon, for example, consists less of the coldly negative and negatively cold qualities Shakespeare assigns to "thou winter wind."[5] The intricate ecologies these winds express include avian ecologies, particularly during migration when the distribution of species is affected directly by weather and climate.

One does not have to be an ecocritic to see the rich metaphoric possibilities afforded by literature about migration—movement, diaspora, return—whether one defines migration "as an annual return movement of populations between regular breeding and non-breeding grounds" or "as a syndrome of behavioural and other traits that function together with individuals" (Dingle 212). Migration has been taken up as an important indicator of species health and population decline in response to global environmental factors. The migratory patterns—and concomitant ecological requirements—of Pacific salmon and caribou, for example, have become integral in discussions of ocean health (not to mention food politics and Indigenous rights) and oil extraction, respectively.[6] But studies of bird migration have changed an understanding of global ecological dynamics in ways that directly affect agriculture and efforts at sustainable (industrial and urban/suburban) development. Early naturalists, for example, used to think that swallows spent winter months not feeding in warm southern climes but hibernating beneath frozen lakes, buried into lake bottoms like so many frogs. With the advent of radio transmitters and satellite technology, researchers like Bridget Stutchbury have been able to track migratory patterns of songbirds, raptors, and shorebirds. Those concerned about songbird populations on the Canadian prairies—a group that shouldn't be confined to farmers and self-proclaimed conservationists—can expand their efforts to research environmental conditions in wintering grounds, including clear-cutting and non-shade coffee plantations.

Avian poetics relies on knowledge of human language and movement as integral to ecological considerations of our impact on the earth. In her discussion of excursion and excursionist figures in McKay's poetry, Susan Elmslie argues for a slippage between the real (the physical world) and the imagination by suggesting that metaphorical excursion—that is, "straying from formal and linguistic conventions"—disrupts language with "formal functions which are designed to rejuvenate language" (83–84). By emphasizing movement in her discussion of McKay's excursionist figure, Elmslie builds upon Alana Bondar's fixation on the "mental migration" undertaken by the "poet-speaker" in *Birding, or desire* ("'That'" 17). Both of these readings reflect Terry Tempest Williams's position in *Refuge: An Unnatural History of Family and Place* (1992): "One can think of migration as merely a mechanical movement from point A to point B, and back to point A," but one might also think of migration as birds' "ancestral memory, an archetype that dreams birds thousands of miles to their homeland" (192–93). In addition to "the motif[s] of flight and migration serv[ing] as an elaborate metaphor for [McKay's] poetic process" (Bondar "'That'" 14), flight and migration inhabit McKay's poetry as ornithological and ecological problems to be taken seriously in humans' ongoing estimation of our place on the earth.

If there is an antecedent to McKay's interest in avian migration in a Canadian context, it would be Fred Bodsworth's *Last of the Curlews* (1959), a short novel that follows a single male Eskimo curlew (*Numenius borealis*) on his migratory flight south to the Yucatan coast and on his return north to Canada's Arctic. Bodsworth's narrative effectively follows the bird and records in unsentimental prose the male's unrequited physiological desire to mate; in other words, Bodsworth's prose closely attends to ornithological and ecological details and patterns without imposing too many human attributes on the bird. He acknowledges, for instance, the integral role weather plays in migration, noting that the curlew's movements, during his nine-month migration, are decided by "the cosmic forces of nature and geography—the winds, tides, and weather. Winds determine[] the direction the birds [...] fly. Tides and rain fall, by controlling the availability of food, determine[] each flight's goal" (98). Bodsworth's book—I have been calling it a novel, but is also a natural history—succeeds, to my mind, because of its sparse narrative and informative yet not overly didactic details of a vanishing species' clandestine behaviour.[7]

Norman Elkins corroborates and extends Bodsworth's observation on bird behaviour in a meteorological context: "The amount of foraging and hunting that diurnal species can accomplish is controlled by daytime light intensity, which may be modified by meteorological factors such as thick cloud" (56). Other climatic factors, such as wind direction and wind speed, affect "the initiation and maintenance of migration" as well as "the performance of the migrant in flight" (Elkins *Weather* 131, 126). In the novel *Birds in Fall*, American author Brad Kessler explains a "behavior, known as *zugunruhe*, or 'migratory restlessness,' [which] has long been observed by bird biologists" in terms of anticipation and eventual acquiescence, weather permitting: "Their disquiet builds for weeks, until finally an evening arrives in September when the skies clear and the wind bears down from the north. When the sun drops precisely six degrees below the horizon, thousands of birds pour into the sky, triggered by a signal not yet completely understood" (23–24). Kessler's deployment of avian migration as operating metaphor in a story about loss, and the process of coping with loss, functions on at least two levels: to introduce the notion of return that inheres in migratory patterns and to embrace, I think, humans' affinity with birds, our animality. Bereft of her husband, ornithologist Ana Gaulthreaux seems to exist in a permanent state of *zugunruhe*, having been left behind and always poised on the edge of leaving.

In "Leaving" (*B* 25), McKay connects wind to migratory monarch butterflies "massing on Point Pelee, / hanging in their thousands, wings folded." Point Pelee, Ontario, the southernmost point of mainland Canada, is renowned for its migratory populations: songbirds in spring; hawks and monarchs in fall. Wind becomes more obviously significant to butterflies because of the poet's associating them with leaves, an association made plausible by monarchs' diminutive and fragile appearance—the title punningly invites a reading of the monarchs as preparing to leave on their migration south to Mexico and of the wind making them "look like dun dead leaves." It is the wind that "stirs some from their branches" prior to "their tiny / minds all reaching south in one long / empty line of poetry across the dark waves of Lake Erie." The monarchs' migration fascinates in part because scientists have difficulty fully explaining how these tiny creatures manage to travel such long distances and arrive at the same mountain year after year; bird migration, though easier to explain physiologically, poses similar challenges regarding energy expenditure and navigation. Like an "empty line of poetry" that reveals little of its meaning, migration requires at least a modicum of what Keats termed "negative capability" in order for those of us observing and writing about it to avoid utter confusion vis-à-vis such seeming contradictions.

When Bodsworth describes migration behaviour, his lack of sentimentality does not preclude moments of comparative anthropomorphism, although such moments accord with Tempest Williams's idea of ancestral memory: when the time comes for the Eskimo curlew to begin the return flight to his nesting ground, Bodsworth writes that "[t]he essence of what the curlew felt now was a nostalgic yearning for home" (80). Any "negative" effects of Bodsworth's anthropomorphism are surely offset by his primary project of checking a larger imbalance as a result of human arrogance.[8] Compare, for example, the anthropomorphism in the final couplet of Charles G. D. Roberts's sonnet "The Waking Earth," in which the human soul, amid "Praise for the new life" of spring, "fetterless," "is flown abroad, / Lord of desire and beauty, like a God!" (94). Both Bodsworth and McKay provide ample evidence—extinction and *matériel*, respectively—for what such god-like behaviour has historically wrought. Recounting the nearly sixty-hour non-stop flight from the coast of Labrador to the "savannahs abutting the Orinoco," Bodsworth explains that "in less than three days each bird had lost ten to fifteen percent of its weight," approximately two ounces of fat; "at the same rate of fuel consumption, a half-ton plane would fly one hundred and sixty miles on a gallon of fuel instead of the usual twenty miles" (73). The remarkable fuel economy adds to our wonderment—and envy—in the face of birds' aerial abilities, to be sure; nevertheless, such considerable weight loss explains how the white-throated sparrow in McKay's "Load" has come to be so utterly exhausted, even if its journey across Lake Erie pales in comparison to the curlew's six-thousand-mile migration. (The size difference between sparrows and curlews—17 cm and 26 g versus 30 cm and 270 g, respectively—helps account for the relative difference in long-distance performance.)

In contrast to Bodsworth's faithful rendition of the Eskimo curlew's aerial and migratory achievements, some of McKay's poems that overtly signal migration as their subject tend to invite symbolic readings in addition to ornithological ones. The three-part "Migratory Patterns" (*B* 69–72) and "Nocturnal Migrants" (*AG* 29–30), in particular, enact movement between ecological observation and metaphorical abstraction. "Migratory Patterns" returns to the same geographic region as Point Pelee, even if the national park is not named. Beginning with the speaker lying awake at 2 a.m. and experiencing his own version of *zugunruhe*—he "grieves early closings everywhere" and wonders, by way of Villon,[9] "où sont les // restaurants nocturnes d'antan"—the poem shifts to a description of what birders are likely to see while watching Souwesto skies during fall migration.[10]

>   weather
> tightens and they drift beat soar
> and harry south, the Marsh hawk
>
> tilts a rufous breast, a white patch
> flashing, stoops upon its prey, pressure, Kestrels,
> trim and lethal, Sharp-shins, Red tails,
>
> funnelled by the Great Lakes into concentration, genius
> swells toward catastrophe along
> Lake Erie, wind in the northwest we watch the blank sky
> burst, aboil with, someone breathing christ the Broadwings,
>   hundreds,
> more, soar toward us swift and still and
> still without one wingbeat turn
> and spiral even higher, climbing in their kettle so far into blue
>   the eye
> is sucked up through the lens into its element
> and blinded
>   pitched past all capacity (69–70)

Once again, the birder-poet provides field marks to identify an impressive list of migrating raptors; he also employs a stream-of-consciousness style (the entire poem is free of full stops) that mimics the birds' literally unflappable soaring, turning, and climbing. Once again, the speaker finds himself spinning beneath these birds as if on a plate. And once again, McKay acknowledges the influential role of wind and weather in affecting migratory movements, suggesting in the process an intelligence at work, consisting of elemental and avian "concentration," beyond anything humans can comprehend. The blinded eye recalls David Quammen's definition of a good poem as "a one-eyed glimpse of a bird in flight" (188). The eponymous "patterns" are, like the "genius" of bird and weather, impossible to know fully and with certainty, yet, paradoxically, one-eyed glimpses and dreamlike images help us get closer. The beginning of the poem's second section, "shifts in seeing, gifts, / suddenly your eyes where your ears had been," implies an ontological movement toward *being* bird (another possible permutation of the gerundive *birding*, though not one that McKay tends to favour). The implication might be there, the gesture toward, but, as Méira Cook suggests, "tactfully, reverently, McKay's watcher never 'becomes' bird" fully (x); if he comes close, he is "pitched past all capacity" to complete the leap necessary to imagine himself inside the mind of an Other. Were McKay's birder-poet to become bird, the desire central to his poetics would no longer impel him to watch and listen.

"How to Imagine an Albatross" (*SD* 93–94) represents McKay's most sustained poetic meditation on becoming bird and, fittingly, it is not a poem that invokes the birder-poet (or watcher, as Cook has it). Instead, the poem invokes the spirit of the how-to guide, but a guide with a knack for the slightly surreal spackled with bits of ornithological detail. The juxtaposition aligns a physical avian feat—long-distance pelagic flight—with an attempt to imagine life as another species. Both exemplify albatrossian achievement while foregrounding imaginative excess. In other words, the difficulty of imagining an albatross marks the bird's aerial accomplishments as qualitatively beyond human ken. To imagine life as a creature that "never needs / to beat the air into supporting him but / thoughtlessly as an idea, as a phrasemark holding notes / in sympathy, arcs above the water," a mind would have to "widen to the breadth of the Pacific Ocean / dissolve its edges to admit a twelve foot wingspan soaring" (93). The challenge (and the poem's argument) lies in Paul Shepard's reminder that "birds are not like ideas, [...] they are ideas" (*Thinking* 34), that avian behaviour has no need to be thought or imagined by humans in order to occur or accrue meaning. The centuries-long project to know or control birds and other phenomena through language has itself become an albatross around writers' necks. To imagine a (Coleridgean) albatross, try to imagine a (real) albatross. The tautology threatens chaos only if we cling desperately to the belief that human thinking and language are adequate to the task of defining the world. To imagine a (real) albatross, let go of the assumptions that direct behaviours responsible for the exploitation and plundering of ecosystems that others inhabit.

As the poem goes on, the argument supports a McKavian poetics of specificity and humility while suggesting that physical proximity—in the form of fieldwork and precise, accurate descriptions—might not be the only way to enact such poetics. What is required to imagine an albatross is nothing short of (atomic) decreation, a willingness to release the rage "which holds this pencil in itself, to prod things / until their atoms shift, rebel against their thingness, chairs / run into walls, stones / pour like a mob from their solidity" (93). Meaning itself must shift; the chaos described by quantum physics must migrate from meaningful "thingness" to utter flux. Outside of a lab or a war zone, this can happen only in the imagination, which has itself enabled physicists and poets to acknowledge the indeterminate structure of the universe. As Dana Phillips notes, "[c]haotic phenomena like turbulence ... no longer figure in the scientific imagination as something to be explained away so that our sense of an orderly universe can be preserved" (79). Observing patterns and attending the world, the birder-poet does not necessarily expect to find order, much less to impose it on whatever scape he finds himself inhabiting. Chaotic phenomena complement and define more stable phenomena, and they often enable observers (scientists and poets, perhaps) to question assumptions on balanced nature, humans' place in nature, or the boundaries between ecosystems and species.

The gesture toward becoming bird in "Migratory Patterns" seems less egoistic when considering the poem might be taking place during a dream. "Nocturnal Migrants," too, has the speaker occupying a space between sleep and wakefulness: even when asleep, or on the edge of sleep, the birder-poet wants to be with the birds so much that on the way to the bathroom his "bare feet step / into a pool of moonlight," turn into fish, and "swim off, / up" to join the "night fliers" (*AG* 29). (That his feet turn into fish and not birds reinforces McKay's reluctance to become bird.) When he is in his kitchen, "footless," he thinks about his feet flying "among the night fliers – Snow Geese, swans, songbirds," and about the way they used to be perceived by "early radar techs [who] discovered / ghostly blotches on their screens" and assumed they were "angels": McKay might call them "water-souls" (29–30). Ana Gaulthreaux, ornithologist-protagonist of Kessler's *Birds in Fall*, provides a biological explanation that would seem to support McKay's naming: "Birds, like humans, are mostly moisture—they're ninety percent water—and a flock of finches on a radar screen shows up like a small weather system: one or two green dots. On a night of heavy migration in autumn or spring, a radar screen blossoms with fleeting spectral dots" (115). Despite the obvious differences between birds and humans, similarities abound beyond the developmental characteristics outlined by Margaret Morse Nice and elucidated by Susan Fisher. Moreover, McKay's and Kessler's reference to flocks of birds appearing on radar screens provides at least anecdotal evidence for birds' physiological reality directly influencing an imaginative representation. Birds have the capacity to be both dream and reality, to be ninety percent water and ninety percent yearning. That the numbers do not quite add up, furthermore, points to another way the human mind can be "pitched past all capacity," stretched to its limit.

Migration offers a particularly apt phenomenon for testing the limits of human imagining. In a biological sense, the mechanics and ecology of migration are difficult to imagine. That difficulty transforms, by analogy, to the pain of loss in a poem by Karen Solie. In "Migration" (54), Solie recounts a series of typical natural and cultural occurrences on the way to elegizing a friend and lamenting the mistreatment of the earth. Though enough evidence exists to condemn destructive human habits,

> and though it's illegal to idle one's engine
> for more than three minutes, every one of us will idle
> like hell. After all that's happened. We're all
> that's left. In fall, the Arctic tern will fly
> 12,500 miles to Antarctica as it did every year
> you were alive. It navigates by the sun and stars.
> It tracks the earth's magnetic fields
> sensitively as a compass needle and lives
> on what it finds. I don't understand it either.

Solie accomplishes multiple things with these lines. She evokes the act of return inherent in migration while simultaneously portraying death as migration without the promise (or possibility) of return. She connects the politics of the everyday, apathetic and detrimental behaviour, natural history, and personal loss. The enjambment of "as it did every year / you were alive" poignantly shifts the tone from one of incredulity in the face of environmental crisis to one of resigned sadness in the wake of a friend's death. If the movement in these lines resists certainty even as it enacts return, the poem achieves much more than the formal convention might suggest. The fact that arctic terns routinely travel the farthest of any bird—save for sooty shearwaters, which complete 46,000-mile pelagic figure eights each year—defies the speaker's comprehension, and, she presumes, ours, too, as that terminal "either" suggests.

The ability to understand, Solie suggests in "Migration," has achieved a dubious ontological status—to the extent that who we are parallels, post-Enlightenment, what we know. If we understand that excessive idling contributes to air pollution—creating local effects (smog) and global effects (atmospheric warming)—and we idle anyway, it seems that knowledge by itself fails to convey meaning free of personal and political biases. If we fail to understand how birds (weighing less than the nozzles that deposit the gasoline we idle away) manage to survive epic journeys, then it seems that lack of knowledge conveys perspective, at the very least. That terns continue to migrate is more important than whether we understand how, precisely, they do it. More important, certainly, than the continued maltreatment of the earth despite a living (and dying) archive of "all that's happened." The apparent innocuousness of the passive voice in the phrase "After all that's happened" troubles an ontological reading of environmental crises. The extent to which humans are responsible for what has happened, and continues to happen, exists concomitant with our persistence as a species. Solie's enjambment of the lines "We're all / that's left" enacts the personal and political dynamic of the poem as a whole. To imply that humans are all—all-important, all-encompassing, all-pervasive—and immediately to suggest that our existence persists at the expense of all others would seem to contradict the information about Arctic terns later in the poem. But if we consider the difference between the terms "left" and "leave" as they pertain to migration, the contradiction disappears. The migrating terns leave and return; the speaker's friend has left (and left the speaker behind), never physically to return.

Migration strikes elegiac notes, tells stories that sometimes end with return and sometimes with loss. Watching the hawks gather at Point Pelee, the speaker of McKay's "Migratory Patterns" observes that in the approaching winter air "death begins to blossom" (69). Something about those hawks preparing for migration enables the paradox of blossoming death to occur, something both forward-looking and nostalgic about the seasons continuing to change. Migration in McKay's poems often functions as a metaphor for movement at the same time it uncovers a human desire to fly as freely as the birds, to move across political boundaries without the concomitant bureaucratic responsibilities. As Malcolm Lowry writes of "the northwestern redwing"[11] in "The Bravest Boat," "like all birds" it "may feel superior to man in that he is his own customs official, and can cross the wild border without let" (32). More importantly, by reinforcing our status as ground-dwellers whose ecological impact—contributing to global warming, habitat destruction, air pollution—is attributable in part to our own aerial "achievements," McKay's migration poems highlight an anthropocentric hubris that makes the mythical Daedalus and Icarus's—not to mention Sumner and Zak's—daring attempt to defy gravity seem trivial. In the process, McKay effectively enacts a gestural poetics that points toward a world outside language and invites readers to pay attention after they have put down their books.

ecotone two

> Birding and other forms of nature observation seem to be a symptomatic response to the disjunction between human life and nature typical of modern societies.
> – Andrew Durkin, "A Guide to the Guides: Writing about Birds in Russia in the Nineteenth Century" (6)

FIELD GUIDES

> He would be a bird book full of
> lavish illustrations with a text of metaphor.
> – Don McKay, "Field Marks" (*B* 15)

> Because it is an ecology unto itself.
> – Steve McOrmond, "Field Guide" (39)

For the third day this week, BC lingers in bed listening to the early-morning traffic on 4th Avenue. Hundreds of people move past his apartment on their way to work, or back from work, or to school, in the time between the ringing of his alarm and his first cup of coffee. The past few mornings, the sun has insinuated itself with a welcome vitality. He imagines the starlings roosting in the building next door, having finally mastered the red-winged blackbird song they've been practising for weeks, throwing the sunlight through the window onto his bedsheets. *Starlings defenestrating sunlight.* But no; he stops mid-thought: "defenestration" means to throw something (or someone) *out* of a window. What's the opposite? Has there ever been a need to describe the act of throwing something (or someone) *in* through a window?

Birds and words: the two things that have been occupying BC's mind lately.

As he begins to rise (so he can look up "defenestrate"), he hears another sound that has become familiar, a sort of whistling that he's assumed was coming from a traffic cop directing vehicles at the intersection. But he hasn't seen a traffic cop on his morning walks with Mackenzie, and it seems unlikely that the traffic lights would malfunction around the same time each day. He decides to skip the coffee—well, postpone it—and head out with the dog right away, energized by the notion that there is work to be done. The possibility that there are birds to be found.

As a literary critic interested in how his work might effectively participate in environmental, ecological, and (related) political discourses, BC often feels like the stereotypical environmentalist defended by historian Richard White. Responding in part to a bumper sticker with the offensive rhetorical question "Are You an Environmentalist or Do You Work for a Living?" White challenges those intellectual, philosophical approaches to environmentalism that consider work—specifically physical labour—in opposition to conservation. Most environmentalists, offers White, "equate work in nature with destruction. They ignore the ways that work itself is a means of knowing nature while celebrating the virtues of play and recreation in nature" (171). This resistance to physical labour—farming, fishing, logging—not only ignores certain ways of "knowing nature" but presumes a particular way of knowing to be more important than others. It also assumes, rather arrogantly, that no farmers, fishers, or loggers work in a sustainable manner on a local scale. Like White, who admits "not hav[ing] to face what [he] alter[s]" because of his urban, academic position, the birder-critic (BC) consequently "learn[s] nothing from" the physical world beyond his office walls, beyond words on the pages he reads daily, and beyond his own supposedly limitless imagination (184). But that is changing as BC spends more time walking around his Vancouver neighbourhood, listening to, looking for, and learning from field marks. He turns to bird books that are "written to instruct the novice," aware that "a minimum degree of assimilation to the work of birdwatching is required" (Law & Lynch 285). Birding—not unlike gardening—occupies a space between physical outdoor labour and imaginative indoor work.

Except for the familiar birds—crows, rock doves, starlings, and Steller's jays—BC has a hard time identifying a number of species he sees and hears on his walks. He saw a hawk one morning bathing in Tatlow Park. It looked odd standing in the water, dipping its head into the creek before lifting and tilting its neck so the water trickled down its back; it looked, as hawks seldom do, like a giant sparrow having a dust bath. It looked vulnerable—as hawks seldom do—and yet there was no murder of crows chastising and chasing as there usually is in the park. Was it a Cooper's hawk or a sharp-shinned? And what is that tiny brown bird that seems always to be perched on top of a bush singing a complex song full of buzzes and trills? It looks a bit like a pointy-tailed chocolate Timbit. Feeling he has come to know these birds without actually having learned their names, BC resists naming them himself, resists the urge to join a community of names and namers. His curiosity about where they've come from—whether they're year-round residents or spring migrants—sends him to a field guide. For guidance. He recalls David Wagoner's question after reading a posted warning, "Do Not Proceed beyond This Point without a Guide" (170): "Why should I take a guide along / To watch me scaring myself to death?"

Unwilling simply to open a book and search, though, BC often roots around the library for articles about birdwatching behaviour in humans. Sociologists John Law and Michael Lynch write that field guides operate on "a set of commitments: that bird species exist in nature; that they can be identified and indexed on the basis of sensory (mainly visual, but also audible) evidences; that separate species can be represented in paradigmatic illustration and described in texts" (277). In this context, field marks operate as components of a deliberate representational strategy: guides employ "a tacit 'picture theory' of representation: an idealization of the potential correspondence that can be achieved between a representation in the text and the 'bird in the field'" (Law & Lynch 277–78). As a novice, BC remains aware that he must to a certain degree rely upon the authority of the guide, in spite of his tendency to distrust the authority of the written word. Despite the unavoidable incompleteness of field guides—they cannot list "every species or variant that might *possibly* be seen," that is—"the text remains authoritative in the hands of the novice unless strong external grounds are found for denigrating its completeness or adequacy" (Law & Lynch 277). Walking into the field with a guide does not guarantee instant access. But time spent in the guide necessarily informs time spent in the field. Both have the capacity to inform time spent in a poem.

Busing out to Jericho Beach in search of migrating warblers one day, BC flips through Sue Wheeler's *Habitat*. In the opening poem, "Understory" (11), which she dedicates to Don McKay, Wheeler responds to McKay's avian-inspired writing with the following:

> To walk out of the field guide
> and listen. To wait
> for the world to approach with its dapple and hands.
>
> … … … … … … .
>
> There's an understory here, shades
> of meaning, tale told by a rock
> signifying everything.
>
> To open the grammar of being seen
> and let the creatures name *you*.

Wheeler's infinitives coupled with the poem's title (which appears in the poem between two vague markers of place: there, here) reflect a tentativeness BC wants to emulate. The listening. The waiting. The birding. The ontological shift when he allows himself to be named in a language he will never understand. BC keeps coming back to a particular collection of essays on place, wilderness, and poetry, in which McKay reveals an interest in "the possibilities for reverse flow in a relationship that has been so thoroughly one-way" (*D* 18). Reverse flow represents a complex postcolonial, environmental relationship, a conscious willingness to admit complicity and desires yet still manage to work (against the mainstream) toward a more equitable relation to other humans and nonhumans. BC is an actor in the saga of place even as he resists complicity by learning the names of things in place. McKay's reverse flow echoes Tim Lilburn's notion that humans in a new place "should learn the names for things as a minimum" gesture, "as acts of courtesy … entering the realm of decorum" ("Going" 184). One does not respectfully engage in a dialogue with another person and begin, for example, "Hey, what's-your-name! Let's talk about this land you claim belongs to your ancestors." The saga of place can take place in the realm of decorum. BC is convinced he can start, as ecopoets and ecocritics have started, by learning the names for birds, trees, winds, and the people who live and have lived on this coast.

    Walking with some colleagues on campus during a break from marking, BC moves through rainforest toward coast and waves; salal and Oregon grape border the trail, interrupted by "illegitimate, superfluous," occasional yet persistent bursts of Himalayan blackberry, an introduced *Rubus* cultivar courtesy of famed horticulturalist Luther Burbank (Robertson 125). Arbutus trees point nakedly toward sun and waves. He is looking for a bird-poem, a hybrid creature like himself. But what does it mean to be walking like this? Like Wordsworth walking the Lake

District in an earlier time, "imaginatively and physically" BC "is always moving around"—unlike Wordsworth, BC considers his relation to the natural world with a healthy dose of humility. If "motion is," as John Elder claims, "the integrating dimension of a quest" (*Imagining* 137), BC sees his walking, his moving through the landscape, as a participatory gesture. Otherwise, the quest is likely to become a conquest. As if in response to a poet's bird-word playfulness, birds become participial modifiers, gerunds, continuing actions in the present—*meaning, birding*—and to look at them thus becomes a way of looking at and knowing "trees and rocks and seas and all that weaves itself into habitat" (Bringhurst & Ricou 93). BC moves from the specificity of recognition and nomination—Steller's jay, check—to an inclusive consideration of linked entities and of a process of connection between *this* Douglas fir, *that* spotted owl, and his own desiring gaze. The task is difficult, but as Gabriele Helms suggests, "the interconnectedness of all the environment, of the human and the nonhuman world, its interdependence and mutual implication, make it possible for the [birder-critic] to come to an answer to her/his own impatience and frustration" (51–52). The answer often rests unobtrusively in a space, in a moment, between not-knowing and knowing; BC necessarily hesitates, delays the action of naming in order to pay homage to the named.

Leafing through some papers on his desk, BC comes across the following aphorisms from Ricou's "Field Notes and Notes on a Field": "The typical guidebook formulation defines gross characteristics" (24); "It gives basic information, often in sentence fragments, for the identification of species" (24); "Slight shifts in a repeated formula signal a thematic development" (25). If BC fails, perhaps it is the fault of the field guide. Perhaps he is like the hypothetical birder who, looking at a bird he cannot name, "recognized that it was like the other one but [...] forgot what its name was" (Law & Lynch 272). As Law and Lynch would have it, such failure is a result of what Wittgenstein calls "aspect blindness"—BC suffers "not from a defect of eyesight or an inability to see or optically resolve birds in the field, but rather from *an inability to collect and re-collect species identifications*" (273). Like many of the birder-poets whose work he has encountered, BC is not a particularly good birder. He can be, however, quite an adept critic in spite of and perhaps because of his shortcomings at birding. Or at the kind of birding that encourages obsessive list-making and expensive equipment and trips abroad. Instead of mitigating the failure that results from consulting field guides and "encounter[ing] innumerable frustrations, uncertainties, and quandaries"

(Law & Lynch 291), BC acknowledges the value of such failure. And he might, as birder-poets often do, end up writing about it eventually.

Hitting the street coffee-less to track down the mystery whistle-birds, BC becomes acutely aware of two things: the possibility that he won't succeed, and the luxury he enjoys that enables both the attempt and the capacity to learn from failure. He's solidly middle class, or as solid as one can be as a contract worker. He's an educated bourgeois male walking a dog past million-dollar waterfront properties toward beaches and mountains in one of North America's most expensive cities. It's not that he feels guilty about these details of his existence, but insofar as his research and teaching pretend to address environmental concerns, he wonders how much of his life contradicts his work. The past decade or so during which BC has been working toward the Ph.D. and the prospect of a tenure-track job at a university has left little time to ponder the political and economic implications of his career trajectory—and little power to challenge from the inside. Or so he tells himself. Better to do the work, establish some expertise, and secure a job first; once he achieves a position of relative power, he can put that power to use. But of course he's already in a position of *relative* power. Still, he has to eat, to pay rent, to provide care for Mackenzie. Mackenzie.

Should he, as an ecocritic, feel more vexed than he does about his relation to, relationship with, his dog? *His* dog. The possessive suggests much about unequal power relations between species. BC once asked a professor if he thought that the act of riding other animals—horses, elephants, ostriches—for transportation purposes made us distinctively human. Because, aside from parasites (which hitch rides for nutritional purposes), that doesn't seem to happen among other species. The professor responded by wondering, in contrary fashion, whether such behaviour didn't make us *less* human. By which BC understood him to mean less humane. Less a part of the natural world by staking claims on its constituent parts. By not simply announcing difference between us and them but measuring it. It's an intriguing idea, albeit one that lovers of horses would flat-out reject. BC prefers to think about the possessive in terms of familial relationships. My sister. Her uncle. His husband. Your dog. Not as a claim of ownership, but as a declaration of relatedness. That he loves this dog, his dog, is beyond doubt. Is that enough to explain away the naysayers who might question his credibility as an ecocritic, or would he need to add empirical evidence? That his partner rescued the dog from the humane society; that dogs have evolved alongside humans, effectively domesticating us as we have domesticated them.

Mackenzie has stopped walking, so BC jerks to a halt in the midst of these reflexive thoughts. He looks back, expecting to see the dog sniffing a shrub or pissing on lavender. Instead, she's looking into an alleyway, head cocked. Or not looking so much as listening. Once the line of cars passes them by, BC hears what he came to find, the whistling he's been hearing each morning this week (which the dog can hear clearly beneath the traffic noise). Returning to Mackenzie's side, he peers down the alley, mouth slightly agape. (He's read that lowering your jaw opens the passageways in your ears, making it easier to hear certain sounds.) The whistling is louder here, and he can see movement in a tree near the end of the lane. In his haste to get outside, he forgot to bring his binoculars, so he begins to approach the tree slowly. He's more interested in seeing one of the birds than hearing it at this point. If he gets a good look, he'll try to identify the species at home in his bird guide. And then he'll try to find it in the pages of a book.

But how is it possible to represent birds as birds in the pages of literature, or in a poem? How is it possible for the birder-critic to negotiate the layers of representation and, in reading McKay's "Song for the Songs of the Common Raven" (*S/S* 27), for example, write about actual ravens? One answer, an easy one, is "It can't be done." Even field guides, with their ostensible "capacity ... to put the reader or viewer in touch with the environment" with their "stylized images" and mimetic representations, necessarily fail to achieve scientific or literary realism (Buell *Environmental* 97). BC is not interested in debating how real things are in themselves, though. Reality he takes for granted; but he understands that his experience of the real, how he perceives things, removes him from the experience of things in the world. Helms puts it this way: "From a constructivist point of view, I do not deny the existence of an ontological, non-textual reality; what I deny is the possibility of making a statement about its 'real' nature" (45). BC feels impoverished by the proximity he seeks, not by the birds. He wants to know more about the birds because he is relatively new to this place, their home. His presence alone informs an ongoing history of colonial presence, and it also inheres in an even older history of humans' misunderstanding and destruction of the more-than-human world. Familiarity on the way to recognition, then. He is learning that "users of [all] guides will encounter innumerable frustrations, uncertainties and quandaries. Such 'troubles' are typically experienced by committed birders as temporary problems arising within a personal and situational relationship to 'reality'—problems with perspective, acuity and luck" (Law & Lynch 291). Knowing includes being known:

but the moment of recognition, of realization, is constantly changing. Familiarity takes time. BC longs to achieve the familiarity expressed by P. K. Page in "Only Child" (*Planet* 114–16), a poem about a mother (a "noted naturalist") and "her very affectionate and famous son." The son, interested neither in learning Latin binomials nor in knowing the common names for the birds he and his mother encounter, nevertheless gains a familiarity through proximity afforded by walking with his mother: "he knew / them by their feathers and a shyness like his own" (114). His guide is polymorphous.

And yet such familiarity is singularly developed. In the absence of noted naturalists, BC must train himself. Dana Phillips analyzes Roger Tory Peterson's field-mark system of bird identification, what Buell identifies as "highly abstract renderings that have proved, in the experience of veteran birders, to enable the student to identify the originals more effectively than would a denser mimetic image, such as a photograph in the Audubon Society field guide" (*Environmental* 97). Responding to Buell's description of Peterson's field-mark system, Phillips criticizes Buell's "assumption that the images in the *Field Guide* have something of crucial importance to do with 'originals'" (174). Buell's use of the term "original" is problematic, to be sure; however, BC has little ethical difficulty in accepting that Buell refers to a bird or species of bird that existed prior to any representation, image, or description, whether mimetic, abstract, or verbal. In poet Karen Solie's words, "It's what it was before the naming / that the proper name refers to" ("Frontier" 66). While Phillips and Buell agree on the irony implicit in Peterson's *Field Guide* being "not only mimetically parsimonious, but visually impoverished, too, and deliberately so" (Phillips 174), they disagree on the value and success of his minimalist aesthetic. Phillips remains unconvinced of the guide's ability to put its reader "in touch with the environment," since Peterson's "*merely adequate*" images, which require the "birder to become a reader," push the birder to consider "another image, and yet another, while returning, now and again, to the environment for fresh impressions" (178, 179). In other words, Buell privileges a too-simplistic version of literary realism that Phillips, in his critical appraisal of ecocriticism, seeks to complicate:

> Every transaction entails further action: the birder will have to engage in a lot of back-and-forth between text and world, and world and text, and between stylized image and bird, and bird and stylized image, if she really wants to know what kind of

> chickadee she saw. I think it is precisely this going back and
> forth between text and world, and between nature and culture ... to enable [identification], which gives a notion like
> getting 'in touch with the environment' whatever worth it may
> have. (179)

It is also such back-and-forthing, BC thinks, that Buell would privilege as a way to lead readers back to the physical world and not away from it (Buell 11). Phillips's acknowledgement of a world that exists independently of text is promising, in spite of his sustained and bellicose critique of both ecocriticism and the science of ecology. That he uses chickadees and Peterson's *Field Guide to Birds* to do it is significant for another reason—namely, that it illustrates the central importance birds—*real* birds—have in the ongoing problem of environmentally conscious literature and criticism.

Yet for all that BC wants to demonstrate how learning about the biology and ecology of birds can help to develop a less anthropocentric model of critical inquiry, Ricou reminds that "something in us resists a guide. Hence the sometimes hectoring tone, as the poet-guide has to persuade his companion to see it his way. We would rather go it alone" (*Field* 22). If the poet is guide, BC must learn how to read the guides, must learn the nuances of the genre. In contrast, Andrew Durkin notes that the typical "'consumer' of a [field] guide is not a reader in the usual sense but a user"; not until "the establishment of a reciprocal relationship between the technical means to produce well-illustrated, relatively inexpensive books on an enormous scale ... did the bird guide take on what might be called its modern paradigmatic form," of which Peterson's field guides are most representative (5).

Unlike Phillips, Ricou impels readers of his own *Field Guide to "A Guide to Dungeness Spit"* to "read the 'field' of Dungeness Spit" in David Wagoner's poem. "Pause there, and listen to the echoes of local knowledge. [...] The best plan is to alternate routes" (19). For the birder or the birder-critic reading McKay's poems, the impulse is necessarily different. Land(scape) is not the initial ground of the poetry; air and air's denizens are. Granted, McKay walks myriad trails; but often their specificity is less significant than birds' identities. BC knows that "a cardinal / whistling in the poplars" and "bleeding into the trees" ("Longing" *B* 79) does so not in Victoria, B.C., where McKay lived and worked for ten years or so. But identifying the poplar referred to as *Populus balsamifera* L. (balsam poplar), *P. alba* (white poplar), or *P. nigra* (black poplar)—the likeliest candidates—BC cannot determine whether the poem takes place in Ontario or New Brunswick. To get closer to that truth, he must consult extant biographical data and surmise that, since McKay wasn't living in New Brunswick at the time *Birding, or desire* was published, the cardinal is whistling in the poplars somewhere in southern Ontario. If ecologically precise poetry can invite readers into closer proximity to the outside world, surely setting takes on great significance. In the end, though, this brief lyric poem doesn't provide any "echoes of local knowledge." There is no field to read, in part because of the poem's brevity, in part because the poem does not recount or describe a field or a route through a field. In its lyric simplicity, "Longing:" provides a variation on its title, equates that cardinal whistling in a poplar with "an angel / calling his dog," both of which are examples of a "radical unwinding of the heart" (*B* 79). Love is rough terrain, and the lyric has historically offered a guide to love's many contours. But is lyric poetry capable of functioning as a field guide? On its own the lyric seems ill suited for guiding readers through real-world terrain.

Jan Zwicky defines "lyric insight" as "*this*ness, the whole grasped in the particular" (*Wisdom* Left 70). In this sense, lyric offers McKay a particularly suitable mode of "ontological attention" as he writes about "*this* porch, *this* laundry basket, *this* day" (*Wisdom* Left 52), about horned larks ("Drag"), common snipes ("The Wolf"), and snowy egrets ("Field Marks"). Elsewhere Zwicky suggests that "[l]yric humility is isomorphic to ecological humility" and "[t]he awareness that lyric intuits, and that lyric thought attempts to render, is ecological in form" ("Bringhurst's" 110). Such metaphorical possibilities, though, suggest that poems themselves are "ecosystems, precariously adjusted to the surrounding biomass" (Rasula 7). If BC can manage to negotiate the terrain of an ecopoem—by consulting field guide entries and making trips to science libraries—then listening to the world outside will become easier and more meaningful. As John Elder writes, "poetry is in ecological terms the *edge* between mankind and nonhuman nature, providing an access for culture into a world beyond its preconceptions" (*Imagining* 210). The access Elder writes of, as BC sees it, is attainable only when he puts the poem down (or stuffs it in his pocket) and straddles the ecotone between "mankind and nonhuman nature." Poetry is not enough on its own; nor is science or a life lived either indoors or out. As with the biosphere, diversity is perhaps key.

What other guides might we turn to? While Lilburn claims Euroamericans are not quite capable of being "autochthonic" the way, say, Cree people in Saskatchewan or Haida in British Columbia are ("Walking" 45), BC wants to keep an ear tilted toward available stories, available strategies for attempting the world. There is a danger, though, he realizes, in the way simply "speak[ing] of Native Americans in relation to place, earth, land, or any other geographic location courts cliché," but as Kathryn W. Shanley argues, "the definition of 'indigenous' entails place" (137). During one of his visits to a library across campus—the First Nations House of Learning, or X̱wi7x̱wa Library—BC encounters Leroy Little Bear's Foreword to Gregory Cajete's *Native Science* (2000). To "the Native American mind," Little Bear suggests, the significance of land goes beyond mere affinity or identification with Nature as stereotypical constructions of Indianness would have it. BC has come to a stark realization regarding the emergence of a North American environmental consciousness. Though in the academy and in literature it represents thoughtful responses to centuries of abuse both Euroamericans and Natives have perpetrated on the earth and its inhabitants, the colonization of the Americas by European settlers effectively upset(s) the precariously balancing dynamism theorized and practised by the continent's First Peoples, a dynamism that emphasizes respect for, and participation with, the natural world—a dynamism developed and maintained across generations through the act of storytelling. Indigenous communities, even in the seemingly mundane domestic act of cultivating their gardens, BC learns once he gets past Little Bear's Foreword, express by way of an "attitude of reverence for their food plants ... the central foundations of Native science—participation and relationship" (Cajete 132). Despite current consensus that acknowledges Native North Americans' role in unsustainable hunting practices and the extinction of "four-fifths of all large vertebrates in North America" (Glavin 123), Western scientists—and Western literary (eco)critics and academics—who refuse to acknowledge the parallels between Indigenous and Euroamerican cultures, refuse to acknowledge and consider the efficacy of "participation and relationship" in the development of their theories, including ecocriticism, refuse to acknowledge their own complicity in the world's ill health. Stories that are of a particular place, that are chthonic, can still tell us something about how to live in the world. "Unless the cultural/ecological context of a relationship is understood," however, "one cannot fully comprehend a particular Indigenous technology" (Cajete 125). BC wonders at the seemingly innocuous slashing together of culture and ecology in Cajete's phrasing; surely it's a significant typographical and theoretical decision, as if to say culture can be defined in terms of a particular geographic region and the practices of a particular tribe living in that region, but the cultural practices are not exclusive of a broader ecology.

Cajete endorses Native science as "a metaphor for a wide range of tribal processes of perceiving, thinking, acting, and 'coming to know' that have evolved through human experience with the natural world." "To gain a sense of Native science one must participate with the natural world. To understand the foundations of Native science one must become open to the roles of sensation, perception, imagination, emotion, symbols, and spirit as well as that of concept, logic, and rational empiricism" (2). Cajete's emphasis on participation, irrespective of the role of storytelling, reminds BC of Lawrence Buell's call for literature to lead readers back to the physical world rather than away from it (*Environmental* 11). Native science, as Cajete has it, sounds like a version of ecocriticism that values participatory observation and scientific thinking. For now, though, BC will stick to hiking around outside with his field guides and keeping *Ecology* and *Ornithology* to hand when reading poetry inside.

And his field guides. Back home from the morning walk, while the dog eats her breakfast and the coffee percolates, BC leans against the kitchen counter. He got a fairly decent look at the birds whistling (buzzing?) in the tree, but not a great one. The sun had risen high enough to put the birds in silhouette, but he could see dark heads and wings with orangeish bellies. He turns to Baltimore oriole and considers the likelihood that he's seen his first. The markings seem close enough … but a glance at the range map disproves his hunch. Baltimore orioles seem to occur nowhere west of the Rockies. Oddly, they're year-round residents in southern Ontario, where he grew up, yet he can't recall ever seeing one. The Bullock's oriole might reach this portion of southwestern B.C., but the male depicted in the guide shows too much white on the wing, not enough black on the head. Females more yellow than orange. Working his way back in the book—Mackenzie, sated, asleep on the couch—he sees it. Sees an adequate representation of the birds he just saw in the field. Definitely a western species, the varied thrush looks and sounds the least thrush-like of the typical thrushes. Its slender striped neck and its tendency to be, as BC's guide says, "more secretive" than American robins mark varied thrushes as mysterious residents, that morning's revelation of their identity notwithstanding. Sipping his first coffee of the day, BC chuckles at the parallels between his morning's search and the Greek myth of the sirens, bird-women whose songs compelled sailors to seek them out, often at their peril. He realizes now that the mariners, led by their curiosity, were wholly responsible for the danger they found themselves in. BC wonders how much his own efforts to satiate his curiosity by following the varied thrushes' song contain possibilities for similarly perilous actions, wonders whether this morning has been a miniature version of what has been happening on Earth at least since the Enlightenment. But long since birds have been sending their music through sunny morning windows. *Birds adfenestrating song*, he writes on a slip of paper.

part three

Trying to understand the words
    Uttered on all sides by birds,
I recognize in what I hear
    Noises that betoken fear.
– W. H. Auden, "Bird Language" (174)

And of course there must be something wrong
    In wanting to silence any song.
– Robert Frost, "The Minor Bird" (177)

Chapter Six

Notes

> Poetry is what I start to hear when I concede the world's ability to manage and understand itself. It is the language of the world: something humans overhear if they are willing to pay attention.
> – Robert Bringhurst, "Poetry and Thinking" (192)

If bird flight has inspired revolutionary moments in ornithology, physics, and engineering, not to mention poetry, birdsong has perhaps played a greater role in the growth of birding as a popular activity for experts and amateurs alike. There are few places on the planet where humans cannot hear birds singing for at least part of the year (and part of the day). In the next three chapters, I examine the differing ways birdsong has been interpreted by poets, scientists, and philosophers. Positioning McKay's writing about birdsong alongside and against the lyric tradition, I argue that McKay's attention to aural wilderness, particularly birdsong, iterates an attentive relation to the nonhuman world by modelling an active, respectful style of listening. The ability to listen well, as any birder will insist, informs the act of birding: many sightings begin with—indeed, some consist entirely of—hearing a call or a song and locating the source. Unlike field ornithology, though, literary criticism has not developed a theoretical mode of listening to the natural world. Early ecocritics' preference for "realistic" texts as the best indicators of human–nonhuman relations privileges sight over other sensory experiences. Masami Raker Yuki acknowledges this historical and theoretical lacuna and seeks to rectify it in her doctoral dissertation, "Towards a Literary Theory of Acoustic Ecology: Soundscapes in Contemporary Environmental Literature." My discussion of soundscape and acoustic ecology in the remaining chapters, while indebted to Yuki's main theoretical tenets regarding acoustic ecology's capacity to offer "an antidote to the vision-dominant worldview of modern societies" (ii), focuses on how listening functions metaphorically in McKay's writing as "receptivity to others' natures and histories" and as "an escape from both egotism in the human realm and anthropocentrism in a broader context" (Bartlett "Two Pianos" 8–9). Rather than reproducing a sonic environment for purely aesthetic reasons, McKay enacts a listening on the page through the combination of form and content, particularly by employing a specific mode of linguistic play that cultural anthropologist Donna Haraway calls "metaplasm." Equal parts anagram, palindrome, and pun—abide, abode; listen, glisten; underneath, underearth; loop, pool; earth, hear; owning, knowing—metaplasm, according to Haraway, refers to "a change in a word … by adding, omitting, inverting, or transposing its letters, syllables, or sounds" (20). In several poems about birdsong—from poems in which birdsong can be heard as one sound among many in a constructed soundscape to poems devoted to the songs of individual species—McKay simultaneously pays homage to avian singers and measures the distance—the difference—between their songs and his literary response to them.

Birdsong's mixture of familiarity and strangeness distinguishes birds from other animals, as does the ability to fly. Moreover, birdsong sounds, to human ears, "almost like speech, even expressive of human feelings, and yet it is a communication stranger than speech and not quite the same as music" (Lutwack xi). Poets, to be sure, have tended to find the human aspects of birdsong appealing: the connection between the music of the woods and the music of the lyre is an ancient one. The story, recounted by Leonard Nathan, of Vālmīki inventing poetry after hearing krauñchas and witnessing their murder at the hands of a low-caste hunter provides one example of the ancient link between birdsong and poetry. The answer to the question of which came first, birdsong or human music, according to Don Stap, "is less important than the question" itself, since the long list of references to singing birds in ancient literature—including the Sumerian Tilmun myth and "the oldest secular English music, 'Sumer Is Icumen In'"—supports the notion "that some kind of relationship exists" (138). Even Donald Kroodsma, one of the leading experts in avian bioacoustics—the scientific study of birdsong, which often requires creating and studying sonograms—admits to sharing a history with songbirds "dating back not just 30 years" to Kroodsma's first recordings of Bewick's wrens in his backyard "but to the origins of life itself" (22). In this chapter, I trace some of the more well-known poetic treatments of such singing birds as the nightingale in England and the mockingbird in North America, emphasizing the Romantic tradition that elevates birdsong "to near-angelic status" (McKay "Shell" 53) while examining the ways birdsong has historically connected humans with the avian world.

In her groundbreaking contribution to the early environmental movement, Rachel Carson draws explicitly on the perceived value of birdsong. With its allusion to Keats's "La Belle Dame Sans Merci"—"The sedge is wither'd from the lake / and no birds sing"—*Silent Spring* is widely considered an urtext of modern-day environmentalism. In the chapter devoted entirely to the death of birds as a result of air and water pollution (caused by DDT, the pesticide she focuses on throughout her book), Carson includes reports published in the quarterly *Field Notes*[1] by "seasoned observers who have spent many years afield in the particular areas and have unparalleled knowledge of the normal bird life of the region" (98). These are people whose daily lives are influenced by the song of birds and diminished by the ripple effects of massive spray campaigns against the "so-called Dutch elm disease" (Carson 99). For "millions of Americans," Carson notes, the first robin of the season signifies the end of winter; yearly they "listen for the first dawn chorus of the robins throbbing in the early morning light" (99). Yet by the late 1950s the robins' choruses—indeed, the notes of many species—were being silenced, an indication of more widespread ecological devastation that humans were wreaking on the environment.[2] Birdsong has historically represented more than the coming of spring, and many societies have sold caged birds to people who want to hear pleasing avian sounds year-round.

In the February 2007 issue of *The Walrus*, Larry Frolick contributes a story about a unique pastime in Guyana. Appearing in the magazine's "Field Notes" section, Frolick's story concerns a community of men in Georgetown, Guyana's capital city, who raise native songbirds to compete in clandestine nocturnal matches with other birds, mostly seed finches. According to the driver Frolick hires, "people catch them wild, out in the fields down south. And little by little, they train them to sing. Every Sunday they have these races. Only they don't fly them—it's about the rackle" (17). The rackle in this case has little to do with the Old English adjective that means hasty, and a lot to do with the songs sung by competing birds every Sunday. The diminutive birds—scientific name *Oryzobourus crassirostris*; common name large-billed seed finch or twa twa;[3] local name "bastard," for being "tough as concrete nails"—represent status in the community and cost upward of US$5,000–10,000: "Dey more valuable den a car!" (18). As a cultural outsider, Frolick cannot get much closer to this practice; his driver will not take him since "they not lookin' for visitors" (20). He is left to wonder how these birds sing competitively (he is able to hear them sing from cages on the street) and how the competitions unfold among human participants. Caged singing birds are nothing new, of course. Beryl Rowland reports that the "century-old bird market off Kalitnikivskaya Street, Moscow [is] an enterprise entirely praised in the West as one of the few free commercial activities permitted in the Soviet Union,"[4] and he imagines a thrush eyeing passersby "sadly from the closely packed cages of singing birds that daily line the left bank of the Seine in Paris" (174–75). The persistence of such bird markets from antiquity to the present as a venue for "birders" to procure songsters for personal use, and not necessarily for culinary use, implies a more sophisticated, less violent relation between the people who purchase birds and the birds themselves. To be sure, these birds are not being forced to fight each other as in cockfights or dogfights; however, the practice of capturing birds perpetuates a widespread ecological and environmental violence.

While Frolick's "field notes" are interesting for the intrigue surrounding how the men involved in the singing competitions are said to "have some secret way of judging which bird sings the most melodically" (17), they are also attuned to a much bigger, potentially damaging ecological problem in Guyana. Research by the Iwokrama International Centre for Rain Forest Conservation and Development supports local Guyanese who fear the native songbird population is declining, primarily as a result of trapping to sustain the national songbird trade and, by extension, the competitions. Birdsong continues to be valued in ways that translate into financial gain for part of the human population and threaten the populations in the wild. I am reminded of a scene from the documentary film *Winged Migration* (2003), in which a hyacinth macaw avoids being taken to market by cleverly escaping from its cage while on a raft floating down the Amazon River. Though it focuses on the macaw's escape, the scene cannot but emphasize the continuing prevalence of the exotic animal trade: various monkeys, parrots, and toucans are not so lucky as to escape, whether on camera or not. In *Waiting for the Macaws and Other Stories from the Age of Extinctions* (2006), Terry Glavin provides some context that adds to the scene's power, noting that the blue macaws have suffered more than most: "Like the glaucous and Spix's macaws, the hyacinth macaw is a blue macaw … once common throughout much of Brazil and from Bolivia to Paraguay. During the 1980s, about 10,000 hyacinth macaws were sold in the big-money bird markets of the world. The twentieth century ended with perhaps 2500 remaining outside of cages" (57–58). While the difference between Guyanese seed finches and Brazilian hyacinth macaws lies in the extent to which the latter are commodities destined for collectors beyond South America's borders, both birds are desired for their vocal abilities. "Like all parrots," Glavin reminds us, "macaws are highly social animals … famous for their oddly humanlike characteristics, such as an astonishing capacity for [vocal] mimicry" (57). I find it sadly ironic that this "astonishing capacity" has led to the decline in so many bird populations, especially if I consider the late-twentieth- and early-twenty-first-century proliferation of literature relating to birds and birdsong.[5]

Although one of McKay's poetic projects invites a radical reimagining of humans' abusive treatment of the nonhuman world, McKay avoids sentimentality by writing about birds not obviously connected to such devastating practices as pesticide use and the exotic pet trade. The brief "Song for the Song of the Chipping Sparrow" (*S/S* 25) offers an instructive example of a poem about a bird that holds little symbolic, mythological, or environmental cachet: the chipping sparrow is neither in danger of becoming extinct any time soon nor likely to win any song races with its staccato rackle. Though not as recognizable as the ubiquitous house sparrow or the melodious song sparrow, the chipping sparrow nevertheless maintains a healthy population throughout North America and benefits greatly from urbanization and other human modifications. McKay employs numerous imperatives in his poem, offering a rapid-fire variation on the phrase "Let us pray"—

> Let's go. Let's gargle into song. Let's
> clear our phlegm-clogged
> fucked-up throats let's stutter our
> dumb way into what
> comes next.

The contraction of the prayerful "Let us" simultaneously quickens the pace and subsumes an inclusive relation between sparrow, speaker, and readers, though the "phlegm-clogged" stuttering might accurately describe the song of the chipping sparrow. In *The Singing Life of Birds: The Art and Science of Listening to Birdsong*, Donald Kroodsma explains that a chipping sparrow song typically consists of "a simple rattle or trill, a single split-second phrase repeated many times over" (315), a description in keeping with McKay's lyric version: "Take death rattle, take / automatic rifle fire, take t-t-t-t- Tommy Moss / day after day in grade two failing / to finish his name." None of these metaphors, despite their aural accuracy, resonates in particularly positive ways, and yet the tone and pace of the poem, not to mention its emphasis on the diminutive, relatively little-known chipping sparrow, counters the negativity associated with imminent death, war, and childhood embarrassment and failure. By repeating the imperative "Take," the speaker reveals the ease with which birdsong can inspire associative thinking; by suggesting what to do next—after having taken these images and sounds as possible metaphors—he reveals an awareness of metaphor's limitations. In other words, this poem invites the question Of what use is an accurate aural metaphor if it leads us away from the physical world by imposing inaccurate, inappropriate meaning on a moment, a species, a sound?

The poem's speaker addresses this problem by suggesting that we take the metaphorical versions of the chipping sparrow song and

> wrench them from their torments,
> pass them through this skull-capped
> bright-eyed sparrow in the spruce and into
> morning's rah-rah for itself. Let's go.
> For we shall be changed.

The sparrow itself is capable of modifying a human propensity for free-associative thinking that borders, in the case of written literature, on imposition. McKay rescues this poem from careless anthropomorphism by admitting an incongruence that does not necessarily get him (or his readers) into closer proximity to the chipping sparrow; here, the lie employed by the poet in the interest of truth, and not the song of the chipping sparrow, resembles the memory of Tommy Moss's failure to articulate his name in grade two. In the extreme, the lie recapitulates a violent human nature evident in the image of automatic-rifle fire: these metaphors serve to describe the poet more than they do the sparrow. By ending the poem with a reference to the chipping sparrow's morning singing, moreover, McKay satisfactorily resorts to accurate ornithological data.

In his research on the chipping sparrow, Kroodsma must rise hours before sunrise to record and observe this particular species' habit of singing early and of building toward a longer, seemingly more exuberant song: "Before sunrise males sputter brief songs from the ground, up to 60 a minute. Over the next half hour or so the singing rate slows and song length gradually increases, until the ground singing is over and males rise to sing from the trees" (*Singing* 318). One bird's first song after having alighted in a tree is "more than five seconds long, as if all the sputtering [so far that] morning had prepared him for this longer song" (318), as if he has to clear his "phlegm-clogged / fucked-up throat." The whole act seems to recapitulate the circadian rhythm's repetitiveness. The idea of being changed, then, and in such an affirmative manner—*we shall be changed*—comes up against and challenges my initial reading of this poem as one that does not engage the politics of environmentalism.[6]

Taken together, the onomatopoeic versions of the chipping sparrow's song positions McKay's poem in a tradition of poems that attempt to reproduce birdsong linguistically.[7] The death-rattle metaphor, unlike the others, implies that the sparrows are near enough to death to produce the gurgling, rattling sound sometimes thought to presage death in humans, the result of oral secretions pooling in the backs of throats. But, since chipping sparrow populations remain strong, the bird seems to be speaking for humans' and/or all birds' procession toward death. As a warning and an elegy, "Song for the Song of the Chipping Sparrow" recalls a passage from Thoreau's *Walden*: "If we are really dying, let us hear the rattle in our throats and feel cold in the extremities; if we are alive, let us go about our business" (351). The resemblance in both subject (environmental degradation and its human consequences) and in style ("let us" versus "let's") adds a layer of historicity to McKay's brief lyric and inflects a Thoreauvian note of elegy with a McKavian note of hope by way of more specific attention, of what Ross Leckie calls an "attentive poetics of epistemology that is responsive to the requirements of the world" (128). Whereas Leckie applies the notion of attentive poetics to the act of naming in McKay's "Twinflower," I argue that the act of listening is an integral component of McKay's poetic attention and his avian aesthetic.

As he does with bird flight in poems that repeat, with an ecologically aware difference, lyric connections between flight and truth, McKay writes lyric poems that acknowledge a tradition of odes that pay homage to birdsong while challenging the anthropocentric thrust of such a tradition. McKay paves the way for shifting the lyrical paradigm to consider such poetical "techniques" as metaphor, rhythm, rhyme, and other verbal flourishes as "sensors, listening devices like radio telescopes or sonar. It's as though language, which is—so we think—all mouth, were trying to grow ears" ("Shell" 53). McKay echoes Tim Lilburn's claim that "a certain form of speech can be an attempt to hear" (Preface 2). Homage is such a form. By insinuating formal, linguistic, rhythmic, thematic elements from other, earlier texts into his poetry, McKay evokes, and readers can hear, these other texts. When homage occurs within a critique of an intellectual tradition notorious for elevating human emotion over the rest of the world, it participates in an ecocriticism concerned with webs of literary as well as ecological relations. To think of homage as an ecocritical strategy for reading McKay's bird poems and any poem that might participate in a similar relational economy, it is necessary to trace some traditional associations of lyric and birdsong in Anglophone poetry.

In his entry on "Poetry in Shorter Forms" from W. H. New's *Encyclopaedia of Literature in Canada*, poetics professor, critic, and poet Kevin McNeilly acknowledges the etymological history that connects lyric poetry with singing by way of the Greek *lyrikós*. He also acknowledges a trajectory that sees lyric poetry as "a self-sufficient form" that does not require musical accompaniment, paraphrasing Walter Pater's notion that the lyric "is poetry aspiring to the condition of music" (877). While McKay, like many English-speaking poets during the past hundred years, tends not to rely much on conventional forms such as the sonnet, the ode, and the rondeau, he recognizes their historical significance, often paying homage to the traditions at the same time that he employs subtle changes that question the prevalence and canonical status of traditional verse forms. For his part, James Harting, in *The Ornithology of Shakespeare* (1864), acknowledges the prevalence, even from his historical vantage of the mid-1860s, of songbirds in English poetry. "If there is one class of birds more than another," he writes, "to which the poets in all ages have been indebted for inspiration, it is that which includes the birds of song" (123).[8] It makes sense; if poets consider themselves singers, what better animal to associate with than the birds that sing for a living. Milton, in "To the Nightingale," apostrophizes the infamous bird, "O Nightingale," whose "liquid notes … close the eye of Day": "Whether the Muse, or Love call thee his mate, / Both them I serve, and of their train am I" (107). As an apprentice of the Muse and Love, Milton seems to feel an affinity with this particular bird. He is not alone in this.

As Leonard Lutwack does over one hundred years later in *Birds in Literature*, Harting devotes a good deal of space to the nightingale as quintessential literary songster, claiming that "by common consent," the nightingale "stands first" among "all the singers of the woodland choir" (123). Harting cites *The Taming of the Shrew* ("She sings as sweetly as any nightingale") and *Romeo and Juliet* ("It was the nightingale, and not the lark, / That pierc'd the fearful hollow of thine ear"), as well as *Cymbeline*, *Titus Andronicus*, and *A Midsummer Night's Dream*, all three of which refer to nightingales as Philomel (124–25). Lutwack reminds of the Greek story of Philomela, who is raped and mutilated (she has her tongue cut out) by her brother-in-law Tereus. After Philomela seeks revenge with the help of her sister Procne by killing Tereus's son and feeding him in bits to his father, the gods intervene (ostensibly to prevent further bloodshed) and turn the participants into birds: "Procne becomes a nightingale, Philomela a swallow, Tereus a hoopoe,[9] and poor Itys [Tereus' son], reassembled, a pheasant" (1). In the Roman version of the story, the tongueless Philomela inexplicably becomes the nightingale, and that version has most influenced Western writers, including Aristophanes, whose *The Birds* "constitute[s] one of the earliest attempts to represent bird song in language" (Lutwack 8); Shakespeare; Matthew Arnold, who refers to Philomela's "dumb sister's shame" in "Philomela"; and John Clare, who observed wryly that Londoners "fancy every bird they hear after sunset a Nightingale" (Robinson and Fitter 42). Attentive listeners, it seems, they were not.

In "Wordsworth's Ear and the Politics of Aesthetic Economy," Stuart Allen argues that Wordsworth, especially in "The Pedlar and the Ruined Cottage" and *Lyrical Ballads*, reluctantly promotes aural experience over visual experience, constructing "a studied ambivalence towards listening," which represents his "poetry's resistance to the absence of harmony in the world" (37–38). Concluding that "[r]eceptivity to song is a major theme throughout ['The Pedlar and the Ruined Cottage']" (40), for example, Allen notes that the Pedlar and the narrator at the end of the poem "sit together while birds sing 'and other melodies, / At a distance heard, peopled the milder air.'" What Allen refers to simply as birds, however, Wordsworth names with a specificity Clare would likely approve: "A linnet warbled from those lofty elms, / A thrush sang loud, and other melodies" (ll. 933–34). Given that these lines end the poem, I argue the value of the song the Pedlar and narrator "receive" is directly proportional to the song's avian origins. Wordsworth, however, tempers his species specificity by using a verb with obvious anthropocentric implications; these characters do not hear birdsong so much as the birdsong inhabits—anthropomorphically "peoples"—the air and entices those within range to move indoors to "A village inn." McKay actively resists this self-serving lyric posturing, opting instead for a poetic attentive to how language listens by building upon Heidegger's claim that, although "it is language that speaks," poets respond "to language by listening to its appeal" (*Poetry* 216). In "Remembering Apparatus: Poetry and the Visibility of Tools" (*V* 51–73), McKay articulates his own version of Heidegger's claim, announcing that "[f]or a long time before it becomes a speaking ... poetry is only a listening" (66). In his poetry, especially in those poems that directly invoke the songs of particular birds, McKay demonstrates how poetry functions as "a listening" by combining visual and oral aspects of language and poetry, in much the same way Kroodsma does when observing sonograms.

Some of McKay's earlier "songs" that do not acknowledge birds or birdsong in their titles nevertheless construct a mode of listening that anticipates the birder-poet of later poems. In "Song for the Restless Wind" (*NF* 63), "Song for Wild Phlox" (*NF* 64), and "Song for Beef Cattle" (*A* 13), McKay alludes to such poems as Shelley's "Ode to the West Wind," Keats's "Ode on a Grecian Urn," and Whitman's "Song of Myself," yet each poem subtly responds to these canonical texts by redeploying the lyric I, that peon of egotistical declaration, in order to consider "respectful modes of interaction"

(Bartlett *Two Pianos* 7). Containing anthropomorphic language enacted as thoughtfully as possible, McKay's "Song for the Restless Wind" pays homage to an unpredictable force of nature, a "giant" "struggling in her sleep," as if dreaming of a "car chase [that] always overtakes the plot and wrecks it." Whereas Shelley asks the west wind to "make me thy lyre, even as the forest is" (l. 57), McKay wonders "Whose idea was it / to construct a mind entirely of shoulders," effectively anticipating his critique of "Aeolian harpism" crucial to his notion of "poetic attention" in "Baler Twine" (*V* 15–33). Instead of portraying the wind as inspirational breath, McKay acknowledges the wind's physical presence, its ability to "shoulder" its way through the landscape without regard for humans; he, too, is inspired enough to write poetry about wind, but he gives credit where credit is due, content to let a more-than-human intelligence—"a mind entirely of shoulders"—elude his own mind's tendencies to appropriate.

"Song for Wild Phlox" and "Song for Beef Cattle" have as objects of praise unlikely species. In "Wild Phlox," McKay calls phlox a weed and ends up writing a singular account of its ecological presence: "Nothing / we ever did deserves / these weeds, which seed themselves / in places we have honoured with neglect." Depending on how one reads the words "deserves" and "weeds," the poem can be read as a complaint that since humans have not disturbed a particular area the presence of wild flowers that get in the dog's fur is unfair; but it can also be read as a reminder that agriculture is not necessary for these "purple, / purplish, blue, whitish" flowers to bloom. As E. F. Schumacher writes in the Foreword to *The Virtuous Weed*, weeds are organisms "whose wisdom we should be humbly eager to understand" (n.p.); at the very least, we can admit that some things in nature are beyond our ken and our control. In "Song for Beef Cattle," the only poem of these three that mentions song in any way, McKay offers a more overt critique of industrial agriculture and, perhaps for that reason, adopts a more overtly ironic lyrical tone:

> To be whimless, o monks of melancholy,
> to be continents completely
> colonized, to stand
> humped and immune, digesting,
> redigesting our domestication, to be too too
> solid flesh making its slow
> progress toward fast food.

The apostrophic (though lower-case) "o," the clunky consonance, and the direct reference to *Hamlet*[10] all suggest a critical tone that simultaneously challenges a traditional form of "song" and a conventional farming practice. Unlike Romantic pastoral songs, "Song for Beef Cattle" is more elegy than ode; it pays homage to a domesticated breed of livestock by highlighting humans' role in colonizing bovine bodies through artificial selection[11] and commodifying stock through the fast-food industry. Continuing his efforts to challenge the central importance of the self in poetic form, McKay gestures in these early songs toward what he attempts in some of his later "songs for the songs of" poems.[12]

In "Song for the Song of the White-throated Sparrow," birdsong inhabits the air, but the occupation implies a less anthropocentric effect than it does in Wordsworth. Rather than entice the birder-poet indoors, and thus farther away from the song and its singer, the white-throated sparrow's song articulates a version of sky, "a way to pitch a little tent in space and sleep / for five unnumbered seconds" (*AG* 33). The metaphor of pitching a tent in the air curiously acknowledges the impulse to retire indoors and reflect. But the speaker resists this impulse in favour of embracing the unpredictability of remaining outside. While musically the sparrow's song echoes a musical chord whose notes are performed in rapid upward succession—what McKay calls "the obvious arpeggio"—such a comparison is the result of the speaker's hasty "inferences," of a mind that makes metaphorical associations "Before it can stop itself" (33). This self-conscious reflection on the birder-poet's tendency to respond to birdsong metaphorically anticipates the moment, two books later, in "Song for the Song of the Chipping Sparrow" when tormenting metaphor passes through the sparrow's voice into a hopeful anticipation of change. The obviousness of the mind's inferences, while unspoken, likely refers to the common onomatopoeic renditions of the white-throated sparrow's song. David Allen Sibley identifies it as a "high, pure whistle *sooo seeeeeee dididi dididi dididi*" (494), and it has famously been translated as "Old Sam Peabody Peabody Peabody!" and, north of the forty-ninth parallel, as "Oh Sweet Canada Canada Canada!" The first two notes sound, to human ears, like a doorbell's slightly drawn-out ringing, *dinnggg-donngg*, and hence the speaker "leap[s] up inferences"—

> Where there is a doorbell
> there must be a door – a door
> meant to be opened from the inside.
> Door means house means – wait a second –
> but already it is standing on a threshold previously
> known to be thin air, gawking.

Whereas Wordsworth's characters go inside, McKay's speaker begins imagining an indoor space before realizing, as he does in "Chipping Sparrow," the limitations of a metaphor that positions listeners farther away from the physical, outer world. Once he has checked himself, the door rematerializes as birdsong resonating on a threshold between inside and outside. The little tent pitched in midair is a doorway with room for the poet's imagination, "a nook of reverie," a listening post—a human nest (*V* 72). From his listening post, the birder-poet (and the birder-critic) is able not only to enjoy the aesthetics of birdsong, its vocal complexities, but to recognize, as distinct from merely identifying, the birds he hears, thus demonstrating the participatory, active nature of listening.

In his compendium of bird lore and poetry, *The Bedside Book of Birds: An Avian Miscellany* (2005), Graeme Gibson admits to holding certain "highly Romantic notion[s]" in regard to birds and their songs. Responding to Thomas Hardy's "The Darkling Thrush" (Hardy 23–24), for example, in which "An aged thrush, frail, gaunt, and small" proceeds to sing "a full-hearted evensong" and thus "fling his soul / Upon the growing gloom," Gibson writes: "All [the speaker] can conclude is that the bird knows something he doesn't. Despite its decrepit condition, its song is filled with the passionate energy of life; and that, after all, is at the heart of everything, including Hope itself" (305).[13] In nineteenth-century America, John Burroughs wonders whether he will "ever again be able to hear the song of the oriole without being pierced through and through? ... Day after day, and week after week, this bird whistled and warbled in a mulberry door, while sorrow, like a pall, darkened [his] day" (87–88). Burroughs associates the oriole's song with sorrow and not joy—contrary to Auden's claim in "Bird-Language" that other than "rage, bravado, [and] lust," "All other notes that birds employ / Sound like synonyms for joy" (174)—yet the emotional connection remains. The song itself, "a series of melodious whistled phrases" (Elliott *Songs* 110), is not particularly sorrowful by conventional Euroamerican standards; Burroughs, though, internalizes it (in his memory) after hearing it often during a time of grief in his life. Other descriptions in Burroughs's "A Bird Medley" (83–106) have more ecological significance; after noting the "sweet and musical voices" of sparrows, for example, Burroughs refers to the "white-throat [who] has a timid, tremulous strain, that issues from the low bushes or from behind the fence, where its cradle is hid" (100). His attention is often drawn to individual birds, as with a song sparrow "that was a master songster—some Shelley or Tennyson among his kind" and whose music represents for Burroughs "a simple, but very profound summing-up of life" (101). Such unabashedly Romantic sentiments fit the reading of such poets as Shelley, Wordsworth, Hopkins, and Hardy, whose birds typically occupy decidedly symbolic realms, as distinct from ecological ones.[14] I do not, however, want to dismiss an entire tradition of poetry that engages birdsong metaphorically; rather I want to make conspicuous the absence of ecological detail among canonical English-language poets, an absence that McKay increasingly addresses in his "songs" and, even more elaborately, in his "songs for the songs of" series of poems.

Chapter Seven

Birdsong

> To admit some degree of rationality in animals seemed to entail admitting that animals have immortal souls, while to deny them immortal souls seemed to entail denying them not only any degree of rationality but perhaps even the ability to experience pain and pleasure.
> – Angus Taylor, *Animals & Ethics* (39)

> The study of song-learning in birds has begun to alter the long-held image of birds as unintelligent creatures of instinct.
> – Don Stap, *Birdsong: A Natural History* (78)

> Birds have notes in between our notes—you try to imitate something they do and, like, maybe it's between F and F#, and you'll have to go up or come down on the pitch. It's really something!
> – Eric Dolphy, qtd. in Simosko and Tepperman (13)

In addition to poets, ornithologists and musicologists have long been interested in the sounds birds make. According to well-known recorder of wildlife sounds Lang Elliott, "[t]he question of why birds sing can be approached from two perspectives: the scientific perspective, which derives from evolutionary biology, and the poetic perspective, which springs from our emotional experience of hearing birds sing" (*Music* 11). Elliott reinforces the common distinction between scientists' "attempts to describe bird behaviour free of emotion and anthropomorphic interpretation" and poets' concerns "with feelings and the effects of bird song on human emotion" (11). According to Lutwack, "The song of birds is especially cherished by poets, probably because it is the only animal utterance with sound patterns just close enough to those made by people to tease us into the belief that bird song is like human language" (46). More accurately, birdsong is music, which is not to say that birds do not communicate via song. Some birds produce notes humans cannot hear without visual aid in the form of sonograms or computer software that enables us to slow recordings down, effectively stretching notes out to isolate subtle variations in pitch. Ever since a young German boy recorded the song of an Indian shama with a phonograph, hence producing "the first known recorded birdsong" (Stap 28), technological advances have enabled more and more detailed approaches to understanding avian music. Since the development of the audiospectograph, or sonogram, ornithologists have been able to listen to birdsong in entirely different ways by combining humans' visual capacity with our limited ability to distinguish sounds. In *The Singing Life of Birds*, Kroodsma admits that his sense of hearing is "actually pretty pathetic" and that he has "no musical ability whatsoever"; like most humans, however, he has "well-trained eyes, and it is with [his] eyes that [he] hears" (2). As the field of ethology, the scientific study of animal behaviour led by Nobel Prize winner Konrad Lorenz, was developing, so was the sonogram becoming regularized as an instrument fit for fieldwork that could provide insight into the instinctive and learned behaviours of birds. The visualization of birdsong opened up the possibility that birds have evolved cultural traits.

Why some birds have evolved a large vocal repertoire while others have not remains a mystery. Of the birds whose songs McKay pays homage to, chipping sparrows and white-crowned sparrows, for example, sing only one song each; wood thrushes, by contrast, sing twenty songs; and at the far end of the repertoire spectrum, mockingbirds have 250 songs and brown thrashers an "incomparable" 2,000 or more (Stap 89). Ornithologists can safely say, based on years of research, that birds sing and call "to establish territories and to make themselves attractive to potential mates" (Rothenberg 8). McKay addresses the former reason in "Territoriality" (*SD* 89–91), in which he describes how red-winged blackbirds determine and defend their territories:

> they are sewing their imagined patterns
> vertex to vertex perching on the spruce tips
> and the frayed cigars of last year's cattails
> singing konkeree konkeree
> flashing epaulets of red with yellow fringes
> hunching forward
> signalling the outlines of their small and shifting kingdoms
> to the others who are signalling
> the outlines of their small and shifting kingdoms back. (89)

Despite the potential distance insinuated by the multiple metaphors—sewing, vertices, frayed cigars—it seems entirely plausible that these birds are imagining patterns with their famous song *konkeree*, or *conk-la-ree*. To think otherwise would be to reinforce the idea of birds as "unintelligent creatures of instinct"; though instinct doubtless plays a role in how birds respond to external stimuli, research continues to show that birds are among the most intelligent creatures by human standards. "And if," as McKay writes in "Territoriality," "we listened for an evening we would learn to hear." Red-winged blackbirds, to take one example of a species that might have something to teach us in this respect, might not be as demonstrably intelligent as corvids (considered the most intelligent avian group), but their capacity for imagining and maintaining territory requires a keen intelligence we can witness, and listen to, without ever fully understanding.

The opening section of "Territoriality" describes one aspect of the red-winged blackbird's socio-cultural life; the second and third sections extend that aspect metaphorically to consider how humans have taken similar territorial impulses to radically different extremes, namely by "dig[ging] inverted silos" and "stock[ing] them with extinction" in the form of weapons of mass destruction (90). Humans in this poem are "others" who construct "hair-triggered negative / erections, aimed at their enemies" (90). The contrasting effects of ostensibly similar instinctive acts cast doubt on the notion that humans with our culture are inherently superior or intelligent, though compelling similarities do exist. In "Poetry and Thinking," Robert Bringhurst makes a case for the cultural similarities between human and avian life histories by making an appeal to music: "Humans, like birds, are able to make songs and pass them on. Human songs, like birdsongs, are part nature and part culture: part genetic predilection, part cultural inheritance or training, part individual inflection or creation" (163). Elsewhere he writes of birdsong in a similar fashion. Echoing Saint-John Perse's literal-mindedness regarding birds' burning blood, Bringhurst states: "Songbirds sing. That is fact and not a metaphor. Nothing but human arrogance allows us to insist that these activities be given different names. Bird songs, like human songs, are learned. They are cultural traditions" ("Singing" 116–17). The name "song" is a marker of cultural tradition across species boundaries; but so is the notion of arrogance:

> Like other creatures, humans are heavily self-absorbed. We frequently pretend (or self-righteously insist) that language belongs to humans alone. And many of us claim that the only kind of human language, or the only kind that matters, is the

> kind that is born in the mouth. The language of music and mathematics, the gestural languages of the deaf, the calls of leopard frogs and whales, the rituals of mating sandhill cranes, and the chemical messages coming and going day and night within the brain itself are a few of the many reminders that language is actually part of the fibre of which life itself is spun. We are able to think about language at all only because a license to do so is chemically written into our genes. The languages we are spoken in are those for which we speak. (Bringhurst *Solid* 10–11)

In Bringhurst's world view—as in his poetics—humans are spoken into being as much as humans speak the rest of the world into existence. If, as self-absorbed creatures, humans insinuate themselves into the lives of non-humans, they will invariably become part of a cultural history not of their own making. Biologists provide ample support for Bringhurst's claim that humans are not the only species with culture: "song does not suddenly spring up fully formed when a bird becomes mature," write Catchpole and Slater. "It has a developmental history" (45). Songbirds, or oscines, have developed complex musical vocalizations; they "learn their songs in much the same way children learn to speak," unlike most suboscines, which, like birds from orders outside the order Passeriformes (songbirds), "are born with their vocalizations genetically encoded" (Stap 10). The cultural life of songbirds, as indeed of other nonhuman animals, undermines a critical desire to reconsider anthropomorphism by implying that the human characteristics insinuated by the label anthropomorphism are not entirely human.

Temple Grandin takes Bringhurst's idea an evolutionary step further when she writes that "Animals are the originators of music and the true instructors. Humans probably learned music from animals, most likely from birds"; Grandin goes on to provide "evidence that humans copied music from birds, rather than reinventing it for themselves: only 11 percent of all primate species sing songs" (278).[1] Moreover, she states, "[b]irds compose songs that use the same variation in rhythms and pitch relationships as human musicians, and can also transpose their songs into a different musical key. Birds use accelerandos, crescendos, and diminuendos, as well as many of the same scales composers use all over the world" (279). With our big brains, humans have been able successfully to rationalize mimicking birds as an essentially human cultural practice. No human song should forget this origin.[2]

The notion of intelligence—both human and nonhuman—is integral to an understanding of cultural behaviour among nonhuman groups. Grandin makes reference to a recent experiment involving tool-making and use by a species of crow. Published in *Science* in 2002, "Shaping of Hooks in New Caledonian Crows" (Weir, Chappell, and Kacelnik) recounts the results of an experiment during which zoologists at Oxford "placed a single straight piece of garden wire ... on top of [a] tube" of food to observe the crows' reaction. "Out of 10 valid trials (interspersed with seven invalid ones)," researchers found that "the female bent the wire and used it to retrieve the food nine times" (981). In a related experiment, researchers published a report in 2005 that has radically altered the way scientists think about the avian brain. While the study, titled "Avian brains and a new understanding of vertebrate brain evolution" (Jarvis et al.), is predominantly about new nomenclature scientists have decided to adopt in discussing avian neurobiology, the shift in nomenclature is the cumulative result of decades of research that suggest birds are indeed more intelligent than we have typically given them credit for. Even more recently, and of particular relevance for my discussion of avian song, biologists at the University of Chicago have conducted research the results of which seriously challenge the latest attempts by such theorists as Noam Chomsky to delineate linguistic capabilities unique to humans. Contrary to the claim that "the capacity for syntactic recursion [the hierarchical embedding of language units (such as the one you are now reading) within sentences] forms the computational core of a uniquely human language faculty," Gentner and his fellow researchers "show that European starlings (*Sturnus vulgaris*) accurately recognize acoustic patterns defined by a recursive, self-embedding, context-free grammar" (1204).

Given the results of this research on starling intelligence and grammar, the treatment of birds—and by extension other nonhuman animals—in literature is problematic. Critics have tended to consider writing about animals and the natural world, as I have discussed in earlier chapters, in either realist or symbolic terms. South African writer J. M. Coetzee, for example, confronts what theorists call "the question of the animal" in *The Lives of Animals* (1999) and *Disgrace* (1999).[3] According to Canadian writer Dionne Brand, Coetzee, who has developed a reputation as a master allegorist, seems to have taken advantage of the official end of apartheid in South Africa and begun to write in a realist mode he has not previously produced (see *Map* 126). Be that as it may, he is still writing literature, and all literature, South African and otherwise, about animals and not, is to varying degrees symbolic. As Nadine Gordimer writes in her preface to a collection of critical articles on her fellow South African writer's work, "[n]othing is more unreal than the simulation of outward reality; realism, whether in painting or writing, doesn't exist" (xi). Literary critic and animal-rights advocate

John Simons makes roughly the same argument, but he links it more closely to literary representations of animals. In "The Animal as Symbol," Simons distinguishes between cultural reproduction and representation and offers the "proposition that the non-human experience cannot be reproduced but only represented" (*Animal Rights* 86). However, reading animals in purely symbolic terms assists in reinforcing a species boundary that has been used for centuries to maintain cultural and racial boundaries. For example, dogs in Coetzee's novels *Age of Iron* (1990) and *Disgrace* act in symbolic *and* literal ways to initiate a shift in certain characters' ideologies that reflects the political shift, albeit an idealistic one, in post-apartheid South Africa. That only white people deal with dogs sympathetically in *Disgrace* (and, for that matter, *Age of Iron*) attests to the contemporary necessity of a re-emerging sympathetic imagination. While it would be easy to suggest that dogs function as symbolic Others for the white people who care for dogs in *Disgrace* and as literal dogs for the black people who kill dogs in *Disgrace*, I argue that dogs function symbolically and literally for all characters in the novel. Historically, cultural hegemony has been exercised by treating oppressed peoples like animals; indeed, as Tiffin acknowledges,

> The political history of Western racism and its imbrication with discourses of speciesism ... and above all, perhaps, its metaphorisation and deployment of 'the animal' as a derogatory term in genocidal and marginalizing discourses have made it difficult to even discuss animals without generating a profound antagonism in many post-colonial contexts. (32)

Consequently, white people in Coetzee's fiction have the most to gain, fundamentally and ideologically, from learning to treat all living beings equally with respect to a "consideration of their interests" (Singer 87). But, to extend the notion of the sympathetic imagination as it plays out in Coetzee's post-apartheid South Africa, the black people who kill dogs and rape the protagonist's daughter also have much to gain from learning to treat all living beings with equal respect. I am talking about a compassion that observes the potential interconnectedness of all things, both real and imagined, living and nonliving.

The dynamic conversation between *Disgrace* and *The Lives of Animals* enacts a conceptually ecological framework useful for thinking about McKay's avian poetics. This framework is first articulated by a character, Mrs. Curren, in *Age of Iron*: "When I write about him I write about myself. When I write about his dog I write about myself; when I write about the house I write about myself. Man, house, dog: no matter what the word, through it I stretch out a hand to you" (19). Everything is potentially connected to everything else, and in writing about one thing, Mrs. Curren writes (reflexively) about herself and reaches toward, connects with, her daughter. In other words, the house not only represents, or symbolizes, the dog, but the house *is* the dog. This realization is necessary if Coetzee, by way of his characters, has any chance of unsettling the political and cultural, not to mention speciesist assumptions that have informed the Othering process in the West for centuries.[4] This is admittedly a large project, and far from complete. I have devoted this space to discussing dogs in South African fiction for two reasons: to gesture toward another writer working in another genre from (and about) another country, a writer who is, like McKay, thinking about nonhuman animals in a way that invites respect for humans and nonhumans alike; and to acknowledge, as Linda Hutcheon and Susie O'Brien have, a useful point of congruence between interdisciplinary ecocritical and postcolonial concerns and strategies. Simply put, I see very little difference, fundamentally, in the ideological projects of postcolonial and ecological criticism.

Poets and scientists are both engaging the sympathetic imagination in ways that do not necessarily reassert a central human consciousness as the most important consciousness operating in the world, from John Clare, who writes in "The Skylark" (186–87) of young boys encountering a bird and its nest—"O were they but a bird, / So think they while they listen to its song" (187)—to Don Kroodsma, who claims that "the fun part" of studying Bewick's wrens' songs in the field "was to think like a wren" (Stap 48). In a Canadian context, Timothy Findley's magic-realist novel *Not Wanted on the Voyage* invites, somewhat unexpectedly, an ornithological reading of a peacock. In their influential study, Bill Ashcroft, Gareth Griffiths, and Helen Tiffin argue that *Not Wanted on the Voyage* operates primarily as a "radical [postcolonial] interrogation of the story of the flood [in which] the great myth becomes a saga of destruction in the name of minority righteousness and the extension of petty power" (97). Citing an early passage from the novel, Ashcroft, Griffiths, and Tiffin highlight the postcolonial questioning of authority, ritual tradition, and power exerted by Findley's Noah as a method of controlling interpretive modes and events:

> The peacock, still maintaining the display of his tail, now lifted his head very high on his neck and gave a piercing scream.
> "You see?" said Doctor Noyes. "By every sign and signal, my decision [to have Ham perform a ritual sacrifice] is confirmed." ...
> "He's only calling to his mate, for God's sake!" said Mrs Noyes.

> "How dare you!" Doctor Noyes was livid. "How dare you take the name of God in vain. How *dare* you!"
> This sort of rage—more a performance than a reality—was necessary to keep Mrs Noyes in her place. Also, to intimidate the other women, lest they follow her example and get out of hand. (Findley 13)

This performance is also necessary, so far as an ecocritic is concerned, to emphasize Doctor Noyes's inability—or unwillingness—to read nature in non-symbolic ways. In a novel so famously applauded (and rightly so) for its *magic* realism, Mrs. Noyes's accurate ornithological response to the peacock's "scream" stands out in significant ways. Even though she does not have the power to convince her husband of the validity of her observation, she should at least convince readers that one must be careful not to read always and only figuratively. Sometimes a mating call is just a mating call. Mrs. Noyes's corrective, then, signals an alternative way of reading birds in literature, and animals more generally, by raising the question of animals' roles: Is it possible for a peacock's mating call to *be* just a mating call in a work of literature? To borrow from and build upon previous analyses of Findley's novel, I argue that the answer to that question lies in the paradoxical construction of Dr. and Mrs. Noyes's name: No and yes.[5]

While Gordimer and Simons differ on aesthetic grounds—Gordimer, for example, does not allow for reproduction in her prefatory remarks in the same way Simons does—both recognize the imaginative capacity of authors. Simons believes that culture is *reproducible* because humans have "the ability to use complex language and to communicate complex abstract ideas" about their experiences (86). The recent study that reveals starlings' capacity to comprehend recursive grammatical structures notwithstanding, Simons's decision in a book called *Animal Rights and the Politics of Literary Representation* to modify "representation" with "only" seems inappropriate and potentially damaging to his argument. That is to say, he establishes yet another demarcation between humans and nonhumans by suggesting we have culture and nonhumans do not. As I have demonstrated, avian bioacoustics openly and seriously considers song learning as cultural behaviour: "The general processes of song transmission and cultural evolution are not in doubt, but the details remain to be determined [as of 1996] for many species" (Payne 215). As with human language change, the "cultural evolution [of birdsong] is known directly only when touchstone historical records are available, and … attempts to reconstruct the past beyond these records are problematic" (Payne 219). The extensive Bioacoustics Research Program at the Cornell Lab of Ornithology represents the avian equivalent of the

Library of Alexandria, but thousands of birdsongs remain to be recorded and analyzed.

In the meantime, there is no shortage of poets ready to stretch their legs and go for a hike—I mean, undertake research in the field—to hear bird calls and songs to inhabit their poems. For birder-poets, actively listening to birds in the field provides not only contemplative fodder for their poetry, but a chance to articulate a human awareness shaped by birdsong. Paul Shepard provides an evolutionary explanation for this affinity with birds. In *The Others: How Animals Made Us Human*, Shepard argues that human cognition and physiology are the results—at least in part—of *Homo sapiens*' co-evolutionary responses to their environment, namely the nonhuman animals with whom they competed and cooperated. "It required a good brain," he suggests at one point, to hold "pattern[s] in mind—marking the creation of an auditory world in which rhythms and musical phrases such as the successive notes of birdsong are heard as a melody" (16). The ability to distinguish melodic forms of auditoria, for example, helped humans to evolve a particular system of hearing and enabled them to identify species of birds (and, presumably, non-avian species) for various reasons. Similarly, as Grandin suggests, birdsong is believed to be responsible for the development of certain human languages, or parts of languages. According to David Abram, Koyukon "names for birds are often highly onomatopoeic, so that in speaking their names one is also echoing their cries." "[T]he sounds and rhythms of the Koyukon language," Abram writes, "have been deeply nourished by these nonhuman voices" (147). In the Arctic where the Koyukon live, birds name themselves so that "the whirring, flutelike phrases of the hermit thrush, which sound in the forest thickets at twilight, speak the Koyukon words *sook'eeyis deeyo*—'it is a fine evening'" (148). Even though most active languages do not rely explicitly on birdsong or other natural sounds, the example of the Koyukon reveals a functional link, or overlap, between nature and culture. Such studies as Abram's, Bringhurst's, and Coetzee's inform a paradigm shift that is integral to modifying human relations to the nonhuman world. As I have argued earlier, McKay's notion of "wilderness" as a "placeless place beyond the [human] mind's appropriations" contributes to this shift.

A paradigm shift will likely remain incomplete, incapable of fully encompassing the English language's preference for visual metaphors. In other words, I am not advocating for a shift in the linguistic paradigm; it is clear from Marshall McLuhan's discussion of the "role of written words in shifting habits of perception from the auditory to visual stress" (29) that a linguistic shift has already taken place.[6] I am concerned with a perceptual, or phenomenological, paradigm shift that seeks to acknowledge the sense of hearing—and more particularly of an active listening—as an important sense to be engaged when observing phenomena. If, as Yuki suggests in her dissertation on acoustic ecology, hearing is a "key sense for lowering the threshold of sensory experience which has been raised by our daily existence in human-made environments" (4), listening occupies a threshold, or ecotone, between the desire to understand sounds in the environment and our actions—including writing[7]—in response to those sounds. Yuki refers to John Daniel's experience in Yosemite Valley as evidence of hearing as a threshold. In "The Impoverishment of Seeing," Daniel claims that what he remembers from his early hikes in the valley "is no particular thing [he] saw" but rather "a bird [he] couldn't see that called from around the next bend" (46), and this aural memory "leads," according to Yuki, "to a more integrated [sensory] experience" (14). So, the threshold in the case of Daniel's experience is between the call of an unseen "bird" and his memory of that call (though not, it seems, the bird itself). In *Field Notes: The Grace Note of the Canyon Wren* (1994), Barry Lopez offers a variation on this scene.

The opening story, "Introduction: Within Birds' Hearing," announces difference by foregrounding the hearing of birds, thereby positioning the narrator of the story as part of a soundscape. Despite a lengthy discussion of soundscape in *Field Notes*, Yuki does not discuss "Introduction: Within Birds' Hearing," because, I think, she is more interested in developing an understanding of Lopez's "tendency to transform the particular into the conceptual" (26). I, on the other hand, am more interested in how writers articulate precise knowledge about specific species (especially of birds) on the way to reimagining human–nonhuman relations. For my argument, Lopez's introductory story adds depth and breadth to Daniel's memory of "a bird" calling in Yosemite. Recounting a nameless narrator's journey west across the Mojave Desert toward the ocean, Lopez posits a particular bird's song, the grace note of a canyon wren, as saviour. After days of seemingly endless walking, the narrator feels he has "no good day past this one" (10). Desperate, and with bowed head, he feels defeated until, "[i]nto this agony, as if from an unsuspected room, comes a bare cascade of sound" and his "wounds go silent" (10). Recognizing the "falling *tiyew, tiyew tiyew, tiyew*" followed by "a turn at the end, *tew*" as the song of a canyon wren (10), the narrator, invigorated by the familiar notes, "fix[es] its place and move[s] into the night" until he finds himself standing in the "[h]eadwaters of the Oso," which proves enough to rejuvenate him and provides an optimistic ending to this tale of a difficult journey (10–11). Regardless of whether any bird, recognizable to the narrator or not, would have accomplished the same in similar circumstances, Lopez's decision to name the bird indicates the importance of such specificity in the work of a foremost nature writer. It indicates a willingness to concede a wisdom to the birds[8] and to think the relation between humans and nonhumans with a degree of humility and respect.

In keeping with my examination of poetic attention, especially as it functions within McKay's project of reversing the flow of current exploitive relations humans maintain with the world, I want to consider how McKay constructs and observes soundscapes in addition to landscapes. Studying sonic environments and acoustic realms uncovers "problematic aspects of our tendency to privilege vision and literacy in our relationships with the natural world" (Yuki 5), relationships that McKay claims have been "so thoroughly one-way." Not surprisingly, birdsong constitutes most of the sounds recorded by McKay. The act of listening as a mode of attention—what Abram calls "auditory attentiveness" (130)[9]—favours a propositional, as opposed to an impositional, relation to the nonhuman world,[10] contributes to a McKavian desire for proximity, and informs the impulse to move away from the text and into the physical, sonic world. If, as Abram writes, "[l]ooking and listening bring [us] into contact, respectively, with the outward surfaces and with the interior voluminosity of things," a combination of auditory and visual attentiveness reveals a "complex interplay of inside and outside" (128). Abram's choice of the term "voluminosity" to describe a sonic, phenomenological capacity implies just such a complexity.

"Voluminosity" has two meanings, both of which apply to Abram's use of the term and to my reading of McKay's soundscapes through Abram's "auditory attentiveness": (1) extensiveness of writing and (2) an instance of turning or winding. In either case, Abram's use is significant, if slightly awkward, for the way it suggests a cultural component of the more-than-human world—that is, the capacity for things to engage in a form of writing while acknowledging an interiority reminiscent of a McKavian "wilderness" ("the capacity [...] to elude the mind's appropriations"). The dual sense of voluminosity is on display in the soundscape of "Limestone" (*DW* 50–52), a prose piece from the long abecedarian "Between Rock and Stone: A Geopoetic Alphabet" (*DW* 33–73). In "Limestone," McKay contemplates the phenomenon of hearing "waterfalls or rapids break into speech" from inside his tent, functioning in this instance "like a magical ear" (50). Though no birds appear in "Limestone," the poem effectively constructs a soundscape representative of the "two modes of listening" identified by Yuki in her dissertation: "external and internal" (15). External listening refers to such sounds as birdsong, wind, moving water, and rustling leaves, while internal listening refers to the internal life of the listener, to the way a sound's fleeting nature resonates after it has gone; internal listening is related to memory. Both are present in "Limestone" when McKay mentions "the hubbub [...] inflected by the accents of the mystery language," which wakes the speaker and connects the sonic moment "lichened with strange diacritical marks" to the discovery of a fossil while "browsing along a limestone cliff or outcrop" (50–51). The soundscape dominated by the external language of "ordinary water music" extends to include geological memory represented here by the fossil, "the sudden emergence of a *coiled symmetry*, an apparent artfulness that *calls* across the eons, a compelling visual equivalent to being summoned out into the cold air of northern Ontario by one of its middle-sized rapids" (51; emphasis added). Between the water's linguistic qualities and the fossil's winding, "coiled symmetry," both of which call to the speaker—who here becomes a listener—Abram's voluminosity seems not so mystical as it initially does. The soundscape McKay presents in "Limestone" performs a central tenet of acoustic ecology—namely a reimagining of humans' exploitive, abusive relation to the physical world—by drawing attention to humans' "doggedly linguistic" tendency to "naturally process any continuous sound as a language" and thus to reinforce a distal relation to the more-than-human environment (51).[11]

Generally, McKay's soundscapes, like his poems about specific birds, compel a closer proximity to the outdoors, a proximity in sharp contrast to typical "discussions of the aesthetic value of nature and wilderness," which, according to John Andrew Fisher, "often work on an abstract level several steps removed from sensory experience" (233). In "What the Hills Are Alive With: In Defense of the Sounds of Nature," Fisher submits that "the sounds of a bird or a frog, for example, contribute greatly to the soundscape of a particular environment," yet he wants to avoid privileging "aesthetic attention directed to a bird or frog song type *abstracted* from any particular environment in which it may occur," because by filtering out ambient noise such abstraction ignores "how nature actually sounds" (233). While I can appreciate Fisher's desire to retain the integrity of represented soundscapes, I have read enough of Lilburn and McKay to know such desire necessarily, and instructively, fails. To expect a literary soundscape to include all ambient noise is a bit like expecting a painted landscape to include all that lies beyond the frame as well. As with any representation, the poet must make certain choices regarding what to emphasize and when.[12] The proximity enabled by accuracy and specificity more effectively sets in motion a rethinking of human–nonhuman relations than a "realistic" reproduction of a given soundscape (not to mention landscape), even if the latter were possible in written form.

As Fisher claims, though, "[s]ound is a huge and relatively unexplored subject" (233), so it is no wonder "acoustic ecology," not to mention birdsong, has yet to be extensively theorized in literary criticism.[13] McKay's writing, in "Limestone" and other pieces, about how humans imagine themselves in relation to place (and its otherwise) provides ample opportunity to consider listening an act as revealing as seeing. In "Approaching the Clearing" (*DW* 95–110), McKay addresses two well-known literary ideas and brings them together to reconceptualize, yet again, humans' exploitive relation to place, calling "the clearing [...] the wild ancestor of th[e] room of one's own" (97).[14] Introducing the clearing as both an idea and an actual place often experienced, "when walking through the forest," as "a pool of light where the trees relent, a place that combines seclusion with openness" (98), McKay is quick to emphasize its acoustic and imaginative aspects. Approaching a clearing, for example, "we tend to slow down and shut up"; once we arrive, "we can give our attention to other creatures – kinglets in the fringe, ravens overhead, the spotted saxifrage growing on the rock, or to the granite itself" (98). While "attention" does not necessarily imply listening, his reference to kinglets and ravens, in addition to the voluminosity of rock established in "Limestone," foregrounds the possibility that "listening dissolves the tyrannical subject of the eye" (Allen 37).

McKay's clearing is wordless but not silent, contrary to a similar clearing constructed by Archibald Lampman in "In November."[15] Lampman's speaker goes "wandering in the woods" and finds "A clearing, where the broken ground / Was scattered with black stumps and briers, / And the old wreck of forest fires" (142).[16] Although Lampman's clearing seems to anticipate McKay's attention to clear-cuts, there is no sense of human responsibility for the "stumps and briers" in his poem. Moreover, Lampman's clearing differs significantly from McKay's in its eerie silence—"There was no sound about the wood / Save the wind's secret stir" (142)—and its connection to a particular "poetic disclosure," which, according to Ronald Morrison, Thoreau and Heidegger both associated "with a 'clearing' in the forest, [...] in a way that emphasizes the interplay of what stands revealed within the clearing and what remains hidden beyond it" (143). For Lampman, as for Romantic poets more generally, the moment in the clearing represents a transcendent revelation of concealed truth. In my reading of McKay's poetry and poetics, I see the clearing as an ecotone within which the poet might listen for both lyric insight and experiential knowing.

Standing amid dead mullein stalks and goldenrod, Lampman's speaker experiences, while surrounded by "thin light," a dreamlike moment of inspiration during which time

> A moment's golden reverie
> Poured out on every plant and tree
> A semblance of weird joy, or less,
> A sort of spectral happiness;
> And I, too, standing idly there,
> With muffled hands in the chill air,
> Felt the warm glow about my feet,
> And shuddering betwixt cold and heat,
> Drew my thoughts closer, like a cloak,
> While something in my blood awoke,
> A nameless and unnatural cheer,
> A pleasure secret and austere. (143)

The secret uncovered by—awakened in the blood of—the speaker is of such an ambiguous, non-specific quality as to be rendered innocuous, yet another version of aeolian harpism translating spectral sorts of weirdness into nameless, austere pleasures. The speaker is so idle—despite his inexplicable "shuddering betwixt cold and heat"—that he is incapable of paying attention to his surroundings, especially of listening to the sounds that surely would have animated the "silent sober place" in which he stands (142). For Lampman, entering the clearing is like entering a church; for McKay, "[i]t is as though we ha[ve] entered our own listening" (*DW* 98). While McKay acknowledges Heidegger's "understanding of truth as 'unconcealment' (*aletheia*), a condition which, as the word implies, requires a preceding hiddenness" (103), he is not content simply to engage in the act of revealing some ambiguous truth in nature; "once they [nature's secrets] have been discovered," McKay writes, "we put them to use for the betterment of humanity" (102). Listening comes into play here as a mode of attention that "resists the privileging of transcendence that effectively erases the human body from wilderness participation, and avoids Romantic gestures that allow for the returned separation of humanity from nature after the weekend wilderness retreat is complete" (Bondar "Attending" 65).

McKay's poem "Après Chainsaw" (*S/S* 50) offers an instructive alternative to the Romantic notions of Lampman's "In November." "Après Chainsaw" was initially published—sans title—as a verse epilogue to "Approaching the Clearing" (*DW*).[17] As such, it functions as a way out from McKay's discussion about the clearing as acoustic space and contemporary humanity's propensity to create "an openness that is too open, defenceless, stripped of shadows, a clearing that is no longer in relation to concealment" thanks to the "donkey engine, the logging locomotive, the chainsaw, and the logging truck," in short, to "the industrialization of the forest" (107–8). After providing a brief history of the chainsaw,[18] McKay recounts a "time when, thinning out a plantation of white spruce, [he] just kept on cutting past the end of a row, caught up in that snarl of power" having created—a paradoxical term, to be sure—"a clearing that was completely [his]" (109), his own small clear-cut. The poem occurs, as its later title suggests, after this incident. The incident itself is remarkable, I think, for the way McKay admits complicity in ecological destruction (in much the same way he does when discussing his use of language against its own colonizing tendencies) and reminds himself, and us, of the dangers of such power. "Après Chainsaw" brings the poet back into a proximal relation with the clearing he has made, returns him to his "own listening":

> Everything listening at me:
> the stumps oozing resin, the birdsong
> bouncing off my head like sonar,
> the hammered air with its fading
> after-echoes. [...]
> . . . .
> What I want to say is
> somewhere a man steps
> softly into a hemlock-and-fir fringed
> pause. Heart full.
> Head empty. His lost path
> scrawls away behind him. A blue
> dragonfly with double wings zags, hovers,
> zags. A flicker he can't see
> yucks its ghost laugh
> into the thin slant light.[19] (*DW* 110)

This clearing is distinctively different from Lampman's "silent sober place"—the dying stumps are explicit reminders of human violence, as is the air echoing with the chainsaw's "remorseless" roar (109). Despite the fresh destruction, McKay's clearing is a soundscape that includes traces of human-made sound and a northern flicker's "ghost laugh." That the flicker remains unseen emphasizes the value of listening. Its laugh enters "the thin slant light," an echo of the "thin light" that surrounds Lampman's speaker: again, McKay insinuates his work into a tradition, albeit a problematic one in Canadian history, of nature poetry. More importantly, though, this clearing actively listens to—or "at," as McKay somewhat awkwardly and synesthetically has it—the speaker whose reckless actions have impacted the area, a result perhaps of his empty head. That the speaker can recognize the effects his actions have on the surrounding area in addition to the response they elicit from the listening/observing environment adds to a McKavian reversal of the exploitive relationship he mentions earlier: he holds himself accountable by showing respect for the desires and the agency of other-than-human beings.

By recognizing the agency of the more-than-human world, McKay effectively responds to Barry Lopez's complaint that European settlers "never said to the people or the animals or the plants or the rivers or the mountains: What do you think of this?" (*Rediscovery* 18). If birds are capable of "listening at" him, they are surely capable of responding in some way to such a question as Lopez poses, even if the gesture seems, as McKay suggests when he considers reading "the trail guide *to* the creature we are regarding," "both formal and absurd," except when addressed to people (*V* 65). In "Deactivated West 100" (*DW* 111–17), the final essay in the collection of the same name, McKay attempts to "undo the taxonomical ownership of the gesture," as he puts it in his interview with Ken Babstock (McKay "Appropriate" 55). Continuing an acoustic ecological approach, McKay writes about a hike along a deactivated logging road on Vancouver Island where Loss Creek valley meets the Leech River fault: "Juncos jitter in the alders. A varied thrush sends its whistle-buzz to shake and dissolve in the near-echoic air" (115). In addition to the polyphonic echo of the earlier chainsaw echo, drawing a near parallel between the small-scale damage and the wholesale clear-cutting on Vancouver Island, the birdsong here acts as an ecological marker to remind of the persistent interconnections and biodiversity. After witnessing a mother bear and her cubs, McKay heads back to his car:

> With a backward glance in the direction of the bears, he climbs down the embankment. So, he thinks, tell me about it. [...] Their talk [the columbine and saxifrage in rock crevices] is asyntactical, a small presocratic hubbub. A junco flies past him and under the bridge, tossing comments like pebble-dash; the occasional song of a Swainson's thrush postulates another stream that flows uphill; far off, and next door to the heart, the subliminal drumming of a grouse. And containing them all, the live silence of the valley, with its edges of acoustic rock and its core of impacted shadow. (116–17)[20]

The soundscape McKay describes includes the obvious songs and calls of specific birds, although it is not so inclusive as to achieve the acoustic integrity that Fisher apparently prefers. McKay chooses specific birds to identify, recognizing in the scene a set of acoustic ecological principles—the communicating sounds of dark-eyed juncos, Swainson's and varied thrushes, and ruffed grouse—framed by the voluminosity of less obvious elements, such as saxifrage and rock. (Another addition to McKay's series of songs, interestingly, is "Song of the Saxifrage to the Rock" [S/S 10], which I examine in more detail in my concluding chapter.) The "live silence of the valley" resonates with Lampman's "silent sober place" and inflects the earlier, Romantic ideal with an awareness of the various ecological relations taking place, with or without the poet's presence. When he turns his focus to the songs of specific birds, paying homage to avian singers in verse, McKay continues the project of attentive listening.

Chapter Eight

Listening

> by the porch a flock of Cedar waxwings
> has occurred to the cedars like their lost
> tribe, deft and excited, seep
> seep seeping from the frontiers of the audible.
> – Don McKay, "Little Rivers" (*SD* 28)

The closing moments of "Little Rivers" (*SD* 28) resonate clearly with McKavian listening. Presenting an early version of his idea that "[t]he porch is the ear of the house" (*DW* 19), McKay in "Little Rivers" emphasizes the importance of edge effect when paying attention to the world outside the home. The image of the birder-poet standing on a porch and craning to hear the relatively quiet song notes of cedar waxwings fittingly articulates what it means to pay attention in the McKavian sense. Because of the colonial legacies of the English language and the Western human desire for ownership, the birder-poet and the ecocritic must position themselves at the edge and crane toward the more-than-human world, which is always only "seeping from the frontiers of the audible," and listen. The porch offers an apt spot for the birder-poet to experience the outside while comfortably within the house's interior. In "Song for the Song of the Sandhill Crane" (*P* 7), McKay interrogates his own trope—but this time, the porch exists between domestic/wild space *and* between domesticated/wild time. The crane's song pushes at the limits of hearing the way heavy bass at a concert thumps inside chests: "It eschews the ear," says the birder-poet, "with its toolshed, its lab, its Centre for Advanced / Studies in Hermeneutics and Gossip, / to boom exactly in my thorax" (61). The act of listening, important though it is for poetic attention, relies upon a set of cultural markers that more or less distort sounds. The search for meaning and the associations we make when hearing sounds ultimately maintain a distance between us and the sound's source.

The crane's song bypasses the birder-poet's cultural processes, embodying millennia of evolutionary stability while he hovers safely between, a point that forms the poem's crux:

> Why am I standing on this frigid porch
> in my pajamas, peering into the mist
> which rises in little spirals from the pond?
> Where they call from the blue
> has nearly thinned to no-colour-
> clear. Where
> they call from hominids haven't yet
> happened. Garroo: (61)

The question applies to the poem's speaker as well as to the birder-poet—and all birders, all poets, perhaps—more generally. Unlike the waxwings "seeping from the frontiers of the audible," the cranes have been inhabiting the audible since long before the present, booming from beyond and before human language. In eschewing the ear, the crane's song communicates nothing other than its ancientness, its wilderness inviting curious introspection from the edges. The porch and the pond, the latter of which, McKay writes elsewhere, "gathers in its edge" such things as "pollen, heron, leaves, larvae, greater / and lesser scaup" (*S/S* 12), receive the crane's guttural "Garroo," hold it, and don't know what else to do. "[W]ho can bear those star-river distances?" the speaker ponders, referring to the Milky Way's cosmic aloofness. What the listening ear wants is to get closer. Craning from the edge between mist and kitchen, it wants to get closer.

One of McKay's earlier poems, "Listen at the Edge" (*B* 123), succinctly posits listening on a threshold between human language and the more-than-human song that the poet can only gesture toward onomatopoeically. The onomatopoeia, as metaphorical gesture, is a common recourse for the writers of field guides "when attempting descriptions of songs and calls," despite their tendency to consider the language of field guides and reference books "as clinically awe-free" with their "terse asyntactical bursts of fact" (*V* 85). To the contrary, McKay suggests such descriptions—the call of the Swainson's thrush, for example, compared to "the sound of a drop of water in a barrel": *whoit* (85)—are "mini-poems" that often contain "the point of greatest descriptive accuracy" in their ability to stick in the reader's memory; to help him become a better listener (85).

In "Listen at the Edge," both poet and reader stand "At the edge of firelight," where every word is shadowed by its animal, our ears

are empty auditoria for
scritch scritch scritch rr-ronk the
shh uh shh of greater

anonymities the little
brouhahas that won't lie still for type
and die (*B* 123)

Despite all the words humans have for birds and mammals, despite "the information [in] our voices," plenty of space remains in our imaginations for the actual beings and the songs they sing, those "little / brouhahas that won't lie still for type / and die." In this poem I identify a strategy to begin measuring a McKavian resistance to the poststructuralist orthodoxy "to doubt—at least in the seminar room—that there is a world which precedes or exists outside the text" (McKay *V* 62). If McKay, Bringhurst, Zwicky, and Lilburn are listening at all, they are listening to what language represents: "no language is thinkable that bears no relation to the world" (Wittgenstein, qtd. in Zwicky *Wisdom* Right 29). Elsewhere, Zwicky extols the role of imagination in seeing what is there, in "seeing-as"; however, "[f]rom this," she argues, "it does not follow ... that the world 'exists' only in our collective cultural mind" (25). The world exists without human language or understanding. We did not construct that yellow poplar or that barn swallow. We named them, and in having named them we measure their existence in relation to us; we have interpreted, but we have not defined them.

Indeed, as the speaker in "Song for the Song of the Canada Geese" (*P* 5) implies, human language itself might depend upon avian voices. The poem develops this notion of reciprocity around an onomatopoeic rendering of the geese's well-known honk. In the voices of the geese, the speaker hears "something of that famous mortal reed / making an oboe of the throat. / As though the soul / not / so much in pain as under pressure / yelped. Angst, / angst." Both the reference to the mythological reed—the lyre associated with Hermes and Orpheus, or the pipe of Pan—and the word "angst" grant the geese a measure of poetic agency. The onomatopoeia, too, indicates a spectrum of feelings that helps explain the growing distaste on the part of humans for Canada geese that remain in parks and near watercourses instead of migrating south, as is their evolutionary wont. The angst expressed in the birds' voices announces their own anxiety, anguish, and neurotic fear over their vulnerable position in urban space and, perhaps, a sense of uncertainty over their stasis. Also in their voices resides a sense of guilt and remorse that human listeners project onto themselves, as if the geese's "angst, angst" were blaming humans for having altered the natural environment to such an extent that the geese no longer need to take their chances flying south for the winter. Humans have fed geese for years, usually from benches set up within so-called green spaces. The attempt to provide a more natural space for urban and suburban dwellers has succeeded too well: the geese will not leave because they have a continuous supply of food and water, and the geese create quite a mess.

McKay captures the paradox nicely by drawing a fundamental connection between the angstful honking and a human need for speech, which for the birder-poet trumps all else. "So what," he says,

> if they waddle, shit
> goose shit on the grass all summer then neglect
> to migrate? Were the geese to quit
> their existential yammer, talk
> would also cease, each would-be dialogue collapse
> into its own hole. Where there was ivy,
> ice. Ice
> where there was moss.

The suggestion that geese honking amounts to existential yammer resists accusations of simple anthropomorphism because the utterance, which McKay articulates with nasal precision when reading the poem for *Songs for the Songs of Birds*, implicates the listener in a cross-species dialogue that cannot help but be existential. The hole into which potential dialogue would fall in the absence of geese resembles a winter scene bereft of colour and song. For all that the geese annoy and befoul as they adapt to changing environmental conditions (including the offer of food from urbanites), they at least provide a presence against which humans can measure their thoughts and actions. The birder-poet's homage reaches its nadir in the final lines: "All praise to the geese / in their goosiness, to the ragged arrow that is / and isn't eros." Here the birder-poet offers an explicit resistance to the anthropomorphism of the earlier lines: the geese are valuable in and of themselves, because of their goosiness. The arrow characteristic of flocks in flight simultaneously represents a human desire to fly (and, perhaps, to be comfortable and angst-free in our relations to the earth) and signifies itself, an aerodynamic V-formation that enables the geese to cover long distances with minimal effort and to communicate with their existential cries.

"Listen at the Edge" ends with a short line describing bird and animal songs as "ohms of speech." If poetic attention is "a recognition and a valuing of the other's wilderness," if it enacts a form of homage vis-à-vis the Other, the metaplasmic shift from homage to ohmage enables poetry to gesture—without fear of failure—toward the eros of measurement, the desire to know, and so to name, the Other (*V* 28). But because ohmage originates in this context with nonhumans, the current in the human–nonhuman relation is seemingly reversed. However, McKay's poetics is not as evolutionary as Michael Pollan's argument, in *The Botany of Desire*, that "it makes as much sense to think of agriculture as something grasses did to people as a way to conquer the trees" (xxi). McKay's poetics reflects, more accurately, a mode of engagement put forth by J. M. Coetzee's alter ego Elizabeth Costello in *The Lives of Animals* (1999), a poetics that "does not try to find an idea in the animal, that is not about the animal, but is instead a record of engagement with him" (51). McKay's record of engagement with nonhumans, for all his respectful observation and homage, is also a record of the poet's active listening, as distinct from his passive hearing.

McKay extends his understanding of active ecological listening to the editorial and publication process, recognizing "a quality of attention that is the nerves and sinews of community," which he calls "*audience*" ("Common Sense" 235; emphasis in original). His emphasis on the word "audience" resonates with his emphasis on a poem's sound and on how it enacts a listening that readers can identify and to which they can attend. A collection of poetry is effectively a soundscape; poetry is "written with the ear. If you don't hear something, it's not working" ("Appropriate" 47). And if it is not working—aurally, lyrically, ecologically—it ceases to be of any real use in a public context and fails "to make a place for nature within public life" (Latour 2)—that is, in the relations between the world, the text, and the audience.

One of McKay's projects as poet and editor concerns actively engaging with the tensions between language (poetry) and matter (poetic subjects). More specifically, McKay's interests, at least as they play out in his own writing, lie in attempting to portray a humble relation between word and world that calls into question the colonial impulse of the (human) writer while simultaneously paying homage to the (nonhuman) others about which he writes. The measure of this relation, the distance between word and world that manifests itself in homage, occurs in a style of wordplay endemic to McKay's oeuvre—namely, metaplasm. Donna Haraway's notion of "metaplasm," as a term with linguistic and biological implications, operates at the level of poetics by emphasizing McKay's practice of simultaneous homage and what I call ohmage. Where homage is a form of respectful remembrance of and address to another, ohmage is a form of measurement—literally of electrical resistance (ohms) and metaphorically of another's resistance, conscious or not, to being made into metaphor. Ohmage is homage with the current reversed. In other words, both homage and ohmage position poet and reader in relation to someone, or something, else: while the former acknowledges the fact of the relation, the latter attempts to measure the relation, to articulate linguistically a non-linguistic phenomenal relationality.

In *The Companion Species Manifesto: Dogs, People, and Significant Otherness*, Haraway co-opts the term "metaplasm" to articulate a linguistic mode of rethinking humans' relation to the nonhuman world and to refer to what she calls, in her own metaplasmic moment, "the remodeling of dog and human flesh, remolding the codes of life, in the history of companion-species relating" (20). Haraway's attention to linguistic tropes in a book ostensibly about dog training implies a relation between metaplasm and listening toward which McKay often gestures in his writing. I use the term metaplasm in two ways: first, in the tropic sense Haraway acknowledges (from the Greek, *meta*, denoting change, and *plasmus*, to mould or form), to refer to what I recognize as particularly McKavian movements between, for example, homage and ohmage, grave and gravel, loop and pool, thrush and thresh(hold), material and matériel; and second, in the biological sense Haraway neglects to acknowledge (which botanist J. von Hanstein developed into the German *metaplasma*), which refers to the granular, dead portion of cytoplasm within a cell.[1] This dual sense of metaplasm makes space for both the linguistic and the scientific in McKay's poetry; but, more importantly, McKay insinuates the speakers of the poems under discussion into the spaces between each sense of metaplasm, effectively positioning readers between the two meanings and inviting them (the readers) to consider an active correspondence between the metaphorical and ecological aspects of his poetry.

Integral to this ecopoetical project of measuring the distance between, for example, poet and bushtit is the production of both poetry and a listening audience. Much as a reader scans a line of verse, or an electrician measures resistance in a circuit, to position herself in relation to the potential wisdom of the poem, or the kinetic power of the current, McKay cultivates a humble listening (necessary to enact both homage and ohmage) by carefully mentoring other poets whose work will eventually reach an audience. McKay's relation to other poets' work, such as Dennis Lee's critical work on poetry and cadence and Ken Babstock's poetry, exemplifies how poetic lives are informed by and shaped within public culture, particularly that of book publishing and public readings. In addition to following a trail of linguistic and scientific referents in McKay's writing toward an ecological poetics, I am interested in measuring the degree of editorial influence in Babstock's first collection of poetry as a way of determining an ecology of listening. To this end, I borrow from philosopher Bruno Latour a desire to slow things down a bit, "not to save time, to speed up, to synthesize masses of data, to solve urgent problems in a hurry," but rather to spend time, to slow down, to analyze data, to pose urgent questions (6). Such an approach resonates nicely with poet and critic Brian Bartlett's argument that McKay's poems "show what it means to be at once attentive and energetic, provoking and exhilarating. Festina lente [Hurry slowly]" ("Dog's Nose" 129).

Acknowledgements are public (because published)[2] recognition of private listening. Of all the thanks to McKay I have read,[3] Ken Babstock's Acknowledgements at the end of *Mean* offer perhaps the richest way in to a consideration of his editorial presence: "My editor, Don McKay ("UncleLear"), deserves all the credit for transforming a bunch of almost-poems into a book" (83). Babstock signals at least three things about McKay's editorial relation to *Mean* when he names his editor "UncleLear." First, I read this as Babstock's marking of the obvious age difference between McKay (b. 1942) and him (b. 1970) combined with the Shakespearian connotations of King Lear as tragic hero, madman, and blind poet—as someone who, in short, occupies a place of dubious, because human, wisdom gleaned from decades of reading and experience. Second, and this is perhaps a more fittingly aural signal, I read Babstock acknowledging McKay's keen editorial ear; he is Uncle Ear, the one who actively listens. Third, I read, or rather I hear, something that requires a trick of metaplasm, the dropping of two letters, the slurring of a tri-syllabic term into a bisyllabic one so that UncleLear becomes, paradoxically, Unclear. That Babstock's naming communicates all three is germane to my metaplasmic argument: by simply removing the space between Uncle and Lear, Babstock simultaneously pays homage to his editor and performs an act of ohmage, effectively measuring the impact—influential and paradoxical—McKay's listening had on his first collection.

An editor's active listening can be both attentive and unclear; the contradiction, the lack of clarity reminiscent of metaplasm in biological terms, functions to help negotiate the tensions between listening with the ear and on the page, between the clarity of editorial attention and the opacity of linguistic gesture. Haraway has something similar in mind when she uses metaplasm to express an attention to the more-than-human world that resists conventional assumptions about human–nonhuman relations. By extension, metaplasm, in both the tropic and biological senses of the word, enables McKay's notion of *matériel* to develop as a working—as distinct from fixed—component of his ecological poetics.[4]

Listening, then, depends upon the poet's ability to remain on the porch, to position himself on the edge between speech and silence, waiting to hear songs of knowing "seeping from the frontiers of the audible." In "Song for the Song of the Coyote" (*AG* 9), the poet "listen[s] in the tent, [his] ear / to the ground" as the coyotes sing to the "thin / used-up light" of the land: "Riverless. Treeless." The coyotes' song "articulate[s] the buttes and coulees and dissolve[s] / into the darkness which is always listening" and which "Echoes" tremulously in reply (9). The description of the land, according to the coyotes' song and its echo, is more moonscape than landscape, an otherworldly place "that can only wear its scars, every crater etched"; indeed, the poem opens with an address to the coyotes as "Moondogs, moondogs" (9). As one of the central thematic figures of *Another Gravity*, the moon represents a McKavian mode of scanning the world that belies the notion of language as a purely human construct. Acknowledging the limits of language while working *with* language, McKay traces the etymology of "moon," revealing how humans have developed a syntax of measurement, how something outside the text informs the text. In "New Moon" (38), he provides a partial etymology: "*mene* (Gk.) whence menses, month, the first long / measure" so that finally "metre, as measure / enters the sentence" (38). The measurement initiated by the word "moon" is a measurement informed by cyclical phases of the moon, a measurement of time, the "slow pulse" of which recalls the breathing electric energy of birds, or the pulsing rhythm of a wolf sprinting down the middle of a road, to whom McKay's poem pays homage.

This measurement of the distance "between thought and things, or words and world" (Critchley 185)—what I have been calling ohmage—represents phenomenological poetic experience; it functions both as symbolic gesture (metaphor, homage) and as realistic gesture (humility, haecceity). For McKay and Babstock, as for Wallace Stevens, "the poet must not lead us away from the real" (Critchley 186) even as readers, poets, and ecocritics are acutely aware of "the real" as enigma. The paradox is neither debilitating nor simplistic, but rather creative and complex: ecocritics with an eye and an ear to both the phenomenal world in itself and the way in which humans perceive phenomena linguistically are learning to sing, as the wood thrush does, two songs at once when writing about such poetry.[5] When I write of an ecology of listening, I want to invite readers along a trail of referents that include Barry Commoner's first law of ecology—"Everything is connected to everything else" (29)—as well as some version of the standard scientific definition (the study of the relationships between living organisms and their biotic and abiotic environment). McKay's ongoing series of songs for the songs of specific birds enables such an inclusive approach.

In *Vis à Vis*, McKay argues that "a poem, or poem-in waiting, contemplates what language can't do: then it does something with language—in homage, or grief, or anger, or praise" (87). His "Songs" in homage to some of the more-than-human creatures that inhabit his poetry reveal a reverence for the song and its singer, and they attempt to respond with an appropriate poetic gesture. But each song is inevitably an appropriation, albeit one "with the current reversed" (*V* 99); the birder-poet, aware of the perils of appropriation, pays attention to the coyote or the chipping sparrow and enacts a listening on the page, reversing the popular ideological current vis-à-vis the environment. Combining his acumen for metaphor with attention to biological detail that gestures toward natural history, McKay brings readers closer to a particular species and invites them to know that species beyond (perhaps even prior to) its construction as a symbolic entity. Two poems from *Apparatus* exhibit a McKavian enactment of listening: "Song for the Song of the Varied Thrush" (26) and "Song for the Song of the Wood Thrush" (27).

In "Song for the Song of the Varied Thrush," the poet listens to "the single note" and observes "its // un-inflected but electric" line; the poet, in turn, renders his own song as a single sentence broken into single-lined stanzas to show not only what he hears but how he listens. The spaces between each line represent the pauses that follow each of the thrush's single notes and work with the lines themselves to create a ruled look on the page:

> once more on a lower or a higher pitch and
>
> in this newly minted
>
> interval you realize the wilderness
>
> between one breath
>
> and another. (*A* 26)

In this homage to the varied thrush, the electric energy of the thrush's breathing is itself a form of ohmage, a way of measuring the thrush's song and its imprint on the poet's listening. The addressee (the "you") is both an implied listener and the varied thrush himself. In the first instance, the listener learns to appreciate the capacity of the thrush's song to "elude the mind's appropriations" (*V* 21). In the second instance, the thrush, simply by singing his song, makes "the wilderness / between" breaths *real*, makes it matter, makes it mean the way barbed wire in another McKay poem makes "the meadow meadow" by creating boundaries between cultivated and uncultivated land.[6]

The birder-poet is not always comfortable with his poetry, however, because he is aware of the problematics of reference once linguistic composition begins—"that problematic interface between language and the world" ("Appropriate" 46). And yet part of McKay's ecological project attempts to return poet and reader alike to the trail, "to the grain of the experience," prior to its realization as text (*V* 27). McKay articulates this paradoxical position perhaps no more clearly and concisely than in "Song for the Song of the Wood Thrush," when he writes somewhat enigmatically that "Poetry / clatters." Positioned as it is on the page facing "Varied Thrush," "Wood Thrush" certainly *looks* more clattery than the former poem with its full stops ("Varied Thrush" unfolds as one full sentence) and its condensed spacing on the page. Moreover, "the old contraption pumping / iambs" in the poet's chest "is going to take a break / and sing a little something" instead of relying on the strictures of conventional metre (27). The poet's iambs here beat as a heart beats and exceed the limits of measurement, as if elastic, plastic, clattery. Amazingly, though, "[t]he Wood Thrush can sing a duet by itself, using two separate voices" (Greenewalt, qtd. in Gill *Ornithology* 240); instead of hearing a *single* note, the poet acknowledges the avian polyphony and his "ear / inhales the evening." Subsequently, in the face of such acoustic accomplishments, "only the offhand is acceptable" as a human response (McKay *A* 27). Reviewing *Apparatus* in *Books in Canada*, Richard Greene claims that "[t]o declare one's offhandedness in a self-conscious manner is an obvious contradiction, and a pretentious one" (27). Greene, it seems to me, is not paying attention in the McKavian sense. If he were to step outside language for a moment and listen, he might realize that the declaration of Poetry's offhandedness in this particular context is not pretentious at all. Compared to the wood thrush's vocal abilities, the way it transgresses acoustic thresholds humans can barely imagine, the self-interested page-blackening we call poetry clatters *at best*. Consequently, McKay sets the offhand—the impromptu and distinctively *un*pretentious—against Poetry, capitalized here not incidentally as a way to represent and value the more-than-human world with a measure of humility. Far from being idealized by McKay as the *best* way to represent nonhumans, Poetry is clearly, in its orderly, structured manner, *un*acceptable. Instead, McKay's verse, seemingly free yet inflected and infected with traces of pentameter—"The old contraption pumping"—pays homage to the wood thrush's articulation of a "place / between desire and memory," a place humans "can neither wish for nor recall" (27). It is beyond human language, and hence beyond such formalized modes of address as iambic pentameter and book reviews.

The acoustic threshold sung by the thrushes articulates an ecotonal space that invites clumsy attempts at homage. In much the same way, though with perhaps fewer vocal acrobatics, the common loon represents a threshold confronted by the birder-poet. Despite having been co-opted by the nature-porn industry, the loon song remains for McKay a "riveting" example of avian acoustics. As he reveals while introducing "Song for the Song of the Common Loon" (*S* n.pag.), the ubiquitous sound manages to "throw [listeners] subtly into a deep existential longing." Years before composing his homage to/ohmage of the loon's song, though, McKay published "Some Exercises on the Cry of the Loon" (*B* 105). As with many of his poems about birdsong, McKay presents flight and song as twin desires, although in the case of the loon, diving replaces flight. The exercises he suggests demonstrate a characteristic sense of futility, as though no gesture, linguistic or otherwise, will suffice to represent the loon's music. You can "Write a book about it," he suggests, "and tear out all the pages. / Drop your rake and jump into the ditch, then / climb out and continue raking." Somehow the cry of the loon evokes the loon's ability to cross water's threshold to live a submerged existence and return, as if such an act were as common as breathing or drinking. But there is risk involved in these exercises. They should not, for example, be considered while driving (and thus staring into a partially reflective windshield), but rather "while you brush your teeth," when you can observe in the mirror "for that split / second at the break your reflection vanishes / to drink the crystal whisky on the other side." Rather than attempt to mimic the loon's cry, McKay lingers at and on the threshold between what he knows (what's observable) and the unknowable. He imagines the other side as a mystical place to which only the soul has access. Even in the imaginative exercise the speaker recommends sipping the whisky carefully "on the porches of our minds." If this poem evokes the cry of the loon at all, it does so by echoing images of thresholds. But the relative comfort of domestic images—raking leaves, brushing teeth, drinking whisky, sitting on a porch—admits reluctance, indeed a failure on the part of the birder-poet. The exercises remain unsatisfactory attempts for over twenty-five years until McKay writes "Song for the Song of the Common Loon." He is by now, ostensibly, confident enough with his avian poetics to pay homage to/measure ohmage of this most riveting of sounds.

The confidence of a mature poet notwithstanding, McKay has cultivated a voice at once capable of sophisticated metaphorical acuity and skeptical of his language's capacity to articulate precise truths about the physical world. If this paradox, central to his poetics, proves difficult to accept as anything more than contradiction, at best, or lack of skill, at worst, consider the way McKay revisits the call of the loon later in life, the way he patiently hones his craft for nearly three decades before attempting another poetic exercise. Perhaps because the loon call is, as McKay notes, overly familiar yet uncannily riveting, the more recent poem comprises so many McKavian themes in such a concise form. As much as it pays homage to the loon's song, the poem voices a lament for a particularly human behaviour and its concomitant environmental effects. "Song for the Song of the Common Loon" (*P* 10) provides an elegiac explanation for why the birder-poet experiences deep existential longing when hearing it. The song acts like a "feral / ultrasound with its dreadful / diagnostic reverb," revealing in its sadness something of the human condition. The song, having left the listener's ear "full of its emptiness, / bereft," sounds elemental and ancient, as if time itself "has finally found its syrinx and for a moment / lets itself be voice," compelling the speaker to remark: "Jesus, / what perilous music!"[7] The exclamation—appropriately muted in McKay's reading—expresses both awe and bereavement, aware as it is of the loon's diagnosis, to which the birder-poet attends against his better judgment, resigned to "be stricken" by the loon's throat music.

The spectre of diagnosis propels the poem to a conclusion that once again implicates humans in behavioural practices responsible for violence against humans and nonhumans. What does the cry of the loon tell us about ourselves? Why does it—like the bird itself—always seem to have gone before we can locate it properly? To get at an answer, the birder-poet resists the temptation to plug his ears against the always disappearing diagnostic song; he prefers to suspect

> that it is right now flying to star river –
> as the ancients called the Milky Way – that in
> fact it is already there,
> yodelling for no one and
> ignoring us, the collectors,
> with our heads full of closets,
> our hearts full of ovens,
> and our sad feet.

In attempting to determine why loon song throws the listener into a deep existential longing, McKay fashions a response to the related question, which he poses in "Otherwise Than Place": "what am I to the beach?" The answer is, at least potentially, nothing. The song of the loon ignores us, just as the sandhill crane's eschews the ear. And in ignoring, it castigates us for our habit of collecting, which has proven devastating to bird and human populations alike. But the accusatory note with which rational thought and emotional desire are inflected causes less dread than the accusation implied in the final line. Reminiscent of the "sad / dumb sadness" of the hiker's ass as it resigns itself to a life of groundedness, "our sad feet" remind us of our inability to fly like the birds. Desire and the practice of birding (and of writing) enable the birder-poet to accept his limitations; but the thought that a bird willingly ignores humans because they cannot fly seems particularly devastating, as though some connection existed between "our heads full of closets, / our hearts full of ovens, / and our sad feet." The realization that he is nothing to the loon triggers the birder-poet's existential longing. It is a desire to be accepted by the birds that he watches, a desire to complete the gift of homage while enacting ohmage, which is a gesture toward measurement without the numbers and categories associated with earlier collectors.

The poem, as with McKay's poetry more generally, succeeds in communicating his gestural gifts to readers. For those who also "would rather be stricken" by the "dreadful / diagnostic reverb" of the loon's song than remain contemptuous of humans' place in global ecology, McKay's songs for the songs of avian singers offer spaces from which to consider their own uneasy position in the physical world. More and more poets and scholars are listening to what Bringhurst calls "the language of the world" ("Poetry" 162) and making connections between poetry and science, between nature and culture.[8] This is important work if we are to staunch the environmental wound into which we continue to pour the vinegar of our arrogance. One way to continue this work is to slow down and pay attention to the myriad connections we might not be compelled to notice. Otherwise we risk ending up like the speaker in Babstock's "Wolf" who has to "turn in [his] seat to watch / the blur of hind legs" disappear into the poet's imagination, a missed opportunity for seeing the wolf as a wolf, for a change (53). As Latour argues, "In order to force ourselves to slow down, we will have to deal *simultaneously* with the sciences, with natures, and with politics, in the plural" (3). The simultaneity and the plurality of Latour's argument point to a problematics that McKay's poetry is equipped to negotiate. That Latour neglects to include poetry, or the arts for that matter, in his project of bringing the sciences into democracy speaks volumes of the continuing need for sharing ecological consciousness in social spheres that are plural: both public and private, both literary and scientific, both linguistic and kinetic. It seems to me that McKay, through his listening and his writing, through his editorial and his metaplasmic relations, enacts such a plurality while slowing his readers down and offering various trailheads, entrances to paths that lead toward a clearing, a soundscape, an edge from which they might listen and be listened at.

ecotone three

> The act of observation, be it of a micro-particle, a primitive society, or a stretch of deserted landscape, has already altered that which is being observed—altered it by the mere fact of the observer's presence.
> – Dennis Lee, *Savage Fields* (7)

FIELD NOTES

> I forget: why are there broken birds
> behind me; words, goddammit, words.
> – John Thompson, "Ghazal VIII" (114)

> If to record is to love the world,
> let this be an entry.
> – Roo Borson, "Snake" (24)

The field guide might sometimes help with a species identification in the field, but often there isn't time to flip, find, and identify in situ. Often the field guide is of more use after returning from the field. Once BC has had a chance to review whatever notes he's made in the day's margins, as it were. C. Bernstein advises the birder to "[c]ompare your sighting with books only after the notes are made. Having the book at hand during the note-taking will only interfere with the process.... The description often is that of the picture in the book, *not* of the actual live bird seen" ("Details" 2). Once observed, though, identifying characteristics—field marks—have a tendency simply to disappear, as memories often do. Something else is needed, BC thinks, to bring marks and guide together: call it, as Gabriele Helms does, "striv[ing] for affirmative praxis" by way of note-taking (46); embrace Ricou's argument that "the act of writing, and rewriting, is essentially a mode of thinking"

(*Arbutus* 135). Making notes in the field enables a mode of thinking that destabilizes the imperial authority of the written word—and hence of conventional knowledge. Paradoxically, by making notes toward naming, BC engages a "radical process of demythologizing the systems that threaten to define" the natural world, effectively "uninvent[ing] the world," as Robert Kroetsch would have it ("Unhiding" 394). For BC, on first arriving on the west coast, the idea of making notes was persistently absent, even when he consulted *The Sibley Guide to Birds*, which he'd purchased on a whim in Toronto. He made a mental note on the flight pattern of a bird silhouetted against a typical northwest coast sky (grey) and flying from treetop to treetop, the familiar level flight punctuated by brief flapping, with wingbeats almost entirely below the horizontal plane. Reaching page 351 in the Sibley guide, BC saw the Steller's jay and the blue jay side by side for the first time, and saw too for the first time, on the Steller's, that conspicuously ravenish hood—on the page and not in the field. Birds, whether on the west coast of North America or elsewhere, bring us, all of us, closer to the observation of natural life forms if we, all of we, so choose to be brought. This place, this bioregion, strikes BC as both a theoretically and a geographically significant marker of newness relative to human and geological history. Or, not newness exactly, but of the impulse to stop expanding and take a walk in a place newly acknowledged, to turn and look at one's environment.

> Tues 17 Oct,
> walking dog after dinner, noticed long line of crows flying east—hundreds, too many to count; is this a usual occurrence?

> Wed 18 Oct,
> walked dog at same time as yesterday—saw crows again, tho not quite as many—where are they going?

BC consults books, searching for a key or a legend—some piece of a map he doesn't yet hold. He reads George Levine: "I take the arbitrariness of naming as part of the pleasure of birding, a continuing revelation of the ways in which 'nature' and human conventions and consciousness are always intermingled and never in entirely satisfactory relation" (*Lifebirds* 153). Identifying a particular bird correctly, as McKay suggests, does have "its indisputable satisfactions" as "one of the pleasures of system to which us big brains are addicted" (*V* 84), but the name addict might presume his pleasure is more important, ontologically, than it is.

Sitting down in a small clearing, BC recalls reading Martin Heidegger in an undergrad seminar. Heidegger's reading of Stefan George's poem "Words" resonates here, albeit in tension with BC's birding tendencies. George's poem ends with the line "Where word breaks off no thing may be," a claim for the power of language—Western European human language—not only to classify and catalogue things in the world but, by naming, to speak things into existence. This is a long way from Lilburn's sense of courtesy; it's a long way from the idea of birding as a non-violent participatory activity. As Heidegger writes in his reading of the poem, "Where the word is missing, there is no thing. It is only a word at our disposal which endows the thing with Being" ("Words" 141). If a tree falls in the forest, right? BC turns to an early McKay poem, "Black Spruce" (*SD* 10), in which the speaker offers a parody—repetition with critical difference—of the pseudo-philosophical question If a tree falls in the forest, and no one's around to hear it, does it make a sound?

> If the earth moves for two
> people screwing does it stand still for the moose?

Of course not, BC says aloud, shaking his head and smiling at McKay's innovation: it moves for the moose, too. But only to the extent that the earth is always moving. Spinning on its axis. Orbiting the sun. And if it moves for the two people and the moose, it moves for those crows he's been seeing around sunset each night for the past month. In the metaphorical sense that the phrase "the earth moved" has come to imply, however, the earth does indeed stand still for the moose (and the crows). But the moose are likely to hear a tree falling, even if the two people in McKay's poem are too preoccupied to notice.

Other academics—BC occasionally forgets that he's an academic, that he's supposed to be writing a manuscript from the notes he makes each day in the field and the office—have been thinking about the relation between words and birds (well, and the rest of the world). In addition to the Csezław Miłosz bit about jays, BC often returns to a passage by Alberto Manguel, in part because it reminds BC of a bird he can't see in Vancouver:

> *Outside my window is a cardinal.* There is no way of writing this sentence without dragging in its tow whole libraries of literary allusions. The frame of the window and the margins of the page entrap the bird that serves as a sign for any bird, just

as any bird serves as a sign for any idea. [...] I wonder, corrupt with reading, if there ever was a moment when this sentence—*outside my window is a cardinal*—was not an artifice; when the blood-red bird on a steel-blue tree was quietly surprising, and nothing urged me to translate it, to domesticate it into a textual enclosure, to become its literary taxidermist. I wonder if there ever was a moment when a cardinal outside my window sat there in blazing splendour signifying nothing. (qtd. in Gibson 17)

Is every linguistic act an act of appropriation and domestication? Are notes gestures of "literary taxidermy"? If so, what are the implications for BC's research? What about SueEllen Campbell's distinction between the postmodern conception of signification and the ecological imperative to acknowledge the apartness of the more-than-human world? BC returns to Campbell's essay, which is in *The Ecocriticism Reader*, the first collection of essays from thinkers who represent something like a community of scholars to which BC feels he might belong. In one passage, she seems to be responding to Manguel's wonderment vis-à-vis cardinals as signifiers: "Lacan sees the human being as a text; Derrida argues that everything is text in the sense that everything signifies something else. But ecology insists that we pay attention not to the way things have meaning for us, but to the way the rest of the world—the nonhuman part—exists apart from us and our languages" (133). Not that ecologists don't use language, too, and often in far less reflexive ways than poets and critics. But the insistence on paying attention, that's key. The proximity BC is looking for can never *not* be informed by language, literary allusions, or even by the biases of supposedly objective scientific research. The extreme alternative would be a complete return to nature, where BC could learn from the birds themselves how they think and act. But that would, in a sense, be a way of ignoring human nature as it manifests in human culture. BC gets up and starts walking home, hoping to see some more birds on the way. Paused to think in the clearing, he was distracted from the work of paying attention.

Days later, more research uncovers some of the mystery of the nightly crow commute, which BC has come to assume ends at a roosting site. The first clue arrives when he is next on campus: a few slips of paper from Lisa Szabo, a colleague researching John "Wildwood" Winson, for her master's thesis, "Wildwood Notes: Nature Writing, Music, and Newspapers," rest invitingly in BC's office mailbox. According to Lisa, Wildwood wrote two columns for Vancouver's *Daily Province* between 1918 and 1954—"Open

Air Jottings" and "Along Wildwood Trails." This particular clue, however, comes not from one of Wildwood's columns but from an article by Donald W. Gillingham on 17 November 1923. Commenting in what looks to have been a regular feature, called "Bird Life in British Columbia," Gillingham remarks that in November "crows assemble in vast number in the Fraser delta, and one would not be far wrong in saying that crows migrate" (26). If the crows BC has been observing were "migrating" to the Fraser delta, though, they would be heading south, not east. Perhaps, over the years, crows choose different nightly roosting sites. This tidbit from Lisa—some of the best field notes come from friends and colleagues—compels BC to find out what these crows are doing and where they are going. The impulse to follow this trail, though, quickly fades—he doesn't have a car—and BC decides instead to look for birds in Donna Bennett and Russell Brown's Canadian-literature anthology.

After dinner he packs the anthology along with a couple of flasks—one with milky Earl Grey, the other with cheap whisky—and heads into the cool autumn evening. Just a few blocks away, the narrow beach provides neither sandy comfort nor the human traffic of Kits Beach to the east or Spanish Banks further west. He's often the only person on this modest strand, watching the sunset, reading a book, walking the dog. (The previous January, BC took Mackenzie down for a walk around midnight. Snow had just begun lightly falling, a rare and welcome occurrence for Vancouver. The sky, mottled with clouds over downtown and Stanley Park, admitted enough light from a waxing moon to illuminate the foreshore. BC and Mackenzie witnessed the scene in sepia tones. A great blue heron stood in the shallows close to shore, waiting for a reason to wade to another spot. It held a familiar pose that night as it stared intently into the quiet water. In all likelihood, this heron was part of the Stanley Park heronry, a colony that nests in a copse between condos, tennis courts, and parking lots. That colony is a story of adaptation that probably annoys some urbanites, a story reminiscent of humans' adaptive abilities. None of these details occurred to BC that January night as he watched the heron look up, pause for a second, and catch a snowflake in its bill, then another, momentarily distracted from whatever it was doing before. Did it take the snowflakes for food, insects descending from treetops across the bay? Or was the heron simply, and not so simply, playing?) This evening, late October, a few walkers make their way along the shore, the low tide allowing access for a long stretch. With just an hour before sunset, BC finds a log to sit on, pours some tea, and starts skimming Bennett and Brown's anthology.

One poem catches his attention (which had begun to flag after reading the excerpt from Sara Jeannette Duncan's *The Imperialist*). E. Pauline Johnson, the notorious poet who performed half of each reading as a refined English lady and the other half as a "Mohawk Princess," wrote a poem called "The Flight of the Crows" (170–71). "The autumn afternoon is dying o'er the quiet western valley," it begins, "and far above some birds are flying by // To seek their evening haven in the breast / And calm embrace of silence" (170). Johnson published the poem in 1895; how long has the nightly crow commute been taking place? BC is happy to see that Johnson, too, wanted to know more than simple, grounded observation allows: "Strange black and princely pirates of the skies," she writes, "Would that your wind-tossed travels I could know!" (170). Far from the "wild lands" that Johnson imagines, however—which, if Gillingham's information is accurate, might have been the Fraser delta in 1895—it turns out the crows are flying to a roost in Burnaby, a suburb of Vancouver.

A few days after reading Johnson's poem, *The Vancouver Sun* runs a front-page story, "Will B.C.'s crows still come home to roost?" (A1–A2). BC is taken aback at the serendipity of events these past few days and is thankful he can avoid the archives for the time being. According to Larry Pynn, the author of the article, "northwestern crows from False Creek, the North Shore and north Surrey gather at their greatest roosting site in B.C., a spot near Willingdon Avenue and Still Creek, just north of Highway 1," and have been doing so since "the 1970s" (A1).[1] Pynn's article deals with the destruction of the roosting site to which the crows fly—the very crows BC has been watching as they perform their evening ritual: "The destruction of the roosting site … for development of a Costco outlet and new Keg restaurant has left one researcher concerned and more than a little saddened" (A1). Having read Johnson's 1895 poem, though, and knowing the tenacity of crows, BC remains hopeful that B.C.'s crows will find another place to roost in the winter. Having learned where they go each night, only to learn that they can no longer go there because of people's lust for cheap goods, regardless of the environmental costs, BC happily lets go of his desire to know and embraces his desire to observe.

Walking with Mackenzie the other day, BC hears what he thinks is a Steller's jay; but it might be a northern flicker, or a starling in mimic mode. Nevertheless, he makes a note on a recipe card—he carries recipe cards in his pocket, and a pen—for later investigation:

Tues 24 Oct,
quick, successive "laughs"; descending, harsh.

He knows this is not enough, that there is something missing. The note lacks coherence, it's too cryptic, and when BC compares it to other notes from the field—notes that share a slight resemblance to notes he makes while skimming journals in the library—he has a hard time piecing a narrative together. He recalls an article from *The New York Times Magazine* that came out in the wake of the ivory-billed woodpecker controversy. Ivory-billed woodpeckers have been considered extinct by most ornithologists since about 1940. In 2005, some ornithologists claimed to have sighted (and heard) ivory-bills in Arkansas.[2] To support their sighting, the ornithologists presented their field notes, which would play as great a role as their grainy video and audio files.

> But the act of birding, ultimately, is an act of storytelling. For instance, if someone said to you, "I saw this cardinal fly out of nowhere with yellow tips on its wings and land on the side of a tree," even the least experienced amateur would counter that cardinals don't have yellow wingtips and don't cling to trees but rather perch on branches. Each bird is a tiny protagonist in a tale of natural history, the story of a niche told in a vivid language of color, wing shape, body design, habitat, bill size, movement, flying style and perching habits. The more you know about each individual bird, the better you are at telling this tale. (Hitt n.pag.)

If birding is storytelling, what writerly activity, BC wonders, cannot be approached as a field in which to take notes? Linda Hutcheon, for example, titles her introduction to the reprint of Northrop Frye's *The Bush Garden* "The Field Notes of a Public Critic." Notes taken in the field of Canadian literature, however, are likely as far removed from the notes BC tentatively makes as Canadian literature is from a field of acacia trees. Besides, as Jan Zwicky writes in an essay, "[s]ome things can be known that cannot be expressed in technocratically acceptable prose" ("Bringhurst's" 109); the idea of story, save perhaps the improvisational storytelling of many Aboriginal cultures, seems too linear, too structured, to embody the frantic, hesitant notes of a birder as he stands shivering, just past sunrise, watching and listening for signs of avian life, head cocked, mouth slightly agape, pen at the ready.

Leafing through a pile of papers in his office, BC stumbles across another piece of writing by Laurie Ricou, an essay called "Field Notes and Notes in the Field: Forms of the West in Robert Kroetsch and Tom Robbins" that helps to alleviate the frustration brought on by his incomplete note: "Field notes. The form is the form of absence, defined by what it is not" (119); "Field notes are the unrealized raw material of art, not the achieved object.… [They] are fragmentary, cryptic, ostensibly scientific and factual and empirical. This form suits [poets, critics, birders] who despise words, who want to, who must, keep rein on their imagination" (120). The form invites careful observation of a fragmentary world, a world that does not defer to a master narrative, either natural or artificial. No note can ever be entirely factual or complete or accurate because the world and its inhabitants—Steller's jays, Haida sculptures, black spruces, plastic bags, ecocritics—are never entirely certain or complete or whole. The note about the descending, harsh notes will suffice until BC gets home. After that, who knows?

In his introduction to Robert Kroetsch's *Completed Field Notes*, Fred Wah urges readers to "think of 'field notes' as temporary, as momentary gestures that interpenetrate possibility. Perhaps even as investigations into the potential for narrative" (xii). Similar to McKay's corpus of bird poems, BC's nascent list of birds remains even less "completed" than Kroetsch's field notes, "announced *in medias res* as continuing," yet "in its acceptance of its own impossibilities, completed" (Kroetsch "Author's" 251). Where Kroetsch's impossibility manifests in the poet's inexorable reflexivity and self-doubt, in an endless deference to the symbolism of words, BC's failure to know for sure recapitulates a desire to consider other ways of knowing—BC wants to defer to the authority of schists, shrubs, and shrikes; of terranes, terrain, and towhees; of faultlines, forests, and flickers. This act of deferring, of accepting the possibility of failure in the process of learning about the field, in the field, positions BC as patient observer, as part of a naming that "will be quiet, useless, broken maybe" (Lilburn "Going Home" 184). Insofar as birding comprises identifying field marks, reading field guides, and writing field notes, its connection to reading literature remains.

Sitting down one morning with John Pass's poetry collection, *Stumbling in the Bloom*, yet another passage from Ricou's essay comes to BC: "The field notes are in prose, but their cryptic factuality … keep[s] turning them toward poetry. Here lies the potential and, conversely, the limitation of the form" (120). What could better describe the precision BC identifies with Don McKay's avian poetics better than "cryptic factuality?"

Ricou's passage comes to mind in connection with McKay because John Pass dedicates one of his poems to McKay. In "Notes on the One Note of the Unknown Bird" (107–8), BC recognizes a play on McKay's series of poems with titles such as "Song for the Song of the Varied Thrush" and "Song for the Song of the Common Loon." With his title and the allusion to McKay's "songs," Pass punningly extends the concept of field notes to include musical notes, a connection others writing about field notes haven't, to BC's knowledge, made. BC finds it intriguing that Pass celebrates in this poem the unknowability of the bird—"better not to know," he writes. "Better nameless" (107). While the resistance to name echoes the notion that language equals knowledge, the call, or note, of the bird is "Not strange" but "Familiar in dawn waking, early / spring" (107); the poet here acknowledges familiarity, even a degree of proximity, by way of close attention to the

>   Almost whistle.
> Each instance the same and new to itself, singular
>
> as the smallest increment
> of thought or query. Plea? Not answering.
> A sort of regularity. No rhythm. (And then not missing
>
> a beat the dilemma of attention—the trees (107)

Despite his joy at having stumbled upon this poem, its relevance to his project, BC is not sure what to do with these notes—the poet's or the bird's. Surprisingly, he finds himself guessing at the bird's identity—varied thrush? rufous-sided towhee? starling?—though such nominalization is surely not the purpose of the poem. Or maybe it is; to test the reader's desire to identify. If so, BC wonders if he would pass or fail the test. Or if, like the identity of the bird, it doesn't really matter.

> Fri 27 Oct, note to self—
> those mountains upmaking behind you
>   aren't your mountains—
>   those bushtits, dark-eyed juncos,
>   Steller's jays are not your
> birds—
>
> you're all escarpment and shield—
>   cardinals, grackles, and blue jays—

> you have no idea, though you're starting
>   to understand—
>   who you are in this place
>   is who you were
>   there, but different—

    Another story about birds comes to BC's attention, in spite of his decision to stop looking for more stories and to start spending more time writing. Reluctantly, on his way out of the department office, BC stops to read the latest *UBC Reports*. In the cover photo, a student holds a winter wren. Even though winter wrens have been on his mind lately, BC is prepared to walk away—having enough material to ponder and beginning to think that his research has the potential to provide myriad trailheads leading to infinite trails. This story, though, brings together his recent thoughts about being displaced from eastern to western Canada and about field and musical notes. He takes a copy from the office to read on the bus home. "Divided by glaciation during the Pleistocene Epoch 1.8 million years ago," he reads, "winter wrens have evolved into different subspecies with distinct songs and genetic codes" (Lin 1). This information, while certainly interesting from an evolutionary point of view, is not what grabs BC's attention. The different subspecies have been identified as eastern and western winter wrens, with the former living "as far west as Alberta," while the latter "inhabit the Pacific coastal belt between Alaska and Oregon" (1). Researchers, it seems, have discovered the long-theorized contact zone where these two distinct subspecies share habitat.

    BC gets off the bus early and heads to the pond at Jericho Beach. Standing on the bridge, he notices the ubiquitous mallards and pigeons floating and flying about. Come spring, while standing on this same bridge, BC will watch barn swallows performing aerial acrobatics in their search for food while red-winged blackbirds sing their territorial boundaries. For now, though, he finds a bench and continues to read about the wrens. Professor Darren Irwin found the "elusive contact zone" in a town called Tumbler Ridge, B.C., with the help of a group of dedicated amateur birders. The South Peace Bird Atlas Society had recorded the presence of winter wrens in Tumbler Ridge, and Irwin determined after studying the population that there were both eastern and western winter wrens in the area. He was able to make this preliminary determination based on the notes he heard, as both subspecies were "singing their own special songs within 100 metres of one another" (1). BC starts thinking that winter wrens' notes, which form one of the most complex of all birdsongs, have more to offer ecocritical thought than his notes, which form a fragmented jumble of incoherent thoughts. But maybe they aren't so different. Maybe, if he can allow himself to think about ecology as it applies to environmental systems and as it applies to metaphorical systems of thinking, his field notes might perform ecologically. As concise records of relational experience, some field notes occupy a literary ecotone between the field and the poetry they—resonant, echoic—keep turning toward.

Perhaps field notes keep turning toward poetry because poetry inheres in the things they record. Everything, not just words, has the potential to be poetry. "When you think intensely and beautifully, something happens. That something is called poetry. If you think that way and speak at the same time, poetry gets into your mouth. If someone hears you, it gets in their ears. If you think that way and write at the same time, then poetry gets written. But poetry *exists* in any case. The question is only: are you going to take part, and if so, how?" (Bringhurst "Poetry" 160).

BC takes part by taking notes; the wrens take part by making notes. In the field, of the field. He has enough material now, enough impetus to keep returning to the field with his guides and binoculars, his recipe cards and snippets of verse. But he also needs to spend more time inside, in front of the computer, reading and writing. The notes will continue to accumulate; the poetry will continue to speak:

> Wed 3 Nov, note re: new taxon, *Apsaravis ukhaana*
>
> *Distal to the area of the hypotarsus, an ossified tendon lies against metatarsal III. Semi-articulated pedal phalanges (Figs 1 and 3) decrease in length distally.*
> —M. Norrell and J. Clarke, "Fossil That Fills a Critical Gap in Avian Evolution"
>
> *Fig. 1*
> A bird remains a bird
> until that click of aural recognition
> when you pit
> tititichichichi
> versus
>   chick-a-dee dee dee dee—
>
> You listen in the pause between air
> and song and ear

(songbird and passerine
Regulidae and Paridae
kinglet and chickadee)

wondering about the specimen's defective
feet. What would it feel like? Not the break
but the blunt end
of hopping away from prey and lifting
into sky. What solace surfaced as flight
sloughed off this bird's pedestrian career, locomotive bricoleur no more? What might
you find at that breaking point,
Distal to the area of the hypotarsus?

What might you find that hasn't been found already? What
might you find, waiting to hear an old 45, stylus
scratching static between one song and the next, the next
note hovering like an ink stain on the tip of your tongue
from a pen that fills notebooks with names you don't want to forget?

(Regulus Satrapa; Poecile atricapilla)

And when the arm refuses to lift and return (because
your record player is older than you are) you are
reminded of storied collectors and their tote bags,

collectors who walked awkwardly   betraying
a loss of lateral mobility, the use of *an ossified
tendon* unbending toward something
ancient and telling that *lies
against metatarsal III.*

Fig. 3

Get up and out and walk a trail of
Semi-articulated thoughts,
feathers as light as light
through binoculars.

Get up and out and walk, upright
and bi-*pedal*, toward black-
capped golden-crowned

singing in the trees, toward
feathers as light as
cormorant *phalanges,*
solid as gravity, that homeless ecological

arc between practice and theory,
field trip and office, increase and
decrease—

Get up and out
and measure your life
against that fossil, that gathering
growing glacially between
yesterday and yesterday
awfully *in length*—

that song, that bone, that poem
that calls across and places you
centrally and *distally*
in relation—

part four

The spirit of cooperation, interest in one another's disciplinary approach, and willingness to eliminate conventional boundaries that have so often isolated scholars within the narrow confines of their own spheres [is] not only intellectually stimulating but also promising: in the future, combining disciplines may help elucidate and ameliorate the present troubled relationship between humankind and nature.
– Elizabeth Atwood Lawrence, *Hunting the Wren* (xvi)

There is no need to apologize for not being able to live several lives to the full at once. Instead, encounter may be the way through.
– Gillian Beer, "Afterword," *Contemporary Poetry and Contemporary Science*

Chapter Nine

Birder-Poet

> Once, the watcher,
> following a many-breasted warbler into spruce
> was pierced with sudden focus as the raindrops, poised
> on needles, glanced,
> sharpening light.
> – Don McKay, "Finding Silence" (*SD* 92)

He's been here all along. He's been sipping coffee in the middle of the night, been watching wolves in rural Ontario, been encountering sparrows exhausted from long-distance migration, been paused between buildings, been quoting scientific books and field guides, been praising breasts and birds, been making metaphor, been getting closer, been botanising, been watching, been naming, been walking, been craning, been gawking, been longing, been birding. Often I've referred to him with the rather impersonal—okay, academic—moniker "the speaker." This figure represents a McKavian persona I call the birder-poet, a persona that resembles McKay himself as a poet who pays attention and practises birding as he practises writing. Why invent a name when others exist and should suffice? Why risk conflating McKay the person and the poetic voices through which he contemplates the world? In a brief set of comments about his poetry and poetic attention, McKay remarks that in his experience birdwatching "involves a mental set nearly identical to writing: a kind of suspended expectancy, tools at the ready, full awareness that the creatures cannot be compelled to appear" any more than poetry can ("Some Remarks" 858). One goal in developing an ecocritical reading strategy open to the sciences is to negotiate the opposing impulses to listen to scientific data and to critique scientific objectivity and the manner by which findings are communicated. As a figure with interests in both the natural and the linguistic world, the birder-poet embodies this duality.

Introducing "Close-up on a Sharp-shinned Hawk" (B 22), which I discuss in Chapter Four, on *Songs for the Songs of Birds*, McKay refines the analogy, adding that the possibility of birds and words appearing depends upon how canny the birder-poet is, how much he is willing to put himself in the right habitat, including such places as Hawk Cliff, on the north shore of Lake Erie. During a September visit with other birdwatchers who were there to observe hawks migrating south to their wintering grounds[1] and to band birds for research purposes, McKay witnessed the release of a newly banded kestrel. He claims this as a formative moment in his development as both birder and poet. The story includes all of the elements germane to the argument I put forward in this book. The attention of the amateur birder is revealed, much as the kestrel is revealed to McKay, to have practical applications for ornithology and conservation efforts through trapping and banding. The science of ornithology continues to rely upon the passionate assistance of devoted amateurs, a detail that complicates any neat division between modern science and natural history.

Most contemporary bird poetry, like other categories of nature writing and environmental literature, tends to retain both a sense of natural history and an increasing knowledge about the sciences of ornithology and ecology. The environmental movement gained momentum in the 1960s and inspired a range of well-written books by such scientists as Rachel Carson, Stephen Jay Gould, and David Suzuki. The end of the twentieth century and beginning of the twenty-first witnessed more and more texts that consider histories, questions, and problems pertaining to scientific topics (evolution, genetics, physics, the environment) in general as well as particular species of fauna and flora.[2] Popular writing about birds has undergone a marked shift, similar to that which has seen the market growth of popular science literature. Less than a hundred years ago, the distinction between popular science writing and hard science was far less pronounced than it is today: popular works nowadays tend to engage the reader in personal narrative while academic science, as with most academic writing, tends to address an audience with a minimum degree of shared knowledge. In short, hard science tends to be harder than it was a century ago, which makes communicating its findings to non-specialists increasingly difficult.

In *The Rhetoric of Science in the Evolution of American Ornithological Discourse* (1998), John Battalio claims that "amateur discourse, as represented by natural history writing, has persisted as a legitimate form of writing by ornithologists at least through 1970, much longer than would be expected, given the continuing professionalization of American ornithology during the twentieth century" (72).[3] Battalio's book, like other works on the history and philosophy of science, makes it easier for ecocritics to contextualize hard, or what Battalio calls experimental, science when pursuing interdisciplinary edges. The popular scientific discourse—including key works of environmentalism—represents one direction in the evolution of the sciences, despite the seemingly widening "gap between those advocating the preservation of nature, and science, technology, and business advocating progress and profit" (Battalio 158). Battalio might draw too neat a distinction between amateur ornithologists who have been influenced more by Rachel Carson and Barry Commoner—whose books criticize science's complicity in environmental degradation—and professional ornithologists whose research informs a particular social, capitalist agenda. Indeed, it seems as arbitrary as the valuative distinction between literature and science; but Battalio provides ample statistical evidence to support his argument that, as scientific research practices evolved, some scientists took the opportunity to apply their research for financial gain. Between 1910 and 1990, for example, observations and measurements conducted in the field were replaced at a more or less steady rate by laboratory work and theoretical discussions in scientific journals (72–77). In light of this move indoors, literary critics are not the only scholars/researchers to whom the imperative to get out of the office (or lab) and (back) into the field might apply. Because theoretical science discourse is often as difficult for outsiders to comprehend as literary theory can be, the works of Carson, Commoner, Loren Eiseley,[4] Mary Midgley, E. O. Wilson, and their ilk are valuable additions to the ecocritic's library. But the increasing sophistication with which such authors translate the hard theoretical science into more accessible terms, while inviting and refreshing for the non-specialist, must be taken with a healthy dose of skepticism. Their works are, after all, translations, and all translations pose potential problems that are best approached by getting closer to the source material. As McKay has it in "Remembering Apparatus: Poetry and the Visibility of Tools" (V 50–73), "the translator's real power lies in her humility," which "includes not only reverence for the source, but a remembrance of language as apparatus" (63). The birder-poet fulfills the role of translator, mediating between McKay's observations and his readers' imaginations, between ideas and experience.

McKay is not the first to invent such a compelling persona. In his study of birds in nineteenth- and twentieth-century French fiction, James Walling identifies shaman-like figures, or "intercessors," who represent a version of the birder-poet. Since "for civilized, educated Western man, the bird's mind must remain a closed book," in Walling's estimation, French novelists employ the trope of intercessors, "privileged visionaries [who are] aware of the magical and mystical signs which convey the intimate 'soul' of a bird or mammal" and are "psychologically half-way between man and beast" (7). While such psychological betweenness tends to manifest in such a way as to render intercessors socially marginal figures, the extent to which they are granted access to the mysteries of the avian world implies a sense of privilege the birder-poet, especially as McKay presents him, would resist. Nevertheless, McKay does grapple with tensions between "soul" and "spirit" in ways I have not yet discussed—in part because many of those poems offer avenues for contemplating more material aspects of McKay's avian poetics, as in "Song for the Song of the Common Loon," and in part because I've spent a good deal of space thinking about vision's complementary sense, hearing—and that warrant some attention, particularly in light of Bringhurst's comparison of McKay with the visionary poet Halitherses (which I discuss in Chapter One).

McKay's extensive use of the imprecise terms "soul" and "spirit," which he often deploys when referring to an intangible human response to the wonders of the natural world, implies a growing interest in the ineffable qualities of the physical world, qualities that cannot easily be explained by the natural sciences or mere observation. In his preamble to the audio version of "Song for the Song of the Wood Thrush" (*S* n.pag.), McKay admits that the wood thrush's song might be "less ethereal" than that of the hermit thrush, whose pure lyricism was made famous by T. S. Eliot in Part V of *The Waste Land*. It might, he goes on, "be less on the edge of spirit" and more "the voice of soul." For McKay, "soul sticks to the ribs while spirit comes and goes. Spirit's a migratory species" (*S* n.pag.). Distinct from body and mind, yet related, soul and spirit seem to articulate the inexplicable in much the way David Abram examines, say, "The Forgetting and Remembering of the Air" in *The Spell of the Sensuous*. Pursuing an etymological argument, Abram reminds that "the word 'spirit' itself, despite all of its incorporeal and non-sensuous connotations, is directly related to the very bodily term 'respiration' through their common root in the Latin word *spiritus*, which signified both 'breath' and 'wind'" (238). As human constructs that nevertheless provide links to certain religious or shamanic discourse, spirit and soul enable a view of cultural and linguistic qualities alongside ethereal, other-than-human realities.

"As if Spirit, As if Soul" (*S/S* 57–59) narrates the differences between the two concepts. The poem's first section concentrates on spirit's propensity to achieve liftoff, "seizing leave as though / departure were the first act ever, stepping / into air as sigh, as outbreath, hum" (57). Spirit manifests as much as possibilities inhabiting—albeit for a brief time—human consciousness as it does "tossed-off warbler phrases that dissolve in the air before / the voice can manage to corral them" (57). The visionary qualities associated with spirit here merge with auditory and corporeal qualities, an "exquisite thirst" that leads to more and more thirst leading, eventually, to a recognition of a human potential for evil—represented by unquenchable thirsts, or desires; a thirst for knowledge and ownership—and of "the camber of its nothing as it / lifts, as it glances, / as it vanishes" (57). The repeated vagueness of the pronoun "it" refers us to spirit's indistinct relation to the physical world, including its role, indicated by the double meaning of "glances," as something to be looked for—by a birder-poet, say—and something with the capacity to watch. Those warbler phrases are tossed off by warblers, after all. And the birder-poet makes an effort to acknowledge that fact. He often does so by adopting a mode that might be considered praise, which Susan Stewart identifies in its lyrical form as a mode integral to poetical making.

In *The Poet's Freedom: A Notebook on Making* (2011), Stewart writes that "the material world becomes a resource for and, inevitably, an impediment to, our form making, for we are part of nature and finite within its infinity. Our secondariness thereby both evokes our wonder and compels our powers of judgment, binding us to the obligations—at times sacrifices—of praise" (29). Though she's not making an ecocritical argument, Stewart brings up a condition apposite to McKay's ecopoetic project by pointing out humans' "secondariness" vis-à-vis the material world. She does so, in part, in response to a poem by Rainer Maria Rilke, which McKay offhandedly references in "Ascent with Thrushes" (*S/S* 62–63). The hermit thrush, though unseen "Among subalpine fir" (62), is heard in this poem to be "against the best advice / a poet ever gave – / praising the unsayable to the angel" (62–63). The Rilke passage comes from his "Ninth Duino Elegy," which Stewart quotes from Stephen Mitchell's translation: "Praise this world to the angel, not the unsayable one, / you can't impress *him* with glorious emotion; in the universe / where he feels more powerfully, you are a novice" (qtd in Stewart 30). As Stewart notes, the unsayable angel is, in the Hebrew tradition, the Creator, whose name must not be pronounced (30). Human language, even in the form of praise, "cannot approach the scale of the gods" (Stewart 30), but hermit thrushes in the birder-poet's mind ignore such barriers, a testament to their, as it were, primariness. However, I suspect that McKay's reference alludes to a different translation, one that gestures away from the theological reading Mitchell's translation invites (and Stewart adopts for her argument). The hermit thrush praises the unsayable to the angel, not the world to the unsayable angel (i.e., God). This brings to mind Anita Barrows and Joanna Macy's translation: "Praise the world to the angel: leave the unsayable aside. / Your exalted feelings do not move him. / In the universe, where he feels feelings, you are a beginner" (57). Even in the absence in this translation of a deity whose name should not be uttered, humans' profound secondariness remains, which in the light of "Ascent with Thrushes" gives way to a bird's privileged status as primary being. Both the hermit thrush, in a nod to ancient wisdom about auguries and auspices, and the birder-poet, in his attentive and lyric observations, function as intercessors—the former between the world and the ineffable beyond, the latter between the bird and human understanding.

David Quammen identifies Jim Harrison and Robert Penn Warren as intercessors whose "visionary" privilege paradoxically emanates from the poets' partial blindness: "leave a man with one good eye," writes Quammen, "and he is liable to raise it skyward, squint it, focus it into the middle distance.... He is liable to write about birds" (181). The McKavian version of this intercessor is closer to Quammen's "half-blinded poets" than to Walling's "privileged visionary." Indeed, despite the temptation to read the first section of "As if Spirit, As if Soul," with its emphasis on flight and auditory ephemera, as a way to align spirit with avian being, the poem's second section undermines such a reading. The soul—another vague "something" that "settles," "stays," "accumulates"—resembles an emu, which has evolved "into flightlessness" (58), a metaphor that highlights a homological connection between flightless creatures. Even in poems that invoke more symbolic associations than material observations by a birder in the field, McKay writes through a birder-poet who is unrepentingly amateur, a "slightly stumbling, stooped and wandering, peripatetic birdwatcher," as Méira Cook has it (x). Describing soul as something that settles and "sits / in the kitchen listening to us weep" (58), McKay sets up the encounter—discussed at the end of Chapter One—with the house wren that he imagines perched on the fridge. The birder-poet's efforts to help only increase the bird's panic, and both creatures seem out of place in that kitchen at that moment. Better for both to get outside.

Susan Elmslie devotes some space to this figure I'm calling the birder-poet in her discussion of excursion and excursionist figures in McKay's poetry. For Elmslie, "the comical persona 'the watcher,' an amateur ornithologist," is one of McKay's "most notable excursionists" (88). I appreciate the way "excursionist" links McKay to a tradition of nature writers who walk about, or ramble, the way excursionists' "penchant for 'getting out'" anticipates my call for ecocritics to get out of the office and into the field and field guide. I want, though, to extend the birder-poet's history by looking at one of McKay's poems that is often overlooked. "The Rough-legged Hawk, the Watcher, the Lover, the Blind" (*B* 65–66) at once connects the birder-poet to poetic antecedents noted by Quammen and shifts the emphasis away from movement that Elmslie and Bondar attribute to McKay's poems about watching (cf. Elsmlie 89–90). "Getting out" requires movement, of course, and McKay's birder-poet often walks and reflects on walking. In Chapter Four, I discuss walking in opposition to flying as a means of human locomotion. In discussing the birder-poet, however, I want to emphasize patience and stillness and the degree to which much watching occurs within close proximity to domestic space—indeed, as poems such as "Nocturnal Animals" attest, much of McKay's poetry occurs from within, or within close proximity to, domestic space.

Three distinct personalities inhabit "The Rough-legged Hawk, the Watcher, the Lover, the Blind" that correspond with the first three items in the title. The poem begins by identifying the first two: "A Rough-legged hawk hovering / above the field beside the old folks' home / arrests the watcher in his car" (65). That a rough-legged hawk (*Buteo lagopus*)—and not a red-winged blackbird (*Agelaius phoeniceus*) or a blue jay (*Cyanocitta cristata*)—catches the watcher's attention reaffirms the story McKay relates about his experience at Hawk Cliff. Sometimes a bird has the "power to stop time or penetrate or / throw the world to neutral" (65); the hovering hawk "arrests the watcher" who ostensibly would have driven past the old folks' home and the field on his way, perhaps, to a more secluded birding destination. The eponymous lover is a "lover of the field," in this case an occupant of the old folks' home named Henry. Not even the nonagenarian Henry with his distinctive "plaid-rugged knees"—a field mark that curiously echoes "rough-legged hawk"—can know the field "hair scalp follicle and / scruff with the intensity" of the hawk, "whose black wing patches / impossibly still hanging in the air / are staring straight through into earth's / subconsciousness" (65). Still, the watcher remains a creature apart, in awe of the hawk's powers yet conscious of Henry's capacity to remember the field's various "faces." At this point, "the watcher throws himself into l'envers / and takes the tactics of the blind" (65). He demonstrates characteristics of the birder-poet: ready, attentive, aware of his limitations: half blind yet canny.

On the one hand, by assuming "the tactics of the blind," the watcher, in Elmslie's reading of this line, "opts to relinquish all he knows or thinks he knows in order to perceive on another level" (89). I'm not sure the watcher knows anything about this bird and this field that would enable him to relinquish "all he knows" about them; and the notion that he chooses to relinquish all he knows about *anything* is not supported by the poem. If the birder-poet seeks to perceive the scene on another level, he achieves such perception with binoculars, effectively aiding his blindness rather than relinquishing his sight. But using binoculars, which by poem's end are "focussed on thin air" (66), hardly constitutes taking "the tactics of the blind." Quite the opposite. The eponymous blind has a double meaning, referring both to the watcher's inability to fully see the scene before him and to the blind the watcher builds by "sling[ing] his tarp among the apple thorn" (65). This physical blind—a concealed spot from which to observe without being seen—enables the watcher to sit more comfortably on a "lawnchair, elbows / firmly on his knees to balance the binoculars." From this blind he is able to attend "the rough-legged uncles of the wind," a descriptive phrase that admits a degree of ignorance, a lack of knowing that the birder-poet treats as a gap to be filled by learning. If as Laurie Ricou suggests, "the poem is to the critic as the bird is to the ornithologist" (Bringhurst and Ricou 93), then McKay's avian poems are the poetic equivalent of "rough-legged uncles of the wind": hovering avuncular purveyors of intense knowing, which reveal themselves after careful, humble attentiveness, and open themselves to being named. As a namer, too, the birder-poet occupies an uneasy position in McKay's work.

As I discuss in more detail in Chapter Two, naming inhabits McKay's poetics as vexed linguistic act precisely because it is vexed and because as a contemporary nature poet he occupies the role of namer uneasily. It is no coincidence that McKay posits Adam in "A Small Fable" as progenitor of "a cigarette and a cup of coffee" to accompany the sleeplessness experienced by many McKavian speakers (*V* 90). The uneasiness with identifying himself as a namer extends from McKay's destabilizing of nature and wilderness. The world of plants and birds includes objects that have been abandoned by people—a creek "articulates a shopping cart, / the cliché in its throat" ("Inhabiting the Map" *SD* 103); "the Vulcan 0-4-0 saddle tank locomotive" is rumoured to be on a "ridge turning into a humped hill or tumulus" ("Five Ways to Lose Your Way" *DW* 85); wildflowers reclaim abandoned railway tracks.

In "Abandoned Tracks" (*A* 56–58), the third in a series of eclogues, the birder-poet identifies plant species in pairs and in relation to an aspect of the built environment, emphasizing that no single organism has dominion over any other. Having been abandoned, the railway tracks invite hikers to "walk the ties" and experience "their awkward / interval[s]," spaces measured with the movement of trains in mind, not of mammalian bipeds. The awkwardness indicates the lack of ecological foresight involved in such a human endeavour as building a railway, a mode of transporting people, raw materials, and goods within a network of industrial economies. In the poem's present, however, "Cow Vetch and Mustard get in the way / and hide the ties" (56). Species that would have had little opportunity to thrive while the tracks were in use have begun to reclaim the narrow swath the tracks still occupy, albeit absently: "Bindweed and Wild Grape / curl around the rails" (56); "Hawkweed / and Daisies / sharpen their hardihood on gravel" (56); yellow warblers articulate their "pointillist attention / in the Rock Elm" (57); "Milkweed with its lavish / muted blooms" produces "the milk that feeds the larvae / of Monarch Butterflies and makes them / poisonous to birds" (57). Complex webs of interaction revealing "So much intricate tenacity" take place with implications far beyond the space of the tracks. The poem is partly about botanical and avian tenacity over time, about the capacity of plants and birds to overcome human intervention and adapt. McKay uses two examples, like parallel tracks, to symbolize tenacity. One is a story of his dog, Luke, which was hit by a train—the "spot is occupied by Bladder Campion now" (57)—and survived "ready for round two" (58). The other story envelopes the one about Luke, documenting the life cycle of the monarch butterflies that will "feed and flit and pollinate their hosts, / by accident, and after an infinitude of flits / wind up precisely in one Mexican valley" (58). I think McKay's fealty to specificity seeks to pay homage to the tenacity and precision of nonhuman intelligence represented by those two stories. "Abandoned Tracks" is also about humans' relative insignificance, the earth's ability to continue the process of breaking down and reclaiming place for itself. The poem ends with an inversion of human intention: "Everything the tracks / have had no use for's happening / between them" (58). The exclusivity of the tracks—their one-track mind, as it were—makes the inclusivity of the surrounding habitat that much more compelling. The tracks might not disappear for another half a million years, give or take, but they have been reclaimed, because of their uselessness, for wilderness.

To continue naming in the face of its limitations is to grasp at specificity on the verge of inaccuracy: no name can express the totality of a thing. But naming can express relations between things named, and McKay often writes *about* naming in his poetry to engage an ecological view that includes cultural as well as natural phenomena. If ecocritics are themselves to engage this ecological view, I suggest, their work can be enriched with an understanding of species' names and, by extension, their ecologies.

Like "The Rough-legged Hawk, the Watcher, the Lover, the Blind," other poems in *Birding, or desire* contribute to fleshing out the birder-poet persona whose identity can be taken for granted by the time he appears in

"Abandoned Tracks" (*A* 56–58). The opening poem in the collection, "Field Marks" (15), and the related "Field Marks (2)" (75) both focus attention on the birder-poet as a central figure. The poem titles refer to the system of bird identification made popular by Roger Tory Peterson in his celebrated *A Field Guide to the Birds* and "widely regarded as the most efficient and most effective way to identify birds under the poor conditions, such as color-obscuring glare, often encountered outdoors. A field mark is any distinctive feature setting one species of bird apart from others, especially its near congeners: barred tail feathers, eyebrow ridges, a curved bill, an unusual flight pattern, and so on" (Phillips 173). In the first "Field Marks," McKay provides an abbreviated, ontological field-guide entry for the birder-poet: "just like you and me but / cageless, likes fresh air and / wants to be his longing. / Wears extra eyes around his neck" (*B* 15). The birder-poet here is restless, full of desire for identifying birds and for an unidentified woman, the "shape and texture of" whose thighs he "spends days attempting to compare" to "a snowy egret's neck, elegant / and all too seldom seen in Southern Ontario" (15). This attempt at precise comparison anticipates that of the speaker in "'The Bellies of Fallen Breathing Sparrows'" and demonstrates the extent to which the birder-poet himself "would be a bird book full of / lavish illustrations with a text of metaphor" (15). The more effective metaphor in both poems relies on intimate knowledge of the natural history of birds as recorded in field guides. Ending with "He wings it," a line hovering on the edge of cliché, "Field Marks" fits a McKavian world full of birding and desire, ecological and linguistic edges.[5]

"Field Marks (2)" offers a more extended version of the birder-poet. In both poems McKay is characteristically self-deprecating: while in the first poem the birder-poet is an unimpressive egghead, in the second he is "Distinguished from the twerp, / which he resembles, by his off-speed / concentration: *shh*" (75), the mildly pejorative "twerp" resonating onomatopoeically with avian calls and songs. Resemblance to "the twerp" indicates a strategic humility on the part of the speaker, one that McKay cultivates in his writings about the limitations of language. Moreover, in attempting "to become / a dog's nose of receptiveness" (75), the speaker embodies a theriomorphic proclivity evident in much of McKay's work. Not only does the metaphor provide "a more familiar directness" (Bartlett "Dog's Nose" 124) in spite of its obvious unreality—a human is *not* a dog's nose—it also implies respect for the unique physical (and intellectual) abilities of nonhumans.

This entry on the birder-poet combines a respectful acknowledgement of nonhuman intelligence and (inherent) value with McKay's interest in what he calls, in "Baler Twine: Thoughts on Ravens, Home & Nature Poetry," "poetic attention." A coinage in which McKay "feel[s] the falsity (and in some way the transgression) of nomination," poetic attention is "a sort of readiness, a species of longing which is without the desire to possess, and it does not really wish to be talked about" (*V* 26). McKay here recalls Bringhurst's repetition, in "Gloria, Credo, Sanctus Et Oreamnos Deorum," of "Knowing, not owning," and the movement toward "Sharpening, honing / pieces of knowledge, / pieces of earth" that Bringhurst's poem articulates (154–55). Knowing, though, requires a genre of attention, especially by the birder, that can be, or can seem to be, didactic and boring—

> Later on he'll come back as the well-known bore
> and read his list (Song sparrows: 5
>   Brown thrashers: 2
>   Black-throated green warblers: 1)   omitting
> all the secret data hatching on the far side of his mind:
>
>   that birds have sinuses throughout their bodies,
>   and that their bones are flutes
>   that soaring turkey vultures can detect
>   depression and careless driving
>   that every feather is a pen, but living,
>
>   flying (B 75)

In Bartlett's savvy reading, this poem, because of its attention to attention and its interest in listing, represents a particularly McKavian style. In my reading, the list is key because it shows the birder making his field notes; the shape of the list, its epistemology, is not as important as what the birder-poet does with it and what the list enables beyond identification and classification. The birder's list here becomes parenthetical, unlike the listing of "bindweed, spiderweb, sumac, / Queen Anne's Lace" found earlier in the poem. While he omits "all the secret data hatching on the far side of his mind," he includes the secret data for readers to see, an aesthetic choice in keeping with Bartlett's claim that the list is "a common poetic device to evoke multiplicity" ("Dog's Nose" 133).[6] The "secret data" hence gesture tellingly toward a poetic style attuned specifically to the biologies and ecologies of the birds themselves.

Granted, the scientific—"that birds have sinuses throughout their body"—slides effortlessly into metaphor—"that every feather is a pen"—but the transition, indeed the translation, avoids simplicity. In numerous poems, as Bartlett points out, "McKay's avian precision moves from bird-guide delineations to metaphor" and "from metaphor to fieldguidisms" (124); the field guide represents one intertextual referent toward which a McKavian trail might lead. It also offers a particularly interesting example, especially in the case of bird books, of biological, ecological specification meeting metaphorical, representational description. Interdisciplinary reading practices are required if, as Gabriele Helms writes in "Contemporary Canadian Poetry from the Edge: An Exploration of Literary Eco-criticism," viewing "ecologically aware poetry as created in [*sic*] an edge under the influence of both writers and their environment opens a way for writers and readers to advance the shift from an intellectual anorexia and complacency that prevents holistic views to an increasing awareness of the importance of our environment" (58). Thus a return to the concept of ecotone helps articulate an interdisciplinary space from which ecocritics might "strive for an affirmative praxis" (Helms 46)—by which I take Helms to mean an attempt to make conventional reading practices relevant within and applicable to a world outside the text. The birder-poet thus represents a figure capable of occupying the ecotone in critically rewarding ways, particularly as he struggles with his desire to get closer to the birds he sees by knowing their names.

I have devoted a good deal of space to those poems of McKay's that pay attention to organisms other than birds, both here and elsewhere in this book, in order to position his poetry within a larger historical, critical context of science and literature, to show that science functions as intertext in poems that feature twinflowers, saxifrage, red pines, and quartz, as well as hermit thrushes, ravens, goldfinches, and peregrine falcons. But birds overwhelmingly occupy McKay's poetics, helping to shape a lyric ornithology informed by science and desire alike. In "Identification" (*B* 91), for example, McKay writes about a moment when someone digging potatoes happens to see "a hawkish speck / above the cornfield moving / far too fast" to enable a positive identification. The speaker names the speck which has quickly "stooped and / vanished / *Peregrine*." He doesn't record the name confidently, though; he writes it down "because [he] might have gone on digging the potatoes / never looking up" and "because / such clarity is rare and inarticulate as you, o dangerous / endangered species." Alanna Bondar suggests that the speaker, since he does not have time to get his binoculars and identify field marks, "forces meaning onto the situation" ("'Every Feather'" 25) by naming the bird. If the repetition of "because"—it appears six times in the poem as part of the phrase "I write it down because"—functions, as Bondar claims, as "a vacillation in meaning, an attempt to pinpoint the reason why he writes down 'Peregrine' when he is not sure he even saw more than 'a hawkish speck'" (24–25), then the poem's title refers more to the speaker than to the bird: the act of naming identifies the poet-speaker as someone who is satisfied with the "bright / reticulated snaps of system" that inevitably occur, as they do in "Twinflower," when the speaker is able to place the twinflower "among the honeysuckles" (*A* 5). But the naming in "Identification" remains tentative, and the upper-case "P" and the italics, furthermore, articulate the speaker's hopeful desire to have seen a endangered species. I think he is attempting to pinpoint the reason why he writes down anything at all. The impetus to "write it down" reflects more a desire for a moment of clarity that might help the peregrine falcon recover from its population decline than it does the satisfaction of having established the identity of a distant "hawkish speck." Identification, this poem suggests, is a process; the identity the birder-poet ultimately settles on and writes down simultaneously reveals a human desire to name and the potential danger of such a desire.

Since the act of writing down for the birder-poet poses questions about naming as ownership, McKay advocates a latter-day textual version of decreation that echoes the speaker of "Identification." No longer content to explain why he writes anything down, McKay's birder-poet acknowledges the paradoxical tension between presence and absence in what becomes a ritual linguistic gesture throughout *The Muskwa Assemblage* (2008): "Write it down, cross it out." (n.pag.). The pronoun's antecedent is deliberately vague—it refers to "[t]he struggle of language with itself, its sojourn in the wilderness, its fast" (*M* n.pag.); it refers to caribou crossing a river; it refers to birds; it refers to "the paradoxical thirst of words for seclusion, for animal intimacy, that parenthetical embrace" (*M* n.pag.). Recalling the reluctant birder of "Load" (*AG* 10) and invoking a fear of extinction as the ultimate absence (as in "In Aornis" [*S/S* 66], which I discuss below), here McKay brings language and the desire for proximity together. The intimate parenthetical embrace occurs during moments of seclusion when the birder-poet is (at least nominally) alone in the world, paying attention to his surroundings and accepting the paradoxes at play all around.

Both "Load" and "In Aornis" touch upon the dangerous potential for damage that underlies much of McKay's poetics. Inherent in a lyric attention that incorporates field guide details and a degree of scientific understanding, this potential harkens back to the latent violence in the birder-poet's urge to get out from domestic space. In "Saxifrage punctata, Raven"—one half of the essay "Robert Bringhurst's 'Sunday Morning': A Dialogue" (Bringhurst and Ricou 88–100)—Ricou identifies an ecocritical model apposite to McKay's avian poetics and turns his critical attention to influential field guide publisher Roger Tory Peterson, according to whom birding provides access to flora, fauna, bodies of water, and rocks (Bringhurst and Ricou 93). Birding enables a more comprehensive ecological mode of knowing despite the necessary focus on creatures that can weigh as little as one-tenth of an ounce. Nature writer David Quammen captures this paradox in a brief homage to poet Jim Harrison. For Harrison, birding "implies paradoxically a seizure, a connection, a participatory relationship that nevertheless doesn't violate the bird's tetherless untouchability" (182). For most poets and critics searching for ways to read and write about birds as birds, a similar paradox applies; birds' untouchability is part of what makes them so vital as subjects for poetry and so indispensable as living members of the physical world.[7] But science, or what scientific research and methods can provide to amateur birders and naturalists, nevertheless remains part of a long humanist, epistemological tradition that goes back at least as far as the Enlightenment and its consequent influence on imperialism and colonialism.

Broadly speaking, science's impulse to reduce and objectify has been criticized for making possible such violations as Harrison mentions. Ironically, much of the current popular science about birds addresses endangerment and population declines—which have been caused, predominantly, by scientific and technological advances in industrial agriculture and urbanization. As works such as Bridget Stutchbury's *Silence of the Songbirds: How We Are Losing the World's Songbirds and What We Can Do to Save Them* (2007) and Trevor Herriot's *Grass, Sky, Song: Promise and Peril in the World of Grassland Birds* (2009) attest, massive numbers of birds are facing unprecedented pressures from myriad fronts, and many are unable to adapt. The science behind each of these books (Stutchbury is an ornithologist whose book springs from her own research; Herriot is an amateur naturalist who relies on others' studies) tells of a bleak situation, whether you are a bird lover or not. McKay ponders a future without birds in the short lyric "In Aornis." I am tempted to call McKay's poem "speculative lyric" for the way it imagines a post-avian world in verse. McKay's use of negative words and suffixes portends a time when the distance between humans and birds manifests as extinction. So much in Aornis is *not*, is *un*. The prospect of utter loss resonates in frightening ways throughout the poem. Aornis translates, as the poem's speaker tells us, as "birdless land." This is a land whose "*un*inflected sky extends / like rhetoric to the horizon," as if the landscape itself were defined by the presence of birds. Bushes and trees still contain tangles, but they are not nests; the wind still carries flying objects, but they are not birds. They are machines presumably controlled by humans, but not necessarily. It seems Aornis is birdless *and* humanless land. It seems McKay is suggesting that the absence of birds indicates bad times ahead for people, as well. Humans exist in the poem as spectres: if not flying those machines, we are presumably responsible for their construction; if not present in the landscape proper, we are at least remembered by one of the branches that "now and then" shrugs to "shed its load" of snow. Likewise, and more to the point, the single mention of a specific bird resonates like an echo in an empty room. The branches—and note the double negative sound—"know / no junco will descend to instigate / the tiny blizzard like a sneeze / which frees them." This is a world in which birds are present only as fading boreal memories and where absence manifests in calm, matter-of-fact tones. The "unsung sun, / it turns out, comes up anyway" while flying machines ride like cyborg Icaruses on the empty wind.

That image of the wind being ridden by machines instead of birds hints suggestively at a Heideggerean critique of technology.[8] As the only human product in the poem—unless we consider the absence of birds as something we will have produced—these flying machines represent the most direct way humans have used birds. The science that informs aerodynamics and the engineering technology that enables powered flight both rely upon knowledge of bird physiology and biology. This is one way we have posited birds as tools in the Enlightenment narrative called progress in an attempt, however unwitting, to extend our grasp and touch the avian other.

In "Load," McKay grapples with these conflicting desires and facts, articulating a version of the "bird's tetherless untouchability" by incorporating his amateur-birding observations and a scientific knowledge into his depiction of an avian encounter. When the birder-poet sees a white-throated sparrow on Lake Erie's shore "exhausted from flight," he thinks

> of the muscles in that grey-white breast,
> pectoralis major powering each downstroke,
> pectoralis minor with its rope-and-pulley tendon
> reaching through the shoulder to the
> top side of the humerus to haul it up again;
> of the sternum with the extra keel it has evolved to
> anchor all that effort

The biological information *about* the sparrow in these lines does not serve to express the poet's mastery over the avian world, to *know* the bird, but to contemplate *this* sparrow's mastery over the air, a mastery that, like all knowledge, is limited and temporary. The *metaphoric* touches in "Load" are almost as delicate as the exhausted bird recovering from its flight over Lake Erie, despite the heaviness one typically associates with ropes and pulleys, with anchors. Incidentally, the scientific literature also uses the pulley metaphor to refer to flight morphology in birds. The metaphoric paradox in the poem pays homage to the phenomenological paradox of bird flight—namely that creatures weighing less than an ounce routinely fly across such vast distances, crossing political and bioregional boundaries with enviable ease. I am less interested in whether this poem successfully represents bird flight (metaphorically) *or* presents bird flight (realistically) than I am in whether and how the poem succeeds in both cases. Its vocabulary, the result of ornithological research, demonstrates the precision and exactitude for which McKay, as a "sharp-eyed and unselfishly meticulous" poet, is renowned (Bartlett "Dog's Nose" 124). The names of muscles and bones are not common in field guides; so while "McKay's avian precision moves from bird-guide delineations to metaphor" and "from metaphor to fieldguidisms," his desire for precision takes him to scientific literature as well (Bartlett 124). The results are at once fastidiously descriptive, metaphorically deft, and fully aware of "the pretensions of accurate description" that seek to measure "the distance between language and bird" (125).

But for all McKay, his speaker, and the ecocritic might use "Load" to get in *touch* with white-throated sparrows, the bird remains essentially and significantly untouchable. Epistemological distance resonates in the dual meaning of not grasping the sparrow. The poem's concluding confession reinforces this distance: "I wanted / very much to stroke it, and recalling / several terrors of my brief / and trivial existence, didn't" (169). The poet resists the desire to know the bird materially. The science that explains the bird's presence, accomplishment, and exhaustion compensates here for the poet's lack. The bird that remains untouched in verse persists in being a bird—which can be known, partially, but not to the point of ownership. After all, as Gillian Beer warns in her contribution to *One Culture: Essays in Science and Literature* ("Problems" 1987), "[k]nowledge is not a solution [and] the power to perceive connections may itself be a trap which has no issue" (50). But the possibility of entrapment "allows the poet," by way of "scientific and technical knowledge," "to contemplate with fresh intensity" questions that poets have been contemplating for centuries (52). Although she does not make an explicit connection to the science of ecology in her article "Problems of Description in the Language of Discovery," Beer's emphasis on the obstinacy of linguistic and epistemological connectivities echoes the difficulties ecologists face in attempting to understand—and then to explain—connections/relations in the ecosystems they study. Simultaneously, Beer offers language as a *metaphorical* ecology that is necessary for scientists to recognize "multiple simultaneous levels of event and meaning" by having "recourse to the linguistic dexterity, and ... instability of reference" common to literary language (56). Such multiplicity is important for both scientists and poets to resist or "outwit the tendency of description to stabilize a foreknown world and to curtail discovery" (56). Carefully realized metaphor, in other words, is a way of articulating an attention to, and engagement with, the world represented in scientific as well as poetic writing because of its instability. As McKay argues, "With a metaphor that works, we're immediately convinced of the truth of the claim *because* it isn't rational. The leap always says … that language is incommensurate with the real, that leaps are necessary if we are to gain a sense of the world outside it" (*V* 69). The notion of incommensurability in this context might seem at odds with the rationality expected of science, but such leaping as McKay espouses isn't far off from the lateral manoeuverability that enables both interdisciplinary and intertextual knowing.

In "Pine Siskins" (*S/S* 64), we witness the birder-poet taking notes on birds he does not see. He accepts pine siskins' hiddenness as a comfortable distance between himself and the birds, stressing the importance of recognizing and maintaining distance between observer and observed. As if reversing the call to write it down before crossing it out, the poem begins with a version of visual absence. But McKay's poetic attention does not rely upon sight alone: "Unseen in the pines the pine siskins / are unlocking the seeds from the pine cones, click / click click." These negative prefixes do not have the same effect as they do in "In Aornis." Here they indicate avian agency and intelligence—the birds exist beyond the birder's field of view and eat their meal as if unlocking the secrets of life. In their absence they provide the birder-poet with material to write about, namely the pine cone seeds they are consuming and the patterns the cones' scales create as they fall. The chaff that "freckles the air, / the lawns, the parked cars, / and the notebook" in the poet's lap enters the notebook as "fallout" and "dross" and "dun-coloured memos from entropy" (64). Each description invokes the energy exchange taking place in the pines, the clicks that release the protein to keep the siskins warm and that deliver the waste, no longer filled with potential heat, to gravity and the earth below. Midway through the poem, the speaker abruptly halts his metaphorical musings, as if to prevent himself from overwriting and writing over the pine siskins. He reminds in the poem's second half that birds are cultural beings who play and make music. Unseen in the pines,

> the siskins party on, now and then
> erupting into siskin song – upswept
> ardent buzzes, part
> wolf whistle, part raspberry, part Charles Ives'

> "Unanswered Question":
> tragic-comic operas crammed
> into their opening arpeggia [*sic*]. (64)

The speaker explains siskin song with a complexity typically reserved for describing Mozart concertos or Thelonious Monk performances. But it seems to be a complexity humans are not entirely capable of comprehending. The tragicomic aspect is easy enough to understand—we are in many ways an ironical species willing to appreciate the come-hither qualities of wolf-whistle that get undermined by the childish raspberry. But we might have difficulty comprehending how these competing sounds come together as a full opera "crammed into" an opening arpeggio. It's a little like trying to imagine an entire novel stuffed into its first sentence. Of course, humans are physiologically incapable of hearing birdsong as birds hear it. For that we need advanced recording and playback equipment. Just as the poet's perception does not rely on sight alone, however, so his rendering of the siskin song does not rely on sound alone. The siskins' operatic performance comprises their song and their opening act—eating seeds—so that they become not just singers but song. The way they erupt into song, which the speaker describes as *ardent* buzzes, completes the energy transfer begun in the first lines. As lichenologist Trevor Goward eloquently puts it, everything alive engages in metabolic process by necessity; "and what is metabolism if not physiological burning carefully controlled: a kind of pale Nabokovian fire: a flame that burns slowly away inside the objects its burning somehow animates" (200). They eat in order to sing; they sing in order to live. At least that's what evolutionary theory implies—some questions remain unanswered.

Chapter Ten

Science

> Perhaps that old pair of antagonists, science and poetry, can be persuaded to lie down together and be generative after all.
> – William Rueckert, "Literature and Ecology: An Experiment in Ecocriticism" (107)

> The greatest enterprise of the mind has always been and always will be the attempted linkage of the sciences and humanities
> – Edward O. Wilson, *Consilience: The Unity of Knowledge* (8)

> I feel fortunate to live in a time when a growing number of scientists are increasingly inclined to consider the work of poets, and vice versa.
> – Gary Paul Nabhan, *Cross-Pollinations: The Marriage of Science and Poetry* (39)

American biologist and poet Gary Paul Nabhan recalls early criticism he received from colleagues with whom he shared some of his poems: "'If you squander all your time reading poetry,' one mathematics teacher admonished me, 'you'll never be able to master the rigors of science'"; "'Your poetry will become even more unintelligible if you continue to burden your free verse with the weight of scientific terms'" (11). A scientist first and a published poet later, Nabhan eventually followed different advice, namely to "use metaphor as well as technical precision" in his writing (12). Poetry and science both offer ways of looking at the world; if the former has a unique ability to examine humans' relation with the phenomenological world by bringing us closer to it via metaphor, the latter has the benefit of engaging more directly with the phenomenological world. Scientific language uses metaphor, yes, but arguably does so in ways that distance readers from the objects of scientific study. Between them, metaphor and scientific observation—Nabhan's "technical precision"—provide an intertextual base from which to consider how to think and write human–nonhuman relations.

In "Landscape, Untitled," Canadian critic John Moss argues that "[t]hrough words the poet merges the experience of things and things themselves" (66). Of course, the poet's primary dilemma then becomes deciding which words will enact a successful merging of experience and things. I have been arguing that if the poet writes about ecological relations, as McKay does, then field guides and scientific texts provide an ample, species-specific, and ecologically accurate vocabulary. "If appropriate language is not at the poet's command," according to Moss, "then the world from his or her perspective and for those who share it is quite literally beyond comprehension" (66). For McKay, no language, no word, seems appropriate enough; McKay's "gift for metaphor" (Coles 55–58) vies with his persistent uneasiness with the supposed authority of human language to produce objective knowledge. As a result, his poetry often speaks to a desire for an ecologically attuned mode of thinking, and it draws upon both symbolic and scientifically accurate language to celebrate the phenomenological world while simultaneously admitting the impossibility of ever fully knowing the species and objects it describes. McKay is searching for the "appropriate gesture" that approximates a merging of things and their ideas ("Appropriate" 44–61). East-coast Canadian writer John Steffler echoes Moss's claim regarding poetry's interest "in human experience, in capturing what feel like the important moments in being both human and part of the world" (49). In expressing the merging Moss refers to and capturing the moments Steffler refers to, "poetry's basic method might seem not very different from that of science. Both involve observation, analysis, and some form of expression or reporting" (Steffler 49). I agree with Steffler's basic argument regarding the similarities between science and poetry, but I take issue with his use of the term "method": poetry has no method like the scientific method. However, both science and poetry need to use language to communicate their observation and analysis.

American poet Alison Hawthorne Deming usefully points out a key difference in what scientists and poets expect from language. Although metaphor and narrative have been used by poets and scientists alike to articulate "the unknown, to develop an orderly syntax to represent accurately some carefully seen aspect of the world," scientists have a tendency to count on the uncomplicated specificity of words' literal meanings (188). Deming describes this paradox as a "beautiful particularity and musicality of the vocabulary," even if poets and scientists tend to use language in distinctively different ways (185). If scientists use words with as much precision as possible to articulate something of the unknown (even if their use of metaphor can appear accidental and imprecise), poets use language that is deliberately imprecise (if we think of a metaphor as "a lie in the interest of truth"); or rather, so precise and compact as to invite more than one meaning. In 2001, Maurice Riordan contributed a short essay to *Nature* about how "science supplies poetry with a register of words outside common usage" (457). For Riordan, who has edited two anthologies of science-related poetry,[1] scientific language has the potential to "exist in a state of sensitive relationship with everything else in a poem" and, when successful, to "increas[e] the surface tension of the language" as "part of the poem's imaginative exertion," which he calls language's "promiscuous agility" (457). This agility prevents, or at least discourages, poets from writing "earnest, educative poems about science" and encourages instead imaginative engagement "with words and ideas that derive necessarily from a materialist model of the world." Most significant for my argument about the role of scientific naming in ecocriticism is Riordan's claim that poetry engaged with a scientific view of the world "produces a version of reality at odds with orthodox thinking" (457). As a response to a section of Donne's "The Second Anniversary," Riordan's language cannot escape religious connotations; however, the idea of poetry such as McKay's producing a version of reality at odds with orthodox thinking anticipates McKay's own desire to articulate the "possibilities for reverse flow in a relationship that has been so thoroughly one-way" (*DW* 18). Whether the relationship is spiritual, ontological, ecological, or political, the contemporary ecopoet's challenge to it retains epistemological, and I might add pedagogical, urgency.

Both Deming and Riordan are poets interested in science. What do scientists think about the linguistic divide? The editors of *Keywords in Evolutionary Biology* (1998), Evelyn Fox Keller and Elisabeth A. Lloyd, waste no time easing their readers into the discussion: "Unlike poets ... scientists expect and indeed generally assume that their language is (or at least ought to be) both precise and clear.... In the traditional model for scientific language ... terminological ambiguity, uncertainty, and double entendre are generally seen as evidence of scientific inadequacy" (1). The desire for clear communication between and consensus among researchers necessitates the expectation of singular meaning. This makes a certain sense, of course, regardless of how stilted it often makes scientific writing seem: it wouldn't do to persist in referring to phlogiston while developing fire-retardant building materials, whatever the poetic (and historical) resonance of the term. Deming cites Miroslav Holub, an immunologist *and* poet, who makes the point succinctly: "For the sciences, words are an auxiliary tool," by which he means they give support to ideas not easily expressed in language (188).

Consider, for example, the following comments about intertidal zones, one from a biology journal and the others from poems:

> (A)
> largely because of the steep gradient in thermal and desiccation stresses that is presumed to occur during low tide, the rocky intertidal zone has long been a model system for examining relationships between abiotic stresses, biotic interactions, and ecological patterns in nature" (Helmuth 837)

> (B)
> December, it's dark when the water's out
> but today is June: sun heats
> the pavement of clamshell and pools
> a tiny shadow at her feet. Her step
> on the mudflat sends the shy heron
> flapping and *gronking* over the headland.
>
> Did she think she could walk here
> with no disturbance?
>
> (Wheeler, "The Tide" 56)

> (C)
> At ebbing, the abandoned pier reveals
> turmoil, seven purple starfish
> spread-eagled against the creosote,
> barnacles, mussel-clusters,
> clutching like 4-year-olds
> in front of a stranger, touch and cold
> exposure straining them, the seize
> of sun, the lap of stippled ocean.
>
> (New, "Bird Landing" 58)

While passage A clearly communicates the significance of low-tide observations in determining ecological patterns, it does not combine such discursive elements as aesthetics, pathos, and politics, all of which scientific discourse has a propensity to exclude (Battalio 81). In passages B and C Laurie Ricou's comments regarding the intertidal zone as "an ideal metaphor for a place in constant transition.... a place of deposition, of layering, of a mix of communities, of crevices and hidden pools" rings true (*Arbutus* 142). Wheeler's heron, flapping at the poet's disturbance, and New's exposed barnacles and starfish, evidence of common ecological turmoil, include the "literary" elements excluded in the more scientific prose. Biotic (heron, mussels, four-year-olds) and abiotic (sun, clamshells, pier) coexist to reveal ecological patterns in a nature that includes humans and nonhumans alike. These poems readily assume the intertidal zone as an important system for examining both metaphorical and ecological relations.

In his memoir, Leonard Nathan dramatizes for narrative purposes the typical tensions between arts and sciences. During a typical debate between Nathan and his friend Lewis (an ornithologist), Nathan essentially reinforces Deming's and Holub's comments regarding differing uses of language by scientists and poets. Nathan sees a turn toward abstraction in scientific language, for example,

> toward birds as an example of race, species, genus, ultimately as confirmation of natural law. [Scientific] language is constituted to do that. But there's another language, dedicated to articulating the sense or feel of an experience. In order to perform that task, it must sometimes break with straightforward language, resort to violations of grammar, syntax, and logic; it must exploit devices like hyperbole, understatement, paradox, oxymoron, irony, strong patterns of meter and rhyme— (127)

The information scientists are attempting to communicate is often ill served by such structurally reflexive strategies as Nathan lists. If studies demonstrate aggressive behaviour in red-necked grebes toward other species of grebes, it behooves the scientist to write "Red-necked Grebes are fierce, and in the breeding season they attack all other grebes entering their territory" (Fjeldså 57) rather than some such attempt as:

> Red-necked Grebes   attacking
>   attacking   attacking
>   while new flowers
>   sway in early rain,
>   attracting Red-necked Grebes

Hypothetically my strained attempt at versifying the data should communicate the same as the original: red-necked grebes are fierce (hence the repetition) and territorial (hence the visual spaces surrounding "attacking") during breeding season (represented, sort of, by images of flowers and spring rain). But, the bathetic quality of my verse notwithstanding, the information gains nothing from the structural inconsistencies. Perhaps we can attribute the difference between Jon Fjeldså's version and mine to the different formal conventions of prose and poetry, though prose fiction writers have produced structurally experimental work. The differences do not necessarily assume a valuation of either linguistic strategy. However, Fjeldså succeeds in communicating something specific about grebe aggression in a succinct manner, which is the basic requirement (expectation) of scientific writing.

One aspect of creative language use Nathan does not address is metaphor. As I have just discussed, metaphor is an important component of both scientific and literary writing. In *Wisdom & Metaphor* (2003), Jan Zwicky connects metaphorical and scientific ways of thinking by introducing a mathematical analogy:

> Understanding metaphor is like understanding a geometrical truth. Features of various geometrical figures or of various contexts are pulled into revealing alignment with one another *by* the demonstration or the metaphor.
>
> What is "revealed" is not that the alignment is possible; rather, that the alignment is possible reveals the presence of already-existing shapes or correspondences that lay unnoticed. To "see" a proof or "get" a metaphor is to experience the significance of the correspondence for what the thing, concept, or figure is. (L36)

Yet while metaphor importantly, if inconspicuously, populates scientific writing it also has the ability, in the service of a poet such as McKay, simultaneously to describe and question the accuracy of description. This ability is precisely what Brian Bartlett refers to when, discussing McKay's shift from "fieldguidisms" to metaphor and back, he writes that "[d]escription in Don McKay's poems isn't limited to pictorial details" ("Dog's Nose" 124). By way of example, Bartlett quotes a line from "A Morning Prayer Ending with a Line Borrowed from the Holiday Inn" (B 59): "A treeful of starlings, speckled and / oily as comic book germs or high school wiseguys" is, according to Bartlett "more idiosyncratic and exact than a *treeful of gaudy, iridescent starlings*" (124), a bastardization of McKay's lines that resembles my own attempt to versify grebe behaviour ecology.

For all that McKay invites extra-textual excursions into scientific literature and language, he is not a scientist.[2] His poems are not validated by "facts" I as a reader can look up. He reveals his scientific curiosity, though, in an essay, listing ideal companions for an afterlife canoe trip, including Rachel Carson, Stephen Jay Gould, David Suzuki, and Roderick Haig-Brown. If this list is any indication, and I think it is, his poetry works to get past the nature-poet stereotype, the Romantic vision of Man passively observing, describing, and ultimately constructing Nature. The hypothetical canoe trip represents for McKay an opportunity to go back in his writing career and give "full attention to birds, animals, plants, and lichens, not to mention the eloquent glacier-inscribed granite itself" ("The Shell" 56). In *Strike/Slip* (2006) he contemplates a similar return, minus the hypothetical companions, in "Precambrian Shield" (8–9), a nostalgic poem about canoe trips during the speaker's earlier life in Ontario. Responding to the reflexive question "Would I go back to that time?" the speaker says:

> Not unless I was allowed,
> as carry-on, some sediment that has since
> accumulated, something to impede the
> passage of those days that ran through us
> like celluloid. Excerpts from the book of loss.
> Tendonitis. Second thoughts. Field guides.
> Did we even notice
> that the red pine sprang directly from the rock
> and swayed in the wind like gospel choirs?
> Not us. (8)

Here the language of botany and geology occupy the same poem as nostalgic metaphor. Just as "[b]otanical nomenclature is an art of transmission that makes a certain kind of science possible" (Daston 155), so scientific knowledge represents an art of understanding that makes a certain kind of poetry possible. The naming of red pine adds as much poignancy to the passage as references to the ethereal "book of loss" and "gospel choirs," the point being that the speaker and his fellow canoeists were not paying attention to the ecology or geology of the region through which they yearly paddled, and hence would have been unable to devise accurate metaphors about the experience. The turn to rock in this poem reflects McKay's shift to geopoetry in both *Strike/Slip* and *Deactivated West 100*. Though the attention and specificity McKay desires in his geopoetry is similar to the attention and specificity he desires in his ecopoetry, crucial differences exist in the way he positions human intelligence—including imagination—vis-à-vis geologic time. Despite the differences, McKay's geopoetry represents an extension of his interest in the scientific as well as the experiential and the poetic.

Most studies of birds in literature incorporate at least a secondary or tertiary interest in correctly identifying bird species in the literary works under scrutiny. Typically, some knowledge of bird behaviour and habitat, usually provided by natural history rather than an ornithological text, is necessary to such sleuthing. In the editorial in the inaugural issue of *Avian Conservation and Ecology/Ecologie et conservation des oiseux*, Thomas D. Nudds and Marc-André Villard write that "[s]cience is not, indeed, cannot be, the heartless pursuit of objective truth. It is, in fact, a creative human endeavour, and thus subject to all the same foibles as any other human endeavour" (1). Julie Cruikshank, discussing local knowledge production through social and biophysical processes, makes a similar observation when comparing the creative aspects of knowledge production: "For scientists, the creativity comes in the selection of variables and the skilful use of metaphor, rather than in composing a song, but the creative processes may not be so very different" (49). In their attention to the creative aspects of scientific research and writing, Nudds and Villard reflect a small trend in science journals, if issues of *Nature* and *Interdisciplinary Science Reviews* from the first decade of the twenty-first century are any indication.[3] Science, in other words, can operate as literary intertext inasmuch as knowing or "getting" certain scientific references opens up an understanding or interpretation or analysis of a literary text. In this chapter, I articulate an ecocritical theory that posits science as valid intertextual and referential context in literary criticism, in much the same way that history and psychology, for example, are understood as necessary intertextual referents for New Historicist and psychoanalytic approaches, respectively. Desiring more than a general sense of ecology in reading ecocritically, I look to Linda Hutcheon's influential essay about postmodern historiographic metafiction, "History and/as Intertext," as a model of thinking about science as an intertextual trail of referents.

In a 2008 interview, David Reibetanz asks McKay if he thinks "we're moving toward a bridging of [the] gap between science and art" (McKay "Growing" 64). McKay's response is in keeping with his poetic practice: "Oh, I hope so. I hope so. And if you read people on the scientific side, you can see that they're also moving closer to the humanities.... But the two cultures haven't done us any good" (65). The forced, artificial separation of science/technology and arts/humanities has led to, and continues to reinforce, damaging relations between and among humans and the environment. In "Beyond Ecology: Self, Place, and the Pathetic Fallacy," Neil Evernden calls for an intervention by arts and humanities professionals to assist the environmental movement. Evernden points toward a "deep ecological movement"[4]—beyond what he identifies as the limited "shallow ecological movement" advocated by those in the environmental sciences—"that concerns itself with the underlying roots of the environmental crisis rather than simply its physical manifestation" (102). Nature writing is one such intervention, and it represents an in-between zone or "vital edge," according to John Elder: "On one side is the literary scholarship that has largely confined itself to ... declaring texts to be no more than self-referential webs of words. On the other side stretches the domain of academic science" (Foreword vii). The sides are never quite so discrete as Elder suggests, of course, but his hyperbole enacts an effective rhetorical flourish designed more to illuminate the "vital edge" than to castigate either discipline.

The modern-science-and-literature discussion predates Monty Python's Walter Scott sketch (see Chapter Four, note eight) by nearly a century, and it offers an intriguing narrative for thinking ecocritically. Thomas Henry Huxley and Matthew Arnold in the Victorian period, and C. P. Snow and F. R. Leavis in the mid-twentieth century, have all been influential if unwitting participants in the growing discourse of ecological criticism.[5] Huxley's lecture "Science and Culture"[6] sparked one of the earliest public intellectual debates between science and literature. Challenging as it does those who opposed the inclusion of physical sciences in "ordinary education" (the classics and philosophy) (526), Huxley's sardonic riposte to classical scholars and the "practical men" (of whom few apparently remained in 1880) and those who think "that science is speculative rubbish[,] that theory and practice have nothing to do with one another," culminates in Huxley's expression of two convictions he holds very strongly: "The first is, that neither the discipline nor the subject-matter of classical education is of such direct value to the student of physical science as to justify the expenditure of valuable time upon either; and the second is, that for the purpose of attaining real culture, an exclusively scientific education is at least as effectual as an exclusively literary education" (528). Not surprisingly, Huxley's invocation of culture, and "real culture," no less, invokes Arnold, avatar of contemporary anglophile culture. Huxley posits Arnold's oft-quoted definition of culture—viz., that which seeks "to make the best that has been thought and known in the world current everywhere" ("Culture" 475)—as an anti-scientific sentiment and "strongly dissent[s] from the assumption that literature alone is competent to supply this knowledge" of which Arnold writes (529). "That the study of nature," Huxley asserts, "should have any bearing on human life was far from the thoughts of men thus trained" in the Arnoldian sense of culture (531).[7]

Arnold wasted little time fashioning a public response to Huxley, delivering "Literature and Science" as the Rede Lecture at Cambridge in August 1882 and revising it to take on a lecture tour of America (1883–84).[8] Calling for an agreement "about the meaning of the terms" he and Huxley use (490), Arnold aims to describe what is meant by literature: "Literature is a large word; it may mean everything written with letters or printed in a book. Euclid's *Elements* and Newton's *Principia* are thus literature. All knowledge that reaches us through books is literature. But by literature Professor Huxley means *belles lettres*" (490). Whereas Arnold allows that the division between science and literature is not a universal one, Huxley, in his attempt to elevate scientific education to the status of the classics, reinforces the divide. Eighty years after the Huxley–Arnold debate, C. P. Snow resurrects the claim about how "traditional culture, which is, of course, mainly literary," is divided into what he terms the "two cultures." "The separation between the two cultures," he states, "has been getting deeper under our eyes; there is now precious little communication between them, little but different kinds of incomprehension and dislike" (1). Books continue to be published that revisit (and sometimes reinforce) Snow's infamous division, despite Snow's own rethinking of his claim in 1963, allowing for the possibility of a "Third Culture," and in spite of F. R. Leavis's adamant rebuttal, published as "Two Cultures? The Significance of C. P. Snow." It suffices to say that the debate continues, even while some ecocritics insist that the boundaries between disciplines are, like those in ecological systems, membranous and permeable. They remain, to be sure, a reminder of fundamental differences between intellectual fields; but they are not impassable.[9]

More recently, Linda Hutcheon's essay "History and/as Intertext" was part of a landmark collection of essays called *Future Indicative: Literary Theory and Canadian Literature* (1987), a response, in part, to the sense of revolution nurtured by Frank Davey's provocative essay "Surviving the Paraphrase" (1976). As the collection's subtitle indicates, Hutcheon's essay played a significant role in developing a theoretical approach to Canadian literature as distinct from what Davey identified—and lamented—as thematic criticism.[10] "History and/as Intertext" represents Hutcheon's attempt to recognize the paradoxical nature of postmodern theory and to apply it—paradox and all—to works of historical fiction by Canadian writers.[11] In literary critical terms, science is to ecocriticism what history is to postmodernism. Since science cannot really exist for the layperson in anything but textual form, the analogy is apposite. Scientific language, conduit of hypotheses and results, represents a potentially rich discourse from which poets can draw. In other words, "[t]he scientific register is," according to Maurice Riordan, "useful in poetry [as a purely technical resource]. It contributes to the surface variety and overall imaginative exertion of a poem" ("Various Twine" 293). Riordan goes on to quote John Donne's "Of the Progress of the Soul," a poem that he finds interesting primarily for Donne's "use of the new medical language of dissection" (293). Despite Donne's resistance to new scientific discoveries, his poem achieves "something that science also aims for" in the way it alerts readers "to the everyday wonder of the world, to the otherness of its material reality, and to its strangeness" (293). By referring to bodily organs and processes by name, Donne effectively brings readers closer to the human body, albeit not as close as those responsible for the dissection about which he writes.

Much of what Hutcheon and her predecessors have to say about reference, about the writing of the past, resonates with similar ecocritical concerns about the representation of nature. When Hutcheon makes the "commonsense distinction" that "what history refers to is the actual, real world; what fiction refers to is a fictive universe" (169), I hear Lawrence Buell asking "Must literature always lead us away from the physical world, never back to it?" (*Environmental* 11). When she acknowledges that "the past, obviously, did exist," but contests "our ability to know that past by any other means than textualized, interpreted 'reports'" (170), I hear Leonard Scigaj writing that "language is often foregrounded only to reveal its limitations, and this [revealing] is accomplished in such a way that the reader's gaze is thrust beyond language back into the less limited natural world that language refers to" (*Sustainable* 38). And when Hutcheon asks, "How exactly does language hook onto reality?" (170), I recall her own article about Canada's historical relations to colonialism and modernism, "Eruptions of Postmodernity: The Postcolonial and the Ecological."[12] In short, I see numerous points of crossover between literary theory, as it has emerged within postmodern and historicist paradigms, and current modes of ecological and environmental critique, particularly in the way ecocritics announce unease with the limitations—the violence, the imperialism—of language.[13]

In his first collection of essays, McKay suggests that "[t]he nature poet may (should, in fact) resort to the field guide or library, but will keep coming, back, figuratively speaking, to the trail—to the grain of the experience" (*V* 27). I maintain that if the poet refers himself to the field guide, the critic should too. Returning to the trail equipped with names and stories (data) from the realm of science modifies the way we experience the trail. A number of ecocritics have argued for positioning science in a more creative role vis-à-vis literary environmental criticism, among them Glen Love, Joseph Carroll, and Ursula K. Heise. Heise provides perhaps the most convincing rationale, highlighting science's "epistemological power" and "its pervasive cultural influence in the West and, increasingly, other parts of the world" (n. pag.).[14] Heise's focus on science as a descriptive discipline that is both comparable to and different from literature as a descriptive art is key to developing ecocriticism as an interdisciplinary practice. The confrontation between scientific and literary descriptions inevitably occurs in a disciplinary ecotone from which scholars might be able to observe more than one side of a given problem. Heise challenges ecocritics, who for the most part practise traditional literary criticism, to carefully consider our limitations and the limitations of our discipline. The means for such reflexivity inhere in arts' and humanities' willingness to deconstruct cultural and textual constructs, means that rhetoricians of science have usefully employed to draw attention to the complex role of language in science and scientific writing. Resist the urge to occupy "simply a site of resistance against science," Heise implores; examine, in addition, what might be gained by considering how and why literary criticism deviates aesthetically and ideologically. Five years after Heise's contribution to the debate, David Gilcrest notices that "the ecological poem may make use of the precise grammar of ecological science; more often than not, however, [it] reflects a more general sense of ecology" (16). Perhaps the poet, who despite his knowledge of certain ecologies remains a thoughtful amateur, can achieve nothing more than a general sense of ecology with his deployment of precise ecological terms. Technical precision—specific names, accurate interspecies relations—might be enough to start poets, readers, and ecocritics down a trail with multiple opportunities for pursuing scientific data and experiential knowledge.

Knowing (not owning) opens up a route of referents that invites fresh readings: "In literary criticism directed chance arises from the intertext of the critic's repertoire of poetry and the corollary reading the critic makes" (Valdes & Guyon 30). Even though intertextuality "encompasses far more than just source criticism or the study of allusion" (Hubbard 7), critics and theorists have tended to devote intertextual analyses to "cultural phenomena, particularly literature and visual art" (Banting "Angel" 69). In *The Pipes of Pan: Intertextuality and Literary Filiation in the Pastoral Tradition from Theocritus to Milton* (1999), Thomas K. Hubbard examines intertextuality's development from Julia Kristeva's coinage (in *Desire in Language*), by way of Mikhail Bakhtin's dialogism, to other French theorists' refinements. Gérard Genette, for example, prefers "transtextuality" to refer to a movement between literary texts and provides a list of subclasses of intertextuality in *Palimpsests* (1997), which Hubbard compiles into a list:

1) "intertextuality" proper, actual citation of a subtext;
2) "paratextuality," a text's relation to its own apparatus;
3) "metatextuality," commentary or criticism of a subtext, whether explicit or implicit;
4) "hypertextuality," adoption of a subtext as a foil, as in imitation, adaptation, continuation, or parody;
5) "architextuality," relations not to a specific subtext but to a generic convention or type of discourse. (Hubbard 8)

Genette's and Hubbard's discussions of intertextuality reinforce Canadian ecocritic Pamela Banting's claim in "The Angel in the Glacier: Geography as Intertext in Thomas Wharton's *Icefields*" (2001) that most critics consider intertextuality solely on the basis of its, and the text's, relation to culture and cultural tropes. Text presupposes itself as active referent; text begets text in a culturally (pre)determined world of texts. Authorial agency is rendered moot, readers' agency mute. Genette's five subclasses rely upon overt constructions of text and textuality (ostensibly by an author) and could just as accurately be called variations on the theme of allusion, a quirk that is all fine and well but that, in the end, eludes and elides a given reader's chance intertextual discoveries based on her personal reading histories, on relations that an author—much less a text—cannot anticipate.

Without allowing for some sense of unconscious, serendipitous encounters between texts and readers' histories, intertextual theory risks privileging a particular trail of referents by focusing only on texts that are apt to be well known by a wide audience. The act and the process of reading thus risks becoming, if it has not become already, a passive mode of engagement with pre-existing literary and cultural ideals. Michael Cohen, in "Reading after Darwin: A Prospectus" (2007), reasons that such a possibility is unfortunate, since the "point of interdisciplinary work might be that it is collaborative, that it is dialogic and not monological, that it breaks down hierarchies and structures of authority, that it avoids the pitfalls of hero worship ... and iconography" (226). Passive reading closes off the possibility of interdisciplinary authors and astute readers challenging interdisciplinary boundaries. The route of referents conventional intertextuality offers, in other words, is a well-worn path back to some canonical text or ideology, whereas McKay's trail of referents relies simultaneously on readers' knowledge of generic conventions and on their ability to recognize the call to step away from the poem and peer into potentially unfamiliar texts and trails.

What are we to make then of Leonard Scigaj's claim, in *Sustainable Poetry*, that ecopoets "seldom write poems that demand particular knowledge of the technical intricacies of scientific theory" (12)? If ecopoetry "treats nature as a separate and equal other and includes respect for nature conceived as a series of ecosystems—dynamic and potentially self-regulating cyclic feedback systems," as Scigaj claims "we need" (5), why wouldn't ecocritics encourage a literature—and a discourse on that literature—engaged intertextually with "particular knowledge," "technical intricacies," and "scientific theory?" Ecopoets strive for particularity as a way of getting at the core of a problem, a kernel of wisdom approximating—becoming proximal to—truth or a set of truths. Compare, for example, the "unadorned bluntness" of Wallace Stevens's language in his Canadian journals (and subsequent poems). In *Notations of the Wild: Ecology in the Poetry of Wallace Stevens* (1997), Gyorgyi Voros attributes the lack of taxonomical and species specificity to Stevens's unfamiliarity with the "birds, flowers [and] mountains" in British Columbia (48).[15] Rather than criticize Stevens's lack of knowledge as others have done, Voros draws attention to how "his attenuated vocabulary bespeaks the distance and strangeness between him and his new environment" (48). While Stevens's preference for the general over the specific might indicate an early suspicion of language and metaphor vis-à-vis "Nature in its less diluted forms" (Voros 49), linguistic precision precludes neither an understanding of the limits of language nor the role of metaphor in negotiating distance and proximity.

As Nabhan claims, "the technical lexicon of the sciences [is] sufficiently precise to describe just about any phenomenon that we wish to record" and "many poets [are] sprinkling scientific terms into their writing because of [this] very precision" (60). And yet, despite the advancing successes of scientifically precise language, a metaphor remains necessary if poetry—eco, sustainable, and otherwise—hopes to enact a productive, ecotonal link between humans and nonhumans. Relying too strictly on the science, like emphasizing realism at the expense of imagination in ecocriticism, according to Adam Dickinson, "threatens to marginalize lyrical approaches to the natural world that provide an alternative way of thinking ethics, a way that points to a political activism, but not in the terms of any systematic methodology" ("Lyric" 17). Dickinson, whose interest in "alternative ways of thinking" tends to be ethical, stops short of endorsing a readerly interrogation of the scientific language that informs McKay's poetry, even though those poets—Alison Hawthorne Deming and Richard Shelton for Nabhan, Don McKay for me—who handle "biological facts well in their writing" also offer "an altogether different way of making sense of the world, one perhaps complementary to that of the conservation biologist" (Nabhan 68). An understanding of systematic methodologies is not mutually exclusive of either environmental ethics or political activism. In the face of the current global crisis, perhaps they are mutually inclusive. I agree with Scigaj's claim that ecopoets do not "demand" particular knowledge, but rather invite readers to reduce the distance between the written word and the world that is written because of the alternatives such proximity elicits for attempting the world.

Admittedly, not everyone seems as convinced as I am "that the goal of environmental poetry is, as [David W.] Gilcrest states, to put us in closer proximity to the natural world" (Dickinson "Lyric" 38). "If that were the case," asks Dickinson, "wouldn't one be better advised to simply go out into the woods?" (38). I want to answer Dickinson's rhetorical question with a resounding "Yes!" but I recognize (1) its rhetorical intent and (2) that such an answer would position me rather unfavourably alongside Lawrence Buell, whose own rhetorical question—"Must literature always lead us away from the physical world, never back to it?" (*Environmental* 11)—has been the focus of theory-based critiques of the American ecocritic's apparent reification of realism.[16] Instead of my monosyllabic affirmative response to Dickinson's question, then, I offer an extension of it and of Dickinson's own argument "that any relationship metaphor has with 'reality' comes from its articulated ontological ambivalence, or resonance between the 'is' and the 'is not'" (37). Can one not have the "is" and the "is not" of metaphor and of proximity, especially as the latter is rendered by scientific knowing and technical precision? Is truth, which McKay argues might best be approached by way of metaphor-as-lie, not at times a nearness to something beyond the human? Moreover, if ecopoetry and ecocriticism imply a practical relation to the physical—environmental activism, for example—realism might not be such a bad approach. Dickinson, though, focuses less on how ecopoetry represents the real world and more on the potential for ecopoetry to model ways of attempting the real world. He writes:

> I think the goal of environmental poetry is to be generative: it is to enact lyrical thinking that is not limited by systematic logic; it is to make an issue of the unquestioned reality of materiality; it is to think of things and our relation to them otherwise than as single language-games. Poetry cannot give us access to the natural world as such, but it can offer us a model of attention to the material metaphoricity of bodies or things; it can provoke us to think the materiality of the natural world in ways not contained by systematic language. ("Lyric" 38–39)

The access of which Dickinson speaks might be unattainable; however, science's relative proximity to the material world it studies, names, and attempts to explain, improves the possibility of access by "reduc[ing] our level of ignorance" about the physical world (Love *Practical* 47). Provocations to think materially invite readers to seek a way of knowing the world beyond the poem, the book, the office. Science is one way to know the world, and its empirical observations, limited though they are by human bias and error, provide access to the world's materiality using repeatable methods and producing testable results unlike, say, synesthesia, which also provides a way to know the material world. Desire for proximity, in other words, provokes movement away from text and language and toward the material world; so the tension between metaphorical knowing and scientific knowledge instigates in the careful reader a desire to step out.

This tension in McKay's writing represents a literary inverse of physical scientists' gradual retreat from the field to the laboratory, which Battalio acknowledges in his study of ornithological rhetoric. The ecocriticism I argue for requires a subtle shift in the literary critical paradigm, which traditionally positions itself (or gets positioned) against science in public and academic discourse, in order to be successfully interdisciplinary. It requires, and poets such as McKay articulate, a thoughtful respect for what science has accomplished. It also resonates in the duality of Hutcheon's "and/as."

Nearly all areas of intellectual pursuit listen to science and scientific knowledge in explicit ways because the scientific method has enabled "both technological innovations and solutions to practical problems" (Bocking 17). The contributions of the scientific community are indisputable, whether in the field of food science (Louis Pasteur), medicine (Frederick Banting), genetics (Watson and Crick), or locomotion (the Wright brothers). Without scientific research we might still be building houses with asbestos and painting them with lead paint. The paradigmatic shift asks that humanists recognize that science has argued "convincingly for a commonsense realism: that there exists a real world, independent of [humans] and [human] values, and that science, while fallible, can provide true and useful accounts of this reality" (Bocking 17). As others, namely Glen Love and Dana Phillips, have noted, literary critics have tended to focus on the fallibilities of science rather than on its accomplishments. That is not to say the shift should necessarily ignore the fallibilities or that critiques of science have not been valid. Just unbalanced.

In "Turbulence," a short poem in *Another Gravity* (50), McKay incorporates language from a scientific text in order to critique the poor writing and to offer a poetic response to the problem articulated in the text. The poem begins with a passage about turbulence from Sir Graham Sutton's *Mastery of the Air: An Account of the Science of Mechanical Flight* (1965). As

McKay notes when introducing the poem on *Songs for the Songs of Birds* (2008), the book is generally well written and helpful, and he chose the worst sentence to form half of his poem. Sutton claims in this sentence that turbulence cannot be defined; McKay attempts, in the second half of the poem, to prove Sutton wrong by demonstrating how one might define turbulence, deforming Sutton's words and reusing them in a turbulent manner. So, Sutton's claim that "velocity exhibits finite oscillations of a random character" becomes "the ferocity exhibits final / oscar nominations of those random characters"; "kinematics of mean motion" becomes "killer statics of mean motion"; and "coefficient of drag" becomes "co-fishermen of drag." McKay's attempt to define turbulence by disrupting the relentless flow of Sutton's run-on sentence playfully enacts an interdisciplinary strategy that, while not explicitly ecological, demonstrates a mind open to other ways of thinking. His critique of Sutton's bad writing exists concomitant with his interest in what he has to say about aerodynamics in the rest of the book. A turbulent poem about turbulence lingers critically on an edge between two modes of writing and offers an ironic model of risky interdisciplinarity, a space within which to voice reverence and suspicion.

The interdisciplinary stage has been set from early on if ecocriticism "urges its practitioners," as Glen Love suggests, "into interdisciplinarity, into science," if literature already "involves relationships, and ecological awareness enhances and expands [a] sense of interrelationships to encompass nonhuman as well as human contexts" (47). For Pamela Banting, intertextual information in Thomas Wharton's *Icefields* (1995) has the potential to immerse readers "in the geology, history, natural history, and oral history associated with the [geographic] area" around Jasper, Alberta, where the novel takes place. Banting's reading of *Icefields* cannot depend upon a preexisting and comprehensive knowledge of glaciology if she is not a glaciologist. First, Banting, as reader, must follow the compulsion "both to immerse [her]self in books about the history, geography, geology, and literature of the Rocky Mountains and the archival documents and photographs at the Whyte Museum of the Canadian Rockies and to travel to the 'actual' setting around Jasper, Alberta, to learn firsthand about the glaciation, fluvial patterns, trails, plants, and animals of the area" (67); second, she must "take the next step and surrender the notion of the exclusivity of the human subject as author or scriptor" (70) and allow instead for the possibility of, in the case of Wharton's first novel, the landscape as both scriptor and script(ed). To consider such a possibility seriously is to consider the metaphysical alongside the physical aspects of interdisciplinary research. Banting's reading implicates far more than a community of literary critics. It suggests that the act of reading cuts across numerous daily and professional activities, from the obvious act of reading literature—for pleasure, in a classroom, at a conference—to the process of reading the physical world as if it were a text. Interdisciplinarity comes into play precisely because different languages—the language of literary theory, for example, or the language of avian physiology—are needed to contemplate, understand, and articulate different approaches to the world. If we insist on reading the land as text, "the suggestive scrawls and traces" left by "the sinuous calligraphy of rivers winding across the land" and "the black slash burned by lightning into the trunk of an old elm" (Abram 95), we would do well to acknowledge what might be lost as well as what might be gained in enacting the translation. The lack in this case—lack of utter control, lack of linguistic accomplishment—might result in achieving an awareness of said lack. We would do well to learn as much as possible about the "texts" we feel compelled to read, just as we would do well to consider ourselves as "texts" to be "read" by the natural world.

From an evolutionary point of view, such a reversal of anthropocentric epistemology is possible if we consider human evolution in relation to other species with which we have apparently co-evolved. Michael Pollan makes an intriguing case for co-evolution in *The Botany of Desire: A Plant's-Eye View of the World* (2001). Presenting four chapters in which he pairs a human desire with a plant—sweetness/apple; beauty/tulip; intoxication/marijuana; control/potato—Pollan essentially argues that all of "these plant species have found that the best way" of fulfilling the evolutionary imperative to reproduce "is to induce animals—bees or people, it hardly matters—to spread their genes" for them "by playing on the animals' desires, conscious or otherwise" (xv). As a consequence of human desires having become "simply more grist for the evolutionary mill," he proposes, "it makes as much sense to think of agriculture as something grasses did to people as a way to conquer the trees" (xxi). Pollan's co-evolutionary proclamation is of interest to my argument for the way it purports to humble human vanity vis-à-vis the natural world while positioning humans unquestionably within the natural world. McKay attempts a similar revisionary philosophy in "Otherwise Than Place," when he wonders what would happen if "we tr[ied] to define place without using the usual humanistic terms—not home and native land, not little house on the prairie, not even the founding principle of our sense of beauty—but as a function of wilderness" (*DW* 17). As I mention in my introduction, McKay cultivates an understanding of wilderness as both the typical "set of endangered spaces" and "the capacity of all things to elude the mind's appropriations" (*V* 21). A (re)definition of place as a function of wilderness, then, "would involve asking, for example, not 'what's the beach to me?' but 'what am I to the beach?'" (*DW* 17).

According to Leonard Scigaj, Karl Kroeber "affirms that literary criticism ought to seek its theoretical models not in language theory or the aesthetics of consciousness but in the physical sciences, especially biology.[17] By studying the physical sciences one can gain an adequate grasp of nature as an equal other, the necessary referential context where all poetic meditations occur" (14). Moreover, "Carolyn Merchant, in the preface to her 1990 *The Death of Nature*, also suggests that the proper models for environmental inquiry and literature should come from referential reality—the physical sciences" (15). So, ecologically oriented literary critics might have good reason to keep up to date on those aspects of the physical and natural sciences pertinent to the texts they are reading. After reading Christopher Dewdney's *A Palaeozoic Geology of London, Ontario* (1973), for example, my corollary reading might be an article in the latest issue of *Sedimentary Geology* as well as Julie Cruikshank's *Do Glaciers Listen? Local Knowledge, Colonial Encounters, and Social Imagination* (2005). After reading John Clare's "The Pettichap's Nest," I feel compelled to research the ornithological literature (monographs, articles, letters) about pettichap nest-building behaviour, or to record observations of the nesting habits of some local avian species. The resulting ecocriticism serves as a strategy for developing an ecological criticism relevant to other literary texts as well. McKay's poem "Sturnus Vulgaris" reminds me of a recent article in *The New York Times* about avian intelligence, and the *Times* article leads to a recent study in *Nature* about European starlings' ability to comprehend "recursive, hierarchical embedding of language units" (Gentner et al.). (Further research in starlings in North America will reveal cultural and political aspects—namely, how they have been portrayed as pests after being brought from England as part of Eugene Scheifflin's attempt to introduce to North America every bird mentioned by Shakespeare.) Such routes, or trails of referents, that lead readers literally back to the physical world are significant aspects of much ecocriticism, in much the way an understanding of biology, evolution, or ecology is significant. For the most part, though, such aspirations tend to suffer under the substantial weight of interdisciplinary research and its attendant risks of dilletantism. Once the risks of following the trails are identified, enough ecocritics will be willing to search out the rewards, if not of any real conclusions, then at least of entering the ecotone.

ecotone four

> Long pause.　　　Well?
> Then that depopulated silence.
> That darker dark.
> – Don McKay, "Deep Time Encounters," *P* 35

FIELD TRIPS

Pause. Meditation. These related acts often occur in a space between. Pausing in the ecotone—a concise if incomplete description of what BC has been attempting—readies mind and body for encounters that have the potential to lead away from comfortable assumptions about the world. The pause of meditation attentive to the planet's cadences, to the rhythmic patterns of land- and cityscape, requires deliberate focus not unlike the cautious multivalence of much ecocritical work. Stopping at a crosswalk on the way to the office, minus headphones as accompaniment, BC might notice how robins' liquid trills insinuate themselves into an urban soundscape of water dripping from a nearby eavestrough, car brakes squeaking, dogs barking, buskers busking, sirens moving through the city like aural spider silk. He might experience a hill's incline differently when wearing sandals instead of proper walking shoes, and the subtle shift in muscle tension once the ground evens out and reveals a panoramic view of the harbour. He might associate that view, the salty smell of ocean, the slight burn in his calves with the sound of his breathing and the way his heart beats in his ears for a few seconds while he stops to look around.

  The book sits on the desk. Light and shadow combine in Robert Banderheyden's cover photograph to reveal a fossilized trilobite that lived approximately 540 million years ago. *Paradoxides*, the fossil and the book, rest uneasily as works of art "demanding to be read" (McKay *P* 40).

BC wonders about the way McKay's interest in birds and avian poetics shifted to geology and geopoetry. How alike might these seemingly unlike focuses be?

A challenge confronts BC while studying a poet in the midst of his most prolific phase: how to accommodate subtle (or not-so-subtle) shifts in McKay's poetics while maintaining a focus on the announced topic. In both *Deactivated West 100* and *Strike/Slip*, McKay began articulating his geopoetics, a poetry and poetics interested in how geologic forces, and humans' capacity to comprehend geologic time, facilitate thoughtful responses to the more-than-human world. McKay borrows the term "geopoetry" from Harry H. Hess, a geologist who developed a theory of plate tectonics. In "Geopoetry" (*DW* 42–43), an entry in the prose poem/abecedarian "Between Rock and Stone: A Geopoetic Alphabet," McKay writes about Hess's request that other geologists "concede many suppositions in order to entertain the idea that seafloor spreading, driven by magma rising continuously from the mantle, accounts for both the movement of plates and the surprising youth of the ocean floor" (42). "Geopoetry," writes McKay, was a "concession to sceptics," a term that acknowledged the speculative nature of Hess's theory.[1] But in the wake of Hess's theories having been proven, McKay wonders about the potential for geopoetry's renewed relevance during a time when human arrogance threatens to push planet Earth beyond its capacity to accommodate us. "What better term," he asks, "for those moments of pure wonder when we contemplate even the most basic elements of planetary dwelling, and our words fumble in their attempts to do them justice" (42). Geopoetry extends the paradoxical notion that poetry clatters, that words' "greatest eloquence lies in their failure" (*DW* 68). It resonates, too, with what McKay identifies in his foreword to A. F. Moritz's *Early Poems* (2002) as the poet's "profound anarchism, which denies the usual structures of knowing in the interests of opening a wider, phenomenal, sense of the real" ("Shipwreck" 14).[2] By extension, therefore, McKay has been writing geopoetry for years; but he had not articulated it as a key aspect of his poetics until 2005.[3]

As he does with "Twinflower," McKay uses poetry as a "critique of the Romantic idea of the sympathy of all things" and revises the Romantic paradigm rather than simply repudiating or rejecting it (Leckie 127–28). While his project is neither to support scientific practices uncritically nor to challenge them, much of his poetry enables readers to do both should they choose to follow the trail of referents he blazes. The information science provides—information about how three types of faults are produced by differing tectonic movements, for example—sprouts along the edge of a trail BC follows from the poem "'Stress, Shear, and Strain Theories of Failure'" (S/S 33) to *The Geology of Southern Vancouver Island*.

Named for an early geologist's application of a physics theory (about the potential failure of tensiles, ductiles, and brittles relative to the amount of stress exerted on them) to tectonic forces, "'Stress, Shear, and Strain Theories of Failure'" demonstrates McKay's metaphorical skills as well as his ability to integrate language and concepts from the hard sciences. It is also, like "Close-up on a Sharp-shinned Hawk," what BC has come to call an unsonnet. For a poem that announces itself as a sonnet with the line "This sonnet hereby sings," "'Stress, Shear, and Strain Theories of Failure'" accomplishes much more than its glib self-naming suggests by testing the limits of a traditional lyric form against a subject—the earth's crust—that defies simple definition. Though it contains fourteen lines, this sonnet does not adhere to a strict metrical pattern or rhyming scheme, and it is about love, that traditional lyric subject, only in the sense that the poet might, in writing the poem, be making a humble gesture in homage to earth's "chthonic shear." The poem might have been called "Song for the Song of the Failing Lithosphere" for the way McKay plays on the tensions between fault ("The earth-engine / driving itself through death after death. Strike/slip, / thrust, and the fault called normal, which occurs / when two plates separate"), failure (as in the theories of the title), and (human) failing ("Let us fail / in all the styles established by our lithosphere"). The sonnet sustains McKay's suspicion of language, metaphor, and poetry, all of which he argues elsewhere fail necessarily yet instructively.

The traditional sonnet here fails in its attempt to contain the shifting dynamics of the "earth-engine." Beginning the first line with three trochaic feet followed by an appropriately placed catalectic to echo the linguistic "lift," the next three lines attempt to settle into an iambic pentameter but struggle under the "stress shear strain" of metapoetic humility and attention:

> They have never heard of lift
> and are – for no one, over and over – cleft. Riven,
> recrystallized. Ruined again. The earth-engine
> driving itself through death after death. Strike/slip,

Significant for giving the collection its title, this poem challenges conventional wisdom—"orthodox thinking," as Maurice Riordan has it—regarding both lyric poetry and lay geology. The rhythms "clatter" here too, as McKay suggests poetry does in an earlier poem, and the earth itself splits and shifts, as the repetition of "death," the synonymous "cleft" and "riven," as well as "*recrystallization*" and "ruined *again*" indicate. In choosing to resist the sonnet form so explicitly, McKay does not suggest he has somehow found a way not to participate in the colonizing force of the English language. His poems reveal a complicity he feels as a member of North American society and as a poet. It is good "meditative medicine," McKay writes, to consider otherwise-than-place (*DW* 19); it is instructive to consider our relation to the world in ways that reveal, at the very least, our inadequacies as a species and, at the very worst, our arrogance and our violence.

But McKay has been interested in rocks for quite a while, as BC's rereading of earlier works reveals. In "Meditation on a Geode" (*NF* 16),[4] McKay writes about a type of rock "formed, says [an] old geology textbook, from the modification and enlargement of an original void. O," a rock that represents "a tiny ocean in an egg." This "egg" began forming when "a little animal who lived and / died, got buried in the silt and gradually decayed to nothing, which filled up with [salt] water." Freshwater life continues outside the limestone shell, while inside the shell a slow transformation takes place and gives birth to nothing, to void, and yet this transformation enables an infinite set of imaginative possibilities about the egg:

> In which a subtle and irresistible idea, osmosis, unclenches outward against the rock, widening the hole and seeping through the silica until the salts inside and outside balance. And everything (slow gong) crystallizes: : animal, emptiness, ocean, gland : ode of the earth.

"Meditation on a Geode" offers an example of McKay, mid-career, inviting his readers along a scientific trail of referents by combining the language of a geology textbook with the poet's lateral and abstract thinking (BC notes the floating colon that follows emptiness and anticipates the list on the following line). The poem's final phrase, "ode of the earth," succinctly plays on the word "geode"—as a combination of *geo*, from the Greek word for earth, and *ode*, a poem intended to be sung or performed—and implies that even abiotic rocks demonstrate an intelligence constantly at work and worthy of our attention. To comprehend such intelligence and to "think the connections between" such objects as geodes, beach stones, and mountains and the forces that contribute to their ongoing formation requires "a stretch test of the imagination, including what is perhaps the supreme stretch test – geologic time" (*DW*16). Although the stretch test inevitably ends in failure, the attempt (and its failure) function alongside McKay's avian poetics to demonstrate a need for reimagining humans' relations to the rest of the world, for rethinking humans' place in a world that is billions of years older than we are. But, as McKay asks in "Astonished—" (*S/S* 3), a poem that recognizes astonishment's etymological connection to geology, "Are you thinking / or being thought?" The answer, BC thinks, is both. We respond to the phenomenal world by attempting to comprehend it. We also exist as a biological figment of the planet's evolutionary, geologic imagination.

No, McKay's poetics have not simply progressed, in neat chronological fashion, from avian poetics to geopoetics. He has not abruptly finished with birds and moved on to rocks. He has, rather, finally found a way to articulate geopoetry, something he has been thinking and writing about since his first collection. While BC tends to read McKay's fifth book, *Birding, or desire*, as the work of a poet who has found his voice after having written competent but uneven poems for a decade—a vocational progression not uncommon among writers—some of the poems McKay published prior to 1983 show the beginnings of his thinking about the distinction he now makes between rock and stone. In "These Mighty Timbers" (*AOS* 12), for example, McKay writes that

> rocks
> are rocks and are not
> just, or quite,
> when you feel them, take them home
> the granite your hammer chipped
> the circling encircling land you hunger,
>   never to possess.

Here, in 1973, McKay recognizes the capacity of the land—granite—to elude the mind's appropriations, though he has yet to develop the lexicon—or "ecolect," as some ecocritics would have it[5]—to name it wilderness. Having developed his notion of wilderness, McKay is able to return to the vocabulary of rock, which functions in his poetics much like wilderness does: "What happens between rock and stone," he writes in "Rock, Stone" (*DW* 59), "is simply everything human, from the modifications necessary to make homes to, at the other extreme, the excesses of ownership and exploitation which submit all ends to ours.... [R]ock is as old as the earth is; stone is only as old as humanity." Human presence and use, in other words, translate rock into stone—stone hammer, gravel, paving stone, tombstone, milestone—the way "place becomes place by acquiring real or imagined borders and suffering removal from anonymity" (*DW* 18). As McKay's interest in both domesticity and wilderness—the desire for home and the inability to acquire home, respectively—as well as the title of his abecedarian demonstrate, he remains fascinated with what occurs between various ideas, states, worlds.

The distance between rock and stone offers a particularly salient ecotone from which to contemplate one's place in geologic time. A place to pause and meditate. "Otherwise Than Place" begins with an admission: "I keep a rubbing stone in my pocket – a piece of glossy basalt from the west coast of Vancouver Island. It's become my palm's companion, always there in moments of stress or boredom, a reassuring weight that's smoother – thanks to the continual wave action which has kept it rubbing against the other rocks on the beach – than skin" (*DW* 15). Since McKay has taken a rock from the beach, has appropriated it for his own use as a stress reliever and companion, it has, according to his definition, become stone. Apparently he has been carrying, or at least thinking about, rubbing stones since the mid-1980s, when he wrote "Rubbing Stone" (*SD* 27). Again, too early to articulate his geopoetic distinction between rock and stone, this poem nevertheless anticipates the opening of "Otherwise Than Place" and the poem "Philosopher's Stone" (*S/S* 43–44). After providing a litany of possible names for the rubbing stone—jewel, gewgaw—the birder-poet recounts how it came into being:

> this stone slavegirl of the ocean constantly
> caressed and beaten rubble
> rubble at Pacific's lip where deep heave
> crashes into nonsense this stone
>   this stone
> . . . .
> whose dead language is catastrophe this stone
> living in my pocket as its hermit (*SD* 27)

The odd comparison of the stone to a slave girl who is both "caressed and beaten" into a "hard / softness" draws attention to human acts of violence that thoughtlessly mirror the catastrophic, paradoxically creative violence the earth perpetrates against itself. It also points to "the birth of eros," to a human (male) tendency to act on his desires as though they must be fulfilled, as though his desires were all. But the hermit living in the poet's pocket seeks to modify such anthropocentric ways of thinking the relation to other humans, other creatures, and other intelligences. In "Philosopher's Stone," an updated version of "Rubbing Stone," the poet allows for the possibility that he has been adopted by the hermit who is now, as he says,

> living in my pocket as its sage, as my third
> uncanny testicle, the wise one,
> the one who will teach me to desire
> only whatever happens (43)

As the poet rubs this stone in his pocket—sage, philosopher—so is he being rubbed by the stone. Two modes of intelligence are touching each other, which the poet realizes in the poem's closing lines: "it turns out / though it can't be / we both know—" (44). What and how they both know are different; but they can teach each other, too, about desire. This poet learns that desire does not determine what happens. This poet learns about a species of longing that is without the desire to possess ("Appropriate" 54). This poet learns.

And so, with a growing understanding of various fields and the impetus to embark on field trips to libraries and woods alike, does BC attempt to learn. Though a goal might be to cajole McKay himself into taking a field trip to Mistaken Point in Newfoundland, where he's been living since winning the Griffin Prize, BC is content for now to trip into the fields carved by *Paradoxides*. Following the opening section's bird poems, other sections and poems name rocks with a precision BC has come to expect. "Labradorite" (P 36–37) exudes "Frostbitten light," an "oil spill / practising za-zen" "inside otherwise plain / plagioclase feldspar" (36). "Mistaken Point" (P 38), on the contrary, identifies an absence of knowledge surrounding "a fernlike creature" fossilized along the Avalon Peninsula: "What shall we call / this antique frond," the birder-poet wonders, "part fern, part feather, / part Art Nouveau and brand new Braille, / urgent and enigmatic as an oracle?" That he doesn't proceed to name it beyond the metaphorical gestures of the poem indicates a comfort with not knowing. This poet learns. That something so ancient—"Precambrian, pre-Burgess Shale" (38)—should occupy the same imaginative space as an oracle attests to the complex negotiations between material (bodily, earthbound) and ephemeral (spiritual, ethereal) that animate the birder-poet's trips into and reports from the field. More remains to be said about the birder-poet's not-so-secret life as geo-poet; more calls to be learned about the earth engine; more wants to be understood about deep time and humans' arrival in the Anthropocene.

With ears ready to hear, and eyes gazing down, BC heads into the field. His pack is filled with poetry and guides, apples and a Thermos full of iced tea. Binoculars weigh on his belt. Anticipation fuels his imagination. What he has learned exposes gaps in his knowledge, even as he has accumulated more. The question, of course, remains: So what? What will he do with such knowledge, knowing? Closing *Paradoxides* and putting it in his pack, BC sets out. So, he thinks, let's find out.

Ending

> a convenient place to end (though not to conclude).
> – Don McKay, "The Bushtits' Nest" (*V* 106)

RAVENS

> maybe I will find myself back out here with the traffic,
> picking up popcans,
> listening for the moment when a raven takes a piece of sky,
> packs it like a snowball,
> and speaks.
> – Don McKay, "On Foot to the Bypass Esso Postal Outlet" (*A* 55)

To end is not necessarily to conclude. Despite the finite materiality of this book, of all books, the ideas I hope reach beyond the physical boundaries of the page. To do what? To invite others into a conversation. What is a book of criticism if not a constant search for "a convenient place to end (though not to conclude)" (McKay *V* 107)? Perhaps, as the popular Canadian band the Tragically Hip declare, I have been "looking for a place to happen / getting lost along the way." A place to happen is a place to end these ecocritical essays, then, but not to conclude the discussions about ecocriticism and avian poetics shaped by Don McKay's words. Here I offer myself a way out while offering you—reader, student, birder-critic—possible ways back in. To begin looking for your own ways to happen and get lost along the way. McKay's raven poems represent an ecotone where bird and rock, ornithology and geology, speech and deep time come together and put us humans in our place among the most recent of natural phenomena. Here, at the end.

Just as Halitherses demonstrated a capacity for translating what he learned from birds, McKay shares through his poetry what he has learned from birds and stones and trees. More accurately, he shares what he has learned from bushtits and basalt and black spruce and from the various interactions he has observed. He also, as his species specificity, his lyric humility, and his distrust of language suggest, gives credit where credit is due, preferring to sabotage what Keats identified as the "wordsworthian or egotistical sublime" typical of traditional lyric poetry by writing in spite of the faults and failings of a poet. Sometimes the proximity afforded by specificity results in an ironic distancing between poet and subject. A late poem, "Song of the Saxifrage to the Rock" (S/S 10),[1] expresses this irony even as the title announces its link to McKay's homage to and ohmage of birdsong. Uncharacteristically, McKay writes this poem in the voice of a plant addressing a rock, rather than the unnamed birder-poet (or watcher, or excursionist figure) of other poems, who often addresses an unidentified listener. Saxifrage, also called rockfoil, is a fairly common plant native to subarctic, temperate regions. This saxifrage, though, asks a lot of questions, including one about other plants that have attempted to grow on the basalt: "How many fingerholds / have failed, been blown or washed away, unworthy / of your dignified *avoirdupois*, your strict / hexagonal heart?" This song, this homage, sounds like a love song as the saxifrage lauds "Monsieur Basalt" for being heavier with the past than "the twentieth century." The saxifrage sounds, actually, quite similar to McKay's humble birder-poet, especially during the poem's final lines, in which several McKavian ideas come together in an attempt to nudge the rock, respectfully, closer toward stone:

> Listen, slow one
> let me be your fool, let me sit
> on your front porch in my underwear
> and tell you risqué stories about death. Together
> we will mix our dust and luck and turn ourself
> into the archipelago of nooks.

More than simply a poet, the saxifrage is a geopoet whose words obviously "fumble in their attempts" to do the basalt justice. Willing to be the fool, to sit half-naked on a porch, the saxifrage must invent words to express its ecotonal position; the awkward reflexive pronoun "ourself" simultaneously reveals the limitations of language and the creative desire to use language against itself as a method of checking its colonizing tendencies. Articulating an ecological relation, the saxifrage also expresses with the term "ourself" an awareness of individual ontology coeval with a group ontology. The self lives contemporaneously with a diverse, polyphonic community of organisms and other nonliving matter within an "archipelago of nooks." This saxifrage sings as if in response to William Rueckert's question, at the conclusion of his experiment in ecocriticism, about how critics can "move from the community of literature to the larger biospheric community which ecology tells us ... we belong to even as we are destroying it" (121). Singing is one way; playing the fool is another; doing both, as ravens, those quintessential northwest tricksters often do, is still another.

In "Song for the Songs of the Common Raven" (S/S 27), McKay adds to his homage/ohmage repertoire of poems and extends some thoughts he has expressed about the poetry of Dylan Thomas, the subject of his doctoral dissertation. Much of what McKay identifies in Thomas's craft manifests in McKay's own poetry. Like Thomas, McKay "revels in puns and displaced clichés" and can "afford to be as rhetorical and even pompously oracular as he sometimes is, because the trickster's tongue is in the poet's cheek" ("Crafty" 376–77). I do not want to suggest that McKay has built a career attempting to mimic Thomas's craftiness and style; my purpose in introducing McKay's own criticism here at this late stage is twofold: to acknowledge a continuity between his early thinking about the trickster in Thomas's poetry (a continuity that runs parallel to avian and geopoetics); and to highlight the possibility that an ecotone—between critical and creative writing in this case—need not observe a temporal proximity. The "smoke-and-whisky brogue" of the common raven resides in the Latin name, *Corvus corax*. The raven's song, because it seems ancient and heavy with earth, acts as aural link between avian and geopoetics despite the fact that it "says nothing" of "its brutal seismic histories," that it "conspicuously / does not sing" "of the flowing and bending of rock, / of the burning and going down and coming / up again as lava." What, then, does McKay—modern-day Halitherses, twenty-first-century John Clare—learn from these ravens if not about the geopoetry that has formed the earth and informs the poems of *Strike/Slip* and *Paradoxides*? These ravens say many things, hence the plural "songs" in the title, and yet what they say "is hollowed out and rendered terminally / hoarse." The birder-poet does not reveal what he learns; he only guesses that the raven's messages "might / say 'Watch your asses, creatures / of the Neogene' or might say 'Baby, / bring it on.'" These ravens, older than humanity and wiser—based both on what they symbolize through story and myth and on their evolutionary history on the west coast of North America—actively resist meaning.

The intelligence and playfulness—not mutually exclusive qualities—the ravens in McKay's work display characterize them as creatures audibly and acrobatically audacious. If the birder-poet occupies a space between from which to observe and note avian behaviour, as the speaker of "Ravens at Play over Mount Work" (*P* 11–12) certainly does, ravens, too, exploit "the steep / veer that limns the knife edge / hidden in the wind" (11). As the verb "limn" suggests, though, the ravens are all action, their liminal position as "Intro- / aggroverts of small-b being" manifesting as "the improv / at the heart of things" (11). That humans can never quite grasp what's going on in raven minds clarifies their introversion; that, as the earlier raven poem concludes, humans might be the object of ravens' taunting cries confirms the birds' aggro. In the midst of "having scavenged Yiddish, / Irish, !Kung, English, and / Inuktitut" (11), the ravens also observe the birder-poet

> perched on the summit writing
> *yowp*, writing *tók* and *wörk*, writing what
> would it be like to be so casual and acute
> in my little notebook filled with
> phrases, numbers, recipes,
> and to-do lists. (12)

Do "casual and acute" resemble "humble and precise" as terms to describe how birder-poets and -critics might acquit themselves in the field, in the world? Without suggesting an easy homology between ravens and writers, I'd like to think so. This poem brings together observation and experience in ways similar to other poems—"Pine Siskins" and "Field Marks," say—while effectively drawing a portrait of the birder-poet, along with his "little" notebook, shrinking beneath the evolutionary enigma these ravens represent.

These ravens tempt us—critics, writers, humans, creatures of the Neogene—to interpret their croaks and barks, their polyglot palaver, as McKay puts it in "Ravens at Play over Mount Work." Like most other birds, they can handle whatever we have to say, mostly because what we have to say in poems and essays has little or no effect on them. Insofar as our words might, as Susan Fisher suggests, inform "a way of thinking that permits overt forms of exploitation" (50), however, these ravens seem prepared for us to "bring it on." When we do, I think it wise to bring along a companion or two, books and writers that model an attention and a desire to know the world in its myriad complexities without the urge to simplify, own, or destroy. Listening closely to these companions and to the more-than-human world they write about might just lead us toward a more thoughtful, respectful set of relations than we currently inhabit. The work of Don McKay is one such companion.

Appendix

Bird Concordance

COMMON NAME	SCIENTIFIC NAME	POEM	BOOK, PAGE
Albatross		How to Imagine an Albatross	SD 93
Auk, Great	Pinguinus impennis	First Philosophies	S/S 26
Blackbird		The Confession: Notes Toward a Phrenology of Absence	L 16
		Lependu Nearly Materialized by His Blackbirds	L 28
Blackbird, Red-winged	Agelaius phoeniceus	To Sing and Feed	B 92; C 31
		Territoriality	SD 89
		Inhabiting the Map: (i) For Laurel Creek	SD 99
		A Morning Song	B 19
Bluebird		Sanding Down This Rocking Chair on a Windy Night	SD 36
		Sturnus Vulgaris	SD 82
Bufflehead	Bucephala albeola	Icarus	AG 45; C 172
Bunting, Indigo	Passerina cyanea	Meditation on a Small Bird's Skull	NF 22
Bunting, Snow	Plectrophenax nivalis	The Snow Buntings over on the Ninth	B 38
Cardinal, Northern	Cardinalis cardinalis	Longing:	B 79; C 21
		Cardinal and Cat	B 76
		Le Style	SD 75
		Sturnus Vulgaris	SD 82-83
Catbird, Gray	Dumetella carolinensis	The Laugh	A 29; C 126
Chickadee, Black-capped	Poecile atricapilla	Midwintering	SD 20; C 47
		Plantation	NF 58[1]
		Chickadee Encounter	A 10

227

COMMON NAME	SCIENTIFIC NAME	POEM	BOOK, PAGE
Chicken		The Trout	L 24
		Canadian Tyre	NF 55
		Le Style	SD 76
		Specific Gravities #76 (Marble)	S/S 29
		Descent	P 77
Crane, Sandhill	Grus canadensis	Song for the Song of the Sandhill Crane	P 7
		"And of moose, speak no more the brawn"	M n. pag.; ST 101
Crane, Whooping	Grus americana	Tuning Up for the Elegy	B 58
Crow, American	Corvus brachrhynchos	But Nature Has Her Darker Side	B 120; C 38
		Descent	P 77
Dipper, American	Cinclus mexicanus	Dipper at Parkinson Creek	S/S 60
Dove		Descent	P 77
Dove, Mourning	Zenaida macroura	Mourning Doves	B 108; C 32
Dove, Rock (Pigeon)	Columba livia	Alias Rock Dove, Alias Holy Ghost	B 57; C 17
		Camouflage	NF 19; C 117
		Nothing There	AOS 20
		[untitled]	MC n. pag.
Duck (Mallard)	Anas platyrhunchos	Icarus	AG 45; C 172
		Inhabiting the Map: (i) For Laurel Creek	SD 99
Eagle		The Canoe People	V 77; S/S 23
Eagle, Bald	Haliaeetus leucocephalus	Tuning Up for the Elegy	B 58
Egret, Snowy	Egretta thula	Field Marks	B 15
		Field Marks (2)	C 27
Eider, Common	Somateria mollissima	Kinds of Blue #41 (Far Hills)	AG 32; C 181
		As If	P 1
Falcon		[untitled]	LBB 7
		The Canoe People	V 78; S/S 24
		Le Style	SD 77
		Identification	B 91
Finch, Purple	Carpodacus purpureus	Song for the Song of the Purple Finch	P 14
Flicker, Northern	Colaptes auratus	Sturnus Vulgaris	SD 82
		Après Chainsaw	S/S 50

COMMON NAME	SCIENTIFIC NAME	POEM	BOOK, PAGE
Gannet, Northern	*Morus bassanus*	A Kerry Stream	*SD* 25
		Taking the Ferry	*P* 73-75
		Paradoxides	*P* 39-40
Goldeneye		Goldeneye, Diving	*A* 11
Goldeneye, Barrow's	*Bucephala islandica*	Nostra	*NF* 73
Goldfinch, American	*Carduelis tristis*	A Barbed-Wire Fence Meditates on the Goldfinch	*B* 95; *C* 26
		Grey Matters at 7:45 AM	*LBB* 14
		Three Eclogues: (iii) Abandoned Tracks	*A* 56; *C* 154
		September, Cyprus Lake	*B* 124
		Sturnus Vulgaris	*SD* 85
Goose		October Edge	*LBB* 31; *B* 18
		How to Make a Fool of Yourself in the Autumn Woods	*LBB* 59; *B* 17
		Sanding Down This Rocking Chair on a Windy Night	*SD* 31
		Seven Honks for the Wawa Goose	*AOS* 14-15
		Thingamajig: To Rock (2)	*P* 68-70
Goose, Canada	*Branta Canadensis*	Alluvium	*S/S* 11
		Song for the Song of the Canada Geese	*S* Tr. 10; *P* 5
Grosbeak, Evening	*Coccotraustes vespertinus*	Running Away	*AG* 22
Grouse, Ruffed	*Bonasa umbellus*	Camouflage	*A* 14; *C* 117
Gull		Via, Eastbound	*SD* 51; *C* 50
		Recipe for Divertimento in D, K: 136	*NF* 65; *C* 74
		Eddy Out	*P* 26-28
Harrier, Northern	*Circus cyanus*	Migratory Patterns	*B* 69
		On the Barrens	*P* 17-18
Hawk		Air Occupies Space	*AOS* 21
		Concerto for Violin and Orchestra	*LBB* 21; *B* 119 *AOS* 27;
		Taking Your Baby to the Junior Hockey Game	*LBB* 61; *B* 40
		The Trout	*L* 24
		Some Last Requests	*S/S* 71
Hawk, Broad-winged	*Buteo platyperus*	Icarus	*AG* 44; *C* 171
		Migratory Patterns	*B* 69

230 • Appendix

COMMON NAME	SCIENTIFIC NAME	POEM	BOOK, PAGE
Hawk, Red-tailed	*Buteo jamaicensis*	Icarus	A 44; *C* 171
		Migratory Patterns	B 69
		Concerto for Violin and Orchestra	LBB 21; B 119
Hawk, Rough-legged	*Buteo lagopus*	The Rough-legged Hawk, The Watcher, The Lover, The Blind	B 65-66
Hawk, Sharp-shinned	*Accipiter striatus*	Close-up on a Sharp-shinned Hawk	B 22; *C* 4
		Icarus	AG 44; *C* 171
		Migratory Patterns	B 69
Hawk, Swainson's	*Buteo swainsoni*	To Danceland	A 78; *C* 157
Heron, Great Blue	*Ardea herodias*	The Great Blue Heron	LS 138; LBB 52; B 32; *C* 5
		Scrub	B 16
		Pond	S/S 12
		Migratory Patterns	B 71
		Three Eclogues: (i) Sunday Morning, Raisin River	A 51
Hummingbird		50-50 Draw	A 76
		[untitled]	MC n. pag
Hummingbird, Ruby-throated	*Archilochus colubris*	Ode to My Car	A 62; *C* 147
		Le Style	SD 78
Jay, Blue	*Cyanocitta cristata*	Sparrows	B 54; *C* 16
		A Birthday	B 60
Junco, Dark-eyed	*Junco hyemalis*	Song for the Songs of the Fallen Leaves	S/S 61
		In Aornis	S/S 66
		Slow Spring on Vancouver Island	P 6
		Juncos	P 13
Kestrel, American	*Falco sparverius*	The Boy's Own Guide to Dream Birds	B 47; *C* 13
		Kestrels	B 98; *C* 28
		Kestrels, Encore	SD 58
		Setting the Table: (ii) Fork	A 73; *C* 152
		Sturnus Vulgaris	SD 82
		Accidentals, Exotics, and Escapes	B 26
		Migratory Patterns	B 69
		Styles of Fall: (i) Buckling	SD 67
		Inhabiting the Map: (iv) Reception	SD 107
Killdeer	*Charadrius vociferous*	The Man with Itchy Teeth	B 80

Bird Concordance • 231

COMMON NAME	SCIENTIFIC NAME	POEM	BOOK, PAGE
Kingfisher, Belted	*Cercye alcyon*	Icarus	*AG* 43; *C* 170
		Off the Road	*LS* 142
Kinglet		Three Eclogues: (ii) On Foot to the Bypass Esso Postal Outlet	*A* 54
		First Philosophies	*S/S* 26
Lark, Horned	*Eremophila alpestris*	February Willows	*SD* 19
		Inhabiting the Map: (iv) Reception	*SD* 107
		Drag	*AG* 6; *C* 164
Loon, Common	*Gavia immer*	Bone Poems (iv)	*NF* 32
		Driftwood	*NF* 23
		Icarus	*AG* 45; *C* 172
		Nostra	*NF* 75
		Sanding Down This Rocking Chair on a Windy Night	*SD* 35
		Inhabiting the Map: (i) For Laurel Creek	*SD* 101, 102
		Some Exercises on the Cry of the Loon	*B* 105
		Song for the Song of the Common Loon[2]	*S* Tr. 21; *M* n. pag.; *ST* 111-12; *P* 10
		Thingamajig: To Clasp (3)	*P* 59-60[3]
Meadowlark, Western	*Sturnella neglecta*	But Nature Has Her Darker Side	*B* 120; *C* 38
Merlin	*Falco columbarius*	Icarus	*A* 44; *C* 171
Nighthawk, Common	*Chordeiles minor*	Softball:	*SD* 23; *C* 53
Nightingale	*Luscinia megarhychos*	Falcon	*P* 8-9[4]
Nuthatch		Sanding Down This Rocking Chair on a Windy Night	*SD* 37
Nuthatch, Red-breasted	*Sitta canadensis*	Vespers	*S/S* 53
Oriole, Baltimore	*Icterus galbula*	A Toast to the Baltimore Oriole	*B* 88; *C* 22
		Juncos	*P* 13
Osprey	*Pandion haliaetus*	Migratory Patterns	*B* 71
Ovenbird	*Seiurus aurocapillus*	Sanding Down This Rocking Chair on a Windy Night	*SD* 37
Owl		Alias Rabbit, Alias Snowshoe Hare	*P* 19-20
		Sleeping Places	*P* 31-32

COMMON NAME	SCIENTIFIC NAME	POEM	BOOK, PAGE
Owl, Barred	*Strix varia*	Hush Factor	*AG* 53
		Forlorn	*P* 8-9
Owl, Great Grey	*Strix nebulosa*	Edge of Night	*SD* 69; *C* 64
Owl, Great Horned	*Bubo virginianus*	Mourning Doves	*B* 108; *C* 32
		But Nature Has Her Darker Side	*B* 120; *C* 38
Owl, Northern Saw-whet	*Aegolius acadicus*	Finding Silence	*SD* 92
Owl, Short-eared	*Asio Flammeus*	Ravens at Play over Mount Work	*S* Tr. 27; *P* 11-12
Owl, Snowy	*Nyctea scandiaca*	But Nature Has Her Darker Side	*B* 120; *C* 38
		Snow Moon	*AG* 31; *C* 180
Peacock	*Pavo cristatus*	Reading a Rapids on the Gens de Terre	*LS* 135
Peewee, Eastern	*Contopus virens*	Sturnus Vulgaris	*SD* 82
Phoebe, Eastern	*Sayornis phoebe*	Sturnus Vulgaris	*SD* 82
Pigeon (*see* Dove, Rock)			
Puffin [stuffed]		Taking the Ferry	*P* 73-75
Raven, Common	*Corvus corax*	Matériel: (iv) Stretto	*A* 47; *V* 48; *C* 141
		Nostra	*NF* 73
		Three Eclogues: (ii) On Foot to the Bypass Esso Postal Outlet	*A* 53-55
		Song for the Songs of the Common Raven	*S/S* 27
		The Canoe People	*S/S* 23; *V* 77
		Dipper at Parkinson Creek	*S/S* 60
		Batter—	*P* 24-25
		Ravens at Play over Mount Work	*S* Tr. 27; *P* 11-12
		Thingamajig: To Clasp (3)	*P* 59-60[5]
Redstart, American	*Setophaga ruticilla*	Inhabiting the Map: (i) For Laurel Creek	*SD* 101
		The Many Breasted Warbler	*B* 103
Robin, American	*Turdus migratorius*	Matériel: (iii) The Base	*A* 44; *V* 42; *C* 138
		Ascent with Thrushes	*S/S* 63
Sandpiper		"Rapt, sitting on a rock by the shore"	*M* n.pag.; *ST* 113
Sanderling	*Calidris alba*	Feather	*AG* 48

COMMON NAME	SCIENTIFIC NAME	POEM	BOOK, PAGE
Scaup, Greater	*Aythya marila*	Pond	*S/S* 12
Scaup, Lesser	*Aythya affinis*	Icarus	*AG* 45; *C* 172
		Pond	*S/S* 12
Siskin, Pine	*Carduelis pinus*	Pine Siskins	*S/S* 64
Snipe, Common	*Gallinago gallinago*	The Wolf	*NF* 19; *C* 71
Sparrow		Spring Turned Raw	*B* 96
Sparrow, Chipping	*Spizella passerine*	Song for the Song of the Chipping Sparrow	*S/S* 25
Sparrow, House	*Passer domesticus*	Sparrows	*B* 54; *C* 16
Sparrow, Song	*Melospiza melodia*	Field Marks	*C* 3
		Field Marks (2)	*B* 75
		Nocturne Macdonald-Cartier Freeway	*NF* 36; *C* 84
Sparrow, White-throated	*Zonotrichia albicollis*	Drinking Lake Superior	*SD* 96; *C* 48
		Load	*AG* 10; *C* 168
		High Noon on the Pre-Cambrian Shield	*B* 110
		Song for the Song of the White-throated Sparrow	*AG* 33; *C* 182
		Vicky	*LBB* 42; *B* 117
		Thingamajig: To Clasp (3)	*P* 59-60
Starling, European	*Sturnus vulgaris*	Sturnus Vulgaris	*SD* 82-86
		Tuning Up for the Elegy	*B* 58
		A Morning Prayer Ending with a Live Borrowed from Holiday Inn	*LBB* 36; *B* 59
Swallow		Swallowings	*LBB* 54-58; *B* 83-87
		L'Hirondelle	*B* 29
		Dreamskaters	*B* 48
		Inhabiting the Map: (v) A Mouth	*SD* 109
		Streaks of Bird Music	*B* 97
		Le Rêve du pendu	*L* 8
Swallow, Barn	*Hirundo rustico*	Icarus	*AG* 46; *C* 173
		Three Eclogues: (i) Sunday Morning, Raisin River	*A* 52

COMMON NAME	SCIENTIFIC NAME	POEM	BOOK, PAGE
Swallow, Cliff	*Tachycineta cyaneoviridis*	Alibi	*A* 19; *C* 119
		Suckering the Silver Maples	*SD* 22
Swan		Inhabiting the Map: (i) For Laurel Creek	*SD* 100
		Black Box	*A* 32
Swan, Trumpeter	*Cygnus buccinator*	Acoustics of the Conical Tube	*A* 66; *C* 149
Swan, Tundra	*Cygnus columbianus*	Icarus	*AG* 43; *C* 170
		Inhabiting the Map: (iv) Reception	*SD* 107
Swan, Whistling		Accidentals, Exotics, and Escapes	*B* 26
		Slow Landings	*B* 90
Thrasher, Brown	*Toxostoma rufum*	Field Marks	*C* 3
		Field Marks (2)	*B* 75
Thrush, Hermit	*Catharus guttatus*	Styles of Fall: (v) Some Functions of a Leaf	*SD* 71; *C* 56
		Ascent with Thrushes	*S/S* 62-63
Thrush, Swainson's	*Catharus ustulatus*	Ascent with Thrushes	*S/S* 62-63
Thrush, Varied	*Ixoreus naevius*	Song for the Song of the Varied Thrush	*A* 26; *C* 124
		Loss Creek	*S/S* 7
		Cirque	*A* 6
		Ascent with Thrushes	*S/S* 62-63
Thrush, Wood	*Hylocichla mustelina*	Song for the Song of the Wood Thrush	*A* 27; *C* 125
Turkey, Wild	*Meleagris gallopavo*	The Old Wino Will Not Go Away	*AOS* 13
Vulture, Turkey	*Cathartes aura*	Field Marks	*C* 3
		Field Marks (2)	*B* 75
		On Seeing the First Turkey Vultures of Spring	*B* 78; *C* 20
		Adagio for a Fallen Sparrow	*B* 55; *C* 24
Warbler		Concerto for Violin and Orchestra	*LBB* 21; *B* 119
		Summer at Leith	*SD* 55; *C* 51
		Finding Silence	*SD* 92
		As if Spirit, As if Soul	*S/S* 57
		Concerto for Violin and Orchestra	*LBB* 21; *B* 119
Warbler, Bay-breasted	*Dendroica castanea*	The Many Breasted Warbler	*B* 103

COMMON NAME	SCIENTIFIC NAME	POEM	BOOK, PAGE
Warbler, Black-and-white	*Mniotilta varia*	The Many Breasted Warbler	B 103
Warbler, Blackburnian	*Dendroica fusca*	"The Bellies of Breathing Fallen Sparrows"	B 93; C 25
		Bird Thou Never Wert	B 45; C 11
Warbler, Black-throated Green	*Dendroica virens*	Field Marks	C 3
		Thingamajig: To Clasp (3)	P 59-60
		Field Marks (2)	B 75
Warbler, Yellow	*Dendroica petechia*	Three Eclogues: (iii) Abandoned Tracks	A 57; C 155
		Homing	AG 20; C 176
		The Many Breasted Warbler	B 103
Warbler, Yellow Rumped	*Dendroica coronata*	Thingamajig: To Clasp (3)	P 59-60
Waxwing, Cedar	*Bombycilla cedrorum*	Little Rivers	SD 28
Whip-poor-will	*Caprimulgus vociferous*	Listen at the Edge	LBB 19; B 123; C 34
		Summer at Leith	SD 55; C 51
Woodpecker, Pileated	*Dryocopus pileatus*	Three Eclogues: (i) Sunday Morning, Raisin River	A 54
Woodpecker, Red-headed	*Melanerpes erythrocephalus*	Sturnus Vulgaris	SD 82
Wren		The Canoe People	V 77; S/S 23
		Hiking with My Shadow	S/S 51
Wren, House	*Troglodytes aedon*	As if Spirit, As if Soul	S/S 59
Wren, Winter	*Troglodytes troglodytes*	Black Spruce	NF 13
		Eddy Out	P 26-28

1 I base this entry on the lines "waiting for the black-capped // nothing-at-all to flirt up / perch on my finger." Both the black-capped vireo (*Vireo atricapillus*) and the black-capped petrel (*Pterodroma hasitata*) are unlikely possibilities: the former, while slightly smaller than the black-capped chickadee, resides in Texas and Mexico (Sibley 346); the latter, while geographically proximal to New Brunswick, where McKay was living at the time *Night Field* was published, with a 16-inch-long body and a 37-inch wingspan (Sibley 35; weight unknown), can hardly be called a "nothing-at-all."
2 In *The Muskwa Assemblage*, this poem is called "Song for the Song of the Loon."
3 This refers to a soapstone carving of a loon.
4 This reference is to Keats's poem.
5 This reference is to the Northwest Coast Peoples' trickster figure.

Notes

Notes to Beginnings

1 Not everyone agrees on what ecocriticism is or whether the term—concise and functional though it is—sufficiently encompasses the ideas and practices that resonate in comparable names: environmental literary criticism, ecologically oriented/attuned/conscious criticism, sustainable poetics, ecopoetics, green literary studies, evolutionary literary criticism (evocriticism, for short), ecofeminism, practical ecocriticism. Further, a critical mass of theory offers possibilities for individuals to focus, to (re)name, to fashion working definitions: Cheryll Glotfelty and Harold Fromm's foundational anthology (and Glotfelty's Introduction, which includes the concise definition of ecocriticism as "the study of the relationship between literature and the physical environment" [xviii]); Laurence Buell's trilogy of American ecocriticism; Greg Garrard's *Ecocriticism*; numerous anthologies that seek to push the emerging discipline's boundaries, take it farther afield, highlight its relevance to earlier times and literatures (Milton, Shakespeare, the Bible), not to mention other disciplines and cultures—all offer explanations and extrapolations on ecocriticism that render any attempt to summarize too cumbersome and, what is more, unnecessary and redundant.

   Among the numerous ecocritical publications are many that do not succumb to the urge to define—studies, in other words, that simply get down to the work of ecocriticism. I'm thinking of John Elder's *Imagining the Earth: Poetry and the Vision of Nature* (1985) and *Reading the Mountains of Home* (1998); W. H. New's *Land Sliding: Imagining Space, Presence, and Power in Canadian Writing* (1997); Laurie Ricou's *Arbutus/Madrone Files: Reading the Pacific Northwest* (2002) and *Salal: Listening for the Northwest Understory* (2007); Jenny Kerber's *Writing in Dust: Reading the Prairie Environmentally* (2010); and scores of articles that offer readings of texts and cultural practice that fit nicely, if uneasily, into the wonderfully amorphous field of ecocriticism.

2 Broadly, I draw upon natural history and taxonomy, and I often refer to science in general when setting up a cross-disciplinary reading of a poem. While my appeals to natural history and taxonomy serve as much to satisfy my interest in language as to fulfill an ecocritical imperative, the language I appropriate tends to be highly specialized. Natural history, though in many ways still a thriving discipline, occupies a historical place in the trajectory of Western science; taxonomy represents a particularized language that enables natural historians and scientists alike to identify and study organisms with minimum confusion. An awareness of individual species taxonomies, of the function of the Latin binomials attached to all identified species of flora and fauna, indicates a critical interest in, if not utter acquiescence to, a system of organizing the world that seems foreign to most literary critics. That said, I do not devote much space to critiquing science and scientific language. As Glen Love writes, "If science has been employed for harmful and

destructive purposes, then that needs to be recognized and challenged as bad *policy*, not as an excuse for attacking 'science'" ("Science" 71). Instead, I offer an experiment in listening to what scientists have to say about their encounters with avian, animal, botanical worlds.

3 "Birder," as George Levine comments, is "the noun birders use to describe themselves. There is a related verb, 'to bird,' which I use a lot, and there's a participial noun built from that verb, 'birding,' which is what most of the essays in this book are about" (*Lifebirds* 3).

4 At times throughout this book, I find it necessary to refer to a poetics or aesthetics as uniquely McKay's, that is, to deploy a proper adjective to indicate an association with him. For most writers, the adjectival form rolls off the tongue without the need to qualify the inflection: Derridean, Dickensian, Whitmanesque, and even Frygian have entered the critical vocabulary. For McKay, however, the inflection proved more complicated. I finally settled on McKavian rather than McKagian or McKayesque; I like the "avian" echo—its musicality and precision given McKay's interests in birds and birding.

5 This is not to suggest that McKay is particularly elusive as a subject. Indeed, he has always seemed to make himself visible by giving readings and talks, has made himself available by taking up writer-in-residence positions and mentoring writers, and has engaged in discussion by giving interviews and chatting amiably with graduate students and aspiring writers. Given this openness, it was impossible for me not to have encountered McKay at some point during the writing of this book. However, I made a conscious decision early on not to request any interviews, not to run particulars of my research by the subject of my research. I wanted *Ornithologies of Desire* to be a study of the poetry and poetics more than a book about the poet. I feared, despite my relative lack of personal contact with McKay, that I would succumb to a temptation to praise too much, a danger that has remained real enough, as it surely must for all scholars who admire the work they study.

6 Intriguing avian literatures in languages other than English flourish just beyond the edge of this book. See, for example, James Walling's study of birds in French fiction, Steven Feld's study of birds and weeping in Kaluli expression, and Robert Bringhurst's translations of Haida masterworks.

7 Harting titles his introduction "Shakespeare's General Knowledge of Natural History" and his chapters "The Eagle and Larger Birds of Prey," "Hawks and Hawking," "The Owl and Its Associations," "The Crows and Their Relations," "The Birds of Song," "The Birds under Domestication," "The Game-Birds and 'Quarry' Flown at by Falconers," "Wild-Fowl and Sea-Fowl," and "Birds Not Included in the Foregoing Chapters" (xix–xxii).

8 Ecology of knowledge refers to the bare minimum of information—regarding weather, food, shelter, and sources of danger—all species have in order to survive, or at least to compete for resources. Ecology of knowledge also refers to the wide range of knowledges available to the student/scholar of collaborative research.

9 I am thinking here about Hardy's "Shelley's Skylark," a lyric reflection on the existence (and death) of the actual bird whose voice inspired Shelley to pen his famous poem. Hardy's poem, published in 1901 and subtitled "The neighbourhood of Leghorn: March 1887," simultaneously acknowledges the lark as a lark and the lark as immortal(ized) symbol of Romantic enlightenment:

Somewhere afield here something lies
In Earth's oblivious eyeless trust
That moved a poet to prophecies –
A pinch of unseen, unguarded dust:

The dust of the lark that Shelley heard,
And made immortal through times to be; –

Though it only lived like another bird,
And knew not its immortality:

Lived its meek life; then, one day, fell –
A little ball of feather and bone;
And how it perished, when piped farewell,
And where it wastes, are alike unknown.

Maybe it rests in the loam I view,
Maybe it throbs in a myrtle's green,
Maybe it sleeps in the coming hue
Of a grape on the slopes of yon inland scene.

Go find it, faeries, go and find
That tiny pinch of priceless dust,
And bring a casket silver-lined,
And framed of gold that gems encrust;

And we will lay it safe therein,
And consecrate it to endless time;
For it inspired a bard to win
Ecstatic heights in thought and rhyme. (18)

Hardy recognizes the poetic immortality of Shelley's skylark but acknowledges that it "lived like another bird," mortal and meek.

Notes to Chapter One

1. McKay's breakthrough collection, *Birding, or desire*, includes poems from all four of McKay's previous collections: two poems from *Air Occupies Space* (1973), two from *Long Sault* (1975), one from *Lependu* (1978), and twenty-six from *Lightning Ball Bait* (1980). In A Note on the Text (*B* 127), McKay acknowledges that some poems have been reprinted, noting that the high number from *Lightning Ball Bait*, which was still in print at the time, "belonged thematically in *Birding, or desire* as well." He claims that twenty-five poems from *Lightning Ball Bait* reappear in *Birding*; however, I count twenty-six: "How to Make a Fool of Yourself in the Autumn Woods," "October Edge," "There's a Kind of Terror Which Can Seize You," "At Thirteen a Serpent" (which originally appeared in *Air Occupies Space*), "The Great Blue Heron" (which originally appeared in *Long Sault*), "Dusk," "Fridge Nocturne," "A Piece of Rose-Coloured Quartz," "Taking Your Baby to the Junior Hockey Game," "Snow Sadness," "Nocturnal Animals," "I Scream You Scream," "A Morning Prayer Ending with a Line Borrowed from Holiday Inn," "Hoar Frost," "In Blizzard," "March Snow," "Our Last Black Cat," "Returns," "Swallowings," "White Pine," "Drought," "Simply Because Light," "Blood," "Vicky," "Concerto for Violin and Orchestra," and "Listen at the Edge."
2. The phrase "attempting the world" is my way of expressing one's attempt to understand, comprehend, explain, live in, sustain, and respect all the nebulous aspects of the physical world. The phrase recognizes "the world" as an entity that poses challenges and requires attempts or, as the title of this book implies, essays (from the French *essayer*, to try); thus, attempting the world is akin to attempting the rapids, attempting the jump, or attempting the climb.
3. Richard Rorty discusses texts and lumps—"a division which corresponds roughly to things made and things found" (8)—in an attempt to call into question the lazy pseudo-philosophizing of literary theory in the early 1980s. He links, by way of E. D. Hirsch, Jr., texts and lumps to literary criticism and science, respectively, echoing Hirsch's claim that

"the much-advertised cleavage between thinking in the sciences and the humanities does not exist" (qtd. in Rorty 8).

4 An extensive comparison of Clare's and McKay's avian and ecological poetics would require another 200 pages (at least), and therefore lies outside the scope and practical constraints of this book. In addition to this historical comparison, I would also like to see McKay's work read alongside more contemporary poets whose avian poetics merit more comparative study: Mary Oliver, Jorie Graham, Robert Adamson.

5 Such is the ornithological accuracy of Clare's bird poems, particularly his bird-nest poems, that W. J. Keith notes Clare's tendency to retain specific birds at the centre of his poems and to consult W. H. Hudson's *British Birds* when reading "The Thrush's Nest." Keith also identifies "a highly selective Clare [speaking] in his role as local ornithologist and guide" (57). Cf. Keith, *The Poetry of Nature: Rural Perspectives in Poetry from Wordsworth to the Present* (1980).

6 For a discussion about personal ecology as the first in a set of "nested ecologies"—the others being social, environmental, and cosmic—see Edward T. Wimberley's *Nested Ecology: The Place of Humans in the Ecological Hierarchy* (2009).

Notes to Chapter Two

1 See, for example, Julie Cruikshank's investigation into whether "there [are] ways of speaking about global issues such as climate change that accord weight to culturally specific understandings as well as to universalizing frameworks of science" (*Do Glaciers Listen?* 47).

2 Critics such as Albert Goldbarth describe an Edenic past when "the sciences and the arts were at peace, were one" (ix). Goldbarth goes so far as to suggest that Western culture succumbed to this momentous linguistic shift circa 1827, and he notes the significance of this year by recording three key moments: (1) a meeting between Wordsworth and Sir Humphry Davy, "neither side with a key to the other's tongue" (x); (2) the death of William Blake, whose "poems and paintings exhibited a heated, lifelong grumble against the work of Newton, its logic, its willingness to explore by ruler and callipers," and yet whose vision, ironically, "was arguably an experiment in cosmology" (xi); and (3) the supposition that "scientists turn[ed] their back on the practitioners of art of their day" (xi). In much the same way, John Battalio argues natural history developed into differing scientific practices, the back-turning to which Goldbarth refers instigated (or was at least an instance of) a divergence of *praxis*; that is, while scientists and artists interested in the natural world follow different modes of inquiry and use different names for the objects of their inquiry, the basic act of naming on the way to knowing, however imperfectly, remains the same.

3 The title is taken from Leonard Cohen's "Beneath My Hands," but McKay has (perhaps mistakenly) transposed the two modifiers. Cohen's poem begins "Beneath my hands / your small breasts / are the upturned bellies / of breathing fallen sparrows" (16). The discrepancy was rectified neither when the poem was reprinted in *Camber: Selected Poems, 1983–2003*, nor when it was recorded for *Songs for the Songs of Birds*.

4 Indeed, the majority of published articles on McKay's writing focus on his use of metaphor (see especially Bushell, Dickinson, Dragland, and Susan Fisher).

5 One of the central ecocritical challenges that has arisen is that of realistic versus imaginative representation. Lawrence Buell builds upon the notion of environmental representation (his preferred term to "realism") in the third of his trilogy of ecocritical texts, *The Future of Environmental Criticism* (2005), by emphasising "a certain kind of environmental referentiality" (32). This referentiality, inspired in part by Scigaj's "neo-Derridean

theory of *référence*" (39), inheres in the "conviction that contact (or lack of contact) with actual environments is intimately linked ... with the work of environmental imagination, for both writer and critic" (31).

6   "The Butterfly" first appeared in A. J. M. Smith's foundational *Oxford Book of Canadian Verse* in 1960, though it was included later that year in Avison's first book, *Winter Sun*. In *A New Anthology of Canadian Literature in English*, editors Donna Bennett and Russell Brown include the revised version, along with Avison's note. Bennett and Brown add their own note by providing biblical quotations Avison alludes to in *her* note and reprinting three lines, which Avison removed for the revised version, from the second stanza. The editors justify their attention to the biblical aspect of the poem(s)—even though no such detailed attention is paid to the changed lines Avison herself notes—by claiming that "Avison's revision of the original poem goes beyond correcting the 'moth' of the first version" (535). This impulse to push a reading of Avison's poem (and of her revision) "beyond" the nominal correction—beyond, that is, the poet's focus on the natural, lepidopteral world—strikes me as odd. It implies a resistance to appreciating poetry concerned with accurate documentation of the natural world, especially if we consider the comment about Avison's revisions alongside Bennett and Brown's assessment, in the same anthology, of McKay's status as a nature, or an eco-, poet. McKay's "intense responses to the natural world," they write in a headnote, "have brought him a reputation as an ecological poet, but it is more than just a depth of appreciation for nature that gives power to his writing" (861).

7   Mia Anderson makes the following statement while pursuing the "the implications of Avison's struggle with modern astronomy" in *Winter Sun*: "The artist is notoriously lax about facts, but Avison is practically never scientifically inaccurate, a precision arrived at without recourse to poetic licence. (I mean to exclude her metaphors, *façons de parler*, from this licence)" (121). Ultimately, Anderson's article remains within a Christian reading of Avison's poetry. See also Margaret Calverley's "'Service is joy': Margaret Avison's Sonnet Sequence in Winter Sun." For more on the ecological aspects of Avison's poetry, see Merrett and Quincey.

8   For an example of a poet who engages the field of lepidoptery more fully than does Avison, see a. rawlings in *Wide slumber for lepidopterists*.

9   Originally published in *Books in Canada* in 1983, the review was revised by Bringhurst in 1999. The revised version, "The Antithesis of Rape, Which Is Not Chastity: The Voice of Don McKay," is included in *Don McKay: Essays on His Works*, edited by Brian Bartlett. Page references are to Bringhurst's piece as it appears in the Bartlett collection.

10 For an example of a literary critic—an ecocritic—focusing on the biological and ecological details of a single species, see Michael P. Cohen's *A Garden of Bristlecones: Tales of Change in the Great Basin* (1998) and Laurie Ricou's *Salal: Listening for the Northwest Understory* (2007).

11 For a reading of evolution in early Canadian poetry, see Gerald Noonan's "Phrases of Evolution in the Sonnets of Charles G. D. Roberts," in which Noonan moves away from Desmond Pacey's and W. J. Keith's insistence on a Wordsworthian nature poetic as a measure of Roberts's success as a poet.

12 As Phillips takes Glen Love to task for his "antitheoretical" stance, Murphy singles him out for his privileging of a type of nonfictional pastoralism (as opposed to the fiction Murphy privileges in his book) in the early stages of developing an ecocritical discipline. Small wonder that Love constitutes a more "positive" touchstone for my approach to ecocriticism as interdisciplinary strategy: that he has been both one of the most adamant critics in favour of ecocriticism and one of the most attacked for his particular

biases solidifies in my mind his approach as the riskiest, and thus as the most potentially rewarding.

13   In the first place, though not necessarily in the last place, Coetzee suggests readers stop to consider the real-world correlation between literary animals and the animals they represent. This urging in no way endorses an end to metaphorical reading. Rather, Coetzee's challenge to the critical tendency to read a text's interpretive layers enables readers to reconsider animals' (and, by extension, all nonhuman beings') place in literature. If the animals themselves, or if human relations with them (whether through "realistic" ethological observation or "unrealistic" dialogue), point toward a repositioning of animals-as-Other—that is, as valid subjects for inclusion in, for example, postcolonial, political, and cultural discourses that have typically been reserved for humans—then perhaps reading strategies are getting closer to building an arc between two seemingly disparate theoretical approaches to literature.

14   Both Love and Carroll refer to the influence of I. A. Richards in this context; see especially *Principles of Literary Criticism* and *Practical Criticism*, from which Love derives the title of his book.

15   One useful area of congruence between scientific and New Critical modes is reductionism. As E. O. Wilson writes in *Consilience*: "Critics of science sometimes portray reductionism as an obsessional disorder.... That characterization is an actionable misdiagnosis.... It is the search strategy employed to find points of entry into otherwise impenetrably complex systems. Complexity is what interests scientists in the end, not simplicity. Reductionism is a way to understand it" (54). One might also suggest that complexity is what interests New Critics, insofar as their focus on the ambiguity of modern poetry stems from "a close attention to the language of the text, to show a pattern of formal and thematic features that ... [arguably] are fundamental to understanding the meaning of the work as a whole" (Searle 530). By way of reductionism, consider the epistemological value of starting with specifics and working outward to consider a host of contextual affiliations: a poem, a plant (Garry oak or purple loosestrife), a bird (pileated woodpecker or house sparrow), a cell (stem or blood). For more on the value of a Wilsonian approach to ecocritical studies, see Laura Dassow Walls, "Seeking Common Ground: Integrating the Sciences and the Humanities" (Ingram et al. 199–208).

16   Dennis Lee offers another way of conceptualizing dualistic thinking. In *Savage Fields: An Essay in Literature and Cosmology* (1977), Lee discusses "the interaction of world and earth" in some Canadian novels (7). The savage field of his title emerges wherever "world and earth are trying to destroy each other" (8), which is virtually everywhere at all times, since "Planet obliges us to see it as world and earth simultaneously" (10). Imbued with complexities that, according to Lee, the corresponding terms "civilisation" and "nature" lack, world and earth inhere in cosmological literary readings. That is, literary history and the history of ideas inform and are informed by events and developments that are independent of cultural consciousness.

17   D. M. R. Bentley bases his argument in *The Gay]Grey Moose: Essays on the Ecologies and Mythologies of Canadian Poetry 1690–1990*, an example of ecological literary criticism in Canada, on this distinction. Baseland is roughly equivalent to metropolitan/urban; Hinterland is roughly equivalent to rural.

18   This is particularly true of McKay's writing about "burlesque[s] of 'natural' phenomena," such as suburbs and strip malls, that are occasionally "named after the very white oaks or crystal creeks lost or compromised in their construction" (*V* 88). See, especially, the poems *Long Sault* and "Inhabiting the Map" (*SD* 99–109) and the essay "The Bushtits' Nest" (*V* 83–106).

Note to Ecotone One

1 Though European starlings (*Sturnus vulgaris*) are now common across North America—thanks to Eugene Scheifflin, who endeavoured to introduce to the New World all the birds mentioned in the works of Shakespeare—and thus not unique to the west coast, they are not common in BC's hometown.

Notes to Chapter Three

1 In recommending books to act as "a companion to the world" during midsummer, Campbell suggests Americans Washington Irving, Donald G. Mitchell (a.k.a. Ike Marvell), Maurice Thompson, and John Burroughs, as well as Norse writer Björnstjerne (*Mermaid* 111–12).

2 Foremost among Bentley's assumptions in his book, though it is hardly his alone, is that "despite its geographical diversity and lack of a formal manifesto, the group did have a centre, a credo, and a duration," enough to warrant their historical and critical status as a group (Bentley 5). However, as W. H. New states in *A History of Canadian Literature*, "[t]hey constitute a 'group' more for the purposes of literary classification than for any shared cause, though they were all shaded by the late-Victorian romanticism of Tennyson and the American Transcendentalists" (114).

3 A glance at an 1865 issue of *The Canadian Farmer*, for example, reveals the following exchange between a letter writer and the magazine's editor: "A WORK ON CANADIAN BIRDS WANTED—'N.A.P.' writes as follows.—'You would confer a favour if you would inform me, through your valuable paper, if there is any standard work published, in Toronto, on Canadian birds and their eggs, or on the latter only. If so, how can I obtain it? Please answer as soon as possible, as this is the season for birds to build.'
"ANS.—There is no Canadian work published on the subject alluded to. Audubon's celebrated work is, however, quite applicable to this country, but it is costly. 'Wilson's American Ornithology' is a cheap octavo work, but we do not know if it is kept in stock by Canadian booksellers" (168).

4 One hundred years prior to *At the Mermaid Inn*, in 1792 Alexander Mackenzie wrote about his encounter with unfamiliar, local birds:

> I was very much surprised on walking in the woods at such an inclement period of the year, to be saluted with the singing of birds, while they seemed by their vivacity to be actuated by the invigorating power of a more genial season. Of these birds the male was something less than the robin; part of his body is of a delicate fawn colour, and his neck, breast, and belly, of a deep scarlet; the wings are black, edged with fawn colour, and two white stripes running across them; the tail is variegated, and the head crowned with a tuft. The female is smaller than the male, and of a fawn colour throughout, except on the neck, which is enlivened by an hue of glossy yellow. I have no doubt but they are constant inhabitants of this climate, as well as some other small birds which we saw, of a grey colour. (134)

In his article about nature writing in *The Cambridge Companion to Canadian Literature*, Christoph Irmscher suggests the birds Mackenzie describes are "most likely pine grosbeaks" (95).

5 Literary guides to cities, regions, and countries offer one example of interest in how land and landscape influences literature. For recent examples, see Jeanette Eve, *Literary Guide to the Eastern Cape: Places and the Voices of Writers* (2003); Helen Moffett, *Lovely beyond Any Singing: Landscapes in South African Writing* (2006); Daniel Hahn and Nicholas

Robbins, *The Oxford Guide to Literary Britain and Ireland* (2008); and Noah Richler, *This Is My Country, What's Yours? A Literary Atlas of Canada* (2006).

6. Stahl also discusses metaphors used in physics that have no real-world corollary. For example, the term "quark," which has come to refer to groups of subatomic particles that constitute matter, was apparently drawn from James Joyce's *Finnegans Wake*. Murray Gell-Mann, the physicist who appropriated the term, provides an explanation in a letter he sent to an editor of the *Oxford English Dictionary* (see http://www.oed.com; quark, n. 2). Coincidentally, the passage from which Gell-Mann takes the term depicts a group of seabirds singing a chorus. A section of the novel opens with some lines of verse: "Three quarks for Muster Mark! / Sure he hasn't got much of a bark / And sure any he has it's all beside the mark." We learn that the song is sung by "seaswans. The winging ones. Seahawk, seagull, curlew and plover, kestrel and capercallzie. All the birds of the sea they trolled out rightbold when they smacked the big kuss of Trustan with Usolde" (Joyce 383).

7. Thanks to Mike Healey for suggesting this analogy between hypothesis and metaphor.

8. Following scientific and experiential trails of referents would mean, for example, reading up on the ecology of varied thrushes (*Ixoreus naevius*) and going out into the forest (or the park, or the back lane with a few yew trees) to see and hear (or see and touch, if you've been reading about a plant).

9. Though it is rare and obscure, "abide" as a noun means the same as "abode": a dwelling place, a place to remain. As a verb, "abide" means to wait, a meaning which "abode," as a noun, also implies, albeit obscurely.

10. I am tempted to give Jean Chrétien and Donald Rumsfeld (or the latter's speech writer) more credit for their well-known speeches about evidence ("a proof is a proof") and intelligence ("there are known knowns, and known unknowns"), respectively; perhaps they have both read Don McKay.

11. Åkesson and Hedenström admit that "[o]rientation research is still very much concerned with the different compass mechanisms and senses.... [and ornithologists] still do not know how the different cues are integrated in wild birds, and the sensory mechanism for the magnetic compass sense remains obscure, though it is likely to be associated with photoreception in the eye" (132).

12. Ornithologists do more than imagine avian physical feats; for example, the notion of fuel deposition rate (FDR) helps explain physiological mechanics of migration. See Shaub and Jenni (2000). N.B.: FDR (Fuel Deposition Rate/Franklin Delano Roosevelt) is the second ornithological acronym to copy the initials of an American president. The other is LBJ (Little Brown Job/Lyndon B. Johnson).

13. This resistance would seem to be in keeping with Hodgins's concerns regarding Canadian identity, which are negligible. As a west-coast short-story writer and novelist who emerged in the 1970s (in the decade following a surge in literary and cultural nationalism), Hodgins represents a Canadian voice from the geographic margins of the country. If anything, he has been (perhaps unfairly) pigeonholed as a regional writer. His criticism of Victorian empire in *Innocent Cities* marks perhaps his most overt engagement, albeit an ironical one, with notions of Canadian identity.

14. For more on Hodgins's use of gardening language—trellis, native plants, landscaping/land escaping—as narrative trope, see Mason and Roberts, "(Accurate) Metaphor and (Visceral) Wisdom in *Distance*: A Dialogue across Distances," in Guernica Press's writers' series (2010).

15. I borrow this notion of absence, or whiteness, begetting creativity as a method of overcoming absence from P. K. Page's poem "Stories of Snow" (*Planet* 161–62)—though other Canadian authors, including Robert Kroetsch, have developed similar ideas. Page's

poem privileges the telling of stories in a snow-laden place, like Canada (although the poem itself, like many of Page's poems, is set in Brazil). The narrator of the poem states:

> In countries where the leaves are large as hands
> where flowers protrude their fleshy chins
> and call their colours,
> an imaginary snow-storm sometimes falls
> among the lilies. (161)

As one can gather from her title, Page's poem is about, in part, storytelling. It marks a line (perhaps imaginary) between the obvious, unimaginative "countries where great flowers bar the roads" and "the area behind the eyes / where silent, unrefractive whiteness lies." There is an irony inherent in Page's mention of the "silent, unrefractive whiteness" that posits a sound on the other side of silence, reflection on the other side of unrefraction, and colour on the other side of whiteness. Reinforcing this creative irony in Hodgins's *Innocent Cities*, Kate mentions in a letter to her sister in Australia that her husband is away for an indefinite period of time: "so," she says, "I have decided to fill up his absence with writing to you" (219).

16 Thanks to Laurie Ricou for suggesting the various formal possibilities.

17 Hunting does not figure much in McKay's writing, and thus I limit my discussion of it to this brief note. The potential violence of anthropocentric language does correlate with McKay's anxieties regarding human violence to the land and to animals. The raven, for example, that forms the basis for McKay's discussion in "Baler Twine: Thoughts on Ravens, Home & Nature Poetry" (*V* 15–33) is the closest McKay gets to writing about hunting. The raven "was hung up by the roadside at the entrance to a lane, a piece of baler twine around one leg, wings spread. There was a shotgun hole in its back just above the tail, which was missing altogether" (18). Despite the mention of the shotgun, this discovery "doesn't fall into an ethic of hunting" category because ravens are not game birds, and the dead bird was not killed for food or for economic reasons (though its display might be considered a version of trophy). McKay views the combined act of shooting the raven and displaying it as evidence of a disturbing human impulse to control through appropriation. Characteristically, he implicates himself in the perpetration of the act by claiming an uneasy understanding of the raven's death: "we all know, each of us, the sinister delight in casual brutality and long-distance death" (18–19). For more detailed discussions of hunting and writing in a Canadian context, see Misao Dean, "'The Mania for Killing': Hunting and Collecting in Seton's *The Arctic Prairies*" (290–304), and Wendy Roy, "The Politics of Hunting in Canadian Women's Narratives of Travel" (305–32) in Fiamengo, ed.

18 Levine was series editor of the University of Wisconsin Press's Science and Literature series, which, according to the UWP website, is closed. In print are *The Nuclear Muse*, by John Canaday; *One Culture*, by George Levine; *Natural Eloquence*, by Barbara T. Gates; *Gaston Bachelard, Subversive Humanist*, by Mary McAllester Jones; *Seeing New Worlds*, by Laura Dassow Walls; *The Word of God and the Languages of Man*, by James J. Bono; *Science in the New Age*, by David J. Hess; *Sexual Visions*, by Ludmilla Jordanova; and *Fact and Feeling*, by Jonathan Smith. Out of print are *In Pursuit of a Scientific Culture*, by Peter Allen Dale; *Writing Biology*, by Greg Myers; and *Realism and Representation*, by George Levine.

19 I am not marking a distinction between tactic and strategy in the way Michel de Certeau does in *The Practice of Everyday Life*. I am interested in the way Levine's use of "tactic" interconnects with an interdisciplinary notion of "strategy" and offers a space (another ecotone?) from which to read ecocritically.

20 The passage from *Walden* reads as follows: "I think that we may safely trust a good deal more than we do. We may waive just so much care of ourselves as we honestly bestow elsewhere. Nature is as well adapted to our weakness as our strength. The incessant anxiety and strain of some is a well nigh incurable form of disease" (266).

21 This strikes me as a good place to stop and consider one way in which birders and hunters are more closely aligned than many contemporary natural historians would like to acknowledge. John James Audubon, among other naturalists, achieved his popular representations of birds by killing them by the hundreds, placing metal wire inside the dead bodies, and positioning them in "realistic" poses. By contrast, the "meditative medicine" McKay prescribes by way of thinking about "otherwise than place," resembles "[s]omething like a modification of the practice of fishing from trophy hunting to meat acquisition to catch-and-release" (*DW* 19).

22 *Hope Is the Thing with Feathers* is a natural history of six extinct species of birds (including the recently spotted ivory-billed woodpecker, which had not been seen since 1935). Cokinos is aware of how important it is to include science as well as material that might be considered more conventional for a creative writer: "Perhaps unlike a professional historian and more like the poet I have been, I have found myself drawn to the oddments, the margins, so that a cookbook's reference to Passenger Pigeon pie looms as importantly in this book as, say, logging statistics. A settler's account of how Carolina Parakeets in sycamore reminded him of Christmas in Germany—that matters to memory as much as facts of biology" (3).

23 Orography is the study of the formation and relief of mountains, hills, and other elevated land masses. Orographic lift occurs when air rises after encountering such land masses.

24 Penguins have solid bones; some flying birds, such as cormorants and loons, have solid bones to help them dive underwater for food.

25 Despite that pilots of most planes do not have the ability to control a wing's fundamental shape beyond manipulating flaps and ailerons.

26 To be fair, Fisher acknowledges that Leonard Scigaj appropriated the term first, in his discussion of A. R. Ammons's *Garbage* in *Sustainable Poetry*.

27 Fisher's reading of homology in McKay's poetry represents a significant contribution to evolutionary literary studies. To date, such studies have primarily examined evolution as a cultural narrative that has influenced/informed written narratives, particularly in Victorian fiction. See Levine, *Darwin and the Novelists: Patterns of Science in Victorian Fiction* (1988); Carroll, *Evolution and Literary Theory* (1995) and *Literary Darwinism: Evolution, Human Nature, and Literature* (2004); and Beer, *Darwin's Plots: Evolutionary Narrative in Darwin, George Eliot, and Nineteenth-century Fiction* (2000).

28 For a provocative, sympathetic portrayal of one man's attempt to train a red-tailed hawk, see Julian Goldberger's film *The Hawk Is Dying* (2006), based on Harry Crew's novel of the same name.

29 Given the relatively low number of avian species (approximately 10,000) compared to other evolutionary classes, birds do not seem to be overly successful. Although approximately 5,000 species of mammal exist, approximately 40,000 species of crustaceans, 70,000 species of mollusk, 100,000 species of fungi, 280,000 species of plants, and over 1,000,000 species of insects have been identified.

30 Strictly speaking, birds are of the kingdom animalia, the phylum chordate (with a backbone), and class aves (bird). The class aves is organized (currently) into 23 orders and over 220 families.

Notes to Chapter Four

1. Still, ass is a name as much as "Harebell," "Naked // Mitrewort," "Pale / Corydalis, Bluebead Lily, Starflower, Butterwort" and "Gay Wings" (9, 11); the hiker does not, despite having access to a "flower book," resort to the Latin when identifying these flora.
2. Thanks to Laura Moss for pointing this out.
3. The format remains the same in *Camber: Selected Poems* (163 and 164).
4. According to W. J. Brown, "[t]he art [of augury] died out slowly, as people became more educated, and Christianity helped to kill it" (136). Ironically, environmentalists such as Rachel Carson in *Silent Spring* might be closer to the augurs of that past. In lamenting the increasing absence of bird species Carson and her acolytes have been (and continue) observing and predicting the decline of avian and hominoid life on earth.
5. This is not, as one critic suggests, one of McKay's neologisms. Snickersnack is the sound made by the "vorpal blades" in Lewis Carroll's "Jabberwocky." I suppose turning a neologistic noun into a verb is a form of neologism.
6. See "L'Hirondelle" (*B* 29), "Dreamskaters" (*B* 48), and "Alibi" (*A* 19) for other references to swallows.
7. The nearly identical, though slightly larger, Cooper's hawk (*Accipiter cooperii*) and the northern goshawk (*Accipiter gentilis*) are the only other North American representatives in the genus *Accipiter*. Cooper's weigh 450 g, goshawks, 950 g.
8. This year also saw the debut of a Monty Python sketch called "Rival Documentaries," which aired on the television program *Monty Python's Flying Circus*. It neatly dramatizes some of the challenges that face ecocritics. It begins with a man (John Cleese) standing before the camera in rural England, microphone in hand, asking the audience a question: "Was Sir Walter Scott a loony, or was he the greatest flowering of the early-nineteenth-century Romantic tradition?" Another man (Michael Palin) soon steps into the shot, points to the microphone, and asks to borrow it. The first man kindly obliges, only to witness the second journalist proceed with a documentary of his own: "These trees behind me now were planted over forty years ago, as part of a policy by the then Crown Woods, who became the Forestry Commission in 1924." The sketch moves back and forth between these two "rival documentaries," and the following exchanges between Cleese and Palin result in some of the physical comedy the Pythons are known for. In typically absurdist fashion, the sketch that began with a believable, albeit improbable, difference of opinion, ends with a Hollywood-inspired car chase complete with flying bullets and the sounds of a car crash as the rivals speed around a corner.

   This dramatization of a rivalry between different approaches to the landscape—one literary, the other botanical and political—is, I suggest, familiar to (mostly early) ecocritics, scholars whose inclination is to see such opposing perspectives as complementary. Even though the "forty thousand acres of virgin forest" each man stands before was at one point "Sir Walter Scott's country," the two narratives cannot coexist peacefully in the Pythons' world (which is, of course, an absurdly accurate version of the world). "Rival Documentaries" is as good a metaphor as any to describe the practical resistance to truly interdisciplinary research. Granted, ecocriticism's story does not include—at least not yet—a car chase, but the challenges remain analogous.

   While I am tempted to suggest "Rival Documentaries" anticipates ecocriticism, it actually appeared a year after the publication of Joseph Meeker's influential book *The Comedy of Survival: Studies in Literary Ecology* (1972). Meeker's main argument is that the classical genres of tragedy and comedy influence a human tendency toward extinction and survival, respectively. Since comedy recognizes humans' insignificance—and examines it to comic effect—it most adequately reflects a humility necessary to check our egotistical behaviour, which is in part responsible for environmental degradation. *The Comedy of Survival* has been substantially revised twice since 1972, with different subtitles: *In Search of an Environmental Ethic* in 1980; and *Literary Ecology and a Play Ethic* in 1997. For a reading of Don McKay's poetics by way of Meeker, see Sophia Forster's "Don McKay's Comic Anthropocentrism: Ecocriticism Meets 'Mr. Nature Poet.'"

9   While *Long Sault* and *Lependu* are McKay's only book-length long poems, he has continued to include shorter long poems in many of his books. These pieces often include passages of prose poetry and occasionally reflect the surrealism identified by Davey. See "Sanding Down This Rocking Chair on a Windy Night" (*SD* 29–44); "Bone Poems" (*NF* 27–35); "Matériel" (*A* 37–48); and "Five Ways to Lose Your Way" (*DW* 85–93). Actually, this last poem was published as a chapbook (in an edition of 75 copies) by Jack Pine Press in 2004, prior to the publication of *Deactivated West 100*. The chapbook includes illustrations designed by McKay and Dorothy Field, and comes with a piece of orange tape used by loggers to denote a "Falling Boundary."

10 It seems worth mentioning that Bentley, Davey, and McKay all taught English at the same institution, The University of Western Ontario.

11 I realize one might argue that my imagination and my pen have just brought both the Douglas fir and the kinglets into existence for the reader—but this existence is textual and not, in the final analysis, really existence at all, at least as far as the fir and kinglets are concerned. Whether or not the reader knows of their existence, textual or otherwise, is irrelevant to their actual existence. Trees and birds don't care if we see them, or write them (except insofar as we actively participate in their proliferation or extirpation; see Michael Pollan's *The Botany of Desire* for more).

Notes to Chapter Five

1   Grey identifies a modification in Keats's ode between the manuscript and the published version, suggesting that the change has produced better metrics but less accuracy. "Keats first wrote 'Magic casements opening on the foam of *keelless* seas in faery lands forlorn,'" Grey notes. "This is the epithet that agrees best with magic casements in faery lands, but it drags upon the ear. Keats scratched it out and wrote 'perilous' instead: but it must have cost him something to sacrifice the sense of keelless" (72n).

2   Cook mistakenly writes "coefficiency" instead of "coefficient." The former means cooperation; the latter, when combined with drag, refers to an equation used to measure "the relative 'dragginess' of differently shaped objects *independent of size*" (Alexander 15). "The beauty of the drag coefficient," according to David Alexander, "is that it is dimensionless: the numerator and denominator are both forces, so the units cancel" (15). I imagine this dimensionlessness is of immense poetic interest to McKay.

3   For a discussion of the myth of Daedalus and Icarus as postcolonial allegory in a Canadian context, see Eva-Marie Kröller's "Fear of Flying? The Myth of Daedalus and Icarus in Canadian Culture."

4   The turn in Hopkins's poem, which sees the kestrel begin his plummet toward earth (and, ostensibly, his quarry), also represents the fall of humankind. The kestrel's flight prior to buckling, in other words, invokes a pre-lapsarian state of purity and innocence.

5   Of the winds listed in "Without a Song," the last one, mistral, comes closest to meeting the bard's descriptive criteria. A katabatic wind, the mistral is a "cold, dry wind blowing from the north over the northwest coast of the Mediterranean Sea." It can reach speeds of between 80 and 200 miles per hour. In "Katabatic Wind," a section of his abecedarian "Between Rock and Stone: A Geopoetic Alphabet" (*DW* 33–73), McKay suggests that to experience a katabatic wind "is to feel the full weight of winter, winter so profound it has broken from the other seasons and no longer even registers their absence" (49).

6 See the National Film Board (NFB) film *Being Caribou* (2004), for example, which documents Karsten Heuer and Leanne Allison as they follow a herd of caribou across the Arctic tundra. (Heuer's *Being Caribou: Five Months on Foot with an Arctic Herd* [2006] is a print version of the same trip.)

7 The American Broadcasting Corporation's series of "After School Specials" began showing an hour-long animated version of *Last of the Curlews* in 1972. Produced by Hanna-Barbera Productions, it was the first of many "After School Specials" intended "to encourage in children a sense of awareness and curiosity about the world they live in," according to a blurb on the Northern Prairie Wildlife Research Center website.

8 In "National Species: Ecology, Allegory, and Indigeneity in the Wolf Stories of Roberts, Seton, and Mowat," Brian Johnson posits Bodsworth alongside Charles G. D. Roberts, Grey Owl, and Farley Mowat, writers who often make "the case for conservation by contesting the notion of a 'species boundary' between human beings and animals" (Fiamengo 334–35). For each of these writers, Johnson argues, anthropomorphism functions self-consciously to support respect for the nonhuman world by implying affinities between humans and nonhuman animals. See Fiamengo, ed. (333–52).

9 McKay returns to Villon's "classic statement" regarding "the idea of oblivion," "*Mais ou sont les neiges d'antan?*" in "Otherwise Than Place" (*DW* 13–31). In characteristic fashion, McKay applies Villon's question, "which is presumed to be rhetorical," to a hike along "the trail up to the Bow Glacier in Banff National Park" (23). Such a hike would take one "through the boulder field and across the recessional moraine" to the foot of the glacier where, McKay argues, "[t]hese *neiges* are truly vintage *d'antan,* dating back to the Wisconsin glaciation," and Villon's question is rendered "obviously not rhetorical" (23).

10 Souwesto is the geographic area, southwestern Ontario, where McKay lived and taught when he began his career as teacher and poet.

11 This is one of many common names for the red-winged blackbird.

Notes to Chapter Six

1 *Field Notes* was a quarterly published jointly by the National Audubon Society and the United States Fish and Wildlife Service. It is now a section of *Audubon Magazine.*

2 I say *were* being silenced as a concession to the changes put in place to help restore songbird populations following the publication of Carson's book. All, however, is not well in the avian world, as Bridget Stutchbury makes clear in her book, an updated version of *Silent Spring* that Wayne Grady calls "a thoroughly researched and elegantly written call to arms" (D10).

3 Both large-billed and lesser seed finches compete ("ramp" or "race") in Guyana. The lesser seed finch is known locally as towa towa. See http://www.iwokrama.org/business/songbirds.htm.

4 An indication of the political and cultural climate during which Rowland was writing *Birds with Human Souls* in 1978, this reference to the wonders of free-market capitalism resonates with insidious implications, given this Moscow bird market's twenty-first-century associations with bird flu. *The Moscow Times* reported in February 2007 that "[v]eterinary workers wearing masks and white protective suits carted off refuse and burned it [...] inside the quarantined section of the popular Bird Market" in response to "an outbreak of the deadly H5N1 strain of avian flu" (Delany 4).

5 I shall resist the temptation to develop a further connection here between Glavin's phrase "astonishing capacity" and McKay's notion, explored in *Deactivated West 100* and *Strike/Slip*, of "astonishment" as a contemporary version of the sublime. Much of McKay's later writing shifts from his earlier focus on "wilderness," birds, and ecopoetry—though

each remains an integral component of his poetics—to astonishment, rock/stone, and geopoetry. I examine this shift in Ecotone Four.

6. The phrase "we shall be changed" echoes the biblical verse from 1 Corinthians 15:51–52: "Behold, I show you a mystery; We shall not all sleep, but we shall all be changed, In a moment, in the twinkling of an eye, at the last trump: for the trumpet shall sound, and the dead shall be raised incorruptible, and we shall be changed."

7. See, for example, E. B. White's "A Listener's Guide to the Birds" (McClatchy 194–97), which incorporates popular versions of birdsong in fanciful verse.

> Nothing is simpler than telling a barn owl from a veery:
> One says, "Kschh!" in a voice that is eerie,
> The other say, "Vee-ur," in a manner that is breezy.
>   (I told you it was easy.)
> . . . .
> Let us suppose you hear a bird say, "Fitz-bew,"
> The things you can be sure of are two:
> First, the bird is an alder flycatcher (*Empidonax trailii
>   trailii*);
> Second, you are standing in Ohio – or, as some people
>   call it, O-hee-o –
> Because, although it may come as a surprise to you,
> The alder flycatcher, in New York or New England,
>   does not say, "Fitz-bew,"
> It says, "Wee-bé-o." (197)

8. Harting's wording is a bit off: birds as a whole make up the class Aves; songbirds constitute the taxonomic order Passeriformes within the class.

9. A hoopoe plays a significant part in Salman Rushdie's fantastical *Haroun and the Sea of Stories*. Though a lengthy discussion of this postcolonial text is outside the scope of the present work, my sense is that Rushdie's hoopoe, a mechanical talking bird, functions as a catalyst of story and storytelling.

10. Although "Song for Wild Phlox" and "Song for Beef Cattle" appear in two different collections, they share a connection to Hamlet's soliloquy, to which McKay alludes in the latter poem:

> O that this too too sullied flesh would melt,
> Thaw, and resolve itself into a dew,
> Or that the Everlasting had not fixed
> His canon 'gainst self-slaughter. O God, God,
> How weary, stale, flat, and unprofitable
> Seem to me all the uses of this world!
> Fie on't, ah, fie, 'tis an unweeded garden
> That grows to seed. Things rank and gross in nature
> Possess it merely. (1.2, 129–37)

The pun on a dew/adieu takes on a different meaning in a poem about beef cattle preparing for slaughter (decidedly not "self-slaughter"); moreover, the idea of the world as an unweeded garden, which rank and gross things (humans) merely possess, is in keeping with Bringhurst's notion, oft repeated in McKay's poetics, of "knowing not owning."

11. Beef cattle are usually cross-bred over successive generations to "produce an animal with faster growth rates, heavier carcass weights, an improved ratio of lean carcass meat to fat, maximum fertility, improved lactation, and greater stress tolerance compared to the

two contributing base breeds," as is the case with Beefmaker cattle, raised in New South Wales. See http://www.ansi.okstate.edu/breeds/cattle.

12 I have deliberately avoided discussing the ways in which McKay, as poet, might be construed as birdlike in his "songs" because the notion of becoming bird, like other arguments, lie just beyond the edge of this book's argument. I am content at this point to acknowledge that these poems, as representative of the non-bird poems of McKay's repertoire, nevertheless add to an understanding of McKay's avian poetics.

13 The relation between birds and hope is perhaps most strongly affiliated with Emily Dickinson's "Poem 254," in which she writes,

> "Hope" is the thing with feathers –
> That perches in the soul –
> And sings the tune without the words –
> And never stops – at all –

14 Hardy's "Shelley's Skylark" is an intriguing exception.

Notes to Chapter Seven

1 Grandin's claim also looks back to Paul Shepard's claim in *Thinking Animals* that human song "may even have evolved from the avian example as prehuman groups moved toward group consciousness and cultural diversity" (74).

2 I borrow this notion from Anne Michaels's *The Winter Vault* (2009): "We made our paints from the bones of the animals we painted. No image forgets this origin.... With the first grave ... the invention of memory. No word forgets this origin" (n. pag.).

3 In *The Natural Science of the Human Species*, Konrad Lorenz suggests that "one should never construct sentences with 'the animal' as the subject. [Oskar] Heinroth used to interrupt such sentences with the mild and friendly interjection: 'Are you referring to an amoeba or a chimpanzee?'" (260).

4 This is not to suggest that these texts articulate formulae for (re)solving speciesist, racist, colonial problems; rather, they articulate a mode of questioning categories that remain prevalent in the Western imagination.

5 Though literary and cultural studies have been taking the question of the animal quite seriously in the past decade or so, birds are rarely considered. In the two special issues of *Mosaic: A Journal for the Interdisciplinary Study of Literature* on animals in literature, for example (vols. 39.4 and 40.1), only one article deals with birds. Masood Ashraf Raja's "The King Buzzard: Bano Qudsia's Postnational Allegory and the Nation-State," as the title suggests, reads an international conference of the birds in Qudsia's Urdu novel as an allegory for "the national and postnational tendencies of the Islamic world in general and Pakistan in particular" (95).

6 The extent to which this earlier shift can be considered complete is debatable. Assuming oral cultures are necessarily primitive or birds are not a part of a cultural soundscape, for example, ignores complex questions regarding the persistence of oral storytelling and the possibility that "[h]umans, like birds, are able to make songs and pass them on" (Bringhurst "Poetry" 163).

7 I include this parenthesis to acknowledge the work of writing that we often consider disembodied. For a thoughtful discussion of the ways writing can be considered a form of physical labour, framed as a response to Richard White's well-known article "'Are You an Environmentalist or Do You Work for a Living?: Work and Nature,'" see Randall Roorda, "Antimonies of Participation in Literacy and Wilderness," *ISLE: Interdisciplinary Studies in Literature and Environment* 14.2 (Summer 2007): 71–87.

8   See also Lopez's essay "The Passing Wisdom of Birds" (*Crossing* 193–208), in which he recounts Spanish conquistador Hernando Cortés's destruction of Mexican aviaries in 1519.
9   See William Gaver's essay "What in the World Do We Hear? An Ecological Approach to Auditory Event Perception" for his distinction between "musical listening"—paying attention to the "pitch and loudness" of a sound, for example—and "everyday listening"—"the experience of listening to events rather than sounds" (1). Gaver is interested in developing a way to determine how humans distinguish between these two types of listening, and is particularly curious about how everyday listening functions: How, for example, do we identify the location, size, and direction of a thing—such as a car—that makes a sound?
10 I borrow these notions from Yuki, who develops them through her reading of Barry Lopez's work: "If an imposition is an act of refueling what is established," she writes, "proposition is an effort to break down the established, to disturb the existing systems, and to create a common ground on which to start developing a sustainable relationship with the other. As it is epitomized in the expression "What do you think of this?," proposition involves a physical … gesture of listening" (30). In short, the difference between impositional and propositional understanding mirrors the difference between imposing and proposing ideas.
11 McKay's choice of modifier offers a nice contrast to Wordsworth's use of the verb "peopled" to describe birdsong filling the air.
12 A notable attempt to complicate the singularity of voice typically at work in conventional poetry is evident in Dennis Lee's notion of polyphony and in Robert Bringhurst's innovative polyphonic texts. Simply put—for the sake of concision: Lee's polyphony is anything but simple—for Lee, "[p]olyphony in writing is the art of orchestrating successive voices across a work." "It moves from one tonality to another, and on through consecutive voices" (*Body* 54). Bringhurst offers a slightly more practical definition in "Singing with the Frogs": it is "singing more than one song, playing more than one tune, telling more than one story, at once" (114). In numerous works, Bringhurst enacts polyphony by utilizing typographic and print technologies to produce text on a single page meant to be read/performed by multiple voices. See especially "The Blue Roofs of Japan: A Duet for Interpenetrating Voices" (*Calling* 169–79); "New World Suite No. 3: Four Movements for Three Voices" (*Calling* 181–230); and *Ursa Major: A Polyphonic Masque for Speakers & Dancers*.
13 In music theory, acoustic ecology has been discussed for much longer, thanks to the innovative compositions of R. Murray Schafer, pioneer of acoustic ecology. In addition to his work with the World Soundscape Project and his book *The Tuning of the World*, see (or rather hear), especially, Schafer's Quartet No. 10, Winter Birds.
14 See Ronald P. Morrison, "Wilderness and Clearing: Thoreau, Heidegger, and the Poetic," which offers a good reading of how the clearing functions in nature writing, albeit one that suggests "[b]eing a seer even takes precedence over being a writer" (149).
15 Note that Lampman has a sonnet with the same title; it is not discussed here.
16 This scene both echoes and contradicts a scene in Catharine Parr Traill's *The Backwoods of Canada*. Traill names with precision a number of tree species—"pines, cedars, hemlock, and balsam firs"—as she "enjoy[s] a walk in the woods of a bright winter day" (127). Like Lampman after her, Traill notices stumps that "look quite pretty, with their turbans of snow; [and] a blackened pine-stump, with its white cap and mantle" (128). Unlike Lampman, however, who refers to the mullein stalks he sees in the clearing as "hermit folk, who long ago, / Wandering in bodies to and fro, / Had chanced upon this

lonely way" (142), Traill writes that Canada "is too matter-of-fact [a] country for such supernaturals to visit.... No Druid claims our oaks" (128).
17 Although the title "Après Chainsaw" does not appear until its publication in *Strike/Slip*, I will use the title when referring to the poem, since it appears in *Deactivated West 100*.
18 Two other poems in *Deactivated West 100* deal explicitly with the logging industry: "Five Ways to Lose Your Way" (83–93), about the poet-speaker getting lost while searching for an old "Vulcan 0-4-0 saddle tank locomotive that rumour has it is up [...] on the ridge turning into a humped hill" (85); and "Waiting for Shay" (75–82; *S/S* 19–21), about the Shay locomotive, which was prevalent on the railroads of Vancouver Island and was "Four-fifths animal," "the brand-new neolithic monster for the job" of clearing the land of trees (*DW* 81). For more on logging poetry and the logging industry in general, including a more detailed history of the chainsaw, see the following: Laurie Ricou's "Woodswords File" and "Afterfile: Woodswords" (*Arbutus* 117–36, 194–99); McKay's Foreword to *Haunted Hills & Hanging Valleys: Selected Poems 1969–2004*, by British Columbia's best-known "logger poet," Peter Trower; John Vaillant's *The Golden Spruce: A True Story of Myth, Madness and Greed*; and David Lee's *Chainsaws: A History*.
19 Aside from adding the title, McKay makes two minor changes to the poem as it appears in *Strike/Slip*: "the hammered air" on line 4 becomes "the bludgeoned air," suggesting in the later version a more insidious action with murderous implications; and the margin at line 17—"What I want to say is"—moves from left-justified to indented, enacting, perhaps, a typographical clearing that gives readers room to pause and listen.
20 This drumming is produced by the rapidly beating wings of a ruffed grouse. Sibley's description supports McKay's "subliminal" modifier: "this low-pitched 'drumming' is often felt rather than heard" (146).

Notes to Chapter Eight

1 In biological terms, metaplasm refers to the contents of a cell other than the protoplasm, to the dead rather than the living material, to the unclear rather than the clear.
2 Both "public" and "publication" share an etymological link with the Latin *publicus*, to make public, of the people.
3 As McKay has benefited from readers attending to his work over the years, so have others benefited from his listening. In his Foreword to *Don McKay: Essays on His Works*, Brian Bartlett compiles a list—"far from complete"—of twenty-seven poets who thank McKay in the acknowledgements section of their books, including Ken Babstock, Roo Borson, George Elliott Clarke, Barry Dempster, Sue Goyette, A. F. Moritz, Sue Sinclair, John Steffler, and Anne Simpson (9–10). Looking forward to a time when McKay's "role not only as poet, but also as editor, mentor, and friend" will inform an "appreciation of McKay's place in Canadian poetry," Bartlett suggests that McKay "may be the most valued poetry-editor in Canada" (9–10).
4 *Matériel*, defined as the material portion of art and as a term for the collective machinery and supplies for the army, becomes for McKay an extreme version of death: "Unmortality Incorporated" (*V* 48). Thus, the site of the first hydrogen-bomb test, the Pacific atoll Elugelab, is decimated and has "No shadow. All day / it is noon it is no one. All day" (48). The metaplasmic play between "noon" and "no one" here recognizes *matériel* as a severe form of biological metaplasm: not simply the dead, granular material that takes on meaning based on its negative relation to life, to protoplasmic transparency, but the human "rage for immortality" that results in the "denial of death altogether, as in the case of things made permanent and denied access to decomposition" (*V* 20). This, for McKay, is the supreme marker of Western civilization's arrogance; it is anti-ecological, anti-poetic.

5   Don Stap writes that the song of the thrushes he studied "contained harmonically unrelated notes that overlapped in time" (75–76).
6   See "A Barbed Wire Fence Meditates upon the Goldfinch" (*B* 95), which McKay writes in the "voice" of barbed wire and begins by addressing an ambiguous listener:

> More than the shortest distance
> between points, we are
> the Stradivarius of work.
> We make the meadow meadow, make it
> mean, make it yours.

7   The epithet, "Jesus," does not appear in print in either *The Muskwa Assemblage* or *Paradoxides*. McKay uses it in the recorded version of the poem on *Songs for the Songs of Birds*.
8   Scholarly examples include Scottish poet Robert Crawford's *Contemporary Poetry and Contemporary Science*, American ecocritic Glen Love's *Practical Ecocriticism: Literature, Biology, and the Environment*, and Canadian ecocritic Laurie Ricou's *Salal: Listening for the Northwest Understory*; poetic examples in Canada include Adam Dickinson's *Kingdom, Phylum*, Don McKay's *Strike/Slip*, and angela rawlings's *wide slumber for lepidopterists*.

Notes to Ecotone Three

1   Subsequent conversations have confirmed sightings of roosting crows just south of Highway 1 as well.
2   See Jerome A. Jackson's *In Search of the Ivory-Billed Woodpecker*, updated after the controversial rediscovery.

Notes to Chapter Nine

1   As McKay notes in his preamble, hawks generally avoid crossing large bodies of water, so in fall migration many hawks that breed in Ontario follow the north shore of Lake Erie west and leave Canada near Amherstburg, Ont., before dispersing to continue their journey over dry land.
2   Reaktion Books, in the UK, has begun an Animal series consisting of dozens of titles, including *Ant, Bear, Cockroach, Crow, Elephant, Falcon, Oyster, Rat, Salmon, Tiger*, and *Whale*. The books purport to offer an examination of individual species and their cultural and natural place in human history. Other books provide historical and cultural context for a pair of relatively commonplace birds: *Pigeons: The Fascinating Saga of the World's Most Revered and Reviled Bird*, by Andrew D. Blechman, and *Hunting the Wren: Transformation of Bird to Symbol*, by Elizabeth Atwood Lawrence.
3   Battalio focuses primarily on *The Auk*, American ornithology's major journal, and the shifting methodologies and rhetorical strategies in the published articles. Between 1890 and 1930, for example, bird subjects were observed in the field no less than 40% of the time; by the 1970s, however, that number falls to below 5%. In contrast, the use of theoretical systems, mathematics, and complex models increases from 2% in 1890 to 10% in 1970, peaking at 85% in the 1990s (73).
4   For a discussion of birds in Eiseley's writing, see Dimitri N. Breschinsky, "Flights of Fancy: Birds in the Works of Loren Eiseley," *ISLE: Interdisciplinary Studies in Literature and Environment* 15.1 (2008): 39–73.
5   In *Camber: Selected Poems, 1983–2000*, "Field Marks (2)," renamed "Field Marks," opens the collection, while the original "Field Marks," renamed "Field Marks (2)," appears later. This switch, which suggests a renewed favouritism for the birding strategies explored in the original "Field Marks (2)," appears to coincide with McKay's developing avian poetics

between 1983 and 2000. Although Méira Cook returns the poems to their original titles in her recent selection of McKay's poetry, she acknowledges their significance by naming the collection *Field Marks: The Poetry of Don McKay*.
6. W. H. New writes of lists in "Writing Here": "treasure (or maybe junk) collection goes by other names: bibliophilia, for example, or lexicography, or life writing. I came to understand that it's the collecting that matters, the making of lists, and therefore the category of use ('what use is it?' some people ask, whether of plastic souvenirs, or pearls, or poetry) and to reclaim it for creativity and value" (5).
7. This approach contrasts sharply with the practice, common among early ornithologists, of killing birds in order to identify, categorize, and study them.
8. In "The Question Concerning Technology," Martin Heidegger claims that "[m]odern science's way of representing pursues and entraps nature as a calculable coherence of forces" (*Basic Writings* 326). While pursuit implies a distance to be overcome and entrapment suggests a mode of overcoming that presumes to measure and comprehend (explain) "nature," the possibility of a "calculable coherence of forces" threatens, in Heidegger's formulation, to collapse distances in dangerous ways. From an ecological perspective, Heidegger's critique of technology, which he links through the Greek *technē* to the craft of poetry, points out the danger of humans relying too heavily on a set of practices—technological, poetical—that removes the world of its mystery. What Heidegger calls "enframing," which he identifies as the essence of technology, "starts man [*sic*] upon the way of that revealing through which the actual everywhere, more or less distinctly, becomes standing-reserve" (329). In other words, the danger of technology lies in its tendency, as Catherine Frances Botha notes, to usurp "all other modes of revealing. With everything standing in reserve for our use, 'distance' disappears" (162). The disappearance of distance is, I argue, simultaneously a dangerous proximity and an absence, both of which find their ultimate home in extinction.

Notes to Chapter Ten

1. Riordan and Turney, eds., *A Quark for Mister Mark: 101 Poems about Science* (Faber 2001) and Riordan and Burnside, eds., *Wild Reckoning: An Anthology Provoked by Rachel Carson's Silent Spring* (Calouste Gulbenkian Foundation 2004).
2. Like most ecocritics, I have had no formal training in science, environmental or otherwise. If my methodology borrows from other subdisciplines that consider, say, the history of textile manufacture when contextualizing a reading of Victorian fiction, it differs in the degree of congruity between the types of knowledge I consult. I am aware that my attempts to engage dialogically with the sciences might fail because of my focus on scientific *writing* rather than on the graphs and equations that represent data incapable of being uttered clearly in words. Dana Phillips acknowledges this risk, worrying that there might be "a danger that those who, like [him]self, are interested in ecology, but whose training is not scientific and who must cope with an entirely different set of difficulties, will gloss over or minimize the significance of the problems ecologists face in understanding the natural world" (51). While I admit skepticism of my own capacity to comprehend ecologically oriented literature's complexities and nuances—steeped as I am in a discipline that traditionally studies human artistic achievements in language and has been known to posit language as necessary for the world to exist—I am equally skeptical of any one discipline's capacity to comprehend ideas and objects from beyond conventional bounds. But any reverence in these pages is directed toward the biological and ecological wonders of avian behaviour, rendered clearly in prose and verse, and even that reverence is, I hope, muted. By embracing the language and knowledge of science, I want to encourage, not uncritical reverence, but open-mindedness and a willingness to

transgress conventional ways of thinking and writing about literature, which is admittedly far from anarchic.
3   In 2001, *Nature* published an article by Maurice Riordan about some of the ways (and words by which) science provides material for poets. More recently, *Interdisciplinary Science Reviews* dedicated an entire issue (30.4, in December 2005) to science and poetry.
4   For more on deep ecology, see Garrard, *Ecocriticism* (20–23), and Sessions, *Deep Ecology for the 21st Century*. *The Trumpeter: journal of ecosophy* can be accessed online: http://trumpeter.athabascau.ca/index.php/trumpet/index.
5   Ecology did not enter serious or popular discourse until late in the nineteenth century, despite Ernst Haeckel's coining of the term *oikology* (from the Greek *oikos*, house) in 1864.
6   Given at the opening of Sir Josiah Mason's Science College on 1 October 1880.
7   The nature–culture debate is nearly parallel (contiguous) to the science–literature debate. Raymond Williams traces the etymologies of both terms in *Keywords*; Terry Eagleton picks up on Williams's work, beginning with *The Idea of Culture* (2000), by iterating the problematic yet similar etymological lineage of both terms: "'Culture' is said to be one of the two or three most complex words in the English language, and the term which is sometimes considered to be its opposite—nature—is commonly awarded the accolade of being the most complex of all" (1; cf. Williams 87, 219). Both Williams and Eagleton acknowledge the originary link of "culture" to the biotic world, i.e., as in the practice of cultivating the soil (whence "agriculture," "horticulture"), as well as each term's etymological fealty to *process* as opposed to *product*.
8   Quotations here from "Science and Literature" are taken from the revised version as reproduced in Buckler (1958).
9   In the closing decades of the twentieth century and the opening of the twenty-first, scholars have revisited the shifting ground. George Levine has contributed much to the resurgence with his studies of Darwin's influence among Victorian writers (*Darwin and the Novelists: Patterns of Science in Victorian Fiction* [1991]) and his edited collections of essays (*One Culture: Essays in Science and Literature* [1987], and *Realism and Representation: Essays on the Problem of Realism in Relation to Science, Literature, and Culture* [1992]). See also Shaffer, ed., *The Third Culture: Literature and Science* (1997); Brown, ed., *The Measured Word: On Poetry and Science* (2001); Gould, *The Hedgehog, the Fox, and the Magister's Pox: Mending the Gap between Science and the Humanities* (2003); and Crawford, ed., *Contemporary Poetry and Contemporary Science* (2006).
10 A full account of Davey's influence on decades of literary criticism in Canada falls beyond the scope of my argument. For a riposte to Davey's essay and a critique of the disciplinary shift it engendered, see Lecker, *Making It Real: The Canonization of English-Canadian Literature* (1995).
11 The slashing of "and" and "as" in her title enables a reading both of history as "ontologically separate from the self-consciously fictional text (or intertexts) of fiction" and of history "*as* intertext" whereby "[h]istory becomes a text, a discursive construct upon which literature draws as easily as it does upon other artistic contexts" (169–70).
12 Hutcheon links postcolonial and ecological concerns by asking, among other things, "how does one deal with what Frye himself called 'the tension between the mind and a surrounding not integrated with it' (*Bush* 200) without that act of integration being considered a violation, an imposition, a colonization of nature?" (155).
13 I do not advocate simply replacing "history" with "nature writing" or "the past" with "the physical world" in the preceding excerpts, though. Nor do I suggest historiographic metafiction is an inherently ecological form of literature. (Perhaps some such term as ecographic metapoetics would suffice to articulate the uneasy relation between ecocriticism and postmodern theory?) But if science produces texts closely bound to the physical

world as subject, much as history produces texts closely bound to the past as text, why not look to science for intertextual insights the way literary critics have been looking to historical documents? Why not follow an intertextual route of referents from birds in Don McKay's poetry back (or across) to ornithological monographs? For Scigaj, what I suggest aligns itself with what he articulates as ecopoetry's interdisciplinary preoccupations, its "referential concern with environmental context," which leads to "the reverse of the free play of *différance*" (37). Echoing Derrida's neologism, Scigaj calls "this process ... *référance,* from the French verb *se référer,* which means 'to relate or refer oneself to'" (38).

14 Heise perceives a need for ecocriticism to confront scientific descriptions of nature:

> This confrontation enables not only an assessment of how scientific insight is culturally received and transformed (rather than "constructed"), it also allows the critic to see where literature deviates—or, in some cases, wishes or attempts to deviate—from the scientific approach in view of particular aesthetic and ideological goals. The text thereby becomes a place where different visions of nature and varying images of science, each with their cultural and political implications, are played out, rather than simply a site of resistance against science and its claims to truth, or a construct in which science is called upon merely to confirm the inherent beauty of nature. (n. pag.)

15 In 1903 Stevens went on a six-week hunting trip with W. G. Peckham in the Kootenays.
16 Realism, of course, is both impossible to achieve and naive to attempt, according to Dana Phillips and others who criticize an ecocritical emphasis on a world that exists prior to language. Buell, Phillips's main object of critique, acknowledges the difficulties inherent in attempting "environmental representation" (*Future* 31) while maintaining an interest in the relational tensions between words and world. My own interest in specificity has less to do with McKay's mimetic propensity (or lack thereof) and more to do with an impulse, situated in a poetry always already impelled by ecological patterns and biological data, to pay as much attention to the world outside as to the worlds inside texts.
17 Strictly speaking, physics, geology, and chemistry are physical sciences while biology is a natural science.

Notes to Ecotone Four

1 As McKay acknowledges, Hess himself borrowed the term from geophysicist J. H. F. Umbgrove, who coined "geopoetry" as "an approbative term for creative speculation" (Oreskes 1038).
2 Also resonant in this context is Simone Weil's notion of "decreation," which McKay glosses in his "geopoetic alphabet": "Decreation calls for attention to release its grip on fixed principles, to risk radical not-knowing without succumbing to the seductive currents which go by the name of nihilism" (*DW* 38). The "subduction of one plate under another," which often results in the melting of ancient rock into magma, represents for McKay a "decreative feature of the rock cycle" (38–39). See also Anne Carson's *Decreation: Poetry, Essays, Opera.*
3 "Between Rock and Stone: A Geopoetic Alphabet" first appeared in *The Antigonish Review* 140 (Winter 2005): 101–26.
4 McKay has written a number of "Meditations" throughout his career, beginning with *Night Field*: "Meditation on Blue" (*NF* 14); "Meditation in an Uncut Cornfield, November" (*NF* 42); "Meditation on Shovels" (*NF* 47); "Meditation on Snow Clouds Approaching the University from the Northwest" (*NF* 60); and "Meditation on Antique Glass" (*A* 61). In his interview with Ken Babstock, McKay acknowledges the influence of Dennis

Lee and Al Purdy on his meditations, in which he claims to enact a "process of thinking inside language with a lyric sensibility.... Instead of the perfect lyric gesture, the meditation is a little more prosy, a little more moosey-faced" ("Appropriate Gesture" 56).

5   Both James McKusick and Gabriele Helms acknowledge Davies as the originator of "ecolect." According to Helms, Davies, in *Wordsworth and the Worth of Words*, introduced "[t]he concept of 'ecolect' as a language 'variation peculiar to a particular household, or kin group'" and McKusick expanded the term in his essay about John Clare, as he "considers the whole earth as the household or home" (47).

Note to Ending

1   This poem reminds me of another of the poems in *Mean* that engages with a McKavian listening and homage/ohmage. Babstock reveals an attention to subtle, slow movement in "To Lichen" (56). Again an observer, the poet describes lichen as "Something's remains refused / by death, learning to spread" (56). Lichen's movement indicates the way Dennis Lee wants to read free-verse poetry; not as a linear movement but as a dissemination in all directions, a stretching across space and time that also enacts a listening, as in these lines that further describe lichen as "Scrapings off rock's / inner ear that's heard epochs / in sound wave striating a sheer / face —" (56). The parallel streaks—striations—of epochal time that lichen articulates while spreading out parallel Lee's "forward/lateral action," which "occurs when one energy propels the poem down the page— and gets ... transected, deformed by a series of lateral gusts.... The effect is to make us experience two or more energies at once" (216). Outside language, energies are rarely experienced singularly. The "sound wave striating a sheer / face," furthermore, echoes the wolf's identification of himself as "scree-slope," effectively drawing an analogy between wolf and sound wave. Wolf's howl, as it resonates across the meadow toward the town's "Storm of sound" (Babstock 54), echoes "out of the valley" to mingle with "lichen-hooded / granite" (Babstock 53). Paradoxically, the poet requires language to reveal his attention to what lies beyond language. This paradox further enacts an ecology of listening that incorporates the poem's aurality, nurtured at least nominally by McKay's editorial ear, with the poem's eventual public/published existence.

Works Cited

Abram, David. *The Spell of the Sensuous: Perception and Language in a More-Than-Human World.* New York: Vintage-Random, 1996.
Åkesson, Susanne, and Anders Hedenström. "How Migrants Get There: Migratory Performance and Orientation." *BioScience* 57.2 (2007): 123–33.
Alexander, David E. *Nature's Flyers: Birds, Insects, and the Biomechanics of Flight.* Baltimore: Johns Hopkins UP, 2002.
Allen, Stuart. "Wordsworth's Ear and the Politics of Aesthetic Autonomy." *Romanticism* 9.1 (2003): 37–54.
Anderson, Chris. *Edge Effects: Notes from an Oregon Forest.* Iowa City: U of Iowa P, 1993.
Anderson, Mia. "'Conversation with the Star Messenger': An Enquiry into Margaret Avison's *Winter Sun.*" *Studies in Canadian Literature* 6.1 (1981): 82–132.
Armbruster, Karla, and Kathleen R. Wallace, eds. *Beyond Nature Writing: Expanding the Boundaries of Ecocriticism.* Charlottesville: UP of Virginia, 2001.
Arnold, Matthew. "Culture and Anarchy: Sweetness and Light." *Prose of the Victorian Period.* Ed. William E. Buckler. Boston: Houghton, 1958. 458–76.
Ashcroft, Bill, Gareth Griffiths, and Helen Tiffin. *The Empire Writes Back: Theory and Practice in Post-Colonial Literatures.* 2nd ed. London: Routledge, 2002.
Atwood, Margaret. *Survival: A Thematic Guide to Canadian Literature.* 1970. Toronto: McClelland, 1996.
Auden, W. H. "Bird Language." McClatchy 174.
———. "Musée des Beaux Arts." *Collected Poems: Auden.* New York: Vintage, 1991. 179.
Avison, Margaret. "The Butterfly." *A New Anthology of Canadian Literature in English.* Ed. Donna Bennett and Russell Brown. Toronto: Oxford UP, 2002. 534–35.
———. "The Butterfly." *The Oxford Book of Canadian Verse.* 1960. Ed. A. J. M. Smith. Toronto: Oxford UP, 1965. 260.
———. *No Time.* Hansport, NS: Lancelot, 1989.
Babstock, Ken. *Mean.* Toronto: Anansi, 1999.
Bachelard, Gaston. *The Poetics of Space.* 1958. Boston: Beacon, 1969.
Bairlean, Franz, and Timothy Coppack. "Migration in the Life-History of Birds." *Journal of Ornithology* 147 (2005): 121.

Baldick, Chris. *The Concise Oxford Dictionary of Literary Terms*. 1990. Oxford: Oxford UP, 1996.

Banting, Pamela. "The Angel in the Glacier: Geography as Intertext in Thomas Wharton's *Icefields*." *ISLE: Interdisciplinary Studies in Literature and Environment* 7.2 (2001): 67–80.

Barnes, Julian. *Arthur and George*. Toronto: Random, 2005.

Bartlett, Brian. "A Dog's Nose of Receptiveness: A Calvinoesque Reading of Don McKay." *Antigonish Review* 139 (2005): 123–36.

———. *Don McKay: Essays on His Works*. Toronto: Guernica, 2006.

———. "Two Pianos Together." Introduction. *Thinking and Singing: Poetry & the Practice of Philosophy*. Ed. Tim Lilburn. Toronto: Cormorant, 2002. 5–15.

Bate, Jonathan. *The Song of the Earth*. London: Picador, 2000.

Battalio, John T. *The Rhetoric of Science in the Evolution of American Ornithological Discourse*. ATTW Contemporary Studies in Technical Communication 8. Stanford, CT: Ablex, 1998.

Beattie, Munro. "Poetry: 1920–1935." *Literary History of Canada: Canadian Literature in English*. Ed. Carl F. Klinck. 2nd ed. Vol. 2. Toronto: U of Toronto P, 1976.

Beer, Gillian. Afterword. Crawford, 204-10.

———. *Open Fields: Science in Cultural Encounters*. Oxford: Oxford UP, 1996.

———. "Problems of Description in the Language of Discovery." *One Culture: Essays in Science and Literature*. Ed. George Levine. Madison: U of Wisconsin P, 1987. 35–58.

Bennett, Donna, and Russell Brown, eds. *A New Anthology of Canadian Literature in English*. Toronto: Oxford UP, 2002. 535.

Bennett, Peter M., and Ian P. F. Owens. *Evolutionary Ecology of Birds: Life Histories, Mating Systems, and Extinction*. Oxford: Oxford UP, 2002.

Bentley, D. M. R. *The Confederation Group of Canadian Poets, 1880–1897*. Toronto: U of Toronto P, 2004.

———. *The Gay]Grey Moose: Essays on the Ecologies and Mythologies of Canadian Poetry 1690–1990*. Ottawa: U of Ottawa P, 1992.

Bernstein, C. "Details on Details: Describing a Bird" *Western Tanager* 50.6 (1984): 1–3.

Bewick, Thomas. *Selections from A History of British Birds*. New York: Paddington, 1976.

"Bird Flight Muscle Arrangement." 9 June 2007. <http://www.cals.ncsu.edu/course/zo150/mozley/fall/ flightmuscle.jpg>.

bill bissett. Untitled poem. *Seagull on yonge street*. Vancouver: Talonbooks, 1983. N.pag.

Blechman, Andrew D. *Pigeons: The Fascinating Saga of the World's Most Revered and Reviled Bird*. New York: Grove Press, 2006.

"Blue Jay." Cornell Lab of Ornithology. (2003) 20 August 2008. <http://www.birds.cornell.edu/AllAboutBirds/BirdGuide/Blue_Jay.html>.

Bocking, Stephen. *Nature's Experts: Science, Politics, and the Environment*. New Brunswick, NJ: Rutgers UP, 2006.

Bodsworth, Fred. *Last of the Curlews*. 1954. Toronto: McClelland, 1974.

Bondar, Alanna F. "'That Every Feather Is a Pen, but Living // Flying' Desire: The Metapoetics of Don McKay's *Birding, or Desire*." *Studies in Canadian Literature* 19.2 (1994): 14–29.

———. "Attending Guilt-Free Birdspeak and Treetalk: An Ecofeminist Reading of the 'Geopsyche' in the Poetry of Don McKay." *Ecocriticism and Contemporary Canadian Poetry*. Spec. issue of *Canadian Poetry: Studies, Documents, Reviews* 55 (2004): 65–85.

Borson, Roo. "Snake." *Water Memory*. Toronto: McClelland, 1996. 24.

Botha, Catharine Frances. "Heidegger, Technology, and Ecology." *South African Journal of Philosophy* 22.2 (2003): 157–72.

Bradley, Nicholas. "Ecology and Knowledge in the Poetry of Pacific North America." Diss. U of Toronto, 2006.

———. "'Green of the Earth and Civil Grey': Nature and the City in Dennis Lee's *Civil Elegies*." *Canadian Poetry: Studies, Documents, Reviews* 55 (2004): 15–33.

Brand, Dionne. *A Map to the Door of No Return: Notes to Belonging*. 2001. Toronto: Vintage, 2002.

Bringhurst, Robert. *A Story as Sharp as a Knife: The Classical Mythtellers and Their World*. Masterworks of the Classical Haida Mythtellers. Vol. 1. Vancouver: Douglas and McIntyre, 1999.

———. "The Antithesis of Rape, Which Is Not Chastity: The Voice of Don McKay." Bartlett, *Don McKay* 29–34.

———. *Being in Being: The Collected Works of Skaay of the Qquuna Qiighawaay*. Masterworks of the Classical Haida Mythtellers. Vol. 3. Vancouver: Douglas and McIntyre, 2001.

———. "The Critic in the Rain." *BC Studies* 147 (2005): 103–7.

———. "Gloria Credo Sanctus et Oreamnos Deorum." *The Calling: Selected Poems 1970–1995*. Toronto: McClelland, 1995. 154–56.

———. *Nine Visits to the Mythworld: Ghandl of the Qayahl Llaanas*. Trans. Robert Bringhurst. Masterworks of the Classical Haida Mythtellers. Vol. 2. Vancouver: Douglas and McIntyre, 2000.

———. "Poetry and Thinking." Lilburn, *Thinking* 155–72.

———. "Singing with the Frogs." *Canadian Literature* 155 (1997): 114–34.

———. *The Solid Form of Language*. Kentville, NS: Gaspereau, 2004.

Bringhurst, Robert, and Laurie Ricou. "Robert Bringhurst's 'Sunday Morning': A Dialogue." *Inside the Poem: Essays and Poems in Honour of Donald Stephens*. Ed. W. H. New. Toronto: Oxford UP, 1992. 88–100.

Brown, Kurt, ed. *The Measured Word: On Poetry and Science*. Athens: U of Georgia P, 2001.

Brown, W. J. *The Gods Had Wings*. Toronto: Macmillan, 1936.

Bryson, J. Scott, ed. *Ecopoetry: A Critical Introduction*. Salt Lake City: U of Utah P, 2002.

Bryson, J. Scott. *The West Side of Any Mountain: Place, Space, and Ecopoetry*. Iowa City: U of Iowa P, 2005.

Buckler, William E., ed. *Prose of the Victorian Period*. Boston: Houghton, 1958.

Buell, Lawrence. *The Environmental Imagination: Thoreau, Nature Writing, and the Formation of American Culture*. Cambridge: Harvard UP, 1995.

———. *The Future of Environmental Criticism: Environmental Crisis and Literary Imagination*. Malden, MA: Blackwell, 2005.

———. *Writing for an Endangered World: Literature, Culture, and Environment in the U.S. and Beyond*. Cambridge: Harvard UP, 2001.
Burnside, John. "A Science of Belonging: Poetry as Ecology." *Contemporary Poetry and Contemporary Science*. Ed. Robert Crawford. Oxford: Oxford UP, 2006: 91–106.
Burroughs, John. *Birds and Poets with Other Papers*. New York: Houghton, 1883.
Bushell, Kevin. "Don McKay and Metaphor: Stretching Language toward Wilderness." *Studies in Canadian Literature* 21.1 (1995): 37–55.
Cajete, Gregory. *Native Science: Natural Laws of Interdependence*. Santa Fe, NM: Clear Light, 2000.
Calverley, Margaret. "'Service is joy': Margaret Avison's Sonnet Sequence in Winter Sun." *Essays on Canadian Writing* 50 (1993): 210–30.
Campbell, Neil A., and Jane B. Reece. *Biology*. San Francisco: Pearson, 2005.
Campbell, SueEllen. "The Land and Language of Desire." Glotfelty and Fromm 124–36.
Campbell, Wilfred, Archibald Lampman, and Duncan Campbell Scott. *At the Mermaid Inn*. Toronto: U of Toronto P, 1979.
The Canadian Farmer 2.11 (June 1, 1865): 168.
Carroll, Joseph. *Evolution and Literary Theory*. Columbia: U of Missouri P, 1995.
———. *Literary Darwinism: Evolution, Human Nature, and Literature*. New York: Routledge, 2004.
Carson, Rachel. *Silent Spring*. 1962. New York: Crest-Fawcett, 1964.
Cartlidge, Neil, ed. *The Owl and the Nightingale*. Exeter: U of Exeter P, 2001.
Catchpole, C. K., and P. J. B. Slater. *Bird Song: Biological Themes and Variations*. Cambridge: Cambridge UP, 1995.
Chaucer, Geoffrey. *The Parlement of Foulys*. 1383. Ed. D. S. Brewer. London: Thomas Nelson, 1960.
Clare, John. *'I Am': The Selected Poetry of John Clare*. Ed. Jonathan Bate. New York: Farrar, 2003.
Cochrane, Mark. "Don McKay." New, *Encyclopedia* 730–31.
Coetzee, J. M. *Age of Iron*. 1990. New York: Penguin, 1998.
———. *Disgrace*. 1999. London: Vintage, 2000.
———. *The Lives of Animals*. Princeton, NJ: Princeton UP, 1999.
Cohen, Leonard. "Beneath My Hands." *Stranger Music: Selected Poems and Songs*. Toronto: McClelland, 1994. 16.
Cohen, Michael P. *A Garden of Bristlecones: Tales of Change in the Great Basin*. Reno: U of Nevada P, 1998.
———. "Reading after Darwin: A Prospectus." Ingram et al. 221–33.
Cokinos, Christopher. *Hope Is the Thing with Feathers: A Personal Chronicle of Vanished Birds*. New York: Tarcher-Putnam, 2000.
Coles, Don. "A Gift for Metaphor." Bartlett, *Don McKay* 55–58.
Commoner, Barry. *The Closing Circle: Nature, Man, and Technology*. New York: Knopf, 1971.
Cook, Méira. "Song for the Song of the Dogged Birdwatcher." Introduction. *Field Marks: The Poetry of Don McKay*. By Don McKay. Waterloo, ON: Wilfrid Laurier UP, 2006. ix–xxv.

Craik, Roger. "Animals and Birds in Philip Larkin's Poetry." *Papers on Language & Literature* 38.4 (2002): 395–412.
Crawford, Robert, ed. *Contemporary Poetry and Contemporary Science*. Toronto: U of Oxford UP, 2006.
Critchley, Simon. "Poetry as Philosophy—On Wallace Stevens." *European Journal of American Culture* 24.3 (2005): 179–90.
Cruikshank, Julie. *Do Glaciers Listen? Local Knowledge, Colonial Encounters, and Social Imagination*. Vancouver: U of British Columbia P, 2005.
Daniel, John. "The Impoverishment of Seeing." *The Trail Home: Nature, Imagination, and the American West*. New York: Pantheon, 1992. 35–46.
Daston, Lorraine. "Type Specimens and Scientific Memory." *Critical Inquiry* 31 (2004): 153–82.
Davey, Frank. *Canadian Literary Power*. Writer as Critic 4. Edmonton: NeWest, 1994.
———. *Reading Canadian Reading*. Winnipeg: Turnstone, 1988.
———. "Surviving the Paraphrase." *Canadian Literature* 70 (1976): 5–13.
Delany, Max. "Masked Workers Clean Up Bird Market." *Moscow Times* 21 Feb. 2007: 4.
Deming, Alison Hawthorne. "Science and Poetry: A View from the Divide." K. Brown 181–97.
Dewdney, Christopher. *The Natural History*. Toronto: ECW, 2002.
Dickinson, Adam. *Kingdom, Phylum*. London: Brick, 2006.
———. "Lyric Ethics: Ecocriticism, Material Metaphoricity, and the Poetry of Don McKay and Jan Zwicky." *Canadian Poetry* 55 (2004): 34–52.
———. "Lyric Ethics: The Matter and Time of Ecopoetry." Diss. U of Alberta, 2005.
Dingle, Hugh. "Animal Migration: Is There a Common Migratory Syndrome?" *Journal of Ornithology* 147 (2006): 212–20.
Dragland, Stan. "Be-Wildering: The Poetry of Don McKay." *University of Toronto Quarterly* 70 (2001): 881–88.
Durkin, Andrew R. "A Guide to the Guides: Writing about Birds in Russia in the Nineteenth Century." *Russian Studies in Literature* 39.3 (2003): 4–24.
Eagleton, Terry. *The Idea of Culture*. Oxford: Blackwell, 2000.
Einstein, Albert. *The World as I See It*. Trans. Alan Harris. London: John Lane, 1935.
Elder, John. *Imagining the Earth: Poetry and the Vision of Nature*. Urbana: U of Illinois P, 1985.
———. *Reading the Mountains of Home*. Cambridge: Harvard UP, 1998.
———. Foreword. Armbruster and Wallace vi–vii.
Eliade, Mircea. *Shamanism: Archaic Techniques of Ecstasy*. Princeton: Princeton UP, 1972.
Elkins, Andrew. *Another Place: An Ecocritical Study of Selected Western American Poets*. Fort Worth, TX: Texas Christian UP, 2002.
Elkins, Norman. *Weather and Bird Behaviour*. 1983. 3rd ed. London: T. & A. D. Poyser, 2004.
Elliott, Lang. *The Music of Birds: A Celebration of Bird Song*. New York: Houghton, 1999.
———. *The Songs of Wild Birds*. New York: Houghton, 2006.
Elmslie, Susan. "Got to Meander If You Want to Get to Town: Excursion and Excursionist Metaphors in Don McKay." Bartlett, *Don McKay* 81–103.

"Eskimo Curlew: Vanishing Species?" Northern Prairie Wildlife Research Center. 2 June 2007. <http://www.npwrc.usgs.gov/resource/birds/curlew/last.htm>.

Evernden, Neil. "Beyond Ecology: Self, Place, and the Pathetic Fallacy." Glotfelty and Fromm 92–104.

Feld, Steven. *Sound and Sentiment: Birds, Weeping, Poetics, and Song in Kaluli Expression.* 2nd ed. Philadelphia: U of Pennsylvania P, 1990.

Findley, Timothy. *Not Wanted on the Voyage.* 1984. Toronto: Penguin, 1996.

Fiamengo, Janice, ed. *Other Selves: Animals in the Canadian Literary Imagination.* Ottawa: U of Ottawa P, 2007.

Fisher, John Andrew. "What the Hills Are Alive With: In Defense of the Sounds of Nature." *The Aesthetics of Natural Environments.* Ed. Allen Carlson and Arnold Berleant. Peterborough, ON: Broadview, 2004. 232–52.

Fisher, Susan. "'Ontological Applause': Metaphor and Homology in the Poetry of Don McKay." Fiamengo, 50–66.

Fjeldså, Jon. *The Grebes, Podicipedidae.* Bird Families of the World. Oxford: Oxford UP, 2004.

Fletcher, Angus. *A New Theory for American Poetry: Democracy, the Environment, and the Future of Imagination.* Cambridge: Harvard UP, 2004.

Forster, Sophia. "Don McKay's Comic Anthropocentrism: Ecocriticism Meets 'Mr. Nature Poet.'" *Essays on Canadian Writing* 77 (2002): 107–35.

Frolick, Larry. "Dem's Fightin' Birds." *The Walrus* February 2007: 17–20.

Frost, Robert. "The Minor Bird." McClaskey 177.

Frye, Northop. *Anatomy of Criticism: Four Essays.* 1957. Princeton: Princeton UP, 1971.

———. *The Educated Imagination.* 1963. CBC Massey Lecture Series. Toronto: Anansi, 1998.

———. Conclusion. *The Literary History of Canada: Canadian Literature in English.* Ed. Carl F. Klinck. 2nd ed. Vol. 2. Toronto: U of Toronto P, 1976. 331–61.

———. *The Bush Garden: Essays on the Canadian Imagination.* 1971. Concord, ON: Anansi, 1995.

Gannon, Thomas C. "The New World Bird as Colonized Other." *The Ampersand* 11 (2002) 15 March 2006. <http://www.mprsnd.org/11/tg001.htm>.

———. *Skylark Meets Meadowlark: Reimagining the Bird in British Romantic and Contemporary Native American Literature.* Lincoln: U of Nebraska P, 2009.

Garrard, Greg. *Ecocriticism.* London: Routledge, 2004.

Gaston, Bill. *Sointula.* Vancouver: Raincoast, 2003.

Gaver, William W. "What in the World Do We Hear? An Ecological Approach to Auditory Event Perception." *Ecological Psychology* 5.1 (1993): 1–29.

Genette, Gérard. *Palimpsests: Literature in the Second Degree.* 1982. Trans. Channa Newman and Claude Dubinsky. Lincoln: U of Nebraska P, 1997.

Gentner, Timothy Q., et al. "Recursvie Syntactive Pattern Learning by Songbirds." *Nature* 440.27 (2006): 1204–7.

Gibbs-Smith, Charles H. "Sir George Cayley: 'Father of Aerial Navigation' (1773–1857)." *Notes and Records of the Royal Society of London* 17.1 (1962): 36–56.

Gibson, Graeme. *The Bedside Book of Birds: An Avian Miscellany*. Toronto: Doubleday Random, 2005.

Gilcrest, David W. *Greening the Lyre: Environmental Poetics and Ethics*. Reno: U of Nevada P, 2002.

Gill, Frank B. *Ornithology*. 2nd ed. New York: W. H. Freeman, 1995.

Gill, Robert E., Jr., Pablo Canevari, and Eve H. Iversen. 1998. Eskimo Curlew (*Numenius borealis*). In *The Birds of North America Online*, 347 (A. Poole, ed.). Ithaca, NY: Cornell Lab of Ornithology. Retrieved from The Birds of North America Online. <http://bna.birds.cornell.edu/bna/species/347/articles/introduction>.

Gillingham, Donald W. "Crows Are Not All Black." *Daily Province* 17 November 1923: 26.

Gingras, Pierre. *The Secret Lives of Birds* [Secrets d'Oiseaux]. Trans. Peter Feldstein. Toronto: Key Porter, 1995.

Glavin, Terry. *Waiting for the Macaws and Other Stories from the Age of Extinctions*. Toronto: Viking-Penguin, 2006.

Glotfelty, Cheryll, and Harold Fromm, eds. *The Ecocriticism Reader: Landmarks in Literary Ecology*. Athens: U of Georgia P, 1996.

Goldbarth, Albert. "Introduction." K. Brown ix–xii.

Gordimer, Nadine. "Preface." *Critical Perspectives on J. M. Coetzee*. Ed. Graham Huggan and Stephen Watson. New York: St. Martin's, 1996. vii–xii.

Gould, Stephen Jay. *The Hedgehog, the Fox, and the Magister's Pox: Mending the Gap between Science and the Humanities*. New York: Harmony, 2003.

Goward, Trevor. "Membrane & Mosquito: A Natural History of Metaphor." *Lyric Ecology: An Appreciation of the Word of Jan Zwicky*. Mark Dickinson and Clare Goulet, eds. Toronto: Cormorant, 2010. 197–208.

Grady, Wayne. "Tweet, Tweet, You're Dead." Rev. of *Silence of the Songbirds: How We Are Losing the World's Songbirds and What We Can Do to Save Them* by Bridget Stutchbury. *Globe and Mail* 5 May 2007. D10.

Graham, Vincent L.E. *Winged Wheels and Lightning Fasteners*. Picton: Gale Crescent, 1977.

Grandin, Temple, and Catherine Johnson. *Animals in Translation: Using the Mysteries of Autism to Decode Animal Behaviour*. New York: Scribner, 2005.

Greene, Harry W. "Improving Taxonomy for Us and the Other Fishes." *Nature* 411 (2001): 738.

Greene, Richard. Rev. of *Apparatus*. *Books in Canada* 27.2 (1998): 27.

Grey, Sir Edward. *The Charm of Birds*. 1927. London: Weidenfeld & Nicolson, 2001.

Groden, Michael, and Martin Kreiswirth, eds. *The Johns Hopkins Guide to Literary Theory & Criticism*. Baltimore: Johns Hopkins UP, 1994.

Halle, Louis J. *The Appreciation of Birds*. Baltimore: Johns Hopkins UP, 1989.

Halpern, Sue. *Four Wings and a Prayer: Caught in the Mystery of the Monarch Butterfly*. Toronto: Vintage, 2002.

Haraway, Donna. *The Companion Species Manifesto: Dogs, People, and Significant Otherness*. Chicago: Prickly Paradigm, 2003.

Hardy, Thomas. *Selected Poems*. Ed. Harry Thomas. Toronto: Penguin, 1993.
Harting, James Edmund. *The Ornithology of Shakespeare: A critical examination and explanation of bird life in Elizabethan times as reflected in the works of Shakespeare* 1864. Old Woking, Surrey: Gresham, 1978.
Hedenström, Anders. "Aerodynamics, Evolution and Ecology of Avian Flight." *Trends in Ecology and Evolution* 17.9 (2002): 415–22.
Heidegger, Martin. *Basic Writings: From* Being in Time *(1927) to the* Task of Thinking *(1964)*. Ed. David Farrell Krell. New York: HarperCollins, 1993.
———. *Poetry, Language, Thought*. 1971. Trans. Albert Hofstadter. New York: Harper & Row, 1975.
———. "Words." *On the Way to Language*. New York: Harper, 1982. 139–56.
Heinrich, Bernd. *Ravens in Winter*. 1989. New York: Vintage-Random, 1991.
Heise, Ursula K. "Science and Ecocriticism." *American Book Review* 18.5 (1997).
Helms, Gabriele. "Contemporary Canadian Poetry from the Edge: An Exploration of Literary Eco-criticism." *Canadian Poetry* 36 (Spring/Summer 1995): 44–61.
Helmuth, Brian. "How Do We Measure the Environment? Linking Intertidal Thermal Physiology and Ecology through Biophysics." *Integrative and Comparative Biology* 42 (2002): 837–45.
Herriot, Trevor. *Grass, Sky, Song: Promise and Peril in the World of Grassland Birds*. Toronto: HarperCollins, 2009.
———. *Jacob's Wound: A Search the Spirit of Wildness*. Toronto: McClelland, 2004.
Herzog, Karl. "Biophysics of the Bird Flight." *Der Schwingenflug in der Natur und in der Technik*. Mechanikus: J. F. Schreiber Verlag Esslingen am Neckkar, 1963. 50.
Hitt, Jack. "13 Ways of Looking at an Ivory-Billed Woodpecker." *New York Times Magazine*. 7 May 2006.
Hodgins, Jack. *Innocent Cities*. 1990. Toronto: McClelland, 1991.
Hopkins, Gerard Manley. "The Windhover." *Poems and Prose of Gerard Manley Hopkins*. Ed. W. H. Gardner. London: Penguin, 1963. 30.
Hubbard, Thomas K. *The Pipes of Pan: Intertextuality and Literary Filiation in the Pastoral Tradition from Theocritus to Milton*. Ann Arbor: U of Michigan P, 1999.
Hutcheon, Linda. "Eruptions of Postmodernity: The Postcolonial and the Ecological." *Essays in Canadian Writing* 51–52 (1993–1994): 146–53.
———. "The Field Notes of the Public Critic." Introduction. *The Bush Garden: Essays on the Canadian Imagination*. By Northrop Frye. Toronto: Anansi, 1995. vii–xx.
———. "History and/as Intertext." *Future Indicative: Literary Theory and Canadian Literature*. Ed. John Moss. Ottawa: U of Ottawa P, 1987. 169–84.
Huxley, Thomas H. "Science and Culture." Buckler 526–37.
Ingram, Annie Merrill, et al., eds. *Coming into Contact: Explorations in Ecocritical Theory and Practice*. Athens: U of Georgia P, 2007.
Irmscher, Christoph. "Nature-Writing." *The Cambridge Companion to Canadian Literature*. Ed. Eva-Marie Kröller. New York: Cambridge UP, 2004. 94–114.
Jackson, Jerome A. *In Search of the Ivory-Billed Woodpecker*. New York: Perennial-Harper, 2006.

Jarvis, E., et al. "Avian brains and a new understanding of vertebrate brain evolution." *Nature Reviews Neuroscience* 6.2 (2005): 151–59.

Jeneid, Michael. *Chaucer's Checklist*. Capitola: Pandion, 1993.

Johnson, E. Pauline. "The Flight of the Crows." *A New Anthology of Canadian Literature in English*. Ed. Donna Bennett and Russell Brown. Toronto: Oxford UP, 2002. 170–71.

Keats, John. "Ode to a Nightingale." *English Romantic Writers*. Ed. David Perkins. 2nd ed. Fort Worth, TX: Harcourt, 1995. 1251.

Keith, W. J. *The Poetry of Nature: Rural Perspectives in Poetry from Wordsworth to the Present*. Toronto: U of Toronto P, 1980.

Keller, David, and Frank Golley, eds. *The Philosophy of Ecology: From Science to Synthesis*. Athens: U of Georgia P, 2000.

Keller, Evelyn Fox, and Elizabeth A. Lloyd. *Keywords in Evolutionary Biology*. Cambridge: Harvard UP, 1998.

Kerber, Jenny. *Writing in Dust: Reading the Prairie Environmentally*. Waterloo, ON: Wilfrid Laurier UP, 2010.

Kern, Robert. "Ecocriticism: What Is It Good For?" *The ISLE Reader: Ecocriticism, 1993–2003*. Ed. Michael P. Branch and Scott Slovic. Athens: U of Georgia P, 2003. 258–81.

Kessler, Brad. *Birds in Fall*. New York: Scribner, 2006.

Kinnel, Galway. "Poetry, Personality and Death." *A Field Guide to Contemporary Poetry and Poetics*. Eds. David Walker and David Young Stuart Friebert. Rev. ed. Oberlin, OH: Oberlin College P, 1997. 255–71.

Krebs, Charles J. *Ecology: The Experimental Analysis of Distribution and Abundance*. 4th ed. New York: Harper, 1994.

Kroetsch, Robert. "Author's Note." *Completed Field Notes: The Long Poems of Robert Kroetsch*. 1989. Edmonton: U of Alberta P, 2000. 251–52.

———. "Unhiding the Hidden." *The Lovely Treachery of Words: Essays Selected and New*. Toronto: Oxford UP, 1989. 58–63.

Kröller, Eva-Marie. "Fear of Flying? The Myth of Daedalus and Icarus in Canadian Culture." *Journal of Canadian Studies* 28.4 (Winter 1993–94): 102–17.

Kroodsma, Donald. *The Singing Life of Birds: The Art and Science of Birdsong*. Boston: Houghton, 2005.

Kroodsma, Donald E., and Edward H. Miller. *Acoustic Communication in Birds*. New York: Academic, 1982.

Kuhn, Thomas. *The Structure of Scientific Revolutions*. 1962. Chicago: U of Chicago P, 1965.

Küppers, Manfred. "Changes in Plant Ecophysiology across a Central European Hedgerow Ecotone." *Landscape Boundaries: Consequences for Biotic Diversity and Ecological Flows*. Ed. Andrew J. Hansen and Franscesco di Castri. New York: Springer-Verlag, 1992. 285–303.

Lampman, Archibald. "In November." Ware 142–43.

Latour, Bruno. *Politics of Nature: How to Bring the Sciences into Democracy*. Cambridge: Harvard UP, 2004.

Law, John, and Michael Lynch. "Lists, Field Guides, and the Description Organization of Seeing: Birdwatching as an Exemplary Observational Activity." *Human Studies* 11 (1988): 271–303.

Lawrence, Elizabeth Atwood. *Hunting the Wren: Transformation of Bird to Symbol*. Knoxville: U of Tennessee P, 1997.

Leavis, F. R. "Two Cultures? The Significance of C. P. Snow." *Cultures in Conflict: Perspectives on the Snow–Leavis Controversy*. Ed. David K. Cornelius. Chicago: Scott, Foresman, 1964. 14–16.

Leckie, Ross. "Don McKay's 'Twinflower': Poetry's Far Cry and Close Call." Bartlett, *Don McKay* 126–44.

Lecker, Robert. *Making It Real: The Canonization of English-Canadian Literature*. Toronto: Anansi, 1995.

Lee, Dennis. *Body Music: Essays*. Toronto: Anansi, 1998.

———. *Savage Fields: An Essay in Literature and Cosmology*. Toronto: Anansi, 1977.

Levine, George. *Lifebirds*. New Brunswick, NJ: Rutgers UP, 1995.

Levine, George, ed. *One Culture: Essays in Science and Literature*. Madison: U of Wisconsin P, 1987.

Lilburn, Tim. "Going Home." Lilburn, ed. *Thinking* 173–85.

———. "How to Be Here?" Lilburn, *Living* 3–23.

———. *Living in the World as If It Were Home*. Toronto: Cormorant, 1999.

———. Preface. Lilburn, ed. *Thinking* 1–3.

———. "The Provisional Shack of the Ear." Interview with Shawna Lemay. *Where the Words Come From: Canadian Poets in Conversation*. Ed. Tim Bowling. Roberts Creek, BC: Nightwood, 2002. 174–83.

———. "Walking Out of Silence." Afterword. *Desire Never Leaves: The Poetry of Tim Lilburn*. Ed. Alison Calder. Waterloo, ON: Wilfrid Laurier UP, 2007. 41–48.

Lilburn, Tim, ed. *Poetry and Knowing: Speculative Essays & Interviews*. Kingston, ON: Quarry, 1995.

———, ed. *Thinking and Singing: Poetry & the Practice of Philosophy*. Toronto: Cormorant, 2002.

Lin, Brian. "Birds of a Feather, Discovered Together." *UBC Reports* 52.11 (2006): 1, 3.

Lopez, Barry. *Crossing Open Ground*. New York: Scribner's, 1988.

———. *Field Notes: The Grace Note of the Canyon Wren*. Toronto: Random, 1994.

———. *The Rediscovery of North America*. Lexington: UP of Kentucky, 1990.

Lorenz, Konrad. *The Natural Science of the Human Species: An Introduction to Comparative Behavioral Research. The "Russian Manuscript" (1944–1948)* [Die Naturwissenshaft Vom Menschen: Eine Enfuhrung in Die Vergleichende Verhaltensforschung. Das 'Russische Manuskript' (1944–1948)]. 1992. Trans. Robert D. Martin. Cambridge, MA: MIT, 1996.

Love, Glen A. *Practical Ecocriticism: Literature, Biology, and the Environment*. Charlottesville: U of Virginia P, 2003.

Lovelock, James. *The Revenge of Gaia*. 2006. Toronto: Penguin, 2007.

Lowry, Malcolm. "The Bravest Boat." *Hear Us O Lord from Heaven Thy Dwelling Place*. 1961. Ed. Nicholas Bradley. Toronto: Oxford UP, 2009. 29–48.

Lowther, P. E., C. Celada, N. K. Klein, C. C. Rimmer, and D. A. Spector. "Yellow Warbler (*Dendroica petechia*)." In *The Birds of North America Online* (A. Poole, ed.). Ithaca, NY: Cornell Laboratory of Ornithology, 1999. 2 June 2007. <http://bna.birds.cornell.edu/BNA/account/Yellow_Warbler/>.

Lutwack, Leonard. *Birds in Literature*. Gainesville: U of Florida P, 1994.

Mackenzie, Alexander. *Voyages from Montreal: on the river St. Laurence, through the continent of North America, to the frozen and Pacific oceans, in the years 1789 and 1793: with a preliminary account of the rise, progress and present state of the fur trade of that country*. London: Printed for T. Cadell, Jun. and W. Davies, Cobbett and Morgan, and W. Creech, at Edinburgh, by R. Noble, 1801.

Mason, Travis V., and Duffy M. Roberts. "(Accurate) Metaphor and (Visceral) Wisdom in *Distance*: A Dialogue across Distances." *Jack Hodgins: Essays on His Works*. Ed. Annika Hannan. Toronto: Guernica, 2010. 207–37.

McClatchy, J. D., ed. *On Wings of Song: Poems about Birds*. Toronto: Knopf, 2000.

McDaniels, T. L., M. Healey, and R. K. Paisley. "Cooperative Fisheries Management Involving First Nations in British Columbia: An Adaptive Approach to Strategy Design." *Canadian Journal of Fisheries and Aquatic Sciences* 51.9 (1994): 2115–25.

McKay, Don. *Air Occupies Space*. Windsor, ON: Sesame, 1973.

———. *Another Gravity*. Toronto: McClelland, 2000.

———. *Apparatus*. Toronto: McClelland, 1997.

———. "The Appropriate Gesture, or Regular Dumb-Ass Guy Looks at Bird." Interview with Ken Babstock. *Where the Words Come From: Canadian Poets in Conversation*. Ed. Tim Bowling. Roberts Creek, BC: Nightwood, 2002. 44–61.

———. *Birding, or desire*. 1983. Toronto: McClelland, 1993.

———. *Camber: Selected Poems 1983–2000*. Toronto: McClelland, 2004.

———. "Common Sense and Magic." Afterword. *Fiddlehead Gold: 50 Years of The Fiddlehead Magazine*. Ed. Sabine Campbell, Roger Ploude, and Demetres Tryphonopoulos. Fredericton: Goose Lane, 1995. 223–38.

———. "Crafty Dylan and the Altarwise Sonnets: 'I Build a Flying Tower and I Pull It Down.'" *University of Toronto Quarterly* 55.4 (1986): 375–94.

———. *Deactivated West 100*. Kentville, NS: Gaspereau, 2005.

———. *Field Marks: The Poetry of Don McKay*. Ed. Méira Cook. Waterloo, ON: Wilfrid Laurier UP, 2006.

———. *Five Ways to Lose Your Way*. Saskatoon, SK: JackPine, 2004.

———. *Foglio a foglia/Leaf to Leaf*. Ed. Branko Gorjup and Francesca Valente. Trans. Sara Fruner and Filippo Mariano. Peter Paul Charitable Foundation Series of English Canadian Poetry. Ravenna: Longo Editore, 2012.

———. "Great Flint Singing." Introduction. *Open Wide a Wilderness: Canadian Nature Poems*. Ed. Nancy Holmes. Waterloo, ON: Wilfrid Laurier UP, 2009. 1–31.

———. "Growing an Ear." Interview with David Reibetanz. *echolocation* 7 (2008): 56–69.

———. *Lependu*. Ilderton, ON: Nairn-Coldstream, 1978.

———. *Lightning Ball Bait*. Toronto: Coach House, 1980.
———. "Local Wilderness." *Fiddlehead Gold: 50 Years of The Fiddlehead Magazine*. Ed. Sabine Campbell, Roger Ploude, and Demetres Tryphonopoulos. Fredericton: Goose Lane, 1995. 173–74.
———. *Long Sault*. London, ON: Applegarth Follies, 1975. Rpt. in *The Long Poem Anthology*. Ed. Michael Ondaatje. Toronto: Coach House, 1979. 125–57.
———. *The Muskwa Assemblage*. Kentville, NS: Gaspereau, 2008.
———. *Night Field*. Toronto: McClelland, 1991.
———. *Paradoxides*. Toronto: McClelland, 2012.
———. *Sanding Down This Rocking Chair on a Windy Night*. Toronto: McClelland, 1987.
———. "The Shell of the Tortoise." Afterword. *Field Marks: The Poetry of Don McKay*. By Don McKay. Waterloo, ON: Wilfrid Laurier UP, 2006. 49–56.
———. "Shipwreck and Clear Sight: A. F. Moritz's Early Poems." Foreword. *Early Poems*. By A. F. Moritz. Toronto: Insomniac, 2002. 14–16.
———. "Some Remarks on Poetry and Poetric Attention." *20th-Century Poetry & Poetics*. Ed. Gary Geddes. 4th ed. Toronto: Oxford UP, 1996. 858–59.
———. *Songs for the Songs of Birds*. Tors Cove, NL: Rattling, 2008.
———. "Song for the Song of the Sandhill Crane." *The Green Imagination*. Ed. Jay Ruzesky and John Barton. Spec. issue of *The Malahat Review* 165 (2008): 61.
———. *Strike/ Slip*. Toronto: McClelland, 2006.
———. *Vis à Vis: Field Notes on Poetry & Wilderness*. Wolfville, NS: Gaspereau, 2001.
McKusick, James C. "'A Language That Is Ever Green': The Ecological Vision of John Clare." *University of Toronto Quarterly* 61.2 (1991–92): 226–49.
McLaren, Leah. "Birdman of B.C." *Globe and Mail* 28 September 2006: R1–R2.
McLuhan, Marshall. *The Gutenberg Galaxy: The Making of Typographic Man*. 1962. Toronto: Signet, 1969.
McNeilly, Kevin. "Poetry in Shorter Forms." New, *Encyclopedia* 877–87.
McOrmond, Steve. *Lean Days*. Toronto: Wolsak & Wynn, 2004.
Meeker, Joseph. *The Comedy of Survival: Studies in Literary Ecology*. New York: Scribner's, 1972.
Merrett, Robert James. "Margaret Avison on Natural History: Ecological and Biblical Meditations." *Canadian Poetry* 59 (2006): 95–110.
Merwin, W.S. "'This *Absolutely* Matters': An Interview with W. S. Merwin." Interview by J. Scott Bryson and Tony Brusate. *Limestone* 6.1 (1998): 1–8.
Miłosz, Czesław. *Visions from San Francisco Bay*. Trans. Richard Lourie. New York: Farrar, 1982.
Milton, John. "To the Nightingale." McClatchy 107.
Morency, Pierre. *A Season for Birds: Selected Poems*. Trans. Alexandre L. Amprimoz. Toronto: Exile, 1990.
Morris, David Copland. "Listening to the Voice from Nowhere: The Surround-Sound of Science and Metaphor in a Postmodern Landscape." *isotope: A Journal of Literary Nature and Science Writing* 3.2 (Fall/Winter 2005): 48–51.

Morrison, Ronald P. "Wilderness and Clearing: Thoreau, Heidegger, and the Poetic." *ISLE: Interdisciplinary Studies of Literature and Environment* 10.1 (2003): 143–65.
Moss, John. *The Paradox of Meaning: Cultural Poetics and Critical Fictions*. Winnipeg: Turnstone, 1999.
Murphy, Patrick D. *Farther Afield in the Study of Nature-Oriented Literature*. Charlottesville: U of Virginia P, 2000.
Nabhan, Gary Paul. *Cross-Pollinations: The Marriage of Science and Poetry*. Minneapolis: Milkweed, 2004.
Nathan, Leonard. *Diary of a Left-Handed Birdwatcher*. San Diego: Harcourt, 1996.
Nemerov, Howard. *The Collected Poems of Howard Nemerov*. Chicago: U of Chicago P, 1977.
New, W. H. *A History of Canadian Literature*. 1989. 2nd ed. Kingston, ON: McGill-Queen's UP, 2003.
———. *Land Sliding: Imagining Space, Presence, and Power in Canadian Writing*. Toronto: U of Toronto P, 1997.
———. "Bird Landing." *Riverbook and Ocean*. Lantzville, BC: Oolichan, 2002. 58.
———. "Writing Here." *BC Studies: The British Columbian Quarterly* 147 (2005): 3–25.
New, W. H., ed. *Encyclopedia of Literature in Canada*. Toronto: U of Toronto P, 2002.
Nice, Margaret Morse. *Development of Behaviour in Precocial Birds*. New York: Transactions of Linnean Society of New York Volume 8, 1962.
Noonan, Gerald. "Phrases of Evolution in the Sonnets of Charles G. D. Roberts." *English Studies in Canada* 8.4 (1982): 452–64.
Nudds, Thomas D., and Marc-André Villard. "Basic Science, Applied Science, and the Radical Middle Ground." *Avian Conservation and Ecology/Écologie et conservation des oiseaux* 1.1: 1–4. <http://www.ace-eco.org/>.
O'Brien, Susie. "Nature's Nation, National Natures? Reading Ecocriticism in a Canadian Context." *Canadian Poetry: Studies, Documents, Reviews* 42 (1998): 17–41.
———. "Articulating a World of Difference: Ecocriticism, Postcolonialism, and Globalization." *Canadian Literature* 170/171 (2001): 140–58.
Oreskes, Naomi. "Shaking Up Seismology." Rev. of *The Big One: The Earthquake That Rocked Early America and Helped Create a Science* by Jake Page and Charles Officer. *Nature* 431.7012 (2004): 1038–40.
Oughton, John. "Lord of the Wings." Bartlett, *Don McKay* 35–38.
Quincey, Katherine M. "'Our own little rollicking orb': Divinity, Ecology, and Otherness in Avison." *Canadian Poetry* 59 (2006): 111–38.
Packard, William. *The Craft of Poetry: Interviews from the New York Quarterly*. Garden City, NY: Doubleday, 1974.
Page, P. K. "Improbable Concept." *Coal and Roses: Twenty-One Glosas*. Erin, ON: Porcupine's Quill, 2009. 48–49.
———. *Planet Earth: Poems Selected and New*. Erin, ON: Porcupine's Quill, 2002.
Pass, John. *Stumbling in the Bloom*. Lantzville, BC: Oolichan, 2005.
Payne, Robert B. "Song Traditions in Indigo Buntings: Origin, Improvisation, Dispersal, and Extinction in Cultural Evolution." Kroodsma and Miller 198–220.

Peattie, Donald Culross. *Singing in the Wilderness: A Salute to John James Audubon*. London: Allen & Unwin, 1936.
Perrins, C. M., and T. R. Birkhead. *Avian Ecology*. Glasgow: Blackie, 1983.
Perron, Paul, et al., eds. *Semiotics as a Bridge between the Humanities and the Sciences*. Language, Media & Education Studies 16. New York: LEGAS, 2000.
Perse, Saint-John. "The Bird." McClatchy, 198–99.
Peterson, Roger Tory. *A Field Guide to Western Birds: A Completely New Guide to Field Marks of All Species Found in North America West of the 100th Meridian and North of Mexico*. Boston: Houghton, 1990.
Phillips, Dana. *The Truth of Ecology: Nature, Culture, and Literature*. Oxford: Oxford UP, 2003.
Pollan, Michael. *The Botany of Desire: A Plant's-Eye View of the World*. New York: Random, 2001.
Press Release. 6 June 2007. Griffin Trust. 9 June 2007. <http://www.griffinpoetryprize.com/ news/gpp2007-winners.pdf>.
Purdy, Al. *Beyond Remembering: The Collected Poems of Al Purdy*. Ed. Sam Solecki and Al Purdy. Madeira Park, BC: Harbour, 2000.
Pynn, Larry. "Will B.C.'s Crows Still Come Home to Roost?" *Vancouver Sun*. 23 October 2006, final ed.: A1–A2.
Quammen, David. *The Boilerplate Rhino: Nature in the Eye of the Beholder*. New York: Touchstone, 2000.
Raja, Masood Ashraf. "The King Buzzard: Bano Qudsia's Postnational Allegory and the Nation-State." *The Animal*. Spec. issue of *Mosaic* 40.1 (2007): 95–110.
Rasula, Jed. *This Compost: Ecological Imperatives in American Poetry*. Athens: U of Georgia P, 2002.
rawlings, angela. *Wide slumber for lepidopterists*. Toronto: Coach House, 2006.
Relke, Diana M. A. *Greenwor(l)ds: Ecocritical Readings of Canadian Women's Poetry*. Calgary: U of Calgary P, 1999.
Richards, I. A. *Poetries and Sciences: A Reissue of Science and Poetry (1926, 1935) with Commentary*. New York: W. W. Norton, 1970.
———. *Practical Criticism: A Study of Literary Judgment*. 1929. New York: Harcourt Brace, n.d.
———. *Principles of Literary Criticism*. 1924. London: Routledge, 2001.
Ricou, Laurie. *The Arbutus/Madrone Files: Reading the Pacific Northwest*. Edmonton: NeWest, 2002.
———. "Ecocriticism." New, *Encyclopedia* 342.
———. *A Field Guide to "A Guide to Dungeness Spit."* Lantzville, BC: Oolichan, 1997.
———. "Field Notes and Notes in the Field: Forms of the West in Robert Kroetsch and Tom Robbins." *Journal of Canadian Studies* 17.3 (1982): 117–23.
———. *Salal: Listening for the Northwest Understory*. Edmonton: NeWest, 2007.
———. "So Big about Green." *Canadian Literature* 130 (1991): 3–6.
Rilke, Rainer Maria. "Duino Elegies." *In Praise of Mortality: Selections from Rainer Maria Rilke's Duino Elegies and Sonnets to Orpheus*. Trans. and Ed. Anita Barrows and Joanna Macy. New York: Riverhead-Penguin, 2005. 29–64.

Riordan, Maurice. "The Suspense of Strangeness." *Nature* 409 (2001): 457.

———. "Various Twine." *Interdisciplinary Science Reviews* 30.4 (2005): 291–95.

"Rival Documentaries." *Monty Python's Flying Circus*. Episode 38. 1973.

Roberts, Charles G. D. "The Tantramar Revisited." Ware 74–77.

———. "The Waking Earth." Ware 94.

Robertson, Lisa. *Occasional Work and Seven Walks from the Office for Soft Architecture*. Astoria, OR: Clear Cut, 2003.

Robinson, E., and R. Fitter, eds. *John Clare's Birds*. Oxford: Oxford UP, 1982.

Rorty, Richard. "Texts and Lumps." *New Literary History: A Journal of Theory and Interpretation* 17.1 (1985): 1–16.

Rothenberg, David. *Why Birds Sing: A Journey into the Mystery of Bird Song*. New York: Basic-Perseus, 2005.

Rowland, Beryl. *Birds with Human Souls: A Guide to Bird Symbolism*. Knoxville: U of Tennessee P, 1978.

Rowlett, John. "Ornithological Knowledge and Literary Understanding." *New Literary History: A Journal of Theory and Interpretation* 30 (1999): 625–47.

Rueckert, William. "Literature and Ecology: An Experiment in Ecocriticism." Glotfelty and Fromm 105–23.

Schumacher, E. F. Foreword. *The Virtuous Weed*. By Joy Griffith-Jones. London: Blond & Briggs, 1978.

Scigaj, Leonard M. *Sustainable Poetry: Four American Poets*. Lexington: UP of Kentucky, 1999.

Searle, Leroy F. "New Criticism." *The Johns Hopkins Guide to Literary Theory & Criticism*. Ed. Michael Groden and Martin Kreiswirth. Baltimore: Johns Hopkins UP, 1994. 528–34.

Seymour, David. "In the Absence of Birds." *Inter Alia*. London: Brick, 2005. 81.

Shaffer, Elinor S., ed. *The Third Culture: Literature and Science*. European Cultures: Studies in Literature and the Arts 9. Berlin: de Gruyer, 1997.

Shakespeare, William. "As You Like It." *The Norton Shakespeare, Based on the Oxford Edition*. Ed. Stephen Greenblatt et al. New York: Norton, 1997. 1591–656.

Shanley, Kathryn W. "Writing Indian: American Indian Literature and the Future of Native American Studies." *Studying Native America: Problems and Prospects*. Ed. Russell Thornton. Madison: U of Wisconsin P, 1998. 130–52.

Schaub, Michael, and Lukas Jenni. "Fuel Deposition of Three Passerine Bird Species along Migration Route." *Oecologia* 122 (2000): 306–317.

Shelley, Percy Bysshe. "To a Skylark." *English Romantic Writers*. Ed. David Perkins. 2nd ed. Fort Worth, TX: Harcourt, 1995. 1094.

Shepard, Paul. *The Others: How Animals Made Us Human*. Washington, DC: Island, 1996.

———. *Thinking Animals: Animals and the Development of Human Intelligence*. New York: Viking, 1978.

Sibley, David Allen. *The Sibley Guide to Birds*. National Audubon Society. Toronto: Knopf, 2000.

Silko, Leslie Marmon. *Yellow Woman and a Beauty of the Spirit: Essays on Native American Life Today*. New York: Simon-Touchstone, 1997.
Simons, John. *Animal Rights and the Politics of Literary Representation*. New York: Palgrave, 2002.
Simosko, Vladimir, and Barry Tepperman. *Eric Dolphy: A Musical Biography and Discography*. 1974. Cambridge, MA: Da Capo, 1996.
Sinclair, Sue. "The Animal Inside the Instrument." Bartlett, *Don McKay* 104–10.
Singer, Peter. Reflection. Coetzee, *Lives* 85–91.
Snow, C. P. "The Two Cultures." *The Scientist vs. The Humanist*. Ed. George Levine and Owen Thomas. New York: Norton, 1963. 1–6.
Solie, Karen. "Frontier County." *Pigeon*. Toronto: Anansi, 2009. 66.
———. "Migration." *Pigeon*. Toronto: Anansi, 2009. 54.
Solnit, Rebecca. *Wanderlust: A History of Walking*. New York: Penguin, 2000.
Spiegelman, Willard. "Jorie Graham Listening." *Jorie Graham: Essays on the Poetry*. Ed. Thomas Gardner. Madison: U of Wisconsin P, 2005. 219–37.
Stalh, Frieda A. "Physics as Metaphor and Vice Versa." *Leonardo*. 20.1 (1987): 57–64.
Stap, Don. *Birdsong: A Natural History*. Toronto: Oxford UP, 2005.
Steffler, John. "Language as Matter." Lilburn, *Poetry* 45–51.
"Steller's Jay." Cornell Lab of Ornithology. 2003. 20 August 2008. <http://www.birds.cornell.edu/AllAboutBirds/BirdGuide/Stellers_Jay.html>.
Stewart, Susan. *The Poet's Freedom: A Notebook on Making*. Chicago: U of Chicago P, 2011.
Stutchbury, Bridget. *Silence of the Songbirds: How We Are Losing the World's Songbirds and What We Can Do to Save Them*. Toronto: HarperCollins, 2007.
Sullivan, Rosemary. Untitled essay. *Foglio a foglia/Leaf to Leaf* by Don McKay. Ed. Branko Gorjup and Francesca Valente. Trans. Sara Fruner and Filippo Mariano. Peter Paul Charitable Foundation Series of English Canadian Poetry. Ravenna: Longo Editore, 2012. 16–19.
Taylor, Angus. *Animals & Ethics: An Overview of the Philosophical Debate*. Peterborough, ON: Broadview, 2003.
Thompson, John. *John Thompson: Collected Poems & Translations*. Ed. Peter Sanger. Fredericton: Goose Lane, 1995.
Thoreau, Henry David. *The Portable Thoreau*. 1947. Ed. Carl Bode. New York: Penguin, 1982.
Tiffin, Helen. "Unjust Relations: Post-Colonialism and the Species Boundary." *Compr(om)ising Post/colonialism(s): Challenging Narratives and Practices*. Ed. Greg Ratcliffe and Gerry Turcotte. Sydney: Dungaroo, 2001. 30–41.
Traill, Catharine Parr. *The Backwoods of Canada: Being Letters from the Wife of an Emigrant Officer, Illustrative of the Domestic Economy of British America*. 1836. Toronto: McClelland, 1989.
Trouern-Trend, Jonathan. *Birding Babylon: A Soldier's Journal from Iraq*. San Francisco: Sierra Club, 2006.
Tuan, Yi-Fu. *Topophilia: A Study of Environmental Perception, Attitudes, and Values*. Englewood Cliffs, NJ: Prentice-Hall, 1974.

Valdes, Mario, and Etienne Gyon. "Serendipity in Poetry and Physics." Shaffer 28–39.
van Peer, William. "Sense and Nonsense of Chaos Theory in Literary Studies." Shaffer 40–48.
Vogel, Steven. Foreword. Alexander xi–xvi.
Voros, Gyorgyi. *Notations of the Wild: Ecology in the Poetry of Wallace Stevens*. Iowa City: U of Iowa P, 1997.
Wagoner, David. *Collected Poems 1956–1976*. Bloomington: Indiana UP, 1978.
Wah, Fred. Introduction. *Completed Field Notes: The Long Poems of Robert Kroetsch*. 1989. By Robert Kroetsch. Edmonton: U of Alberta P, 2000. ix–xvi.
Walling, James. *Portrayal of Birds in Selected Nineteenth and Twentieth Century Fiction*. Studies in French Literature 58. Lewiston, NY: Edwin Mellen, 2002.
Walters, Michael. *A Concise History of Ornithology: The Lives and Works of Its Founding Figures*. London: Christopher Helm, 2003.
Ware, Tracy, ed. *A Northern Romanticism: Poets of the Confederation*. Ottawa: Tecumseh, 2000.
Watanabe, Shigeru. "Van Gogh, Chagall, and Pigeons: Picture Discrimination in Pigeons and Humans." *Animal Cognition* 4 (2001): 147–51.
Webb, Phyllis. *Wilson's Bowl*. Toronto: Coach House, 1980.
Weir, Alex A. S., Jackie Chappell, and Alex Kacelnik. "Shaping of Hooks in New Caledonian Crows." *Science* 297 (2002): 981.
Wente, Margaret. "Carson's Toxic Legacy." *Globe and Mail*. 24 May 2007. A21.
Wheat, Jennifer C. "Mindless Fools and Leaves that Run: Subjectivity, Politics, and Myth in Scientific Nomenclature." Ingram et al. 209–20.
Wheeler, Sue. "The Tide." *Habitat*. London: Brick, 2005. 56.
———. "Understory." *Habitat*. London: Brick, 2005. 11.
White, E. B. "A Listener's Guide to the Birds." McClatchy 194–97.
White, Richard. "'Are You an Environmentalist or Do You Work for a Living?': Work and Nature." *Uncommon Ground: Rethinking the Human Place in Nature*. Ed. William Cronon. New York: W. W. Norton, 1996. 171–85.
White, T. H. *The Bestiary: A Book of Beasts, Being a Translation from a Latin Bestiary of the Twelfth Century*. New York: Capricorn-Putnam, 1954.
Williams, Raymond. *Keywords: A Vocabulary of Culture and Society*. New York: Oxford UP, 1976.
Williams, Terry Tempest. *Refuge: An Unnatural History of Family and Place*. 1991. New York: Vintage-Random, 2001.
Wilson, David L., and Zack Bowen. *Science and Literature: Bridging the Two Cultures*. Gainesville: UP of Florida, 2001.
Wilson, Edward O. *Biophilia*. Cambridge: Harvard UP, 1984.
———. *Consilience: The Unity of Knowledge*. New York: Knopf, 1998.
Wimberley, Edward T. *Nested Ecology: The Place of Humans in the Ecological Hierarchy*. Baltimore: Johns Hopkins UP, 2009.
Winged Migration. Dir. Jacques Perrin and Jacques Cluzaud. DVD. Sony Classics, 2003.
Wordsworth, William. "[The Pedlar and the Ruined Cottage]." *William Wordsworth: Selected Poems*. Toronto: Penguin, 1994. 178–203.

———. "The Tables Turned: An Evening Scene." *Poems of Science*. Ed. John Heath-Stubbs and Phillips Salman. New York: Penguin, 1984.
Yeats, William Butler. *Yeats's Poems*. Ed. A. Norman Jeffares. Dublin: Gill and Macmillan, 1989.
Yorath, Chris. *The Geology of Southern Vancouver Island*. Rev. ed. Madeira Park, BC: Harbour, 2005.
Yuki, Masami Raker. "Towards a Literary Theory of Acoustic Ecology: Soundscapes in Contemporary Environmental Literature." Diss. U Nevada, Reno, 2000.
Zwicky, Jan. "Bringhurst's Presocratics: Lyric and Ecology." Lilburn, *Poetry* 65–117.
———. *Wisdom & Metaphor*. Kentville, NS: Gaspereau, 2003.

Index

A
Abram, David, 137, 139, 140, 180, 212
acoustic ecology, 115–16, 138, 140–41, 144, 252n13. *See also* soundscape
albatross, 93
animality, 75, 90
animals, 251n5; cultural life, 131–32, 136; and hunting, 245n17; intelligence of, 6; naming of, 38–41; and ownership, 104, 118; and play, 36, 225; as rational, 129, 133–34; rights of, 134; as symbol, xv, 134, 242n13; *qua* animals, 26
anthropocentrism, 9, 41, 46, 77, 212, 221
anthropomorphism, 39, 91, 120, 124, 129, 132, 150, 249n8
apostrophe, 68–69, 71, 85, 122, 124–25
Aristophanes, 122
Arnold, Matthew, 122, 203–4
Arthur & George (Barnes), 34
Ashcroft, Bill, 135
Atwood, Margaret, xi, 32, 77
Auden, W. H., 113, 126; "Musée des Beaux Arts," 84
Audubon, John James, 246n21
Avison, Margaret, 241n7; "The Butterfly," 23–24, 241n6
awe, xvii, 58, 59, 69, 84, 148, 158, 183

B
Babstock, Ken, 77, 144, 152–54, 159, 258n1
Bachelard, Gaston, 3, 4, 9–11, 245n18
Banting, Pamela, 206–7, 211
Bartlett, Brian, 74, 153, 187, 192, 200, 253n3
Bate, Jonathan, 10–12

Battalio, John, 54, 178–79, 210, 240n2, 254n3
Beattie, Munro, 75
becoming bird, 93–94, 251n12
The Bedside Book of Birds: An Avian Miscellany (Gibson), 126, 163
Beer, Gillian, 175, 192
being bird, 93
Bentley, D. M. R., 46, 76, 78, 243n2
Bewick, Thomas, 17
bioacoustics, 116, 136
biophilia, 48, 54
birder-critic, 31–41, 99–111, 126, 161–71, 215–22, 223
birder-poet, 36, 75, 76, 79, 85, 92–94, 125–26, 136, 147–48, 150, 156, 177–94, 186, 189, 224; as amateur, 182; as mediator, 179–82; as namer, 184
birding, 23, 33–34, 74, 77, 100, 163, 177, 238n3; amateur, 54, 182; as analogous to poetry, 55, 177; and relationship, 190; as storytelling, 167
Birding Babylon: A Soldier's Journal from Iraq (Trouern-Trend), 33
birds: affinities with humans, 36, 57–58, 130, 137; caged, 118; cultural life, 131–33, 193, 251n6; and endangerment, 118–19, 188, 190; intelligence, 36, 93, 131–33, 193, 225; as intercessor, xix, 182; as other, xviii, xix, 8, 150–51, 191; *qua* birds, 56–57, 163–64, 190; as subject for poetry, xviii, 12, 57, 59, 122, 129–30, 190, 202; as symbol, xix, 11, 18–19, 53, 56, 59, 62, 71, 92; as toolmaker, 36; and unknowability, 169; and

277

278 • Index

wisdom, 69, 139. *See also* individual bird names
Birds in Fall (Kessler), 90, 94
birdsong, 11, 38, 110, 115–27, 129–32, 136–45, 148, 158–59, 169, 170–71, 193–94, 250n7; as inspiration for human language, 149–50; as inspiration for human music, 12; and lyricism, 180; polyphonic aspects, 156; and walking, 17
Birds with Human Souls: A Guide to Bird Symbolism (Rowland), 33
birdwatching. *See* birding
bissett, bill, xi
blackbird, red-winged (*Agelaius phoeniceus*), 99, 130–31, 183
Black Mountain Poets, 76
Bondar, Alana F., 23, 89, 188
Borson, Roo, 161
The Botany of Desire (Pollan), 151, 212
Bradley, Nicholas, 23
Brand, Dionne, 133
Breugel, Pieter, 84
Bringhurst, Robert, 7, 24, 31, 115, 131–32, 159, 171, 180, 187, 238n6; and polyphony, 252n12; and Ricou, 24–25, 34, 189
Brown, W. J., 63, 68, 247n4
Bryson, Scott, 10, 41
Buell, Lawrence, 15, 26–27, 37, 47, 105, 106–7, 110, 205, 237n1, 240n5
bunting, indigo (*Passerina cyanea*), 22
Burroughs, John, 27, 46, 55, 71–72, 126
Bushell, Kevin, 49
bushtit (*Psaltriparus minimus*), 36, 169; and nests, 9–10
Byron, Lord, 11, 83

C
Cajete, Gregory, 109–10
Campbell, SueEllen, 164
Campbell, Wilfred, 46
cardinal, northern (*Cardinalis cardinalis*), 35, 163–64, 169
Carman, Bliss, 46
Carroll, Joseph, 26–27, 205
Carson, Rachel, 12, 117, 178, 179, 247n4, 249n2

Chaucer's Checklist (Jeneid), xvii
chickadee: black-capped (*Poecile atricapillus*), 40, 171–72; Carolina (*Poecile carolinensis*), 40
chiffchaff, common (*Phylloscopus collybita*), 11
Clare, John, 7–12, 18, 123, 213, 240n5, 258n5; "The Pettichap's Nest," 11; "The Skylark," 135
clearings, 141–43, 163, 252n14
cockatoo, 53
Coetzee, J. M., 26, 56, 133–34, 151, 242n13
Cohen, Leonard, 240n3
Cohen, Michael P., 207, 241n10
Cokinos, Chris, 56, 246n22
Coleridge, Samuel Taylor, 83, 93
colonialism, 5, 52, 105, 109; and science, 190
Commoner, Barry, 154, 179
A Concise History of Ornithology (Walters), xvii
consilience, 48, 242n15
Cook, Méira, 84, 93, 182, 248n2
Coupland, Douglas, 35
crane, sandhill (*Grus canadensis*), 147–48
Crawford, Robert, 254n8, 256n9
Creates, Marlene, 12–13
crow, xiii, 35–36, 39, 101, 133, 162, 164–66; American (*Corvus brachyrhynchos*), 35–36; New Caledonian (*Corvus moneduloides*), 36, 133; northwestern (*Corvus caurinus*), 35–36
Cruikshank, Julie, 202, 213, 240n1
curlew, Eskimo (*Numenius borealis*), 89–90

D
Davey, Frank, 45–46, 76–77, 204, 256n10
Deming, Alison Hawthorne, 196–97, 199
Dewdney, Christopher, 213
Dickinson, Adam, 20, 78–80, 81, 208–9
Dickinson, Emily, 33, 251n13
dog, 3–4, 38–39, 104–5, 134–35, 152, 165, 185–86
domestic. *See* home
domestic space, 5, 6, 10, 13, 183, 157, 183, 189; the kitchen as, 3, 6, 9, 14, 94, 148, 182; and wilderness, 4, 9, 147, 220

Donne, John: and medical language, 205
dove, mourning (*Zenaida macroura*), 35–36; rock (*Columba livia*), 35–36
duck, ring-necked (*Aythya collaris*), 30, 40

E

ecocriticism, xviii, 5–6, 17, 18, 21–22, 25, 28, 47, 55, 75, 82, 197, 204, 223, 237n1, 247n8; and interdisciplinarity, 55, 188, 210, 255n2; and literary theory, 26, 78, 213; and realism, 78–79, 240n5; and science, 16, 25, 110, 177, 257n14; and unknowability, 10
ecology, 10, 25–26, 60, 69, 84, 88–90, 106, 109, 154, 164, 198–99; acoustic, 115–16, 138, 140–41; avian, 18; human, 8; of knowledge, xvii, 238n8; nested, 240n6; and poetry, 69, 76,108, 206; and taxonomy, 15
ecotone, 31–32, 37, 108, 188, 215; as clearing, 141; literary, 171; as porch, 147, 154, 224
Einstein, Albert, 26, 27
Eiseley, Loren, 179, 254n4
Elder, John, 31, 37, 59, 63, 103, 108, 203, 237n1
Eliade, Mircea, 63, 67
Eliot, T. S., 180
Elliot, Lang, 129
Elmslie, Susan: and excursionist figures, 89, 182; and watching, 183
enjambment, 95, 96
Evernden, Neil, 202–3; and naming, 28
evolution, 50, 57, 60–61, 63, 130, 132, 170, 194, 197, 212, 246n27
experience, 29, 110, 140, 156, 205
experiential knowledge, 22, 141, 206
extinction, 77, 91, 167, 189

F

falcon, 59; 86; peregrine (*Falco peregrinus*), 188
feathers, 60–61
Feld, Steven, 238n6
field guides, 16, 18, 27, 29, 40–41, 99–111, 106–7, 147, 148, 161, 187–88, 192
field marks, 38, 40, 100–101, 106, 161, 186, 188. *See also* identification

field notes, 54, 161–72; John Clare's, 11
finch, 117–18
Findley, Timothy, 135–36
Fisher, John Andrew, 140–41, 145
Fisher, Susan, 58, 95, 226, 246n27
flicker, northern (*Colaptes auratus*), 143
flight, 53, 63–74, 84, 159, 192; inspired by birds, 12, 85, 191; mechanics of, 56–57; and migration, 50–51, 89; as Truth, 82, 84, 88
Frost, Robert, 113
Frye, Northrop, xi, 45, 52, 77, 167; on criticism as field work, 32; on criticism as science, xii; *The Educated Imagination*, xii, 28

G

Gannon, Thomas C., 38; on John Clare, 8
Garrard, Greg, 237n1
The Gay]Grey Moose: Essays on the Ecologies and Mythologies of Canadian Poetry 1690–1990 (Bentley), 76, 78, 242n17
Genette, Gérard, 206–7
geopoetry, 201, 216–22, 257n2
George, Stefan, 163
getting outside, 4, 17, 18, 22, 25, 182–83; *pace* nesting, 14. *See also* hiking; walking
Gibson, Graeme, 126
Gilcrest, David, 206, 209
Gill, Frank, 57, 60, 156
Glavin, Terry: *Waiting for the Macaws and Other Stories from the Age of Extinctions*, 118
Glotfelty, Cheryll, 237n1
Goldbarth, Andrew, 240n2
goose, Canada (*Branta canadensis*), 149–50
Gordimer, Nadine, 133
Gould, Stephen Jay, 18, 178
Goward, Trevor, 194
grackle, common (*Quiscalus quiscula*), 35, 169
Graham, Jorie, 61
Grandin, Temple, 132–33, 137, 251n1
gravity, 82
grebe, red-necked (*Podiceps grisegena*), 199–200
Grey, Sir Edward, 81, 248n1

Griffiths, Gareth, 135
grouse, ruffed (*Bonasa umbellus*), 144

H
Halitherses, 7, 180, 224
Halle, Louis, 55, 57
Haraway, Donna, 116, 151–53
Hardy, Thomas: "The Darkling Thrush," 126; "Shelley's Skylark," 238n9
Harrison, Jim, 182; and birding, 190
Harting, James, 122, 238n7
hawk, 92, 96, 178; Cooper's (*Accipiter cooperii*), 30; rough-legged (*Buteo lagopus*), 183; sharp-shinned (*Accipiter striatus*), 58
Heidegger, Martin, 123, 141–42, 163, 191, 252n14, 255n8
Heinrich, Bernd, 60–61
Heise, Ursula K., 205–6, 257n14
Helms, Gabriele, 103, 105, 161, 188
heron: great blue (*Ardea herodias*), 53, 165, 199; green-backed (*Butondes striatus*), 40–41
Herriot, Trevor, 190
Hess, Harry H., 216
hiking, 40, 64–65, 138, 144. See also getting outside; walking
Hodgins, Jack, 43, 244n13, 244n14
Holub, Miroslav, 199
homage, 36, 86, 121, 150–55, 224–25. See also ohmage
home, 3–5, 9–11, 13, 23, 29, 43, 49–50, 79, 147, 220; *pace* environment, 28; and flight, 51–52, 54; and migration, 51, 89, 91
homology, 8, 58, 226
Hopkins, Gerard Manley: "The Windhover," 86–87, 248n4
Hubbard, Thomas K., 206–7
humans (*Homo sapiens sapiens*), 29; desire for control, 14, 30, 69, 73, 181; desire for knowledge, 15, 17, 40, 73, 150, 181; and fallibility, 19; foolishness of, 22; impact on nature, 8–9, 16, 89, 96, 117, 150, 157, 185; relations to nonhumans, 9, 20, 47, 134–35, 137, 143, 150, 212; as secondary, 158, 181–82, 185

humility, 22, 75, 86, 94, 139; lyric, 224
hummingbird, 59
Humphreys, Helen, 5
hunting, 245n17
Hutcheon, Linda, 28, 135, 167, 210, 256n12; "History and/as Intertext," 202, 204–5
Huxley, T. H., 203–4

I
Icarus, 54, 67, 82, 84–86, 248n3
identification, 24, 36, 40, 106, 110, 137, 162, 169, 170, 171–72, 184–86, 188–89
Innocent Cities (Hodgins), 51–54, 85, 244n13, 245n15
interdisciplinarity, 22, 26, 135, 195–213, 241n12; as reading practice, 55, 188
inter-species relations, 25
intertextuality, 206–7, 211, 256n13

J
jay: blue (*Cyanocitta cristata*), 35–36, 162, 169, 183; and "jayness," 37; Steller's (*Cyanocitta stelleri*), 35–36, 162, 169
John Clare's Birds (Robinson & Fitter), 11
Johnson, E. Pauline: "The Flight of the Crows," 166
Jones, D. G., 45
junco, 144, 169, 191

K
Keats, John, 11, 50, 82, 83, 91, 123, 224; "La Belle Dame Sans Merci," 117; "Ode to a Nightingale," 81, 248n1
Keith, W. J., 240n5
Keller, Evelyn Fox, 197
Kerber, Jenny, 237n1
Kern, Robert, 47
kestrel. See falcon
kinglet, 141; golden-crowned (*Regulus Satrapa*), 171–72
Kinnell, Galway, 29
knowledge, 41, 192; limitations of, 96; and naming, 15; scientific, 22, 25, 27, 47, 191, 201
Krebs, Charles, 25
Kristeva, Julia, 206
Kroeber, Karl, 213

Kroetsch, Robert, 162, 168, 244n15
Kroodsma, Donald, 116, 119–20, 130, 135

L
Lampman, Archibald, 46; "In November," 141–42, 252–53n17
landscape, 51–52, 77, 103, 107, 215; modified by humans, 6, 190
language, 15, 73, 75, 77, 136; and absence, 189; as anthropocentric, 41, 164; and colonial legacy, 36, 147; failure of, 36, 69, 181, 216; influenced by birdsong, 149–50; limitations of, 15, 16, 26, 33, 79, 153–54, 196, 205, 208; and memory, 30; as metaphorical ecology, 192; and naming, 163; onomatopoeia, 40, 57, 120, 125, 137, 149, 186; and parataxis, 55; and poetry, 36; recursion, 133, 213; as representation, 26, 105, 136; and science, 196–99; and starlings, 36, 133, 213. *See also* linguistic imperialism; metaplasm; naming
lark, horned (*Eremophila alpestris*), 67
Last of the Curlews (Bodsworth), 89–90, 91, 249n7
Latour, Bruno, 153, 159
Lawrence, Elizabeth Atwood, 175
Leavis, F. R., 203–4
Leckie, Ross, 17, 121
Lee, Dennis, 152, 161, 242n16; and polyphony, 252n12
Levine, George, 162, 256n9; *One Culture: Essays on Science and Literature*, 54–55; *Lifebirds*, 56, 58–59, 238n3, 245n18
Lilburn, Tim, 20, 28, 102, 112–13, 121; and naming, 28, 162
linguistic imperialism, 28, 29, 36, 217, 224
Linnaeus, Carolus, 15, 17. *See also* taxonomy
linnet, common (*Fringilla linota*), 17
listening, 105, 115–16, 121, 123, 138–44, 147–60, 252n9. *See also* acoustic ecology
Little Bear, Leroy, 109
Lloyd, Elisabeth A., 197
logging, 143, 253n18
loon, common (*Gavia immer*), 30, 157–59

Lopez, Barry, 25, 138–39, 144, 252n8, 252n10
Lorenz, Konrad, 15, 130, 251n3
Love, Glen A., 26–27, 74, 77, 205, 211, 237n2, 241n12, 254n8
Lovelock, James A., 78
Lowry, Malcolm: "The Bravest Boat," 96
Lutwack, Leonard, 57, 61, 71, 82, 129; and myth, 122; on ornithological knowledge, xv
lyric, 79, 83, 85, 108, 121–23, 209, 217, 224, 257n4; etymology, 121–22; limitations of, 156; and praise, 181; "speculative," 190. *See also* sonnets
lyric I, 21, 83, 123

M
Mackenzie, Alexander, 47, 243n4
magpie, 12
Manguel, Alberto, 163–64
matériel, 91, 153, 253n4
McKay, Don: "Abandoned Tracks," 184–86; *Air Occupies Space*, 76, 239n1; "Angle of Attack," 68; *Another Gravity*, 65; "Approaching the Clearing," 4–5; "Après Chainsaw," 142–44; "Ascent with Thrushes," 181; "As if Spirit, As if Soul," 13–14, 180–81; "Astonished—," 219; "Baler Twine: Thoughts on Ravens, Home, & Nature Poetry," 186–87, 245n17; "A Barbed Wire Fence Meditates upon the Goldfinch," 254n6; "'The Bellies of Fallen Breathing Sparrows,'" 18–19, 186, 240n3; "Between Rock and Stone: A Geopoetic Alphabet," 216; *Birding, or desire*, 24, 76, 239n1; "Black Spruce," 64–65, 163; "Buckling," 86–87; "The Bushtits' Nest," 36; "Camber," 65; "Close-up on a Sharp-shinned Hawk," 72–74, 177; "Dark of the Moon," 21; "Drag," 61, 65–67; "Easter 1981," 8–9; "Field Marks," 186; "Field Marks (2)," 186–87; "Geopoetry," 216; "Homing," 49–50; "How to Imagine an Albatross," 93–94; and humility, 22, 41, 179, 186, 224; "Icarus," 84–86; "Identification," 188–89; "In Aornis," 189–91;

"Labradorite," 221; "Leaving," 90–91; *Lependu*, 76, 239n1; "Lift," 65–67; *Lightning Ball Bait*, 76, 239n1; "Little Rivers," 147; "Limestone," 139–40; "Listen at the Edge," 148–49, 150–51; "Load," 22, 91, 189, 191–92; and the long poem, 76, 248n9; *Long Sault*, 76, 239n1; "Meditation on a Geode," 218; "Meditation on a Small Bird's Skull," 22; as mentor, 238n5, 253n3; and metaphor, 58; "Migratory Patterns," 60, 92–93, 96; "Mistaken Point," 221; "A Morning Prayer Ending with a Line Borrowed from The Holiday Inn," 200; *The Muskwa Assemblage*, 189; "Night Field," 19–20, 78; "Nocturnal Animals," 6–7; "Nocturnal Migrants," 94–95; "Otherwise Than Place," 5, 212, 220, 249n9; "Philosopher's Stone," 221; "Pine Siskins," 193–94; "Precambrian Shield," 201; "Ravens at Play over Mount Work," 226; "Rock, Stone," 219–20; "The Rough-legged Hawk, the Watcher, the Lover, the Blind," 183–84; "Rubbing Stone," 220–21; *Sanding Down This Rocking Chair on a Windy Night*, 76; and scientific knowledge, 58; "Simply Because Light," 4; "Sleeping Places," 12–13; "A Small Fable," 29–30; "Smash the Windows," 3–4; "Some Exercises on the Cry of the Loon," 157; "Sometimes a Voice (1)," 67, 82–84; "Song for Beef Cattle," 124–25, 250n10; "Song for the Restless Wind," 124; "Song for the Song of the Canada Geese," 149–50; "Song for the Song of the Chipping Sparrow," 119–21; "Song for the Song of the Common Loon," 157–59; "Song for the Song of the Common Raven," 225; "Song for the Song of the Coyote," 154; "Song for the Song of the Sandhill Crane," 147–48; "Song for the Song of the Varied Thrush," 155; "Song for the Song of the White-throated Sparrow," 125–26; "Song for the Song of the Wood Thrush," 156; "Song for Wild Phlox," 124; "Song of the Saxifrage to the Rock," 224–25; and specificity, 23–25, 27; "'Stress, Shear, and Strain Theories of Failure,'" 217; "Sturnus Vulgaris," 213; "Styles of Fall," 86–88; "Swallowings," 69–70; "Territoriality," 130–31; "These Mighty Timbers," 219; "A Toast to the Baltimore Oriole," 8; "Turbulence," 210–11; "Twinflower," 16–17; *Vis à Vis: Field Notes on Poetry & Wilderness*, 28–29, 75; "Without a Song," 87–88

Meeker, Joseph, 247n8

metaphor, 16, 19, 28, 36, 49, 57–58, 60–61, 78–79, 84, 86, 88, 96, 116, 119–20, 121, 124, 131, 154, 186, 191–93, 200, 209, 221, 240n4; anthropocentric, 9, 46; the birder-poet's distrust of, 19–21, 208; informed by accurate details, 11, 24; and science, 47–48, 195, 244n6

metaplasm, 116, 151–53

Midgley, Mary, 179

migration, 49–51, 81–82, 88–89, 94, 244n11, 244n12, 254n1; ecology of, 95; as metaphor, 96

Miłosz, Cszesław, 37, 163

Milton, John: "To the Nightingale," 122

mockingbird, 71

Monty Python, 247n8

Moodie, Susanna, 47

Morris, David Copland, 37

Moritz, A. F., 216

Moss, John, 196

Murphy, Patrick D., 26, 241n12

N

Nabhan, Gary Paul, 195, 208

naming, 15–30; 28, 39–41, 49, 65, 101–2, 139, 163, 188–89; arbitrariness of, 162; as artifice, 29–30, 187; failure of, 36; as vexed linguistic act, 184–85. *See also* language

narrative, 89–90, 196; and evolution, 246n27

Nathan, Leonard, 34, 56, 86, 116, 199

natural history: as proto-science, xvii

nature, 77, 75, 84, 203; and aesthetics, 140; and culture, 7, 28–29, 203, 256n7;

non-symbolic, 136; unknowability of, 10
Nemerov, Howard: "The Blue Swallows," 68–69, 70–71
nests, 7–14, 71
New, W. H., 121, 237n1, 243n2, 255n6; "Bird Landing," 198–99
New Criticism, 27, 242n15
Nice, Margaret Morse, 57–58, 94
nightingale (*Luscinia megarhyncos*), 11, 81, 122, 123
nostalgia, 4, 21, 30, 35, 63, 67, 75, 91
Not Wanted on the Voyage (Findley), 135–36

O
O'Brien, Susie, 135
ohmage, 151–55, 224–25. *See also* homage
oriole: Baltimore (*Icterus galbula*), 110; Bullock's (*Icterus bullockii*), 110
Ornithologae (Willughby), xvii
ornithological knowledge, 22; and poetry, xvi
ornithology, xvii, 10, 22, 54, 61, 71, 86, 115, 120, 130, 167, 177; and amateur discourse, 178–79; Cornell Lab of, 35; lyric, 188
The Ornithology of Shakespeare (Harting), xvi–xvii, 122
osprey (*Pandion haliaetus*), 60
owl, xvii; great grey (*Strix nebulosa*), xiii–xiv; screech-, 30

P
Page, P. K.: "Improbable Concept," xiii–xiv; "Only Child," 106; "Stories of Snow," 244n15
parrot, 39
Pass, John, 168–69
pattern recognition, 32, 94
peacock, 135–36
Peterson, Roger Tory, 31, 40, 65, 106–7, 186, 189
pettichap. *See* chiffchaff, common
phenomenology, 10, 138
Phillips, Dana, 25–27, 40, 94, 106–7, 255n2, 257n16

pigeon (*Columba livia*), 35. *See also* dove, rock
place, 5–6, 28, 46–47, 74, 108, 212. *See also* landscape
poetic attention, 77, 187, 193
The Poetics of Space (Bachelard), 9–10
The Poet's Freedom: A Notebook on Making (Stewart), 181–82
Pollan, Michael, 151, 212
polyphony, xi, 144, 156, 225, 252n12
postcolonialism: and animals, 32; and ecocritical concerns, 135, 205, 256n12
Purdy, Al: "Breugel's *Icarus*," 84

Q
Quammen, David, 93, 182, 190

R
raven, common (*Corvus corax*), 25, 35, 36, 54, 61, 105, 141, 188, 223, 225–26, 245n17
rawlings, angela, 254n8
Reading the Mountains of Home (Elder), 59
Reibetanz, David, 202
Richards, I. A.: *Poetries and Sciences*, xii
Ricou, Laurie, 16, 25, 65, 103, 107, 161–62, 168, 199, 237n1, 254n8; and Bringhurst, 24–25, 34, 184, 189, 241n10
Rilke, Rainer Maria, 181
Riordan, Maurice, 197, 205–6, 217, 255n10, 256n3
Robbins, Tom, 168
Roberts, Charles G. D., 46, 241n11; "The Waking Earth," 91
robin, American (*Turdus migratorius*), 110
Romanticism, xvi, 8, 62, 81–82, 83, 88, 116, 126, 142, 201, 216; and apostrophe, 71, 85
Rorty, Richard, 239n3
Rousseau, G. S., 54
Rowland, Beryl, 33, 82, 117–18, 249n4
Rueckert, William, 195, 225

S
Schumacher, E. F.: *The Virtuous Weed*, 124
science, 16, 75, 94; and colonialism, 190; distinction between hard and popular,

178; native science, 109–10; and natural history, 237n2. *See also* ecology; ornithology
science and literature, 27, 48, 54–55, 159, 188, 192, 195–213, 240n2, 256n3; as fringe activity, 22
scientific method, 18, 27, 48; and poetry, 196
Scigaj, Leonard, 205, 207–9, 213, 240n5, 257n13
Scott, Duncan Campbell, 46
Shakespeare, William, 88, 122, 153, 250n10
Shanley, Kathryn W., 109
Shelley, Percy Bysshe, 83, 123, 238n9; "To a Skylark," 81
Shepard, Paul, 93, 137, 251n1
Sibley, David Allen, 11, 32, 125
The Sibley Guide to Birds (Sibley), 74, 161
Silko, Leslie Marmon, 20
Simons, John, 134, 136
siskin, pine (*Carduelis pinus*), 193–94
skylark, 81
Snow, C. P., 203–4
Solie, Karen, 106; "Migration," 95–96
Solnit, Rebecca, 64
sonnets, 73, 86, 87, 91, 122, 241n7, 241n11. *See also* unsonnets
soul, 13, 61, 149, 157, 180–82
soundscape, 115–16, 138–41, 143, 145, 151, 160, 215; and oral cultures, 251n6. *See also* acoustic ecology
sparrow, 25; chipping (*Spizella passerina*), 19–21; white-throated (*Zonotrichia albicollis*), 22, 26, 91, 125, 192
speciesism, 134–35
The Spell of the Sensuous: Perception and Language in a More-Than-Human World (Abram), 180
spirit, 13, 180–82
Stahl, Frieda, 48, 244n6
Stap, Don, 38, 116, 129, 130, 132, 135, 254n5
starling (*Sturnus vulgaris*), 35, 99, 133, 200, 213, 243n1
Steffler, John, 196
Stevens, Wallace, 28, 154, 208
Stewart, Susan, 181–82

Stutchbury, Bridget, 89, 190
sublime, 12
Sullivan, Rosemary, 13
Suzuki, David, 178
swallow, 68–69, 89, 247n6
Szabo, Lisa, 164–65

T
taxonomy, 17, 24, 27–28, 45, 62, 237n2; and ecology, 15
Taylor, Angus, 129
tern, arctic (*Sturna paradisaea*), 51, 95–96
thematic criticism, 32, 45
Thomas, Dylan, 225
Thompson, John, 35, 161
Thoreau, Henry David, 55, 121, 141; *Walden*, 246n20
throstle. *See* thrush, song
thrush: hermit (*Catharus guttatus*), 181–82; song (*Turdus philomelos*), 17; Swainson's (*Catharus ustulatus*), 144; varied (*Ixoreus naevius*), 110, 144, 155–56; wood (*Hylocichla mustelina*), 155–56, 180
Tiffin, Helen, 134, 135
Traill, Catharine Parr, 47, 252–53n17
Tuan, Yi-Fu, 9–10

U
unsonnets, 86, 87; "Close-up on a Sharp-shinned Hawk," 72–74; "'Stress, Shear, Strain Theories of Failure,'" 217–18
urban space, 28, 46, 58, 215; and geese, 149–50

V
Van Peer, William, 47–48
Vogel, Steven, 55
Voros, Gyorgyi, 208

W
Wagoner, David, 101, 107
Wah, Fred, 168
walking, 16, 63–64, 69, 103, 138, 141, 162, 182; and birdsong, 17. *See also* getting outside; hiking
Walling, James, 179–80, 182, 238n6
warbler, 181; Blackburnian (*Setophaga*

fusca), 19; yellow (*Dendroica petechia*), 50–51, 185
Warren, Robert Penn, 182
waxwing, cedar (*Bombycilla cedrorum*), 147
weather, 82, 88, 90, 92
Webb, Phyllis: "Imperfect Sestina," 25
Wheeler, Sue: "The Tide," 198; "Understory," 101–2
White, Richard, 100
Whitman, Walt, 123; "Out of the Cradle Endlessly Rocking," 71–72
wilderness, 6, 13, 29, 36, 137, 139, 155, 184, 212; and aesthetics, 140; and domesticity, 49, 147, 220; and language, 15, 69
The Wild Parrots of Telegraph Hill (film), 39
Williams, Terry Tempest, 89, 91
Wilson, E. O., 48, 54, 179, 195, 242n15
Winged Migration, 118
wings, 57
Winson, John "Wildwood," 164–65
wonder, 56, 181, 205, 216
woodpecker, ivory-billed (*Campephilus principalis*), 167
Wordsworth, William, 11, 24, 81, 83, 102–3, 123; "The Tables Turned: An Evening Scene," 17–18, 71
wren: Bewick's (*Thryomanes bewickii*), 38, 116, 135; canyon (*Catherpes mexicanus*), 138; house (*Troglodytes aedon*), 13–14; winter (*Troglodytes troglodytes*), 170–71

Y

Yeats, W. B., 59

Z

zugunruhe, 90, 92
Zwicky, Jan, 48, 108, 149, 167, 200

www.ingramcontent.com/pod-product-compliance
Lightning Source LLC
Chambersburg PA
CBHW071805080526
44589CB00012B/700